Annals of the Reign of
GEORGE III

Annals of the Reign of
GEORGE III

VOLUME ONE

JOHN AIKIN

NONSUCH

First published 1816
Copyright © in this edition 2006
Nonsuch Publishing Ltd

Nonsuch Publishing Limited
The Mill, Brimscombe Port, Stroud, Gloucestershire, GL5 2QG
www.nonsuch-publishing.com

Nonsuch Publishing Ltd is an imprint of Tempus Publishing Group

British Library Cataloguing in Publication Data.
A catalogue record for this book is available from the British Library.

ISBN 1-84588-019-6

Typesetting and origination by Tempus Publishing Limited
Printed in Great Britain by Oaklands Book Services Limited

CONTENTS

INTRODUCTION TO THE
MODERN EDITION

Born in 1747 at Kibworth in Leicestershire, John Aikin's life spanned one of the most turbulent and revolutionary periods in British history. From the shifting fortunes of Britain's colonial ambitions, to the long-term war with Bourbon and then Napoleonic France, Britain found herself challenged on all fronts and, at times, isolated from and threatened by all of her European neighbours. Moreover, during the late eighteenth and early nineteenth centuries Britain's domestic affairs were also in a state of flux. With the advent of the Industrial Revolution, and the large shift of the populace to the industrial centres, the composition of British society was changing from an essentially rural to a largely urban population, while religious freedom was developing as a contentious issue between those of the established Anglican faith and the so-called Dissenters.

Aikin himself was born into the tradition of the Dissenters. His father, also named John, was one of the first tutors at Warrington Academy, one of a series of private academies set up outside the control of the established Church, with the aim of educating young men of every religious denomination in both spiritual and temporal subjects. Brought up in a tradition of Unitarianism, a faith which had developed out of the Protestant Reformation of the sixteenth century and espoused the principles of religious freedom for each individual, Aikin was first educated at Warrington, before going on to study medicine at Edinburgh University, surgery in London and finally achieving the degree of M.D. at the University of Leiden in the Netherlands. However, even in this chosen career of medicine, his faith was to have a major impact.

In 1784 Aikin settled in Great Yarmouth, where he set up an initially successful medical practice. However, Great Yarmouth society was hostile to Dissenters and the growing movement for the repeal of the Corporation and Test Acts, which Aikin supported, was to lead to a breach with the majority of his patients. These Acts had been introduced in 1661 and 1673 respectively, the former excluding non-Anglicans from membership of town corporations, the latter extending this exclusion to holders of civil and military office, thereby prohibiting public office to anyone of Roman Catholic, Jewish or Protestant Dissenter beliefs. Having published two pamphlets supporting the repeal of these Acts anonymously, Aikin's authorship soon became widely known and he was forced to leave Great Yarmouth in 1792 and move to London.

After practising as a physician in London for some years, in 1798 Aikin's medical career was cut short by a stroke of paralysis, after which he retired to Stoke Newington to concentrate on his literary works. He had already devoted much of his free time to literary pursuits and had published a number of works including *Biographical Memoirs of Medicine in Great Britain* and a series of volumes entitled *Evenings at Home* with his sister, Anna Laetitia Barbauld. In 1796 he became editor of the *Monthly Magazine*, which published a miscellany of literature, philosophy, the arts and other intellectual writings, a position he was to hold until 1807. However, he is best known for his biographical works, including works on John Selden and Archbishop Usher, and in particular for his monumental ten volume *General Biography* completed in 1815.

It is perhaps not surprising that Aikin chose to write a contemporary account of the history of Britain during the reign of George III, as these events would have had a particular personal relevance to one who lived through them. The *Annals of the Reign of George III* provide a comprehensive account of significant domestic and international events from 1760 to 1815, a fascinating period which saw Britain, at its lowest ebb, lose its largest colony, then regain its pride in the triumph over one of its greatest opponents and the liberation of Europe from the scourge of French Imperialism.

PREFACE

THE work here offered to the public has no other pretensions than those of a summary of the principal events, domestic and foreign, of the present reign. In its composition, the objects in view have been perspicuity and order in narrative, selection of the most important circumstances, and a strict impartiality, exhibited not only in a fair and ungarbled representation of facts, but in the absence of every kind of colouring which might favour the purposes of what may properly be denominated *party*. This last intention, which has never ceased to guide the writer's pen, did not appear to him necessarily to preclude every expression of his feelings on points involving moral or constitutional questions, but he trusts that he shall be found to have used this liberty with moderation and reserve, and without any effort to enforce opinions in their nature dubious or disputable. Where, indeed, in the records of history can the period be met with, which, to one whose life has passed in contemplating the whole shifting scene, is calculated to inculcate a more impressive lesson against presumptuous confidence in speculative notions, or positive judgment respecting characters and actions?

It will be manifest that the compass of these pages could not afford scope for entering into those conjectures relative to the secrets of cabinets, or those discussions concerning the plans of policy that may be supposed to have influenced sovereigns or their ministers, which usually occupy a large space in professed histories. Perhaps, however, the utility of a historical narrative is not materially impaired by such an omission. Were it possible to attain more certainty with respect to such topics than can come within the reach of a private person, what, in general would be gained, except a nearer insight into a drama of life representing the play of ordinary motives upon ordinary minds — a view of the secondary movements of a machine, the springs of which are acting according to known and obvious laws? In reality, the great series of human affairs is directed by a chain of causes and effects of much superior potency to the efforts of individuals in any station, who, for the most part, are rather the subjects, than the rulers, of events. While men, in continued succession, under a variety of characters, probably at all times existing in nearly equal proportions, are pursuing a course influenced by their passions and interests, changes are operating in the large masses of mankind, the result of combinations of circumstances which the flux of ages has been requisite to produce. It is, from the observation of these, and not from an acquaintance with court intrigues and party manœuvres, that the true philosophy of history is to be deduced; and the impartial record of leading facts is the grand desideratum for obtaining this important addition to human wisdom. Of such incidents, the period which the present work comprehends has been singularly fertile and the intelligent reader cannot fail of drawing inferences from them, which will have more value as the product of his own reflections than as the promptings of a writer.

Although the title of "Annals of the Reign of George III" implies that the affairs of the countries of which he was the sovereign are peculiarly their subject, yet the concerns of all civilized states are so blended, and the events passing in one, exert so material an influence upon the policy of others, that it has been necessary to combine with the record of British history, a sketch of the most important occurrences of which not only the European continent, but a large portion of the inhabited world, was the theatre. Such a comprehensive view was frequently requisite in order to elucidate our own political system; but independently of that consideration, it appeared desirable to associate in a reader's mind, with the memorable events of his native country, those which were simultaneously taking place in other scenes of action. The extraordinary character and momentous consequences of some of these transactions, especially of those which for the last twenty-five years have rendered France the object of universal interest, have sometimes made it difficult to keep this part of the narrative in due subordination to the leading topic; but such a subordination has always been the writer's purpose; and with respect to domestic affairs, in particular, he hopes it will be sufficiently apparent to justify the title given to the work.

Care has been taken to preserve as much as possible the exact application of the word *Annals*, by limiting the narrative of each year to the occurrences within the space of year. In a history at large it may be more advantageous to follow the thread of events of a particular class through the series of causes and effects, without any exact limitation to time; but the design of the present attempt being chiefly to provide, in the most useful form, a repertory of all the important facts of the reign, it was judged expedient to arrange them, as nearly as could be done, in precise chronological order. By such a position they are not only most easily referred to, but they frequently disclose a mutual bearing and connection, which might escape notice if they were removed to a distance from one another in the narrative.

With regard to the point of time chosen for the conclusion of a reign which, in one sense, might be considered as already terminated, and in another, as still subsisting, it is presumed that the circumstance of its being the era at which this country has been relieved from the weight of a war of unprecedented length and difficulty, and the great powers of Europe have agreed upon a definitive settlement of their long embroiled

affairs, will generally be looked upon as rendering it, if not
chronologically exact, the most satisfactory in a historical and
political view that could have been adopted.

1760

1st Year of the Reign

O^N October 25th died suddenly at his palace of Kensington his Majesty King George II, in the 77th year of his age, and the 24th of his reign, in the midst of a war with France, carried on in the four quarters of the globe, with a success, on the part of Great Britain, to which its history affords no parallel. The commencements had been highly unfavourable to this country, and repeated losses and disgraces had produced general despondency and discontent; when the spirit of the nation being at length roused, and its energies being directed by the genius of one of the greatest ministers it had ever known, WILLIAM PITT, the last two or three years had been marked by an almost uninterrupted succession of victories by sea and land. The marine of France was nearly annihilated. The conquest of its North American colonies was in this year completed; and in the East Indies its force was greatly reduced in consequence of the defeat of General Lally by Colonel Coote at the battle of Wandewash. In Germany alone did the French arms maintain at least an equality; and indeed it was chiefly owing to the talents of that consummate general, Prince Ferdinand of Brunswick, that in this quarter they did not become decidedly superior. The king of Prussia, the sole ally of

England, some subsidised German princes excepted, had lately undergone such losses in a most unequal contest with a host of foes, that it exercised all his abilities to preserve himself from being totally overwhelmed. Through these circumstances, the war in Germany had been rendered less popular than any other part of the political system; and although parliamentary opposition to the measures of administration had subsided to a calm scarcely ever before experienced, yet some publications had appeared, and been much read, in which, with respect to this object, the conduct of the ministers had been animadverted upon with great force and severity.

On the day after the king's decease his grandson, George III, was proclaimed with the usual solemnities. This sovereign, born on June 4th, 1738, was son of Frederick, prince of Wales, and Augusta, princess of Saxe Gotha. It appears to have been a leading object in his education to keep him uncontaminated by the allurements which are commonly at an early period laid in the way of the heir to a crown. He was therefore brought up in privacy, and had been introduced neither to the pleasures nor the business of a court. His person and character were little known to the nation; but the accession of a young and native sovereign, decorous in behaviour, and of unblemished reputation, was greeted by the warm affections and sanguine hopes of his subjects; and few in the line of English kings have ascended the throne under happier auspices. No immediate change took place either in the plans of policy, or in the persons entrusted with the conduct of them. Mr. Pitt, as principal secretary of state, remained at the head of the cabinet, other members of which were Mr. Fox, Mr. Legge, the Duke of Newcastle, the Earl of Holderness, and Lord Anson.

One of the first acts of royalty was to introduce into the privy council the Earl of Bute, who had obtained an ascendancy over the mind of his Majesty in consequence of the office he had held in the superintendence of his education. A royal proclamation issued on October 31st, "For the encouragement of piety and virtue, and for preventing and punishing of vice, profaneness and immorality," indicated the sober and religious character which the new reign was about to assume.

On November 18th the subsisting parliament assembled, and was opened by a speech from the throne, the tenor of which gave general satisfaction. One of its clauses was judiciously calculated to operate upon the feelings of the nation, by alluding to a circumstance always desirable in a regal succession, but which was become a novelty in that of the British crown: "Born and educated in this country," said his Majesty, "I glory in the name of Briton." In adverting to the war, a resolution was expressed of prosecuting it with vigour, in order to obtain the object of a safe and honourable peace; and to this end, the zealous concurrence of parliament was relied on in supporting the king of Prussia and the other allies of the nation, and in making ample provision for the demands of the service.

No event, foreign or domestic, worthy of particular record, occurred during the short remainder of the year.

1761

1st & 2d Year of the Reign

ONE of the concluding acts of the parliament, which, according to law, continued to exercise its functions six months after the demise of the crown, was passing a bill to fix the civil list at the clear annual sum of £800,000 payable out of the aggregate find, in lieu of the specific revenues settled on the late king.

Another act, by which great popularity accrued to his Majesty, was introduced to parliament in a speech from the throne on March 3d, for the declared purpose of giving an additional security to the independence of the judges. Although an act had passed in the reign of William III to continue the commission of the judges during their good behaviour, they were legally determined on the death of the reigning sovereign. No instance had, indeed, occurred since that period of the removal of a judge at the accession of a new sovereign; but it was justly considered, that such a power remaining in the crown was a derogation from the perfect independence of that important office. Both houses expressed their gratitude on the occasion by loyal addresses, and a bill was speedily drawn up and passed according to the royal recommendation.

The session was closed on March 19th, and writs were soon after issued for convoking a new parliament. Changes in the ministry and new appointments were now announced. Mr. Legge was dismissed from the office of chancellor of the exchequer, and was succeeded by Viscount Barrington. Soon after, the Earl of Bute was made one of the principal secretaries of state, in the room of the Earl of Holderness. The post of Lord-Lieutenant of Ireland was conferred on the Earl of Halifax.

Early in this year, the negotiations for peace, which had been broken off in the close of 1759, were resumed at the instance of the French court. The parties in conjunction with that court were those of Vienna, Petersburgh, Poland, and Sweden, and their several declarations were signed at Paris on March 25th, and were met by those of Great Britain and Prussia on April 3d. The City of Augsburg was appointed as the seat of a general congress, and Lords Egremont and Stormont, and General Yorke, were nominated as the British plenipotentiaries. As the interests of Germany were the matter to be treated of at Augsburg, it was thought advisable by France and England that the affairs at issue between them should be separately discussed, and for that purpose Mr. Stanley was sent to Paris, and Mr. Bussy to London. The negotiations being likely to run out to length, it was determined by the English ministry in the meantime to urge the operations of war with unremitting vigour.

At the conclusion of the last campaign, the French were left in entire possession of the territory of Hesse, while their advanced points were at Gottingen on one side and at Weser on the other. As early as February 9th Prince Ferdinand assembled his army for the purpose of striking a sudden blow; and pushing on with great celerity, he penetrated to the heart of the French quarters, and forced them to retreat on every side. Various successes followed, and at length the allied troops laid siege to Cassel. The French general, Marshal Broglio, having in the meantime been reinforced, made an attack on the hereditary prince of Brunswick, posted at Stangerode, and defeated him; the consequence of which action was the raising of the siege of Cassel, and the retreat of the allies across the Dymel.

A secret expedition which had been fitting out early in the spring in the English ports, sailed from Spithead on March 29th, under the command of Commodore Keppel and General Hodgson, and arrived off the island of Bellisle on the coast of Britany, on April 7th. An attempt to land on the following day was defeated with loss. It was afterwards renewed with success, and the siege of the chief town of the island, Le Palais, was commenced. The vigorous defence of the commander, St. Croix, protracted the fall of the citadel till June 7th, when it surrendered by capitulation, together with the island.

In Germany, the destruction of the French magazines retarded the movements of their forces so much, that it was the end of June before their commanders, Soubise and Broglio, could avail themselves of their superiority. Broglio at length crossed the Dymel, having previously routed the rear-guard of General Sporken. Various encounters then took place, the principal of which was the battle of Kirch Denkern, on the 15th and 16th of July, in which the attacks of the French were repulsed with considerable loss on their part. The general result of the campaign, however, was that the French were enabled to lay the greatest part of Westphalia under contribution.

The King of Prussia, in this year, far from being able to afford any assistance to his ally, was reduced to a state of languor which did not suffer him to quit his strong camp in Silesia, while his important fortresses of Schweidnitz and Colberg were taken, the first, by the Austrians, the second, by the Russians, who were thereby enabled to take up their winter-quarters in Pomerania. This was the period of the lowest decline of that celebrated Prince, who had so long maintained a conflict against adverse fortune, with a spirit not inferior to that of the greatest heroes in history.

If the events of the war on the European continent were less favourable to the cause of Great Britain in this year than in some which preceded, victory still crowned her arms in other parts. The successes in the East Indies had left to the French no other possession of importance than their capital settlement of Pondicherry, and this, during several months of 1760, was closely blockaded by the land forces under Colonel Coote, and the maritime force under Admiral Stevens. The besieged were reduced to great distress for want of provisions, when, on January 1st, 1761, a dreadful hurricane drove the English squadron from before it, with the loss of four ships of the line, and the crews of two of them, besides other damages. But whilst the commander, Lally, was flattering himself with a complete deliverance, the dispersed fleet appeared again within four days before Pondicherry, and the siege was renewed with redoubled vigour. Lally, however, a man of a violent character, made no proposals to surrender and when, at length, only one day's provision remaining, the town sent deputies to offer terms of capitulation, Lally, alleging the breach of treaties in India by the English, refused to join in the negotiation, and the place was accordingly delivered up at discretion to the British troops.

In the West Indies, the island of Dominica was reduced by an armament commanded by Lord Rollo and Sir James Douglas. The Cherokees in North America were brought to the necessity of suing for peace, by an expedition into their country, in which a number of their towns were destroyed.

The negotiations for peace between the courts of England and France were proceeding in the midst of these hostilities, and proposals on each side were reciprocally made by means of their agents at Paris and London. In general, there appeared to be no great difficulty in settling the terms relative to the conquests made by each nation, according to the basis of *uti possidetis*; but the conduct to be pursued by them with respect to their German allies was a matter of great difficulty, the English minister absolutely declaring their resolution of preserving their faith to the King of Prussia, and refusing to concur in the proposal of a neutrality in Germany. Another difficulty resulted from the demand on the part of France of the restitution of the captures made upon them at sea before the declaration of war, and which they contended to have been directly in contravention of the law of nations. A memorial transmitted by M. Bussy, on July 15th, in relation to these objects, might have conduced to an amicable termination, had it not been accompanied by a paper of a peculiarly offensive nature. The family connexion between the courts of France and Spain had long been a source of suspicion, and the latter, on several occasions during the war, had been charged with a partiality in favour of the former. Some matters of dispute were at this time pending between Spain and Great Britain, which afforded a pretext for the interference of France. The paper in question therefore contained a proposal that the King of Spain should be invited to guarantee the intended treaty, and that, in order to prevent the differences between Spain and England from being the occasion of a new war, they should be finally adjusted in the present negotiation. Great indignation was excited in the English ministry by this proposal; and it was positively declared to M. Bussy, that the King of Great Britain would not in any manner suffer his disputes with the Spanish court to be blended with the negotiations carrying on with France, and that the latter country had no right to intermeddle in discussions between the two former. The French court thereupon made an apology, and propositions were for some time longer reciprocally offered for bringing the treaty to a conclusion; but confidence and cordiality were now banished, and in September the agents on each side were recalled, and the negotiation terminated.

It was, however, productive of an important change in the English ministry. Mr. Pitt, whose influence had hitherto been predominant in the cabinet, became thoroughly persuaded, by the interference of France in the affairs of Spain, and the avowal of the Spanish ambassador, of a close union of blood and interest between the two courts, that the Spaniards were fully resolved to become a party in the contest as soon as they should find themselves in a state of preparation; and he therefore urged an immediate declaration of war by this country against that power, and the sending a squadron to intercept its Plate fleet. This step was strongly opposed by his colleagues, as not only rash, but unjustifiable by any thing that had as yet been made public. Mr. Pitt, incapable, by temper and long success, of bearing contradiction, finding himself unable to carry the point, declared that "he would no longer remain in a situation which made him responsible for measures he was no longer allowed to guide;" and after delivering his reasons in writing, he resigned the seals of secretary into the King's hand on October 9th, his brother-in-law, Earl Temple, at the same time resigning the offices of lord privy seal and cofferer. The eminent services of Mr. Pitt were rewarded (certainly not beyond their deserts) by a pension of £3,000 a year, and the rank and title of Baroness Chatham conferred on his lady. He carried with him in his retreat the regrets of a great part of the nation, and received addresses of thanks for the great benefits he had conferred on his country, from the corporation of London and other public bodies. His successor in office was the Earl of Egremont.

The domestic history of the year was rendered memorable by the pomp and festivity attendant upon royal nuptials and a coronation. In the summer, his Majesty declared in council the resolution of demanding in marriage the Princess Charlotte Sophia of Mecklenburg-Strelitz, second daughter of the late Duke. The negotiation for this purpose was entrusted to the Earl of Harcourt; and the princess, attended by the Duchesses of Hamilton and Ancaster, and the Countess of Effingham, embarked at Cuxhaven, August 23d, on board a royal yacht, convoyed by a squadron under the command of Lord Anson. She landed at Harwich on September 6th, and her nuptials with the king were celebrated, at the royal chapel, St. James's, on the evening of the 8th. The coronation of their Majesties was performed at Westminster Abbey, on September 22d, with all the solemnity and magnificence proper to the occasion.

On November 6th, the new parliament was opened with a speech from the throne, in which his Majesty, after taking notice of the termination of the negotiation for peace with France, declared his resolution to carry on the war in the most effectual manner, adhering firmly to his engagements with his allies, till his enemies should yield to the equitable conditions of an honourable peace.

Their Majesties and the royal family, with a numerous attendance of nobility and the great officers of state, on November 9th, entered the city of London in grand procession, where they partook of a most sumptuous entertainment at Guildhall.

The year had not closed, before the ministry found itself under the necessity of justifying, if not the measure proposed by Mr. Pitt, at least the opinion he had given of the hostile nature of the connection between the courts of France and Spain, and its inevitable tendency to produce a rupture between the latter country and Great Britain. The Earl of Bristol, ambassador at Madrid, had been directed to remonstrate with that court on its extraordinary proceeding in rendering France an umpire in the disputes between two friendly powers, with one of which she was at war; to propose farther terms for settling those disputes; and to require a categorical declaration concerning the final intentions of Spain. While these points were under discussion, a treaty was signed between the courts of France and Spain, which confirmed the family alliance between the two crowns, and purported to preserve the House of Bourbon from oppression, and to maintain its interests. This transaction was for a time kept a profound secret; but as soon as the negotiation with France was broken off, that court studiously circulated a report that Spain would immediately declare war against Great Britain in consequence of the engagements she had contracted. This idea was so prevalent, that the British ambassador thought himself entitled to require satisfaction from the Spanish minister, Don Wall, respecting it; but the Plate fleet being now arrived with a rich cargo, and the arms of France and her allies in Germany possessing a superiority, the tone of the Spanish ministry was changed, and warm complaints of the conduct of England were the chief reply. The British ministry now conceiving that the crisis was come, directed Lord Bristol to signify that a refusal to communicate the terms of the treaty in question, or at least to disavow any intention of taking part with our enemies, would be regarded as equivalent to a declaration of war by Spain. The answer made by Don Wall threw the act of hostility upon the English cabinet, and intimated that Lord Bristol might return when he thought proper; and he accordingly left Madrid on December 17th. The Spanish ambassador soon after departed from London, leaving behind him a manifesto reflecting upon the haughtiness of the late English minister, and the indignity with which his court had been treated, and declaring that the obnoxious treaty contained only a reciprocal guaranty of the dominions of the several branches of the House of Bourbon, with the restriction, with respect to France, that it should extend only to the dominions remaining to her after the conclusion of the present war.

The year thus closed with the certain prospect of a new war to be sustained by Great Britain, against an enemy powerful in resources, and firmly leagued with her most inveterate foe.

1762

2ᵈ & 3ᵈ Year of the Reign

ON the 4th of January war was declared against Spain; and although the nation was lying under the pressure of a heavy debt and vast expenses, though it had no aid to expect from allies, and saw the greatest part of the European continent either directly hostile, or disposed to become so, yet this accession of hazard seemed little to affect the spirits of the public. In fact, a war with Spain has generally been popular in this country, where she has been looked upon, especially by the navy, rather in the light of a tempting prey, than of a formidable antagonist. Past successes, moreover, had inspired confidence; the naval and military forces were in a high state of discipline and ably commanded; and there appeared no deficiency of vigour in the administration, to conduct a war which they had not hesitated to enter upon, under the idea that the honour and interest of the nation rendered it necessary.

The first military operation of the year was the execution of an enterprise determined on at the close of the preceding year, against the island of Martinico, the principal of the French Caribbees. An attempt against this important settlement in the year 1759, had failed of success; but the British arms having now little more employment in North America, and it being obviously a point of great consequence to deprive the enemy of their remaining strong hold in the West Indies, which, in case of a Spanish war, might be rendered a dangerous annoyance as a place of rendezvous, it was resolved to renew the attack with a force that was likely to overcome all resistance. Accordingly, a body of troops, amounting to nearly 12,000 men, under the command of General Monckton, and a squadron of eighteen ships of the line, commanded by Admiral Rodney, assembled at Barbadoes, whence they proceeded early in January to Martinico. A landing was effected without loss, and the army proceeded to the town of Fort Royal, which was protected by a strong citadel, and by batteries erected on two eminences, named Morne Tortenson and Morne Garnier. These were stormed and carried with great intrepidity, and on February 4th, the town and citadel capitulated. The governor-general of the island, M. de la Touche, having retreated to the capital, St. Pierre, he made preparations for a farther resistance; but on the 10th, as the British commander was about to embark for an attack on that place, deputies arrived to offer a capitulation for the whole island. The reduction of Martinico was followed by the surrender of all the dependant islands, which comprised Grenada, the Grenadines, St. Lucia, St. Vincent, and Tobago; and thus the whole chain of the Caribbees was brought under the British dominion.

The effects of the war with Spain were first felt in Europe by the necessity incurred of undertaking the defence of an ancient but feeble ally of Great Britain. This was Portugal, a country naturally weak in extent and position, and from various circumstances, declined from its former power, and reduced to a deplorable state of inability and disorganization. To compel it to renounce that close connection with England, which had so long been a source of commercial advantage to the latter, and of security to the former, and to force it into the confederacy against her, doubtless appeared an easy task to the courts of France and Spain; and should the King of Portugal obstinately remain faithful to his engagements, the pretext afforded thereby of conquering his country, and annexing it to the larger portion of the peninsula, would not fail to gratify the ambitious views of the House of Bourbon. Troops were in consequence early in the year assembled on the Portuguese frontier, and the commerce of corn between the two kingdoms was prohibited. On March 16th, a joint memorial was presented by the ambassadors of France and Spain at the court of Lisbon, inviting the King of Portugal to join the alliance against Great Britain, insisting upon his expelling the English residents in Portugal from his kingdom, and no longer giving shelter to the English shipping in his ports, and offering to garrison his fortresses and maritime towns, in order to protect them from the resentment of England. The Portuguese sovereign having returned a conciliatory answer, in which he expressed his determination to preserve his ancient alliance with England, but to maintain an exact neutrality, the associated powers delivered a second memorial in terms still more imperious, telling him that "he ought to be glad of the necessity which they laid upon him to make use of his reason, in order to take the true road of his glory and the common interest." As his Majesty still remained unshaken, and declared his resolution to continue faithful to his engagements at any hazard, the ambassadors, on April 7th, demanded passports for leaving the country, and soon after, France and Spain jointly issued a declaration of war against Portugal.

No country could be worse prepared for defence. Its army was equally contemptible in numbers and discipline; its fleet was reduced to six or seven ships of the line and a few frigates; and its fortified places were wholly incapable of standing a long siege. In this emergence all its hope was fixed upon the assistance of England, which lost no time in transmitting supplies of every kind. No immediate resistance, however, could be made to the invaders; and a Spanish army having entered the north-eastern angle of Portugal, invested

Miranda, of which, in consequence of the explosion of a powder-magazine, they obtained easy possession on May 9th. Braganza soon after submitted without resistance, and in a short time the whole of Tralos Montes was overrun to the banks of the Douro. A second body of Spaniards entering the province of Beira, reduced Almeida, and proceeding southwards, occupied the territory of Castell Branco, and approached the Tagus. During this time, the Portuguese, though reinforced by British troops, brought to their aid under the command of Lord Tyrawley, had no army in the field capable of encountering the enemy in a battle, and were obliged to confine their efforts to the defence of passes. Lord Tyrawley appears to have been disgusted at the want of due exertion on the part of the Portuguese ministers, and returned to England on the arrival of the celebrated Count de la Lippe Buckeburg to take the supreme command of the forces of Portugal. A third army of combined French and Spaniards assembled in Spanish Estremadura, with the intention of penetrating into Alentejo, and making a junction with the other armies, which would have brought Lisbon into great hazard. In order to frustrate this design, the Count de la Lippe sent a detachment under the command of Brigadier-General Burgoyne, to attack an advanced body of Spaniards which lay at Valentia de Alcantara; the result was a complete surprize, in which the enemy sustained considerable loss. The Spanish army in Beira then made repeated attempts to cross the Tagus, which were foiled by the skill of the Commander-in-Chief; and the British troops gained additional honour by the surprize of a large body of Spanish cavalry near Villa Velha, directed by Burgoyne, and executed by Colonel Lee with distinguished success. In conclusion, the autumnal rains setting in, and the invader finding no prospect of farther success, all the Bourbon troops fell back to the frontiers of Spain, and Portugal was delivered from one of the greatest dangers she had ever incurred.

While the British administration was thus providing for the defence of an ally, they resolved upon striking a home blow at the new enemy, in a part in which he is peculiarly sensible. The Havanna in the island of Cuba is the center of the trade and navigation of the Spanish West Indies, and the station of the principal naval force of Spain in that quarter. Its capture therefore would lay at our mercy the main resources of Spain for the support of a maritime war, and would lead to any enterprize that might be planned against her American possessions. An expedition was therefore prepared early in the year under the command of General Lord Albemarle and Admiral Pococke, which sailed from Portsmouth on the 5th of March. It was joined off Hispaniola by a fleet from Martinico, under Sir James Douglas, when the armament consisted of nineteen ships of the line, eighteen small armed vessels, and one hundred and fifty transports, conveying 10,000 land forces, to which 4,000 were to be added from New York. The fleet passing through the Bahamas arrived off the Havanna on June 5th, and a landing was effected without opposition on the 7th. The first object was the reduction of the strong fort, Moro, by which the harbour is protected, and which was supposed to be almost impregnable. Prodigious difficulties were encountered in making the approaches and carrying on the works for the siege of this place, which were met by the greatest courage and perseverance on the part of the commanders and men, although a severe sickness was added to the other hardships they had to sustain. At length, an attempt from the town for its relief having been frustrated, but no proposals being yet made for a capitulation, on the 44th day from the first operations it was stormed through a breach made by springing a mine, and carried at the bayonets' point, the brave governor, and the second in command, perishing in the defence. Not long after, on the 14th of August, the city of Havanna capitulated, and was yielded to the victors with a district of 180 miles to the west. A richer conquest has rarely been made. Nine sail of the line and four frigates were taken in the harbour; three of the line had previously been sunk by the enemy, and two were destroyed on the stocks; and the plunder, in money and merchandize, was supposed to reach the value of three millions sterling. The glory acquired by this exploit was not inferior to its other advantages.

It is now proper to turn our attention to the events of the year in that part of Europe which had so long been the principal theatre of military action.

The campaign in Germany between the French and the Allies, commenced nearly in the same tract which had been contended for in the two preceding years. The principal French army, under the Prince of Soubise and Marshal d'Etrees, was posted on the Weser, where it was opposed by Prince Ferdinand, who lay behind the Dymel; whilst the other French army on the Lower Rhine, commanded by the Prince of Condé, was watched by the hereditary prince in the Bishopric of Munster. The various and complicated movements which took place within these limits do not admit of an abridged narrative, and no particular action occurred decisive of the superiority of either party. On the whole, however, the bold and skilful manœuvres of Prince Ferdinand were successful in recovering the greatest part of the principality of Hesse; and his efforts not being in the least slackened by the approach of peace, the last event of the war was the recapture of Cassel, which the French army had been obliged to leave uncovered.

The fortune of the King of Prussia in this campaign, and the incidents connected with it, afford more interesting subjects for narration. The loss of Schweidnitz and Colberg had laid that sovereign so much at the mercy of his enemies, that there appeared scarcely a possibility of his deliverance by any efforts of his own, when death suddenly freed him from one of the most formidable of his foes. Elizabeth, Empress of Russia, his inveterate enemy, died on the 2d of January, and was succeeded by the grand-duke Charles Peter Ulric, of the house of Holstein, who took the name of Peter III. He was a prince of a singular character, more German than Russian in his ideas and inclinations, and one of whose passions was an extravagant admiration of the King of Prussia. Among the political changes with which his reign commenced, one was therefore that of a total alteration of the system of conduct adopted by the Russian court towards that monarch. In a memorial delivered on February 23d to the ministers of the allied courts, he declared, that "in order to the re-establishment of peace he was ready to sacrifice all the conquests made by the Russian arms during this war;" and not satisfied with waiting the slow progress of combined negotiations, he concluded a suspension of hostilities with the King of Prussia, on the 16th of March. In the beginning of May he proceeded to the decisive step of making a treaty of peace and alliance with him, in which, without any stipulation for his confederates, he agreed to join his troops to those of Prussia, for the purpose of expelling the Austrians from Silesia. The court of Sweden, now wholly under the influence of Russia, also signed a treaty of peace with Prussia on May 22d.

Frederic was not backward to avail himself of this unexpected change in his condition. His brother, Prince Henry, on May 12th attacked the imperial posts on the frontiers of Saxony, and having obliged the Austrians to evacuate Dipposwalda with loss, secured all that part of Saxony, which was in the possession of the Prussians. The king himself, when joined by his new allies, moved to dislodge Marshal Daun from the eminences which connected his army with Schweidnitz. In this war of posts the success was various; but in the end, Daun, fearing to be cut off from his communication with Bohemia, fell back to the extremity of Silesia, leaving Schweidnitz uncovered, which was immediately invested by Frederic. At the same time detachments of Prussians, and the Russian irregulars, penetrated into Bohemia, and laid the country under contribution.

This tide of success was in some measure checked by the extraordinary revolution which took place in Russia. The innovating spirit of the new czar, uncontrouled by moderation or good sense, and the open contempt which he displayed for all the ancient institutions of the empire, had rendered him obnoxious to the principal orders of the state; and as, under a despotic government, there exists no other mode of resisting pernicious measures, than by a change in the throne, schemes were early meditated for effecting the deposition of Peter. The event was accelerated by the disclosure of his intention of divorcing his consort Catherine and probably of confining her to a monastery, whilst he should raise a favourite mistress to the imperial title. Catharine, a woman of masculine spirit and understanding, was placed by some of her confidents at the head of a conspiracy, which, joined by the body of malcontents, took possession of the person of the emperor. He was put under confinement, and his death speedily followed, July 6th. The empress, though a stranger, the daughter of a petty German prince, was without opposition elevated to the throne of the Russian czars, and invested with all the authority annexed to it. That a change of politics with respect to the alliance with Prussia would follow upon this event, was to be expected; accordingly, Catharine immediately declared to the ministers of that power her intention of recalling all her troops which were serving with those of Prussia. At the same time she professed her purpose of observing inviolably the peace which had been concluded between the two countries; and she caused all the places which had been conquered from the Prussians to be restored. When the orders for the separation of the Russians from their late allies arrived at the camp on July 21st, Frederic, with his usual presence of mind, resolved on an attack upon Marshal Daun before he could be apprized of the circumstance. Falling upon his right wing, which occupied the heights of Buckersdorff, he drove the Austrians from their post with considerable loss, and afterwards laid close siege to

Schweidnitz. In order to save that important place, Marshal Laudohn was sent to attack the Prince of Bevern, who, with a separate corps, was covering the siege. The prince, though his force was much inferior, made a defence which gave time for the King of Prussia to come to his assistance, and Laudohn, placed between two fires, vas routed with great slaughter. Schweidnitz was obliged to surrender on October 9th, its garrison remaining prisoners of war. Hostilities were afterwards transferred to Saxony, where various encounters took place with different fortune between the Austrian generals and Prince Henry of Prussia. The last, on October 29th, was a complete victory on the part of the prince; after which, Prussian detachments broke into Bohemia, Franconia, and Suabia, ravaging the country, levying exorbitant contributions, and spreading terror on every side. This was the state of Germany at the period when the peace between England and France left no other powers but those of Austria and Prussia under arms. To the narrative of this great event, and the circumstances accompanying it, we shall proceed, after a brief notice of some remaining military occurrences of the year in different parts of the globe.

On June 24th a French squadron of four men of war and a bomb vessel, with a body of troops on board, arrived in the bay of Bulls, in the island of Newfoundland, and took with little resistance St. John's and two other forts, destroying the stages and implements for the fishery to a considerable amount. If any neglect had occasioned this disaster, it was soon repaired. General Amherst, the British commander in North America, on being informed of the circumstance, detached Colonel Amherst and Lord Colville with a land and naval force to recover the island; and the troops having successfully attacked the posts of the French near St. John's, and prepared for an attack on St. John's itself, its commander delivered up the place, and surrendered himself and his garrison prisoners of war. The French ships escaped under cover of a fog.

As soon as the intelligence of the Spanish war reached the East Indies, an armament was equipped at Madras under the command of Admiral Cornish and Colonel Sir William Draper, for an expedition against Luçonia, the principal of the Philippine islands. The force consisted of 2300 land troops, European and Indian, and nine men of war and frigates; and the fleet, sailing from Madras on August 1st, arrived off Luçonia on September 19th. A landing being effected on the 24th, the troops marched to the siege of the capital, Manilla; for the defence of which 10,000 of the natives had been collected, in addition to a garrison of 800 men. During the progress of the siege some daring attempts were made to impede the advance of the works, but were repelled with much slaughter. At length, a breach being made in the enemy's works, without any proposal on their part of a capitulation, the place was taken by storm on October 6th. The governor retired to the citadel, where he surrendered at discretion. Although the victors had a right to avail themselves of all the privileges of conquest, they generously admitted the inhabitants to a capitulation, by which their lives, liberties, and property were preserved on the agreement for a ransom of one million sterling. The surrender of the capital comprehended that of the whole country, with all the islands which are its dependencies.

During the siege of this place, the admiral receiving information that the galleon from Acapulco was arrived at the entrance of the Archipelago of the Philippines, dispatched a man of war and a frigate in quest of her. They came up with and captured a large ship which proved not to be the vessel they expected, but a galleon from Manilla, which had been obliged to put back in order to refit after a storm. She was however a prize of very great value, and made a considerable addition to the success of this enterprize.

It will appear from the preceding narrative of military transactions, that the British administration at this time was wanting neither in vigour to conceive, nor power to execute designs calculated to bring the war to an honourable termination. It is however certain, that early in the present year the cabinet began to manifest symptoms of disunion, and that a commencement was made of those party animosities and dissentions which have so much agitated the reign of George III. The preponderating influence of the Earl of Bute over the royal mind, which was branded with the invidious appellation of *favouritism*, was sensibly felt by his colleagues in office; and it was particularly galling to that ancient servant of the crown, the Duke of Newcastle, who now possessed the post of first commissioner of the treasury. His situation was rendered so uneasy, that on May 26th, in consequence, it is said, of a direct intimation that the step was expected, he sent in his resignation. An ample pension was offered him in consideration of his past services, which he declined, with the reply that "if he could no longer be permitted to serve his country, he was at least determined not to be a burden to it." The resignation of the office of Lord Chamberlain by the Duke of Devonshire soon followed. The Earl of Hardwicke also retired in disgust; and several noblemen of distinction ranged themselves on the side of opposition. The vacant place at the head of the treasury, usually considered as that of first minister, was occupied by Lord Bute, who was succeeded in the secretaryship by Mr. George Grenville; but this gentleman soon after exchanged his post with the Earl of Halifax, who had succeeded Lord Anson as first Lord of the Admiralty. These changes and defections were productive of discontents that probably gave some alarm to the administration; of which it may be regarded as some indication, that the King's speech on the prorogation of parliament on June 2d expressed a hope that the members of both houses would continue to diffuse in their several counties that spirit of concord which they themselves had so steadily exerted in parliament. The increased difficulty of continuing the war in the face of a powerful opposition, and the laudable wish of relieving the nation from the burdens under which it laboured, were motives with the ministers for entertaining a sincere desire of the return of peace; and the Bourbon courts concurring in the same desire, it was easy to convey mutual intimations that a renewal of overtures would not be unacceptable. When the French and English courts were come to an understanding on this point, it was agreed, that in order to manifest a full determination to render the negotiation effectual, a minister of the highest class should be appointed on each side: accordingly, the Duke of Bedford nominated by the King of England as ambassador extraordinary and plenipotentiary, and the Duke de Nivernois with the same character from the King of France, were sent respectively to Paris and London in the beginning of September. Former discussions and late events had so far cleared the way that preliminaries were signed at Fontainbleau on the 3d of November. By this treaty, the original cause of the war was for ever removed by the cession to Great Britain of the entire province of Canada, and of all that part of Louisiana which is situated to the east of the Mississippi, together with Cape Breton, and the other islands in the gulph and river of St. Laurence. A right of fishery on the banks of Newfoundland was granted to the French, with the small islands of St. Pierre and Miquelon, for the accommodation of their fishermen. In the West Indies, the islands of Tobago, Dominica, St. Vincent, and the Grenades were retained, and those of Martinico, Guadaloupe, Marigalante, Desirade, and St. Lucia, were restored to the French. On the coast of Africa, Senegal and its dependencies remained in possession of England, and Goree was restored. In the East Indies, all the French factories and settlements were restored, but France agreed to erect no fortifications in Bengal and to acknowledge the Nabob of the Carnatic, and the Subah of the Decan. In Europe, Minorca on one side, and Belleisle on the other, were to return to their former possessors, and the fortifications of Dunkirk were to be demolished.

On the part of Spain, a cession was made to England of East and West Florida, and of all her possessions to the east and south-east of the Mississippi, and a right was confirmed to the English of cutting log-wood on the coast of Honduras, but without erecting any fortification. In return she obtained the restitution of the Havanna, and all other conquests made upon her. The King of Spain further agreed to restore all the lands, fortresses, &c. conquered from Portugal.

The interests of our ally the King of Prussia were so far consulted, that a stipulation was made with France for the evacuation of Wesel, Cleves, and Gueldres, by its troops; and England and France being now withdrawn from the German war, it was thought that the remaining belligerents, Prussia and Austria, might settle their quarrel by themselves.

Such, in substance, was the treaty by which the most extensive and burdensome, but the most glorious and successful war in which Great Britain had ever been engaged, was terminated. It was not to be expected that in the violent conflict of parties which had now commenced, negotiations comprizing so many nice and complicated points could be brought to an issue without leaving much matter for political criticism; and in fact, some very severe censures were passed upon different articles in the parliamentary debates on the subject. But the ministry foreseeing the impending attacks, had prepared for it. Mr. Fox, though possessing only his former post of paymaster to the army, was engaged to conduct the affairs of government in the House of Commons; and by his abilities, and the support given to the court by the great body of the country or Tory party, now enlisted under the royal banners, an address was voted by a large majority in approbation of the preliminaries of peace, notwithstanding the warm invectives of Mr. Pitt and other members in opposition. In the House of Lords a similar address passed without a division. Through the nation at large much dissatisfaction prevailed at what appeared a gratuitous renunciation of so many hard-earned conquests: yet many calm reasoners were convinced that no solid advantages would have accrued from insisting upon higher terms.

Before the close of the year a treaty of peace was signed at Hubertsburg between the courts of Austria and Prussia, by which the latter power was left in possession of all the territories belonging to it at the commencement of the war. Such was the result of seven years of blood-shed and desolation.

In this year, the parliament of Paris, without any opposition on the part of the crown, issued a decree condemning the institution of the Jesuits, releasing the members of the society from their vows, and alienating all the possessions of the order in France; and the example was followed by the other parliaments of the kingdom.

1763

3^d & 4th Year of the Reign

THE latest action of the war with Spain, and the only unsuccessful one, occurred on the first day of this year. A joint expedition of English and Portuguese, consisting of three frigates and some small-armed vessels and store-ships, with 500 soldiers on board, sailed in the preceding August from the Tagus, destined against the Spanish settlement of Buenos Ayres. It arrived at the mouth of the Plata in the beginning of November, and after encountering much difficulty in ascending that great river, reached Buenos Ayres on January 1st, and steered directly for the harbour. The Spaniards, who were well prepared, received them with a fierce cannonade; but at length their batteries were nearly silenced, and the success of the enterprize seemed almost certain, when the commodore's ship, from some unknown accident, took fire, and instantly was all in a blaze. A dreadful scene ensued, which ended in the destruction of the ship, and of more than three-fourths of her crew, the commander included. The ship next in force escaped with difficulty, and the attempt was thus entirely defeated.

The general peace was proclaimed in March, and tranquillity every where prevailed, except at the back of the settlements in North America, where an alarming war broke out with the native Indians, which was carried on with various success during the summer and autumn. It appears to have taken rise from the jealousy of these tribes of the increased power acquired by the English, in consequence of their victory over the French, and the establishment of new forts which encroached upon the Indian hunting grounds, and seemed to threaten them with subjugation. They were even led to believe that a plan had been formed for their total extirpation. The Indians on the Ohio, who had been particularly attached to the French interest, took the lead in the war which followed. A scheme was adopted of a general attack upon the frontier settlements in the time of harvest; and it so far succeeded that numbers of persons were killed, crops were destroyed, houses burnt, and all the frontier country of Pennsylvania, Maryland, and Virginia, from twenty miles inwards was deserted. Several small forts were likewise taken by the Indians, who proceeded to make attempts upon the more considerable fortresses of Detroit, Niagara, and Fort Pitt. A variety of actions, in which much loss was sustained, occurred in this scattered and irregular warfare, but the general result of the campaign was that the savages were foiled in their principal designs.

These remote hostilities were little regarded in England, where a warfare of a different kind soon engrossed the whole public attention. The winding up of the war expences, as usually happens, exhibited large arrears of debt, which new financial measures were required to satisfy. Among the ways and means resorted to for this purpose, one was a tax of four shillings per hogshead upon cyder, to be paid by the maker. Although equity seems to demand that the burdens laid upon the drinkers of beer should be equally partaken by the drinkers of cyder, yet in the collection of the tax there was this difference, that in the first case, the makers of malt alone, who in general are manufacturers for sale, are subjected to the visitation of excise officers; whereas in the cyder counties, that liquor is the production of every farm and orchard, whence it was necessary to arm the officer with authority to enter private houses at pleasure. This extension of a mode of taxation, in itself unpopular, occasioned violent discontents among those on whom the hardship pressed; and the opposition in parliament was ready to use the occasion for inflaming the dislike with which the administration, and especially its head, was viewed by a great part of the public. The cyder bill was carried in parliament, though it was opposed by a strong division in the House of Lords. Petitions against it were presented to both houses by the corporation of London, and these proving ineffectual, that body petitioned his Majesty to refuse his assent to the bill, which, however, passed into a law.

After having weathered this storm, the Earl of Bute, to the general surprise of the kingdom, resigned his place on April 8th, and withdrew into retirement. Reserved in his disposition, little calculated to attach friends or conciliate enemies, and fonder of private than of public life, it was not extraordinary that after having attained the highest point of a subject's ambition, he should withdraw from the odium with which he was pursued, and of which few ministers have encountered a larger share. He was succeeded by Mr. George Grenville, and no alteration in the principles of administration appeared to result from the change. The resignation of Lord Bute was not, however, generally supposed to have diminished his influence over his Majesty's councils, and he and his country were still the objects of much virulent abuse. Of this, a principal vehicle was a periodical publication, entitled, "The North Briton," first set up as a contrast to "The Briton," a paper written in defence of Lord Bute's administration. The editor of the North Briton was Mr. Wilkes, member of parliament for Aylesbury, and colonel of the Buckinghamshire militia, a gentleman, who for several years of this reign, occupied a space in the political annals of the country, for which he was solely indebted to the mistaken measures of his opponents.

The North Briton had long rendered itself distinguished by the virulence of its attacks on the administration, without attracting its notice, till, on the appearance of the 45th number, which contained a direct charge upon the King of uttering a falsehood in his speech from the throne, a general warrant was issued on April 26th by Lord Halifax, one of the principal Secretaries of State, commanding the apprehension of the authors, printers, and publishers of that seditious and treasonable paper. In consequence, the house of Mr. Wilkes was entered in the night by three King's messengers, who searched his papers, and seized his person, when, after examination at the Secretary's office, he was committed to the Tower. A few days after, being brought, by *habeas corpus,* before the Judges at Westminster-hall, he was discharged on the ground of privilege of parliament. A prosecution, however, was immediately instituted against him by the Attorney-general; and in the meantime he was dismissed from his command in the militia, and Lord Temple, as his friend, was deprived of the lieutenancy of Buckinghamshire. On the meeting of Parliament, a message was sent to acquaint the House of Commons with the measures that had been taken with respect to Mr. Wilkes, and the obnoxious number of the North Briton was laid before it; on which, the paper was voted to be a scandalous and seditious libel, and was ordered to be burnt by the common hangman. When the Sheriffs of London proceeded to execute this sentence at the Royal Exchange, a great mob assembled, by which the magistrates were grossly insulted. A riot ensued, which was the commencement of those popular commotions that long attended upon every transaction relative to the contest between Mr. Wilkes and the government. He thenceforth came to be regarded as the champion of the people; and that it was not the lower class alone who espoused his cause, was proved by the negative put in the Common-council, on a motion for returning thanks to the Sheriffs for their spirited conduct in executing the order of Parliament. Mr. Wilkes obtained a legal victory, which was of greater public consequence. Having brought an action against the under Secretary of State for seizing his papers, and the cause being tried before Lord Chief-Justice Pratt and a special jury, he obtained a verdict in his favour with £1,000 damages. The judge in his charge, explicitly declared his opinion against the legality of general warrants, or those in which no names of persons are specified. Some journeymen printers who had been imprisoned on the same account, also brought actions and obtained damages. Mr. Wilkes himself, who had been severely wounded in a duel by Mr. Martin, late Secretary to the Treasury, which laid him up for a considerable time, and thereby prevented him from appearing in Parliament to answer to the charges made against him, on his recovery withdrew to France.

The death of Lord Egremont in August, gave rise to a negotiation for the purpose of effecting a coalition between the leaders of the contending political parties; but it was soon broken off, and the Earl of Sandwich succeeded to the vacant secretaryship. The Earl of Egremont was placed at the head of the admiralty; and the ministry was strengthened by the appointment of that powerful nobleman, the Duke of Bedford, to the post of president of the council. The House of Commons voted, in contradiction to the decision of the court of Common Pleas, that privilege of parliament does not extend to the case of libels; and addresses full of loyalty were presented to the King from both houses of parliament, and from various public bodies.

The most important public event on the continent of Europe in the present year, was the death, on October 5th, of Augustus III King of Poland, and Elector of Saxony, who had lately returned to his electoral dominions, whence the events of the war had banished him for six years. Immediately after his decease, his eldest son and successor to the electorate, declared himself a candidate for the crown of Poland, and was supposed to be countenanced by the court of Vienna; but he was carried off by the small-pox a few weeks after his father.

In this year the Corsicans, under their gallant leader Paschal Paoli, sustained with great vigour their struggle for independence against the Genoese, over whom they obtained a considerable victory. Their cause was popular with the English nation, as being that of freedom; but the ministers, on the application of the republic of Genoa, thought proper to issue a royal proclamation, prohibiting all his Majesty's subjects affording succour of any kind to the inhabitants of Corsica, "in rebellion against the said republic."

This year was also the commencement of those contests between the court of France and the parliaments of that kingdom, which greatly contributed to foster that spirit of liberty and resistance to arbitrary power, whence such extraordinary consequences have since resulted. The King having in April issued an edict for the continuance of some war taxes, and the imposition of others, and for certain regulations respecting the redemption of the crown debts, the different parliaments refused to register them, and made strong remonstrances on the subject. The court, thereupon, sent the governors into the provinces with orders to register the edicts by force; but the parliaments, paricularly those of Rouen, Toulouse, and Grenoble, persisted in their opposition, and even issued decrees for the apprehension of the governors on account of their arbitrary proceedings.

During the course of this year, a war was maintained in the East Indies by the English company against Cossim Ally Cawn, whom they themselves had made Subah of Bengal on the deposition of Meer Jaffier. The difference first arose from certain restrictions imposed by the Subah on the English commerce in his dominions; and although President Vansittart had concluded a treaty with Cossim, acquiescing in the duties imposed by him on the inland trade carried on by the Company's servants, the council of Calcutta, in Jan. 1763, declared their refusal to abide by it. Mr. Amyatt, who was sent to the Subah in order to obtain better terms, was massacred with his suite on his return to Calcutta, which outrage produced a declaration of war against Cossim in the month of July, and a proclamation for restoring the deposed Jaffier to the Subahship. An army took the field commanded by Major Adams, who was joined by Major Carnac; and marching to Moorshedabad, that capital was attacked and taken by storm. A battle was fought on August 2d, on the plains of Geriah, in which the company's troops, though greatly outnumbered by those of Cossim, obtained a complete victory. The conquerors then proceeding to Mongheer, it was surrendered to them on October 11th.

Patna was the only place now remaining to Cossim, in which he had posted a large garrison. He there displayed his barbarity by ordering the murder of near 200 English prisoners in cold blood. This atrocity was revenged by Major Adams, who, advancing against the place, took it by storm on November 6th. Cossim had now no other refuge than the territory of Sujah ul Dowla, Nabob of Oude, and Vizier to the Mogul, who received the fugitive, but refused admission to any of his troops. This was the state of affairs in that quarter at the close of the year.

In this year a commencement was made of those voyages of discovery which have so much distinguished the reign of George III. Two of those expeditions, under the command of Captain Byron, and of Captains Wallis and Carteret, set sail from England during its course.

1764

4th & 5th Year of the Reign

O N the 16th of January the Princess Augusta, eldest sister of his Majesty, was married to the Hereditary Prince of Brunswick-Lunenburg.

The parliamentary year commenced with further proceedings against Mr Wilkes, whose total discomfiture appeared to be an object of the highest importance in the eyes of the ministers. As he still remained in France, his non-appearance to the charge against him before the House of Commons for writing the North Briton N° 45, was voted, on January 19th, a contempt of the House, he was found guilty of the charge, and, after a long debate, was expelled from his seat in parliament by a large majority. On the same day, on the motion of Lord Sandwich, a complaint was brought against him in the House of Lords for "violating the most sacred ties of religion, as well as decency, by printing in his own house a book or pamphlet, entitled, 'An Essay on Woman,' with notes or remarks to which the name of a Right Rev. Prelate, (Warburton Bishop of Gloucester,) had been scurrilously affixed. On this account the House voted him guilty of a breach of privilege, and also voted an address to his Majesty, to direct a prosecution against him in the king's bench, which was instituted on the double charge of libel and blasphemy. Whilst this attack injured his character in the opinion of all the sober supporters of his cause, the sinister artifices made use of to obtain a copy of a work which was privately printed with no intention of publication, and the choice of an accuser at least as notorious for licentiousness as the culprit, gave general offence. The final result was, that Wilkes, not choosing to appear to the indictment, was at length run to an outlawry, and the suits which he had commenced against the secretaries of state, were of course annulled.

In February a motion was made in the House of Commons by Sir William Meredith to declare "that a general warrant for apprehending and seizing the authors, printers, and publishers of a seditious libel, together with their papers, is not warranted by law." The introduction of this proposition was very embarrassing to the ministers, who, while they did not choose to defend the legality of general warrants, were unwilling to be shackled by a direct determination of the point in parliament. At the same time the arguments for the motion were so strong and popular, that no better mode was found for defeating it, after a long and animated debate, than an adjournment of the question, which was carried by much less than the usual ministerial majority. The agitation of this subject proved highly interesting to the public; and the city of London voted its freedom in a gold box to Lord Chief Justice Pratt, in which expression of gratitude to the opponent of general warrants it was imitated by the city of Dublin, and various other principal places in the two kingdoms.

Although ministers might be regarded rather as having sustained a defeat, than as having been victorious, on this point, yet they retained their credit in the general administration of affairs, and particularly in the financial arrangements of the year, which were so contrived as to raise the necessary supplies for extinguishing a remaining debt contracted on account of the war, without the imposition of any new taxes. It is true, the proposed ways and means underwent considerable censure from the opposition writers, especially that part which consisted in the appropriation of a surplus in the sinking fund. It was a much more important circumstance, though little attended to at the time, that the plan was in this year opened of easing the burdens of Great Britain by taxes imposed upon the North American colonies. In March Mr. Grenville proposed to the House of Commons a variety of resolutions respecting new duties to be laid on foreign goods imported into the colonies of North America, which, as commercial regulations, passed with little notice. For levying them, the naval commanders appointed to the American coast were sworn to act as revenue officers, the result of which was the seizure and condemnation of many ships and cargoes, without any power of redress in that country. At this time a very beneficial, though irregular, commerce was carried on between the British West Indies and the French and Spanish colonies. By an act moved for in April this trade was in some measure legalized, but was at the same time burdened with such heavy duties, and laid under such severe restrictions, that it was almost reduced to a nullity, to the great detriment of the colonists. And as if to add to these causes of disaffection to the mother country, the minister procured a resolution for raising a direct revenue from the colonies, and proposed to their consideration a stamp tax, with the offer, however, of substituting any other equally productive which they might prefer. These measures were resisted on the part of the Americans by associations against the use of British manufactures, and for the encouragement of their own.

Amidst these threatenings for futurity, the ministers felt themselves possessed of so much present strength, that they did not hesitate to display their power in the face of the nation by the dismissal of several military officers of rank who had displeased the court by their votes on the subject of general warrants.

On the European continent one of the most interesting political occurrences was the election of a King of Poland. Among the powers of Europe there were two parties, one of which wished that the throne might be filled by a foreigner, the other by a native. Of the latter were Russia, Prussia, and Turkey, which prepared to support their preference by force of arms; in consequence, an army of Prussians entered Poland and marched towards Warsaw, whilst the two others assembled troops on their respective frontiers. The person on whom the choice of these potentates fell, was Count Poniatowski, a member of an illustrious Polish family, and a particular favourite of the Empress Catharine. A party arose against this foreign nomination, headed by the house of Radzivil, and the crown-general Count Branitzki, and the usual tumultuary proceedings taking place at the first elective assembly, the dissentients withdrew from the diet, and afterwards took up arms to assert the national freedom. They were, however, defeated by the Russians, and Poniatowski was elected (if so it could be termed) on September 7th, under the name of Stanislaus Augustus.

Another election, which took place without the least opposition, was that of a King of the Romans, in the person of the Archduke Joseph, who was crowned at Frankfort with great solemnity on April 3d.

A remarkable and tragical incident occurred in this year near Petersburgh. Prince Ivan, the son of Antony Prince of Brunswick Wolfenbuttle and the Princess Anne of Mecklenburg, was proclaimed Emperor of Russia on the death of Anne Iwanowna in 1739. He was then in his cradle, and the Princess Elizabeth having gained possession of the throne, Ivan was deposed, but suffered to live in an obscure condition. Catharine, on her accession, placed him under a guard in the fortress of Schlusselburg, giving strict orders that no one should be suffered to see him. A bold design was formed by one Mirowitz, a lieutenant, of setting this Prince at liberty, and placing him at the head of a conspiracy against the Empress; and after tampering with some soldiers of the garrison of Schlusselburg, he procured himself to be put on guard out of his turn. On July 15th, every thing being prepared, he led his partizans to an attack on the guard of Ivan, and having been repulsed, he brought up a piece of cannon to force an entrance to his apartment. The commanders of the guard, who conceived themselves responsible for the security of the Prince's person, finding no other way of defeating the attempt to carry him off, caused him to be put to death; and then producing his bleeding body, exposed it to the view of the conspirators exclaiming "Here is your Emperor, let him now head you!" Struck with horror and despair, Mirowitz and his associates immediately surrendered, and he afterwards suffered death for his attempt. Of this tragedy the Empress reaped the fruit, but there seems no reason to believe that, as some suspected, it was the result of her contrivance.

The republic of Genoa finding itself unable to contend with success against the Corsican malcontents, concluded a treaty in August with the King of France, by the tenor of which seven battalions of French troops were to be sent to Corsica for four years, where they were to occupy four towns in order to secure them for the republic, but without being engaged in the war against the islanders. In November, the principal of the malcontents assembled at Bastia to deliberate on the expected arrival of these troops, when among other resolutions, Paoli was commissioned to make a respectful remonstrance to the French King, representing the injury that would be done to the Corsicans by sending over forces at the time they were on the point of expelling their enemies from the island; and also, to engage other friendly powers to interpose their mediation with that King in favour of Corsica.

In December an edict was registered in the Parliament of Paris, by which the King of France for ever abolished the society of Jesuits, permitting, however, the individual members to reside in the country under subjection to their spiritual superiors, and putting a stop to all criminal proceedings against any of them.

The war with the savages in America was in this year, though not extinguished, yet greatly limited in extent. In the month of April, Sir William Johnson concluded a treaty with the Senecas, one of the hostile tribes of the Iroquois; and in the autumn, the confederate tribes between Lake Erie and the Ohio were induced to submit on the advance into their country of Colonel Bradstreet from Niagara, and of Colonel Bouquet from Philadelphia.

The East Indies presented during this year an extension of hostilities between the English Company and the native princes. Cossim Ally Cawn, who had taken shelter in Sujah Dowla's dominions, was not at first openly countenanced by that Nabob, but by his own activity and influence was enabled to bring a body of troops into the field, which cut off a small party of English. This success induced both the Nabob and the Mogul King Shah Zada, to declare in his favour, and to support his cause by bringing into the field an army of 50,000 men, with a large train of artillery. Major Adams dying about this time, Major Hector Munro was sent to succeed him in the command, who immediately marched with about 9000 men, of whom a small proportion were Europeans, to meet the enemy. Coming up with them at Buxar, a place about 100 miles above Patna, he attacked them on October 23d, and put them totally to the rout with the loss of 6000 left on the field, 130 pieces of cannon, and their tents and military stores. The Mogul, after this action, threw himself under the protection of the English, and signed a treaty with the Company in the camp. An attack by Major Monro on the fort of Chanda Geer having been repulsed with considerable loss, he encamped with his army under the walls of Benares, where he remained to the close of the year.

1765

5th & 6th Year of the Reign

I N the King's speech on the opening of the Session of Parliament, January 10th, the disputes with the colonies were slightly alluded to by expressing his Majesty's reliance on the firmness and wisdom of both Houses, "in promoting that obedience to the laws, and respect to the *legislative authority of this kingdom*, which is essentially necessary to the safety of the whole."

A renewed attempt was made in the same month, by the opposition in the House of Commons, to procure a resolution against the legality of general warrants, which was productive of a copious debate; but in the end, the decision of the point was eluded by the previous question.

The highly important topic of colonial taxation was brought under discussion, early in the session. It has been mentioned that the resolution of laying a stamp duty on the colonies had been postponed in its effect in order to give them time to propose any other scheme of taxation which they might prefer. None of the colonies however, had authorized their agents either to consent to a stamp tax or to offer a compensation for it; and some of them had transmitted petitions to be presented to the King and both Houses of Parliament, directly calling in question the jurisdiction of the British legislature over their properties. Very warm and strenuous debates ensued in Parliament on this head; and argument was exhausted in proving on one side the reasonableness of the contribution of America to the general expences of the empire, and the natural right of a mother country over her colonies; and on the other, the necessary connection, in a free state, of representation with taxation, and the injustice of a power of taxing others, exercised by a body whose own burdens were to be relieved in proportion to the weight of those they imposed. The point, however, was not to be decided by argument; the ministers were resolved upon carrying the Stamp Act, and it passed into a law on March 22d.

During this period his Majesty had been labouring under an indisposition, now generally understood to have been of the same nature with that which has so deeply afflicted the latter years of his reign. On his recovery he went on April 24th to the House of Peers, and made a speech to the parliament, in which he said, that "his late indisposition, though not attended with danger, had led him to consider the situation in which his kingdoms and family might be left, should it please God to put a period to his life, whilst his successor was yet of tender years." His Majesty therefore proposed to their consideration, whether it would not be expedient to vest him with the power of appointing from time to time either the queen, or any other person of the royal family, usually residing in Great Britain, to be guardian of such successor, and regent of the kingdom, assisted by a council, till the successor should come of age. In consequence of this recommendation, a bill was brought into the House of Lords, framed on the plan of the Regency Act of the 24th of the late king, in the discussion of which, a doubt arising as to the questions, Who were the royal family? it was explained by the law lords to be the descendants of George II, in which construction Lord Halifax, secretary of state, readily concurred, declaring it to be agreeable to the royal intention. When, however, the bill came to the House of Commons, a member, who was a confidential friend of the Earl of Bute, made a motion to insert, after the name of the queen, that of the Princess-Dowager of Wales, who otherwise was excluded from the regency by the above construction. The bill passed with this amendment; but it soon appeared that the prior omission of the princess-dowager greatly indisposed the mind of his Majesty against the ministers, and it was resolved in the secret cabinet to make overtures to some of the leaders of opposition for the formation of a new administration.

At the latter end of May, the Duke of Cumberland (the king's uncle,) held a conference with Mr. Pitt and Lord Temple, in which he acquainted them that the king had determined upon changing his ministers, and wished to engage them and their friends in his service. When conditions, however, came to be treated of, the conference proved unsatisfactory. The ministers being apprized of this hostility against them in the inner cabinet, resolved to keep no measures with the court. Mr. Stuart Mackenzie, brother of Lord Bute, was dismissed, without any reason alledged, from a lucrative post which he held in Scotland; and the Duke of Northumberland, who had married a daughter of Lord Bute's, and Mr. Fox, his steady advocate in parliament, were discharged from their places. A further attempt to engage Mr. Pitt and Lord Temple having failed, the Duke of Cumberland negotiated with the Duke of Newcastle the arrangements for a new administration, which were carried into effect early in July. By this disposition, the Marquis of Rockingham was made first lord of the treasury, the Duke of Grafton and General Conway secretaries of state, Mr. Dowdeswell chancellor of the exchequer, Lord Winchelsea president of the council, and the Duke of Newcastle lord privy seal. Lord Northington was continued in the post of chancellor, and Lord Egremont at the head of the admiralty. The subsequent elevation of Lord

Chief Justice Pratt to the peerage, sufficiently indicated the political complexion of the new ministry.

On October 31st the Duke of Cumberland suddenly died, in the 45th year of his age, much regretted by the nation in general, on account of the generous manliness of his character, and his attachment to the principles of the constitution.

In this year the Isle of Man was irrevocably annexed to the crown of Great Britain, and rendered subject to the revenue laws, its sovereignty having been purchased from the Athol family.

The most important circumstance relative to the state of the British empire, which occurred abroad during the present year, was the manner in which the intelligence of the passing of the stamp act was received in the North American colonies. As soon as it reached Boston, the ships in the harbour hung their colours half-mast high, the bells were rung muffled, and the act was printed with a death's head, and cried in the streets under the title, "Folly of England and ruin of America." Publications of various kinds appeared, to inflame men's minds against the measure, and exhort them to unite in resisting it. The flame spread from one extremity of the continent to the other, and every where the act was treated with the utmost indignity, and its authors with the severest sarcasm. Of the persons who came from England to act as distributors of stamps, some were obliged publicly upon oath to renounce all concern with them, and others thought proper to return. Several residents in the colonies, who were suspected as agents of the British government, and enemies to American freedom, had their houses burnt down, and their property destroyed or plundered. These violences were not confined to the lower classes, but many of the better orders of society mingled with the populace in their tumults. The provincial assemblies declined to give advice to the governors on this occasion, and refused to strengthen their hands by acts of authority. They even avowed their hostility to the act, and established committees to correspond with each other, concerning the general affairs of the colonies. In consequence of these proceedings, on November 1st, the period when the act was to take place, not a sheet of stamped paper was to be met with from New England to Carolina, except a small parcel which the governor of New York had surrendered to the corporation of the place; so that all business, which could not be legally carried on without stamps, was at a stand, the courts of justice were closed, and the ports were shut. The merchants in several of the colonies made solemn engagements with each other to order no more goods from Great Britain, and even not to dispose of such as were sent upon commission, if not shipped before the first day of the year ensuing. Societies were formed for encouragement of home manufactures, and markets were opened for the sale of them; and various resolutions were entered into for lessening the wants of families by the promotion of industry and frugality. In short, the colonists seemed determined to take the experiment how far it was possible to go in resistance to what they considered as a tyrannical imposition, short of actually renouncing their dependence on the mother country. In the West India islands, the stamp tax, though unpopular, forced its way in consequence of their more direct connexion with Great Britain.

The events in the American colonies were adverted to in the King's speech to parliament on December 17th, as demanding the most serious attention of that assembly, with the promise of laying before it the fullest accounts of them as soon as the expected information from different parts of that country should arrive.

Of the occurrences on the European continent, one of the most memorable was the death of the Emperor of Germany, Francis I, on August 18th, who was succeeded on the imperial throne by his son Joseph II. The late emperor acted only a second part at the court of Vienna, as husband to the Empress Maria Theresa; and his successor, during the life of his mother, was only a nominal co-regent of the Austrian states, and inherited no patrimonial dominions.

In France, the parliament of Britany having been dissolved for its contumacious opposition to the will of the court, a commission of 60 members was appointed by the king, with authority to act in its room. A severe prosecution was at the same time instituted against the displaced members; but when sentence was about to be pronounced upon them, it was thought proper to shew lenity, and letters of amnesty were granted in their favour, with an injunction to them of retiring to their estates. Meantime the other parliaments of the kingdom had supported their cause with great vigour, and made spirited remonstrances in their behalf. The parliament of Paris having distinguished itself in these proceedings, the king, on March 3d, unexpectedly coming to the metropolis, went immediately to their grand chamber, and held a bed of justice, in which he expressed himself in the most authoritative style, and prohibited all associations among the different parliaments.

In the East Indies, Major Munro being recalled, the command of the British army lying at Benares devolved upon Sir Robert Fletcher, a major in the company's service, who broke up his camp in January, and marching towards the enemy, they retreated, and finally took to flight. He then determined upon a renewed attack of that fort, before which his predecessor had been foiled; and its garrison being mutinous for want of pay, it was surrendered at discretion by the governor. Sir Robert next proceeded to Eliabad, the capital of the Gorrah country, situated on the Ganges, of which he made himself master. About this time, the restored Subah of Bengal, Meer Jaffier, dying, left his authority to his son Najim ul Dowla, who was waited upon by a deputation from the council at Calcutta, and in February was proclaimed at Moorshedabad. Major Carnac, now arriving to take the command of the army, he made the proper dispositions to secure the conquered territory, and in the latter end of April crossed the Ganges for the purpose of opposing Sujah Dowla. That nabob, though deserted by the Mogul, supported himself with vigour, and engaged a body of Mahrattas in his service. The English general, however, bringing them to an action on the 20th of May, they were totally routed and driven across the Jumna. Sujah Dowla thereupon resolved to throw himself on the generosity of his invader; and having first permitted the fugitive Cossim to escape, he surrendered himself to General Carnac, with no other stipulation than that of awaiting the decision of Lord Clive respecting his fate.

This celebrated commander and statesman had been prevailed upon by the Company to re-visit India, in order to settle their embroiled affairs. Previously to his arrival, the English council of Calcutta, having decided the succession to Jaffier's subahship, in favour of his son Najim ul Dowla, against his grandson, by an elder son, made a treaty with the young prince by which they eased him of the trouble of keeping up an army, which they took upon themselves, on the payment of a portion of his revenue for that purpose. They also insisted upon his discarding his prime minister and favourite Nundcomar, who had held the same post under his father, and receiving in his stead a person nominated by the Company; and by these means Bengal was in effect brought under the British dominion. Lord Clive arrived in India on May 3d, bringing with him full power to act as commander-in-chief, president, and governor of Bengal. There was also a power lodged in a select committee, consisting of his lordship and four other gentlemen, to determine in all cases without dependence on the council. He presently set out for the army, with authority from the committee, in conjunction with General Carnac, to conclude a treaty with Sujah Dowla. It was found expedient to restore him to his nabobship of Oude, and at the same time to satisfy the Mogul, by obtaining for him a more ample revenue, which might enable him to march to Dehli, and take possession of the capital of the empire. This was effected by assigning him a small territory out of Sujah Dowla's dominions: and in return, the Mogul conferred on the Company the *Dewannee*, or collection of the revenue of the provinces of Bengal, Bahar, and Orissa, with the reservation of an annual tribute to himself, and a sum for the maintenance of the Subah, and the expences of his household. In this manner the English Company rapidly advanced to the sovereignty of that part of India.

The concluding month of this year was rendered remarkable by the death of three persons connected with royalty. On December 20th died the Dauphin of France, at the age of 36 years. He was a prince of a benevolent character, and of exemplary piety, but little known in public life.

On the 28th, died in his 16th year, Prince Frederic William, younger brother of his Majesty.

James Francis Edward, known by the title of the Chevalier de St. George, son of King James II, died at Rome on the 30th; in the 78th year of his age. By his consort, Maria Clementina, daughter of Prince Sobieski, he left two sons, Charles Edward Lewis, the adventurer of 1745, and Henry, Cardinal York. He was interred in the church of the Holy Apostles at Rome, with all the insignia of royalty.

1766

6th & 7th Year of the Reign

THE meeting of parliament on January 14th, was opened by a speech from the throne referring almost solely to the dispute with the colonies, now become of so much serious moment. The tables of both houses were soon covered with petitions from considerable commercial and manufacturing towns in the kingdom, complaining of the great decay of trade consequent on the new laws and regulations made for America. They stated that large sums were owing to Great Britain from the colonies, which the latter declared themselves unable to pay, on account of the taxes and restrictions laid upon them, that numerous bankruptcies had been the result, and that the utter ruin of many branches of trade was to be feared, unless some alteration were made in the system. A petition was also presented from Jamaica, setting forth the evils which had attended the imposition of a stamp tax, by the assembly of that island, and which had therefore been suffered to expire. Petitions also were transmitted from Virginia and Georgia, relative to the same subject; the other colonies preserved an ominous silence. This spirit of petitioning was not displeasing to the ministry, who had determined upon the repeal of the obnoxious tax; but the subject was attended with considerable difficulty.

The Grenville ministry who had laid the tax, were of course adverse to its repeal, as a measure of pusillanimity which would encourage the colonies in future resistance to the authority of the mother country. They who were convinced of the necessity of the repeal, divided upon the principle concerning the right of taxation. Some, who were the smaller number, absolutely denied the existence of such a right where taxation was not accompanied with representation, contending that the two were inseparable in a free constitution, and that the maxim "that no man shall be taxed but by himself or his representative," was fundamental in the plan of British liberty. Of this opinion Mr. Pitt was one of the most strenuous supporters; and in the warmth of debate he did not hesitate to exclaim, "I rejoice that America has resisted; three millions of people so dead to all feelings of liberty as voluntarily to submit to be slaves, would have been fit instruments to make slaves of all the rest." But the greater number, among whom were included the ministers, would by no means admit this abstract proposition, and brought many arguments from historical fact to prove that it had not been acted upon, and with respect to the colonies, that they had always been regarded as bound by every regulation of the British parliament, and that the protection they received was a sufficient ground for a right of taxation. So conformable was this idea of superiority to the general sentiments of the members of the House of Commons, that upon the question being put, a declaration of the power of the legislature of Great Britain over her colonies in all cases whatsoever, was carried without a division, the ministers and opposition agreeing upon this point. Upon this resolution a declaratory act was framed and passed which at the same time condemned in strong terms the resistance made in America to the orders of the government, and annulled all the proceedings of the colonial assemblies derogatory to the authority of parliament. This assertion of supremacy was, however, immediately followed by a repeal of the stamp act, carried by a majority of 275 to 167. The bill being brought up the House of Lords by above 200 members, it encountered a vigorous opposition in that assembly, but was passed by a majority of 34, and on March 18th, received the royal assent. This event was hailed by the general joy of the trading part of the nation; and the satisfaction with which it was received in America was little impaired by the declaratory act.

The repeal of the cyder-tax was another sacrifice made by the present ministry to the desire of rendering their administration popular. It was followed by a bill for opening free ports under certain restrictions in different parts of the West Indies; by regulations taking off some of the impediments to which the commercial system of the colonies had been subjected; by a modification of the window-tax, rendering it easier to the lower and middle classes; and (what was more important in a constitutional view) by a parliamentary resolution declaring the illegality of the seizure of persons and papers by general warrants, except in cases prescribed by direct statutes. The ministers had the further merits of concluding an advantageous commercial treaty with Russia; of settling a long contest with the French court relative to bills issued in Canada, the payment of which had been refused; and of making a progress in bringing to a termination the matter of the Manilla ransom, which the subterfuges of Spain had thrown into neglect. It appeared, however, that the sprit of their administration, approved as it was by the nation at large, by no means concurred with the sentiments of those whose favourable opinion is essential to the stability of men in office. Overtures were made by the confidential cabinet to some leading persons for the formation of a new ministry; and on July 30th the public was surprised by the announcement of the following changes: the Duke of Grafton at the head of the Treasury, in the room of the Marquis of Rockingham; the Earl of Shelburne one of the Secretaries of State, in the room of the Duke of Richmond; Lord Camden

(Pratt) Lord Chancellor, in the room of Lord Northington; Right Honourable C. Townshend, Chancellor of the Exchequer, in the room of the Right Honourable W. Dowdeswell; and the Right Honourable William Pitt (now raised to the title of Earl of Chatham,) Lord Privy Seal. It was to the honour of the retiring ministers that they bargained for neither place, pension, or reversion, for themselves or their friends; and the public esteem for the character and conduct of the Marquis of Rockingham was testified by numerous addresses presented to him on his resignation. Of the new ministry, Lord Chatham was regarded as the former and head; and it was no small diminution of his popularity, that he had lent his influence to the overthrow of an administration which had hazarded their seats by the support of principles similar to those professed by himself.

In the autumn, tumults and riots broke out in various parts of the kingdom, in consequence of the high price of provisions, and it was found necessary in several places to call in military aid for their suppression. Many lives were lost, and a special commission was issued for the trial of the apprehended rioters, which acted with all the lenity the case would allow. Government at the same time took measures for remedying the evil, one of which was the laying of an embargo on the exportation of wheat, by the royal authority, parliament at that time being in a state of prorogation. When that assembly met, a bill of indemnity was brought in for the protection of all persons who had acted in obedience to the act of council ordering the embargo, from any prosecution which might be instituted against them on that account. It being remarked as an omission in the bill, that no indemnity was provided for the *advisers* of the measure, but only for its executors, an amendment was proposed for the purpose. This occasioned warm debates, especially in the House of Lords, where it appeared very extraordinary to see Lords Camden and Chatham taking the high ground of prerogative, and arguing for a suspending power in the crown, whilst Lord Mansfield took the contrary ground of the law and constitution. The arguments of the latter preponderated, and the bill passed in its amended form.

The augmentation of the revenues of the East India Company, consequent upon the treaties with the native princes concluded in the last year, produced long debate during the summer and autumn between the directors and the proprietors of India stock, relative to the expediency of an increase of dividend; and it was at length voted by a great majority, that it should be raised from six to ten percent. A great advance in India stock was one result of this measure; and another was, that a message was sent from government to the company, intimating an intention of taking its affairs into public consideration.

This year was marked by internal commotions in various parts of Europe. In France, the rising spirit of liberty, so conspicuous in the late proceedings of the parliaments, still maintained a contest with the arbitrary power of the court, though supported by no other strength than that of opinion. In March, the parliament of Rouen sent a grand deputation to the king, for the purpose of remonstrating against the treatment of the parliament of Britany. Having in their remonstrance reminded the king of his coronation oath, in terms insinuating a compact between sovereign and people, his Majesty in his answer, alluding to it, disclaimed their interpretation, by saying, "The oath, which I have taken, not to the nation, as you take upon you to assert, but to God alone ——." In Britany itself, the spirit of resistance continued unsubdued. The counsellors of parliament refused to obey the king's express order that they should resume their functions; alledging that the oath which they had taken to their parliament, would not permit them to plead before the commission appointed to supersede it. For this contumacy they were punished, by a command that their names should be included in the list of drafts for the militia; and those on whom the lot fell were obliged to join their battalions, and the rest to act as the city guard. The tragical end of Count Lally, the late French commander in the East Indies, was another subject of public interest in France. This unfortunate man was tried before the parliament of Paris, after three years' imprisonment for his misconduct in India to which the ruin of the French affairs was attributed. He was capitally condemned, and was executed three days after, being gagged at the place of execution. Though a man who had always acted under the influence of pride and passion, which had led him to violent and imprudent measures, he was by many regarded as a victim to party and private enmity.

Madrid was in this year the theatre of commotions more serious and daring than could have been expected under an arbitrary government. The King, whose French education and long residence in Italy had alienated him from Spanish manners, and given him a prepossession for foreigners, had brought with him to the crown Spain a number of Italian favourites, and had given his confidence to the Marquis of Squillaci, whom he had made his prime-minister. Being persuaded to undertake the arduous task of new modelling his nation, he published a severe edict against the wearing of flapped hats and long cloaks, the favourite costume of the Spaniards. A young gentleman, on March 23d, appearing near the palace in the prohibited dress, was stopped by a sentinel, and drawing his sword, upon giving a signal, a number of people assembled to his assistance. They were fired upon by the Walloon guard, and several were killed. On the following day they re-assembled in numbers, attacked and overpowered the guard, and then proceeding to the house of Squillaci, entirely demolished it, and pursued the marquis himself who had fled for safety. The riot on the next day took the form of a regular insurrection. A very numerous body went to the royal palace and demanded to see the King, who at length appeared in a balcony. The insurgents required of him to dismiss his Italian ministers, to repeal all the late obnoxious edicts, and to promise amnesty on account of what had taken place. His Majesty found it expedient to comply with these conditions, on which the rioters dispersed, and Madrid became entirely tranquil. On the next day, however, the King withdrawing with his guards to Aranjuez, the populace became more furious than ever; and placing a guard round the city to prevent any one from leaving it, sent a deputation to Aranjuez to complain of the King's suspicion of their fidelity, and to request his return. He declined this proposal, but granted a general pardon, and promised to send away Squillaci and his family. That minister accordingly set out under a strong escort for Carthagena, whence he embarked for Naples. Mutinies afterwards took place in other cities of Spain; but the general result appears to have been a reflux of loyalty, and the King, after an absence of eight months, returned to Madrid, where he was received with general acclamations.

In Poland, religious bigotry was in this year the cause of dissentions highly dangerous to the internal tranquillity of that ill-constituted state. The dissidents of the kingdom, under which name are included all the separatists from the Roman Catholic church, having undergone many oppressions, applied to the courts of Petersburgh, Berlin, Great Britain, and Denmark, as guarantees of the treaty of Oliva, to employ their mediation with the King and republic of Poland in their favour. The treaty in question had secured to the dissidents the free exercise of their public worship, and the continuance of such privileges as they had before possessed; but during the variety of changes which had occurred in the Polish government since that period, the predominant party had framed several constitutions by which the privileges of the dissidents were much abridged. The mediating powers, in consequence of this application, presented memorials in which a recurrence to the spirit of the treaty of Oliva was strongly urged; whilst on the other hand, the Polish majority insisted upon the observance of their laws, of which the above-mentioned constitutions were now a part. On the opening of the diet on September 1st, the Bishop of Cracow, after declaring that by the laws of the kingdom not even the toleration of their worship could be granted to the dissidents, and that they had violated the laws by applying to foreign powers for protection, read the plan of a law to preclude the concession to them of any privileges which they did not now possess; and asking whether it would be agreed to by the two chambers, he was answered by a general acclamation. In the meantime a body of Russian troops advanced towards Warsaw, and the mediating powers renewed their declarations in favour of the dissidents. A strong memorial was delivered to Prince Repnin, the Russian ambassador, against the entrance of the troops; and the diet, in great heat, demanded that the Bishop of Cracow's proposal should be signed. Tumultuary proceedings followed, during which the King and the Prince primate retired from the diet; and at length, the Bishop's plan was again read, approved, and signed. On the last day of sitting, November 29th, the diet seemed to have recovered a degree of calmness, and a resolution was passed, assuring in respectful terms the ministers of the mediating powers that the dissidents would be maintained in all the rights and prerogatives to which they were legally entitled. On the same day the episcopal college signed nine articles, by which the dissidents were allowed the free exercise of their worship in all the places where they had been permitted to erect churches, and in their own houses where there were none; but were however laid under various restrictions denoting a very imperfect toleration.

In Sweden the public peace was for a short time disturbed by an insurrection of some peasants in resentment of the exclusion of one of their members elected to the diet. It was presently quelled with no other loss of lives than the execution of some of the ringleaders. The Swedish diet made a number of economical regulations for relieving the financial difficulties of the country.

On January 14th, died Frederic V King of Denmark in his 43d year, greatly regretted by his people. He was succeeded by his son Christian VII, who being already affianced to the Princess Caroline Matilda, sister of the King of Great Britain, the marriage was celebrated by proxy at St. James's on October 1st. The nuptials took place in Denmark on November 8th.

The Prince of Orange, having arrived at the proper age, assumed, on March 8th, the administration of the United Provinces, as perpetual Stadtholder, amidst general rejoicings.

1767

7th & 8th Year of the Reign

I T had been customary, after the termination of a war, to withdraw any addition made to the land-tax in support of it, and reduce the tax to its established rate; but since the last peace, it had been left at four shillings in the pound, that there might be no necessity of laying imposts which would aggravate the burdens pressing upon the lower classes. The country gentlemen, however, becoming impatient of this innovation, a strong effort was made early in the Session of Parliament to revive the former usage; and a bill for reducing the land-tax from four to three shillings in the pound passed by a considerable majority, in opposition to the ministry; a defeat which was supposed to bode ill for their durability.

A discontented spirit still prevailing in the North American colonies, the assembly of New York had taken upon them to set aside the provisions of an Act of Parliament for supplying the troops in barracks with necessaries, and to substitute regulations of their own. When this circumstance was reported to Parliament, it gave rise to many debates, and measures of rigour were proposed by some of the members. The ministers, however, took the more lenient but decisive mode of introducing a bill by which the governor, council, and assembly of New York were prohibited from passing or giving assent to any act of assembly for any purposes till they had fully complied with the terms of the Act of Parliament. This measure proved effectual.

The most important matter in which Parliament was engaged during this year related to the concerns of the East India Company. It has already been mentioned that the ministers had given them an intimation of its intention of taking cognizance of their affairs, and a committee of Parliament had been appointed for that purpose. Orders were subsequently made to lay before Parliament copies of their charters, their treaties with the country powers, the state of their revenues and expences, their correspondence with their servants, &c. In the course of this enquiry various questions were discussed, among which was the important one (which has never yet been decided) respecting the right of the company to their territorial acquisitions. While things were in this state, a general court of East India proprietors was held, May 6th, at which the dividend for the ensuing half year was declared at six and a quarter per cent; at the same time proposals were agreed upon to be offered for coming to an accommodation with parliament. Of these there were two sets, the second of which consisted of a specific payment to the public of £400,000 a year by half-yearly payments for three years, with an indemnification for any loss the revenue might sustain by granting the advantages which the company required in the tea trade. This was accepted by parliament, with the sole difference of limiting the agreement to two years instead of three, and a bill passed on June 12th, upon these terms.

A message from the ministry to the general court recommending it to the Company to make no augmentation of their dividend till their affairs had been further considered of, failing of its effect, two bills were brought into parliament, one, to regulate the qualifications for voters in trading companies, the other to regulate the making of dividends by the East

India Company. The last of these bills rescinded the act of the Company which had declared an increased dividend, and bound them not to raise their dividends beyond ten per cent till the next meeting of parliament. This was productive of very warm debates, and some of the ministers themselves joined the minority in their opposition to the bill. The Company petitioned against it, and to ward off the blow, offered to restrict themselves from any farther increase of dividend during the term of their agreement with government. The measure was, however, persisted in, and the bill was carried through both houses in face of a strong opposition; the majority in the upper house being only 59 against 44. Of the dissentients 19 joined in a very energetic protest, one article of which touched upon the assumed supposition in the bill that the right to the territory acquired in the East Indies was not in the company, but in the public; and declared it highly dangerous to the property of the subject, and unbecoming the justice and dignity of the house, by extrajudicial opinions, to call into question the legality of such a possession.

The project of raising a revenue from the American colonies being still entertained in the cabinet, an indirect mode of effecting it was proposed by the Chancellor of the Exchequer, Mr. C. Townshend, which consisted in laying a tax upon certain necessary articles imported by them from this country. A bill was accordingly introduced into parliament for imposing duties on glass, paper, painters' colours, and tea, imported into the colonies from Great Britain. It passed with general approbation through both houses, and received the royal assent in June; but when the measure was made known in America it revived the former discontents, being regarded as a kind of experiment, preparatory to future more burdensome financial regulations. At a public meeting of the inhabitants of Boston in October, resolutions were entered into for the encouragement of home manufactures, and the promotion of frugality, by restraining the use of foreign superfluities; and similar resolutions were adopted in the other colonies. On the whole, it was manifest that a spirit of resistance to the controul of the mother country was gaining ground in North America, which every new exertion of authority only tended to exasperate.

During the course of the summer divisions in the ministry became apparent. Lord Chatham, who, though nominally at the head of the administration had, together with his popularity, lost much of his consequence, was reduced by ill health to a state which rendered him entirely incapable of business; and no leader remained of weight enough to give steadiness to the vaccilating frame of government. Soon after the close of the parliamentary session, proposals were made from the court to the Marquis of Rockingham for a coalition with the existing ministry, but the negotiation proved ineffectual. A treaty was then opened with the Bedford party, which was also abortive; and the death of Mr. C. Townshend in September still farther debilitated the administration. At length, without any fundamental change, new members were taken in, by which different interests were united. The chancellorship of the exchequer was occupied by Lord North, son of the Earl of Guilford; and Earl Gower was made lord president of the council.

The high price of provisions continued during this year to occasion much distress, and excite tumults in various parts of the kingdom.

The Duke of York, next brother to his Majesty, being attacked by a fever while making the tour of Italy, died at Monaco on September 17th, in the 29th year of his age.

The most remarkable event that occurred on the European continent in this year was the expulsion of the Jesuits from Spain, and from Naples and Parma, the Italian States dependent on that kingdom; and subsequently, from France.

On the night of March 31st, the six houses of Jesuits in Madrid were surrounded by detachments of troops, which, having obtained admittance, placed a sentinel at the door of each cell. The Jesuits were then ordered to rise, and being apprized of the King's commands, were put, with their travelling necessaries, in hired carriages ready in waiting, and early in the morning began their journey to Carthagena under a strong escort. On the third day after, the Jesuits' college in Barcelona was invested by the civil and military power, and the members were sent off in the same manner as those of Madrid; and at the same hour similar measures were put in execution in every part of Spain where the Jesuits possessed establishments. Ships were provided for their embarkation for Italy, and orders were sent to all the seaports for a strict watch to be kept that no Jesuit in disguise should ship himself for the Spanish Indies. The King then published his pragmatic sanction, or ordinance for their expulsion. Without alleging any other reason than his royal pleasure, the temporalities of the society were declared seized to the King's use, with the reservation of small life annuities to the priests who were natives, which, however, were to be forfeited upon quitting the state to which they were transported, or if any individuals of the society should write any thing derogatory to the submission due to the King's resolution, or attempt to excite any disturbances on its account. Many other articles of great rigour were inserted in the ordnance, which was drawn up in they most arbitrary style. The court of Rome had not recovered its astonishment at the news of this event, before transports convoyed by Spanish men of war arrived at Civita Vecchia, having on board 970 Jesuits. The pope having refused to permit them to be landed, they were sent to Corsica, where, after much demur, and great suffering, they were at length disembarked.

In May the parliament of Paris published an arret, in which the Jesuits were declared foes to sovereigns and to the tranquillity of states; and all of them who had been allowed the liberty of continuing in France by the edict of 1764, were now ordered to quit it within fifteen days, and were forbidden to return on any pretext whatever. The King was also to be requested to apply to the Pope for the total abolition of the society. At Naples the storm fell upon them in November; and from that city, and every part of the kingdoms of Naples and Sicily, they were conveyed to the Pope's territories; an outrage of which the court of Rome justly complained. The orders of the King of Spain respecting them had been conveyed to the American colonies; and in July, those of Mexico, to the number of 700, were suddenly arrested, and placed under confinement till ships could be provided for their deportation to Europe. Their confiscations in that rich province are said to have amounted to an immense sum; the temptation of such prizes out of their property in New and Old Spain was thought to have been no small inducement to the severe measures taken against them.

The dissidents in Poland having no confidence in the moderation of the Catholic clergy, began early in this year to form confederacies in different parts of the kingdom for the preservation of their just rights and privileges. The first act for this purpose was signed in March between the nobles and citizens of the Greek church and the two Protestant confessions of Lithuania. Another confederacy was entered into at Thorn in the same month among the discontented Polish nobility, which was acceded to by the cities of Thorn, Elbing, and Dantzic. For their support the Empress of Russia sent strong reinforcement to her troops already in Poland, with a declaration that orders had been given them to act offensively against all who should attack the confederacies. The King of Prussia transmitted a vigorous remonstrance respecting the manner in which the dissidents had been treated, and their confederacies were also encouraged by the courts of England, Sweden, and Denmark. On the other hand, the Roman Catholic nobility of Poland and Lithuania formed numerous confederacies, many of which, however, had political rather than religious objects in view, whence they bore

the name of malcontents. Of the Catholic confederacies Prince
Radzivil, who had suffered from his opposition to the election
of Poniatowski, was elected marshal; and a coalition between
the general confederacy of the malcontents and that of the
dissidents, took place in September in that prince's palace.
In order to reconcile the different parties, and prevent a civil
war, a general diet of the kingdom was assembled at Warsaw
in October; but the warmth with which the pretensions of
the dissidents were opposed by some of the catholic magnates
and prelates frustrated all attempts for conciliation. In the
meantime the Russian troops were advancing upon Warsaw,
which at length they closely invested; and some of their
detachments entering the city, arrested the Bishops of Cracow
and Kiof, with some nobles of their party, and sent them
prisoners into Russia. At the following meeting of the diet,
after violent tumults, it was agreed that a commission should
be appointed to settle the affairs of the dissidents, under the
mediation of Russia, and a temporary calm was restored.

The Prince Stadtholder of Holland was in this year
married to the Princess Royal of Prussia; an union afterwards
productive of important political consequences.

The Corsicans, under the conduct of Paoli, having effected
a landing on the island of Capraia, belonging to the Genoese,
laid siege to its principal fort, which surrendered in May, after
a long defence.

In the East Indies, a war commenced between the English
Company and a new foe, Hyder Ally, which in the sequel
involved the company in great difficulty and immense
expences. This adventurer, from the condition of a private
soldier, raised himself by his courage and talents to the rank
of a powerful prince, and became master of a considerable
portion of the Malabar coast. He had influenced the Nizam
of the Decan to renounce his alliance with the Company,
and unite with himself in a war against it. On the intelligence of this event, the council of Madras sent an army

into the field, under the command of Colonel Smith, who, on September 26th, brought the confederate forces to an engagement near Trincomalee, and entirely defeated them. The Nizam thereupon deserted Hyder, and concluded a treaty with the Company, by which he ceded to it the Dewannee of the Balagat Carnatic. Hyder withdrew to a mountainous tract, where he maintained himself, and by the superiority of his cavalry, frequently intercepted the supplies sent to the English army.

1768

8th & 9th Year of the Reign

IN the month of January the ministry was consolidated by the appointment of Lord Weymouth to the post of secretary of state, in the room of General Conway; and of the Earl of Hillsborough to that of secretary of state for the colonies, a new office, which the increased importance of colonial affairs was thought to render expedient.

The restraining act, with respect to East India dividends, having nearly expired, and a bill for its renewal being brought into parliament, the Company presented a petition against it, in which they strongly pleaded their right by charter to declare their own dividends, and engaged to make no increase which should not be amply justified by the state of their affairs. The bill, however, notwithstanding a warm opposition, was carried in both houses by a great majority.

A motion made in the House of Commons for leave to bring in a bill for quieting the subject against obsolete claims of the crown, excited considerable interest, both in and out of parliament. It was occasioned by the following circumstance. The Portland family had, in consequence of a grant from King William, been more than 70 years in possession of the honour of Penrith, in Cumberland, with its appurtenances, which last had been regarded as including the forest of Inglewood and manor of Carlisle, though not specifically mentioned in the grant. In the summer of 1767, Sir James Lowther presented a memorial to the lords of the treasury, stating, that he had been informed that this forest and manor had been long withheld from the crown, and praying for a lease of his Majesty's interest in them. The surveyor general of crown lands having given his opinion, without consulting the crown lawyers, that these premises were still invested in the crown, the Duke of Portland presented a memorial to the treasury board, praying to be heard by counsel in defence of his title, before any proceedings were held in consequence of Sir James Lowther's application. He was informed that no steps should be taken to his prejudice without a full investigation of the matter; but whilst the duke's agents were employed in the necessary researches, he received a letter from the secretary of the treasury, acquainting him, that the grant was passed, and the leases to Sir James were signed. Nothing now remained for the Duke but to stop its progress in the exchequer office, where he had entered a caveat; the chancellor of the exchequer, however, being applied to for the purpose, made answer that he could not withhold the seal of his office against a direct order from the treasury to affix it. This was the state in which the affair was brought before parliament, where it occasioned a warm discussion. A motion was made, the object of which was to introduce as an amendment of the law of James I which declared that the quiet enjoyment of property for 60 years *before the passing of that act*, should bar all claims of the crown, the conversion of this *fixed* prescription into a moving limitation, making 60 years possession a bar against such claims in all future times. The ministry found no better method of getting rid of the motion, than by a postponement of it to the next session, which they carried by a majority of 20 only. A bill to that effect, however, passed in the following year.

During the winter, a popular bill passed the Irish parliament, for limiting the duration of the parliaments of that kingdom, which hitherto had only been terminated with the demise of the crown. It was fixed at eight years, and as their sittings were only every second winter, four sessions only were allotted them for the transaction of business.

The metropolis was much disquieted in the spring by riots, particularly among the sailors and coal-heavers, in which many lives were lost; and several of the perpetrators afterwards suffered by the hand of justice.

Parliament was dissolved on March 10th, and the kingdom was for a considerable time kept in a ferment by the election of a new one. Party running high, the electioneering contests were unusually violent, and in many places very serious disorders occurred. Mr. Wilkes, who had been almost forgotten, was again brought into public notice on this occasion. His outlawry had obliged him to reside on the continent, whence he had written to the Duke of Grafton, intreating him to mediate his pardon with the king. His application being disregarded, he ventured on the dissolution of parliament to come over and offer himself as a candidate for the city of London. Being left the last on the poll in the contest, he immediately declared himself for the county of Middlesex, and so high was his popularity, that he was returned by a large majority. After his election, he surrendered himself before the court of King's Bench, which refused to commit him on his outlawry, as moved by the attorney general, and he was accordingly discharged. He was afterwards, however, committed on a writ of *capias utlegatum*; but as the officers were conveying him to the King's Bench prison, he was rescued by the mob. After they had dispersed, he went privately to prison, where he was under confinement at the meeting of the new parliament. A tumultuous mob then assembled, with an intention of conveying him in triumph to the parliament house, and on their disappointment, became so riotous that an order was given to the military to fire upon them. The death of one person, who was singled out and pursued by the soldiers, was brought in by the coroner's jury wilful murder, and the magistrate who gave the order to fire was tried for the crime, but acquitted. The conduct of the soldiers on the occasion received public thanks from the highest authority; whilst the title of *the massacre in St. George's Fields*, was popularly given to the action. Mr. Wilkes's outlawry was afterwards reversed by the court of King's Bench as illegal; but judgment was pronounced upon him for the two publications of which he had been formerly convicted, and he was sentenced to two fines of £500 each, and to imprisonment for the two terms of ten and twelve months.

The new parliament was assembled on May 10th, only for the purpose of passing some necessary bills, one of which was a renewal of the act against the exportation of corn, now near expiring. On the day after, a proclamation was issued by order of the council for the suppression of riots, tumults, and unlawful assemblies, which the disturbed state of the country, particularly of the metropolis, now rendered formidable. Very loyal addresses were presented from both houses of parliament on the occasion, and assurances were given of their concurrence in every measure that might enable his Majesty to maintain the authority of the laws. This short session terminated on the 21st of May.

In this month died the Princess Louisa, second sister of the King.

The North American colonies were during this year in a state of the greatest ferment and disaffection. In February, a circular letter was sent by the assembly of Massachusets-bay to all the other colonial assemblies, the purpose of which was to represent the late acts of parliament as unconstitutional, and to propose a general union among the colonies for counteracting their effects, and for the defence of their natural rights. During a considerable time this colony had been at variance with their governor Bernard: and a letter received by the governor from Lord Shelburne as secretary of state, and which he caused to be read before the assembly, highly inflamed this disagreement. The letter contained severe animadversions on the conduct of the assembly, which that body imputed to misrepresentations transmitted by the governor; and being refused their requisition of copies of the correspondence between him and the secretary of state, they sent to the latter a vindication of themselves, and a charge against the governor. Soon after, the governor, finding himself without influence over the assembly, adjourned it with an indignant speech. On the intelligence of these transactions, the new colonial secretary, Lord Hillsborough, wrote a circular letter to the governors of those colonies which had been addressed by Massachusets, expressive of his Majesty's high displeasure at the combination proposed by that assembly, as a factious attempt to subvert the authority of parliament. In another letter, written to governor Bernard, a requisition was made in the King's name, that the new assembly should rescind the resolution which had given rise to the obnoxious circular letter, and in case of non-compliance he was directed immediately to dissolve the assembly. This demand being laid before them at their meeting, the question was put for the rescinding, which passed in the negative by a great majority. A letter was then voted to the secretary of state, in which the requisition was affirmed to be illegal, and strong remonstrances were made against the late laws; and the assembly was preparing a petition to the king for the removal of the governor, when it was dissolved. The circular letter of the secretary to the other colonies was not attended with better success. The different assemblies returned answers to that of Massachusets expressing high approbation of its conduct; and some of them voted addresses to the secretary, in which they animadverted with great freedom on the requisition made to that assembly, and justified its conduct. Meantime resolutions were entered into by most of the colonies, not to import any more English goods till the laws objected to were repealed.

Previously to the dissolution of the assembly, a serious tumult occurred at Boston, in consequence of the seizure by the custom-house officers, of a sloop belonging to one of the principal merchants. The populace were so outrageous against the commissioners of the customs, that they were obliged for safety to take refuge on board of the Romney man of war, whence they were conveyed to Castle William, a fortress in the harbour. Town meetings were held on the affair, at which the minds of the people were heated by inflammatory speeches, and the greatest aversion and contempt for the authority of the mother country were inculcated. In this disturbed state of things, the report of the expected arrival of two regiments from Ireland, and of the assembling of troops at Halifax, excited a violent commotion at Boston; and a meeting of the people being convened, a committee was appointed to wait on the governor, and desire him to call a general assembly without delay. This being declined by him, a convention was summoned to meet at Boston, to which 96 towns appointed deputies; and the Boston committee proceeded so far as to recommend to the inhabitants to provide themselves with arms and ammunition, on the pretext of apprehension of a war with France. The convention when met, communicated with the governor, who seriously admonished them of the irregularity and danger of their proceedings, and assured them from authority, that the king was determined to maintain his entire sovereignty over the province. That body having prepared a statement of their conduct to be transmitted to their agent in England, broke up on September 29th. On the same day, a fleet from Halifax with two regiments and a detachment of artillery arrived in the harbour. Soon after, General Gage, with the two regiments from Ireland, also arrived, and some difficulties about quartering the troops being compromised, tolerable harmony was established, and the town and province during the remainder of the year were in a state of tranquillity.

It was not to be expected that a ministry so heterogeneous in its composition as that which now governed the affairs of Great Britain, could act with perfect union in the momentous concerns which in this year were brought under their notice. Differences were known to exist among them, which were made public by Lord Shelburne's resignation, in October, of the post of secretary of the southern department, in which he was succeeded by Lord Weymouth from the northern, to whom the Earl of Rochford was appointed successor. Lord Chatham, who had long been treated with disregard, either on account of his infirmities, or his uncomplying disposition, soon after sent in his resignation of the place of keeper of the privy seal, in which he was succeeded by the Earl of Bristol; and so much had this great man declined in consequence, that his retreat passed as an occurrence of no moment.

Many important events on the continent distinguished the present year.

The grand commission in Poland appointed to adjust the affairs of the dissidents, acting under the influence of the Russian ambassador, made a variety of regulations, one of which was a commercial treaty with Russia, very advantageous to that empire. They determined upon suppressing the papal nunciature, and establishing an ecclesiastical synod in its stead; and they resolved that a minister plenipotentiary should be sent to Rome to inform the pope of their motives for re-establishing the dissidents in their ancient rights, and to request his holiness to withdraw his nuncio, and send no other into Poland. These proceedings were strongly resisted by the papal court; and the marshal of the Lithuanian confederacy entered a protest against every thing that should be transacted under the influence of foreign arms. The diet, however, which assembled in February *protected* by a considerable body of Russian troops, ratified almost without opposition the regulations proposed by the commission, and passed others, the tendency of which was to perpetuate the vices of the Polish constitution, and confirm the influence of Russia. It was then declared that the general confederacy of the states, and that of the dissidents, were at an end; and on March 5th, the diet was closed by the king. Tranquillity now for a time appeared to be restored, but this was only a fallacious calm. The bulk of the nation was highly discontented with what had been done, and the court of Rome and catholic clergy used all their efforts to inflame men's minds against the indulgences granted to heretics. A new confederacy was first formed in Podolia, which took possession of the city of Bar, and obtained some success against the crown troops. Several other confederacies were formed, against which the Russians marched in different divisions; and in a short time the whole kingdom was filled with devastation and bloodshed. The detail of this multiplied and cruel warfare will not here be attempted; but no situation can be conceived more disastrous than that of Poland, a prey at the same time to civil discord and to foreign force. Cracow was taken by storm by the Russians in August after a long defence by the confederates; and in general, the Russian discipline and steadiness prevailed against the spirited, but desultory efforts of the Poles. An insurrection of the oppressed Greek peasants in the province of Kiovia and the Ukraine was attended with massacres and cruelties, the narrative of which cannot be read without horror; and irruptions of the Haydamacs or Zaporavian Cossacks added to the calamity of the sufferers. On the approach of winter, large bodies of Russians began to file off to the frontiers of Turkey, with which power hostilities were impending, and in their absence the confederacies revived, and manifestoes were dispersed inviting the Poles to a general revolt, and holding forth promises of the protection of the Porte.

The Ottoman court had long viewed with jealousy the interference of Russia in the affairs of Poland, and had made frequent representations on the subject. On various occasions, Polish fugitives into the Turkish territories had been pursued by the Russians beyond the limits; and in July, a party of confederates having taken refuge at Balta, in Lesser Tartary, the Russians forced an entrance into the town, and indiscriminately massacred all who came in their way. This slaughter occasioned a great commotion at Constantinople, and orders were immediately dispatched for the bashaws of the European provinces in Turkey, to collect their troops and march towards the Niester; whilst warlike preparations were actively carried on in other parts. At length, in October, the Russian resident in Constantinople, according to the barbarous Turkish custom, was sent prisoner to the Seven Towers, and a manifesto was communicated to the foreign ministers, stating the causes of a declaration of war with Russia. It was met by a counter-declaration of the Empress of Russia; each party, as usual, making a solemn appeal to the world for the justice of its cause.

Sweden in this year presented a remarkable scene, the prelude to future important changes. The government of that country had become nearly an oligarchy in the hands of the senate, which equally usurped upon the prerogatives of the crown and the liberties of the people. The taxes which they had laid, proved so injurious and burdensome, that the king, Adolphus Frederic, had made several applications to the senate to convoke an anticipated diet of the nation, in order to inquire into the subsisting grievances, and remedy the disordered state of the revenues. That body persisting in a refusal, and having resolved upon the establishment of a new tribunal to take cognizance of the differences which had arisen between it and the board of treasury, the king went to the senate house and protested against this measure, at the same time renewing his demand for a convocation of the diet. As it was still rejected, he caused a declaration to be entered of his resolution to abdicate the throne, should senate continue its opposition to his desire;

and farther negotiations proving ineffectual, the king publicly declared his abdication on December 13th, and forbade the senate to issue any orders under his name. This step, by which all public business was suspended, threw the senate into great perplexity; and having in vain attempted to prevail on the king to alter his resolution, it came to a trial which of the two parties would be supported by the voice of the nation. In the end, the senate found itself obliged to yield and consent to the convocation of the states. The king, accordingly, on December 21st, signed the letters for that purpose, and resumed the reins of government.

The republic of Genoa finding its efforts for the recovery of Corsica ineffectual, concluded a treaty in this summer with the French court, by which that island was ceded to France, under the conditions, that this power should maintain sixteen battalions in Corsica, that it should secure the possession of Capraia to the republic, and that the latter should have a right of resumption at any time on payment of the expences which France might incur in supporting the cession. In consequence of this compact, about twenty battalions of French troops were landed in Corsica, and hoisted their flag at Bastia on June 24th, as an act of possession; whilst, on the other hand, a general assembly of the Corsicans held at Corte under the influence of Paoli, had entered into a resolution to defend their liberties to the last extremity. In the war which ensued, the French, at first, by the superiority of their numbers and appointments, obtained various successes; and made considerable progress in reducing the districts in their vicinity; but they underwent such serious losses from the gallant resistance of the Corsicans, and the able conduct of their chief, that at the close of the campaign they had little occasion to boast.

The affairs of the small state of Parma were in this year the cause of some extraordinary contests between the court of Rome and the Catholic powers. In that Duchy the ecclesiastics had long enjoyed exorbitant privileges, being exempted from contributing in any manner to the exigences of the state. The applications of the government to the Pope for abridging these injurious prerogatives having proved ineffectual, the Duke (an infant of Spain), published in the beginning of the year a pragmatic sanction, which prohibited all his subjects from carrying any matter of litigation to Rome or any other foreign tribunal; restricted the possession of benefices, dignities, &c. within his territories to his own subjects, and with his permission; and declared all sentences, decrees, bulls, &c. from Rome or any foreign country, null and void. This ordinance struck so directly at the papal authority, that there was no alternative between resisting it, or giving up the supremacy of the holy see; the Pope, therefore, was induced to issue on January 30th a brief against the Duke of Parma, by which he was admonished to desist from his rash enterprize, on pain of an interdict laid upon his territories, and excommunication of his person and his ministers. He moreover claimed the sovereignty of the Duchy of Parma, and declared the Infant to be only his feudatory. The court of Parma so little regarded this menace, that shortly after, all the Jesuits in the duchy were arrested in one night, and conveyed to the states of the church, with a prohibition of ever returning; and the order was declared abolished in Parma. The brief against the duke was highly resented by all the courts connected with him; and the first effect resulting from it was the occupation of Benevento and Ponte Corvo by a body of Neapolitan troops. The ministers of France, Spain, and Vienna, then made a joint application to the Pope for the revocation of the brief, but without success; the consequence of which was, that the King of France took possession of the city and territory of Avignon and the Venaissin, which, though within the French limits, had been long held by the papal see. The King of Naples farther advanced a claim to the Duchies of Ronciglione and Castro, and assembled troops on the frontier of the Ecclesiastical state to support it. The King of Portugal and the republic of

Venice joined in the common cause against the Pope. The Duke of Modena imitated the Duke of Parma in annulling the exemptions of the clergy in his dominions, and expelled the monks of three convents, threatening many others with the same fate; and upon the interference of the Court of Rome, he revived an old claim upon the Duchy of Ferrara. Meantime the rigorous proceedings against the Jesuits were continued. They were expelled from the island of Malta. Their estates in Naples were declared escheated to the crown, and a commission was appointed to search for their effects. When the French had become masters of Corsica, all the Spanish Jesuits who had been in that island were ordered to be sent away, and above two thousand of them were disembarked in the territories of Genoa, whence they were marched in the most wretched condition to the Ecclesiastical state. The question was agitated in a congregation at Rome, whether it would be expedient to abolish a society which was become obnoxious to so many catholic princes, but a majority, with the Pope, declared in their favour. In fine, never was the authority of the church at a lower ebb than in the present year.

The war in the East Indies with Hyder Ally continuing, an expedition was fitted out at Bombay against Mangalore, one of Hyder's principal sea-ports, which succeeded, the forts being taken with small loss on February 25th, and nine vessels of considerable size, besides lesser ones, being brought away. Hyder afterwards ravaged the dominions of the Nabob of Arcot, the English Company's faithful ally, and by his superiority in cavalry was able with advantage to attack several detachments of the force sent against him, and to cut off their convoys. At length, proceeding to the relief of a fort which was invested by a body of troops under Colonel Wood, he was engaged by that officer on October 4th, and notwithstanding his great superiority, was defeated after a very obstinate conflict. The consequences, however, were not important, and Hyder remained in very formidable strength.

Of the domestic events of this year, the institution of the Royal Academy of Arts merits particular notice, as having greatly contributed to that improvement in painting, sculpture, and the kindred arts, which have so much distinguished the reign of George III. It took place in the month of December, and its first president was Joshua Reynolds, still the pride of the English school of painting.

The celebrated navigator Cook, then a lieutenant, sailed on his first exploratory voyage in August, accompanied by Messrs. Banks and Solander.

The King of Denmark employed part of the summer in a visit to England, making a rapid tour through many of the principal towns. He was treated with great magnificence, and partook of a splendid entertainment from the city of London.

1769

9th & 10th Year of the Reign

THE king's speech on opening the session of parliament having particularly directed its attention to the American colonies, the capital of one of which was declared to be in a state of disobedience to all law and government, this subject took the lead in the parliamentary discussions of the present year. A committee of the whole House of Commons had been formed in the session for an inquiry into American affairs, and a great number of papers had been laid before it, which gave rise to frequent and warm debates, in all which the ministers were supported by large majorities. Resolutions were passed in the House of Lords, and adopted by the Commons, declaring illegal and unconstitutional those acts of the assembly of Massachuset's Bay which called in question the authority of parliament to make laws binding upon the colonies in all cases whatsoever, and pronouncing a strong censure on the circular letters sent by that assembly to the other colonies. The conduct of the town of Boston was particularly noted for its audacity and disaffection. An address to his Majesty was voted, expressive of entire satisfaction with the measures that had been taken to support the constitution, and of a firm resolution to concur in such further steps as might be thought necessary to enforce a due execution of the laws; and a request was made that Governor Bernard should be directed to transmit the names of those who were most active in promoting the late disorders, that they might be brought over for trial by a special commission in this country. In the debates on the address this last proposal was animadverted upon with peculiar severity by the opposition, as wholly adverse to the principles of the English constitution.

The agreement with the East India Company, and the act for restraining their dividends, being now near expiring, a long negotiation was entered upon between it and the government, which terminated in a new bill. By this compact the Company was to continue, for five years to come, its annual payment to the public of £400,000 with liberty to increase its dividend during that period as far as twelve and a half per cent; and if from any cause it should be necessary to reduce the dividends, an equal sum was to be deducted from the payments to the public, such payments entirely to cease were the dividend to be reduced to six per cent. Some other stipulations were made for the public benefit.

In February, the first of those deficiencies in the civil list which have occurred from time to time in the present reign was made to parliament by a message from his Majesty, announcing that he had been obliged to incur a debt of £500,000 and relying on their zeal and affection to enable him to discharge it. This demand gave rise to some free discussions, but it was complied with without any particular investigation.

The affairs of Mr. Wilkes again became the topic of much interest both in and out of parliament. That gentleman having got into his possession the copy of a letter written by Lord Weymouth, secretary of state, to the chairman of the quarter sessions at Lambeth, previously to the riot in St. George's Fields, in which an early and effectual employment of the military in case of resistance to the civil power was recommended, published it in the newspapers with a very severe preface of his own composition. Lord W. thereupon made a complaint to the House of Lords of breach of privilege; and the publication being traced to Mr. Wilkes, a complaint was addressed by the Lords to the Commons, and a conference was held between the houses on the subject. In the meantime a petition had been presented to the House of Commons by Mr. Wilkes, complaining of Lord Mansfield's amendment of the information which had been exhibited against him in the court of King's Bench; and on February 1st he was brought from prison to be examined on the subject, on which occasion he boldly avowed himself the publisher of the letter above-mentioned, and the writer of the remarks on it. His petition was voted frivolous and groundless; and on the next day the other affair was taken into consideration, and his introductory remarks were declared a scandalous and seditious libel. This resolution was immediately followed by a motion for his expulsion from his seat in parliament, introduced by Lord Barrington, secretary at war, and seconded by Mr. Rigby, paymaster of the forces, which passed, though not without warm debates.

This unremitting warfare of authority against an individual had the natural effect of inflaming the popular zeal in his favour; and a writ having been issued for a new election for the county of Middlesex, a previous meeting of freeholders was called, where it was resolved to re-elect Mr. Wilkes, entirely without expence to himself. He was accordingly again chosen without opposition; but when the return was made to the House of Commons, a resolution passed, that the election was rendered void by his expulsion, and a new writ was ordered. At this time, as his fortune was known to be greatly impaired by the prosecutions he had undergone, a subscription was opened in London for his relief, and instructions were sent by the electors of Middlesex, London, Westminster, and Southwark, to their representatives, for their conduct in parliament, in which severe censures were passed on several of the late measures. The election being renewed, Mr. Wilkes was again chosen without a competitor, and again rejected as incapable. At length, the ministry, being tired of the repeated contest, procured a military candidate, Colonel Luttrel, who was not to be intimidated by popular tumult from appearing on the hustings. The election proceeded quietly, and terminated in 1143 votes for Mr. Wilkes, and 296 for Colonel Luttrel.

On the return of the writ, a resolution was carried in the House of Commons by a majority of 221 to 139, that Mr. Luttrel ought to have been returned; and the clerk of the crown was ordered to erase the name of Mr. Wilkes, and insert that of Colonel Luttrel in its place. This decision produced more general discontent than any other measure since the commencement of the reign; the popular party regarding it as a flagrant violation of the right of election, to seat a candidate by an arbitrary vote of the house, who had only an inconsiderable minority in his favour. The ferment spread from the metropolis throughout the kingdom, and numerous petitions were carried at public meetings of counties and towns, requesting his Majesty to dissolve the parliament. The county of Middlesex, which considered itself as particularly injured, led the way by a petition presented on May 24th, containing a long list of other grievances, and of charges against the ministry. On the other hand, addresses expressing a detestation of all factious proceedings, and declaring entire approbation of the measures of government were procured by the ministerial party; and this kind of warfare between petitioners and addressers, subsisted through the whole summer.

In November, the long agitated cause between Lord Halifax and Mr. Wilkes, respecting the seizure of the person and papers of the latter, was brought to a trial in the court of Common Pleas, before chief-justice Wilmot. After a full hearing, the jury brought in a verdict for the plaintiff with £4000 damages; and it was thought that a larger sum would have been given, had it not transpired that his Majesty's pleasure had been signified, that all the expences attending this prosecution should be defrayed by the crown.

Violent disturbances took place in the autumn among the journeymen weavers in Spital-fields on account of the price of work, in the progress of which, such outrages were committed, that the magistracy was obliged to interfere. Some of the rioters being apprehended, two of them were capitally convicted, and by their sentences were ordered to be executed at Bethnal-green. Some doubt relative to the legality of altering the usual place of execution having arisen in the minds of the sheriffs, a correspondence took place on the subject between them and the secretary of state, in which they were informed, that the opinion of the judges being taken, the sentence was confirmed by his Majesty. It was accordingly executed in the midst of a riotous assembly, by the civil power alone, the sheriffs having declined the assistance of the military.

At the meeting of the new parliament of Ireland in October, a message was received from the throne, for an augmentation of the troops on that establishment, from 12,000 men to 15,235, which was carried, although it met with considerable opposition. In another matter that parliament was less compliant. A money bill which had originated in the English privy council was sent over to the Irish House of Commons, in assertion of a right claimed under Poyning's law, by which no bills are to pass in Ireland, which have not been ratified from the privy council in England. The present, however, was not a time in which such a claim of authority would be patiently submitted to; and accordingly the bill was rejected upon the sole ground that it had not originated in that house, another money bill for a more liberal supply being unanimously passed. The Lord Lieutenant, Lord Townshend, in his speech on December 26th, after making acknowledgements for the liberality with which the parliament had supported the government, condemned in the strongest terms the rejection of the bill from the privy council, as intrenching upon the rights of the crown, and entered a protest against it in the house of lords. He then suddenly prorogued the parliament to a long day, leaving affairs in great confusion, with all the national business undone.

The campaign between the Russians and Turks opened with an irruption of Krim Gueray, khan of the Tartars, supported by a body of the Spahis, into New Servia, which province he totally ruined, burning its towns and villages, and carrying off a great number of its inhabitants into captivity. About the same time the Polish confederates in Podolia, who were assisted by the Turks, were defeated by the Russians, and driven across the Niester. In April, the Russian general, Prince Gallitzin, having crossed that river, advanced to Choczim, and attacking a large body of Turks in their entrenchments under the walls of that town, drove them to the suburbs of the place. Soon after, however, he found it necessary to quit Choczim, and recross the Niester with precipitation. General Romanzow was in like manner foiled in an attempt upon Oczakow. Gallitzin again advanced to the Niester, and in July having defeated a Turkish army, invested Choczim. Various actions ensued with different success, but at length the Russian general raised the siege of Choczim, and again crossed the Niester. In the meantime Romanzow ravaged the Turkish borders at Bender and Oczakow, and defeated a Turkish detachment. The Turks, under a new grand Vizier, in September, made different attempts to establish themselves on the Russian side of the Niester, but were repulsed with great loss by Gallitzin, and their army was almost ruined. The result was the capture of Choczim, which terminated the campaign in that quarter. In another part the Russians over-ran the province of Moldavia, and took possession of the capital, Jassy, the Greek inhabitants of the province declaring for the empress, and taking the oath of fidelity to her. The same success attended the Russian arms in Walachia, the Turks being obliged to retire to the other side of the Danube. In Tartary and the Ukraine the success was nearly balanced.

The occupation given to the Russians on the Turkish border produced a revival of the Polish confederacies, the nobles of Lithuania taking the lead in a spirited manifesto, in which they declared their resolution of defending to the last extremity their liberties encroached upon by the court of Russia. On the other hand, Prince Gallitzin issued a manifesto in an authoritative style, declaring against all neutrality on the part of the Poles, since Russia was determined to have only friends or avowed enemies. The year accordingly passed in a succession of sanguinary actions between the different confederates and the detachments of Russians remaining in Poland, attended with cruelties and devastations which reduced that unhappy country to a most wretched condition. The king, who found himself a helpless spectator of this misery, sent envoys to the powers who were guarantees of the treaties of Carlowitz and Oliva, to intreat their friendly interposition. Towards the close of the campaign between Russia and Turkey, the former power having more troops at liberty, was capable of acting with greater effect against the confederates, who in consequence underwent some severe losses.

The Emperor Joseph in this year began to display his active disposition and attention to improvement, by a visit to his Italian States, in which he applied himself to the correction of the abuses in the administration; and by a journey to Silesia, where he had an interview with the King of Prussia.

In the Swedish diet, which opened in April at Norkioping, a secret committee brought twenty-four articles of accusation against the senate, the consequence of which was the degradation of all its members except two. Although this was an important point gained by the court, it failed in the attempt to carry some new ordinances which would have made an essential change in the system of government, a resolution passing in the diet that no alterations or amendments should be made in the fundamental laws of the kingdom.

In February the pope died, and was succeeded, after a conclave of three months, by Cardinal Ganganelli, who took the name of Clement XIV. The new pontiff, though a man of great liberality, and no friend to the Jesuits, steadily refused compliance with the solicitations of the southern courts for the suppression of that order, and also with the requisitions of those of France and Naples for the cession of Avignon and the Venaissin, and of the Duchy of Benevento. In consequence, the King of France irrevocably annexed the two former to his dominions, paying a compensation for them to the pope, and the King of Naples kept possession of the latter.

The contest of the Corsicans for their independence was in this year terminated by their total subjugation. The French began by negotiating with some of the chiefs, which however, did not prevent several spirited attempts of the Corsicans to take fortified posts from the enemy, but most of them were unsuccessful. A strong reinforcement of French troops arrived in the island at the beginning of April, and from that time no hope was left of effectual resistance. Corte surrendered in May; and Paoli being surrounded, with a small number of faithful followers, by a greatly superior body of French, after cutting his way through them, got on board an English ship, and was landed at Leghorn. Some chiefs still continued to hold out in inaccessible situations, but the body of the nation submitted to the invaders. The sovereign council of the island was suppressed, and a new one was created under the jurisdiction of the parliament of Provence. Corsica was also declared a member of the Gallican church, and was in all respects considered as a part of the French dominions. The conquest was however obtained at a cost of men and money which rendered it a dear acquisition.

The French East India Company was in this year declared bankrupt, and the trade was laid open. Serious differences took place in the French colony of St. Domingo between the government and the inhabitants, in which blood was shed, and some of the leading people were sent in irons to France.

The war between the English East India Company and Hyder Ally continuing, that adventurous chief eluded the British army in the Carnatic, and appeared in the spring at the head of a body of cavalry within a few miles of Madras. The presidency of that settlement in alarm entered into a negotiation with Hyder, and proposed a truce of fifty days, but he would agree only to one of seven. At the end of that period a peace was signed on the condition of restoration of all places and prisoners taken, a league offensive and defensive, and a free trade between the dominions of each; and thus was terminated a war said to have been less rashly entered into, than ill conducted, by the Company's servants. Its events produced a great fall of India stock; and in order to put a stop to the abuses and mismanagement of the government in India, the directors resolved upon sending over three gentlemen of great respectability, Mr. Vansittart, Mr. Scrafton, and Colonel Ford, with the title of supervisors, invested with a power of controul over all their other servants in every department. While their commission was under consideration, some objections were made to it by government, accompanied by the proposal that the Company should allot a share in the direction of their affairs to the naval officer who was to command a squadron ordered for India at their request. With this proposal the general courts, after long debates, refused compliance, and the operations of the squadron were in consequence limited to the Persian gulf, on the coast of which some disorders had risen, detrimental to the Company's affairs. The supervisors sailed from England in September on board the Aurora frigate, but neither they nor the vessel were ever more heard of.

1770

10th & 11th Year of the Reign

THE King's speech by which the session of parliament was opened on January 9th, began with the notice of a distemper which had broken out among the horned cattle, and proceeded to advert to the disorders still prevailing in the colonies, but was totally silent with respect to the discontents in the kingdom on the subject of the Middlesex election. These, however, were not passed over by the opposition in the House of Commons who introduced a motion for an amendment to the customary address following the speech, assuring his Majesty that they would immediately go into an enquiry into the causes of the discontents. The motion produced a long and unusually acrimonious debate; and though it was rejected by a great majority, the existence of very serious differences in parliament was rendered sufficiently apparent. Farther proof of this fact was given by a great number of resignations which soon after took place, including those of Lord Chancellor Camden, the Marquis of Granby, the Dukes of Beaufort and Manchester, the Earls of Coventry and Huntingdon, Mr. James Grenville, and Mr. Dunning. Mr. Charles Yorke was with great difficulty prevailed upon to accept the seals, and *suddenly* dying three days after, they were put into commission.

On January 28th, the public was surprized by the resignation of the Duke of Grafton. He was succeeded in his office of first Lord of the Treasury by Lord North, who then commenced his long prime-ministry.

In a committee of the House of Commons on the state of the nation, January 31st, a motion was made by an opposition member "that the house in the exercise of its jurisdiction, ought to judge of elections by the law of the land, and by the custom and practice of parliament, which is part of that law." This proposition was meant as introductory to a series of resolutions in condemnation of the decision relative to the Middlesex election. The motion was therefore warmly combated, and an amendment entirely subversive of its purpose was carried by a majority of 224 to 180. In the House of Lords also, the same subject was taken up in a motion by the Marquis of Rockingham, powerfully seconded by Lord Chatham, who appeared now to have recovered his former spirit and vigour. It was however defeated by a contrary motion, in which the interference of that house in a matter concerning which the jurisdiction of the Commons is final and conclusive, was declared a violation of the constitution.

Two other motions in the House of Commons, one for disqualifying certain revenue officers from voting at the elections of members of parliament; the other for the production of an account of the civil list expenditure, were negatived by the efforts of the ministry. A petition having been presented to parliament by the American merchants stating the great losses they had sustained in consequence of the duties imposed upon goods exported to the colonies, the ministers brought in a bill for the repeal of the act which laid a duty on paper, painters' colours, and glass so exported, whilst that upon tea, laid by the same act, was retained, apparently for the purpose of asserting the right of taxation.

This year was distinguished by the passing of that important "Act for regulating the proceedings of the House of

Commons on controverted elections," generally denominated the Grenville bill from its proposer, Mr. George Grenville. Before this time, cases of this kind had been heard at the bar of the house, and decided by the mere votes of the members, which not only interfered with the ordinary business, but was often attended with much partiality, and little regard to the merits of the question. The bill provided for the appointment by lot, of a certain number of members, for the trial of each case, to be reduced by the alternate expunging of names by each party to the number of thirteen and two tellers, who are to form a select committee, sworn to the determination of the matter in dispute. This was so manifest an improvement, that it passed into an act, notwithstanding the opposition of the ministry.

The livery and corporation of London having presented a remonstrance and petition to the king, praying for the dissolution of parliament, and the removal of bad ministers, expressed in terms of extraordinary boldness, to which an answer had been returned, strongly marking the royal displeasure, a motion was made for laying the papers respecting the transaction before the House of Commons, which, after a very warm debate, was carried by a large majority. It was followed by two others, the first, for an address to his Majesty, containing a severe censure of the proceeding of the city of London, and thanks for the reply given to it; the second, for an application to the Lords for their concurrence. Both these were also carried, and the Lords, at a conference, concurring in the address, it was jointly presented.

In April Mr. Wilkes was discharged from his confinement in the King's Bench prison, on giving bond for his good behaviour during seven years; and he was afterwards admitted to the office of alderman for the ward of Farringdon Without, to which he had been previously elected.

A political writer, under the signature of *Junius*, had for some time greatly excited the public attention, by letters printed in the newspapers, distinguished as well by the force and elegance of their style, as by the virulence of their attacks on individuals. Of these compositions the most celebrated was a letter, first printed in the Public Advertiser of December 19th, addressed to the King, animadverting with great freedom on all the supposed errors of his reign, and speaking of his ministers in terms of equal contempt and abhorrence. On its appearance, the attorney general filed a bill *ex officio* in the court of King's Bench, against Woodfall, the publisher (the author himself remaining concealed, as he has been ever since), for uttering a false and seditious libel. The cause came on for trial on June 13th, at Guildhall, before Lord Mansfield, when that judge in his charge to the jury, informed them that they had nothing to do with the *intention,* for that the words in the indictment, *malicious, seditious,* &c. were merely words of course, and that they were only to consider the *fact* of publishing, and whether a *proper construction* were put upon the blanks in the paper; their *truth* or *falsehood* being wholly immaterial. The jury, however, after being out nine hours, found a verdict of "guilty of printing and publishing only," which was in effect an acquittal. Some of the printers and venders of the letter were brought in guilty, and punished with fine and imprisonment, but others were acquitted.

American affairs, though they had been introduced to the notice of parliament in the King's speech, were passed over in silence by the ministers during this session, probably from the difficulty they found in adopting any decided plan of policy towards the colonies, where coercion and indulgence appeared equally hazardous. A riot which occurred at Boston, in March, added to their perplexity, as it proved the danger of attempting to overawe a discontented populace by the presence of a soldiery, whom they would look upon with the most hostile and rancorous feelings. Of the origin of this affray, party has given contradictory relations; but there is no doubt that it arose from the propensity to quarrel upon slight provocations which subsisted between the soldiers and town's people. The result was, that the soldiers being pressed upon by an exasperated mob, were induced to fire, by which several of the latter were killed and wounded. By the efforts of the lieutenant-governor and the principal inhabitants, tranquillity was restored, and no resistance was made to the committing of the officer on guard and three soldiers to prison. A meeting of the inhabitants being held on the occasion, a committee was deputed to wait upon the lieutenant-governor, and request from him a removal of the troops. After some discussion, their desire was complied with, and the two regiments were sent to barracks, in Castle William. Captain Preston, the officer, was afterwards tried for his life, but notwithstanding the exasperation of men's minds, was honourably acquitted, as it did not appear that he had given the order to fire; and indeed the evidence on the trial seemed to prove that the outrages were more on the part of the mob than on that of the military.

On July 27th a fire broke out in the dock yard at Portsmouth, which consumed a large quantity of naval stores, and from various circumstances was supposed not to have been accidental.

In this year an alarm of war disturbed the external tranquillity, which the nation had now enjoyed for a course of years. Soon after the conclusion of the last peace, a project was formed by the British admiralty of establishing a settlement on the isles near the coast of Patagonia, named by us the Falkland islands, by the French and Spaniards the Malouines. In 1764 Commodore Byron was sent out for the purpose of making the proper examinations for this purpose, and in the following year he took formal possession of the islands in his Majesty's name. The French under M. Bougainville had already, in 1764, made a small establishment upon one of the islands, which they ceded in 1766, with all their rights of possession, to the Spaniards, and in that year a Spanish governor with some troops was sent from Buenos Ayres to occupy it. This circumstance was apparently unknown to our admiralty, which directed a settlement to be formed at a harbour which was named Port Egmont, situated on a small island adjoining to the largest of the group; that of the Spaniards, called Port Solidad, being on the smaller of the two principal islands. In 1769, Captain Hunt in the Tamar frigate, cruizing off the Falkland isles, fell in with a Spanish schooner, which was taking a survey of him, and which he warned from the coast, as appertaining to his Britannic Majesty. The schooner soon after returned with letters from the governor of Port Solidad, which asserted the prior right of the King of Spain, and returned upon Captain Hunt the warning to depart. Protests and counter-protests followed, till in February 1770, two Spanish frigates of force, with troops on board, arrived at Port Egmont under pretence of watering, the chief commander of which expressed great surprize at seeing the English flag flying; and the altercation respecting right was renewed between him and Captain Hunt. Though much mutual civility prevailed, Captain Hunt thought it necessary to bring home intelligence of these occurrences, and accordingly arrived at Plymouth on June 3d. The Favourite and Swift sloops were now the only naval force at Port Egmont, and the latter was afterwards unfortunately lost in the straits of Magellan. On the 4th of June a Spanish frigate put in at that harbour, and was soon followed by four others. These vessels brought 16 or 1700 men, soldiers and marines, with a train of artillery and ordnance stores, sufficient for the siege of a regular fortress, and quite ludicrous against a miserable blockhouse, with only four pieces of cannon sunk in the mud. The two English captains, Maltby and Farmer, perceiving the hostile intentions of the Spaniards, made all the preparations for defence that circumstances would admit, and letters mutually passed, asserting the respective rights of each nation. At length the Spanish force by land and sea advanced to the attack; and enough having passed to authenticate a formal hostility, as farther resistance would have been folly, a flag of truce was hung out, and articles of capitulation were concluded. By the terms, the English were permitted, after a limited time, to depart in the Favourite, taking with them such part of the stores as they should choose, an inventory being made of the rest. That this delay might be secured, the great insult, as naval etiquette regarded it, was offered, of taking off the Favourite's rudder. The sloop was detained 34 days, when she set sail, and arrived off Portsmouth on September 22d.

When the account of these transactions first arrived, some ships were put into commission, but warlike preparations were carried on with little activity till late in August. The navy was found to be in a bad condition, and the unpopularity of the ministers, especially in the metropolis, threw difficulties in the way of manning an adequate fleet. The Lord Mayor of London, Crosby, refused to back the admiralty warrants for pressing seamen within the liberties of the city; and an impressed man brought before Alderman Wilkes was discharged. The prime minister however was firm in his seat; and the death of Mr. George Grenville, which left his particular party without a leader, added some recruits to the court party. At the meeting of parliament on November 13th, the tenor of his Majesty's speech evidently showed a desire of leaving to the court of Spain an opening for pacification. The hostility was called "An Act of the Governor of Buenos Ayres," thereby giving the opportunity of a disavowal. Parliament was informed that an immediate demand of satisfaction had been made, and at the same time the necessary preparations for obtaining redress had been ordered, should the court of Spain refuse to grant it; which preparations would not be discontinued until his Majesty had received proper reparation for the injury, as well as satisfactory proof that other powers were equally sincere with himself in resolving to preserve the tranquility of Europe. Very loyal addresses in return to the speech were voted by both houses, though not without debates in which many pointed censures were made on administration relative to the causes of the quarrel, and the unprepared state of the nation. Augmentations to the army and navy passed without opposition.

In the House of Commons, a motion was made tending to restrain the powers lodged in the attorney general for carrying on informations *ex officio*, without intervention of a grand jury or the forms observed by the courts of law in other cases. It was negatived by a great majority; but the opposition being determined to bring on an enquiry into judicial proceedings under another form, a motion was made shortly after, for a committee to enquire into the administration of criminal justice, and the conduct of the judges, particularly in cases relating to the liberty of the press, and power and duty of juries. This was also rejected, after a copious debate, by a majority of more than two to one.

In the House of Lords, a motion having been made on November 28th, by Lord Chatham, relative to the Middlesex election, there arose out of it a digressive discussion concerning the practice of the judges of directing the jury from the bench, and giving judgment in cases of prosecution for libels, in which a particular reference was made to Lord Mansfield's charge on Woodfall's trial. On this occasion, that learned lord entering into a vindication of his conduct, was directly opposed by the ex-chancellor Lord Camden; but the debate was at that time terminated by a motion for adjournment. This attack, together with what had passed in the House of Commons, induced Lord Mansfield to give notice for a call of the house; and when it took place, his lordship acquainted the house that he had left a paper with the clerk containing the unanimous judgment of the Court of King's Bench in the case of the King against Woodfall. The question being then asked, whether it was intended that this paper should be entered upon the journals of the house, and answered in the negative, it was admitted that no notice could properly be taken of such a document. Lord Camden, however, offered to maintain that the doctrine laid down as the judgment of the court was not the law of England; and he intimated a wish to tie the other learned lord to a legal contest on these points; but the matter went no further, to the great disappointment of the public.

Near the close of the year, Lord Weymouth resigned the place of secretary of state for the southern department, in which he was succeeded by the Earl of Rochford.

The war between the Turks and Russians raged in this year with augmented fury. During the winter and spring great efforts were made by the Grand Vizier to recover the provinces of Moldavia and Walachia, in which he was so far successful, that the Russians were entirely driven from the borders of the Danube; and the whole of Walachia, with the lower part of Moldavia were reduced, and the communication with the Tartars was re-opened. General Romanzow, who commanded the Russian army on the Niester, moved in the spring towards the Pruth, and in July drove the Turks from their intrenchments on that river. Pursuing his march towards the confluence of the Pruth with the Danube, a desperate engagement was brought on, August 2d, which terminated in a total defeat of the Grand Vizier, who lost his camp, equipage, ammunition, and a great number of cannon. In the meantime Count Panin had invested Bender, which, after two months' siege, was taken by storm on September 27th, the town being almost entirely destroyed by a conflagration that occurred during the action. Kilia Nova, Bialgorod, and Ibrailow, afterwards surrendered to the Russians, who became masters of the whole northern bank of the Danube.

It had been part of the Russian plan in this war to attack the enemy in the southern part of his empire; and accordingly a powerful fleet had been equipped to act in the Mediterranean, which in the preceding year had been refitted in the English ports. The fleet had wintered in Minorca, and in February sailed for the Morea, under the command of Count Orlof. A negotiation had been carried on with the Greeks during the former year, and arms and ammunition had been sent to them without the knowledge of the Turks. The arrival of the Russians therefore was a signal of open revolt to that people, whose enthusiasm was doubly excited by religious zeal (their faith being the same with that of their new allies), and by the love of liberty. The Mainotes, descendants of the ancient Spartans, flew to arms, and inspired by hatred and revenge, massacred all the Turks who came in their way, without distinction of age or sex. Count Orlof on his arrival had issued a manifesto, in which, according to the spirit of his court, he declared, in the name of the empress, that she looked upon it as a religious duty to free the Greeks from Turkish slavery, and promised reward and protection to all who should join her army, threatening severe punishment to those who should refuse. The Russian forces brought to their assistance were, however, few, and the insurgents were not adequate to the reduction of the places to which they laid siege, and which were bravely defended. That of the castle of Patras was going on, when a body of Turks and Albanians passed the isthmus for its relief; and attacking the besiegers at the same time that the governor of the castle commanded a sally, they made a dreadful carnage, and burned the city of Patras to the ground. The Mainotes were afterwards defeated in various encounters, all the Greeks found in arms were put to death without mercy, and the Russians at length withdrew from the peninsula, while the remaining Mainotes took refuge in the fortresses of their mountains. Meantime the Russian main fleet, reinforced by a squadron under Admiral Elphinston, pursuing the Turkish fleet which had retired to the Archipelago, found it, on July 5th, at anchor in the channel of Scio, which divides that island from Natolia. An encounter ensued in which the ship of the Russian admiral, and that of the Captain Pashaw, fighting yard-arm and yard-arm, and grappled together, both caught fire and blew up. The Turkish fleet then took the advantage of the night to run into the little bay of Cisme on the coast of Natolia, where on the following night, fireships being sent in under the conduct of the English Lieutenant Dugdale, and covered by a division of ships commanded by Commodore Greig, the whole fleet was destroyed, with the exception of a man of war and some gallies towed away by the Russians. This success enabled the Russians to overrun the neighbouring islands; and being joined by a number of the Greek inhabitants, they laid siege to the castle of Lemnos. It, however, was relieved by a body of Turks which, crossing from Romania, put the Russians to the rout, and cut to pieces most of the Greeks. Some attempts of the Russians to pass the Dardanelles were also frustrated; and upon the whole, the consequences of the destruction of the Turkish fleet were less important than might have been expected.

To the disasters which befel the Ottoman empire in this year, was added that of a revolution in Egypt, where an adventurous chief, Ali Bey, threw off the Turkish yoke, and assuming the supreme power, carried his arms into some of the neighbouring provinces of Syria and Arabia.

The distracted kingdom of Poland continued a prey to all the evils of anarchy and civil war, to which, in this year, was added the dreadful scourge of pestilence. The plague first making its appearance in some villages on the Turkish frontier, spread into the adjoining Polish provinces of Podolia, Volhynia, and the Ukraine, parts of which were nearly depopulated. It was an example of the terror excited by this visitation, that the city of Kaminieck, after a great mortality among its garrison and inhabitants, was totally deserted, and continued abandoned for several months, neither Poles nor Russians venturing to take possession of the infected spot. The confederacies were still numerous over the country, and desolation usually followed their steps.

The rapacious spirit which had long characterised the court of Prussia, displayed itself in this year by its treatment of the commercial city of Dantzic. The magistrates of that place having prohibited the Prussian recruiting officers from levying men within their jurisdiction, and the postmaster (who is an officer of Poland and not of Dantzic) having refused to pass without examination some casks of silver sent to the Prussian resident, these acts were made the pretext for sending a body of Prussian troops into the territory of the city, which surprized the out-posts, seized the cannon, and made prisoners of the men; and then, being reinforced, encamped four miles from the city. The alarmed Dantzickers having shut their gates, applied to the foreign ministers for the intercession of their courts; and at length, on agreeing to the payment of 75,000 ducats, and subscribing certain conditions sufficiently humiliating, they were permitted to depute two of their counsellors to make their submission to his Prussian Majesty.

The Danes, having causes of complaint against the Algerines, sent a squadron to demand satisfaction, and the negotiation proving fruitless, an intention was manifested by the Danish admiral to bombard Algiers, and reciprocal hostilities followed for some days; after which the Danish fleet sailed away without having effected any thing. In this year several rapid and unexpected changes took place in the Danish ministry, denoting that weakness in the sovereign which was afterwards too manifestly apparent.

In France, much public commotion arose from the contests between the court and the parliaments. The Duke d'Aiguillon, who had many years been governor of Britany, had incurred great ill-will in the province from his arbitrary administration, and in particular for his vindictive persecution of M. de Chalotais, attorney-general of Britany, a person highly venerated for the zeal with which he had supported the cause of freedom. The parliament of the province, having obtained evidence concerning some of the duke's nefarious proceedings, instituted a prosecution against him, and in the month of April his trial commenced in the presence of the king, the princes of the blood and peers, and the parliament of Paris. In the midst of the proceedings, when papers had been produced which appeared to bring home the charges against the duke, the king interposed his regal authority to prevent all farther enquiries. He afterwards held a bed of justice at Versailles, in which he caused letters patent to be registered, by which a stop was put to the trial, the accusations were suppressed, and all persons were prohibited from taking further notice of them. This manifestation of the royal favour to the Duke d'Aiguillon, did not secure him from other attacks. The parliament of Paris published an arret, forbidding him to exercise any of the functions of the peerage, till the stains of his character should be effaced by a legal trial; which arret was immediately annulled by a counter-decree issued by the king in council. The princes and peers then strongly remonstrated against the arbitrary proceedings of the crown; and the parliament sent to Versailles a solemn deputation to the same purpose, which was answered by a peremptory command to oppose no more obstacles to the duke's enjoyment of the rights of peerage. The parliament, however, on the next day confirmed all its former resolutions. The parliaments of Bordeaux, Toulouse, and Rennes, displayed equal vigour and perseverance in the same cause. A deputation from that of Britany having received permission to wait on the king at Compeigne, were not allowed to speak a word, and two of their members were arrested and sent to the castle of Vincennes. The parliament of Paris having persisted in its remonstrances, the king came suddenly to the capital on the morning of September 3d, and surrounding the parliament house with his guards, held a bed of justice at which, after severely upbraiding the members with their disobedience, he dismissed the chambers of inquests and requests, and calling for all the acts and decrees against the Duke d'Aiguillon, he caused them all to be erased. The Chancellor then, in the King's name, made a speech imposing absolute silence for the future on this subject. Notwithstanding this prohibition, the parliament held another meeting, and issued an arret, in which, after some remarks on the arbitrary power which had been exercised contrary to the letter and spirit of the constitution, an intention was expressed of persevering to carry truth to the foot of the throne. Violent measures were in the meantime carried on against the other parliaments in which officers of the army were sent to compel the registering of the royal edicts, or to tear in pieces the arrets of the parliaments, and banish or confine some of their members. On one side strong remonstrances were made in assertion of privilege; on the other, arrets were issued, laying down maxims of the most unlimited monarchial authority; and these disputes must be always memorable in French history, as sure indications of that rising storm which, in the next reign, was to overthrow the whole fabric of the existing government.

In the month of May, the Dauphin of France was married to the Archduchess Antoinetta Maria. A grand exhibition of fire-works at Paris in honour of the event, was attended, through mismanagement, with a most shocking loss of lives among the crowded spectators.

In Corsica so much disaffection prevailed against the dominion of France, that the governor was obliged in the summer to take the field in order to reduce the malcontents, who had rendered it unsafe to go beyond the walls of the fortified towns. Many of the natives were executed, and others were sent for transportation to the West Indies; but a number still remained in arms in their inaccessible posts.

The Tunisians, who had made a treaty with the Corsicans as an independent people, having, since the conquest of the island, made prize of all Corsican vessels under French colours, and also expelled the African company from a coral fishery on their coasts, a small French squadron was sent against Tunis, which having bombarded Biserta and threatened other places, brought the Bey to terms, and obtained reparation for the injuries committed.

1771

11th & 12th Year of the Reign

A T the beginning of the year Sir Edward Hawke resigned his place at the head of the admiralty, and was succeeded by the Earl of Sandwich. The Earl of Halifax was made secretary of state in the room of the latter, and *his* post of lord privy seal was filled by the Earl of Suffolk. Judge Bathurst was promoted to the office of lord-chancellor with the title of Baron Apsley; and various other promotions took place in the law departments, among which were the names of De Grey, Thurlow, and Wedderburne.

Negotiations had been carrying on with the Spanish court, relative to the dispute between the two nations on the affair of the Falkland islands, which, at the latter end of November, had been broken off and the English minister had been directed to quit Madrid, in the expectation of an inevitable rupture. In the beginning of this year, however, they had been resumed, and on January 22d, a declaration was signed by the Spanish ambassador in London, Prince Masserano, and accepted by the Earl of Rochford, which was laid before parliament. In this declaration, the result of a *convention*, his Catholic Majesty disavowed the violence committed on the subjects of his Britannic Majesty, in obliging them by force to evacuate port Egmont, and engaged to give orders for the restoration of every thing to the state it was previously in; but protested at the same time, that this engagement was in no wise to affect the question of the prior right of the sovereignty of the Malouine or Falkland Islands. On the other side, his Britannic Majesty accepted the said declaration and engagement, as a satisfaction for the injury done to the crown of Great Britain. Together with these documents, there were presented to parliament a number of papers relative to the transaction; but among them were none respecting the claims and representations made by the court of Spain since the first settlement of Falkland's island by the English, nor could any information be obtained, relative to a supposed interference of France in the negotiation. Addresses to procure such intelligence were moved, but were negatived by great majorities. The opposition then made violent attacks upon the convention, as having neither satisfied the insulted honour of the nation, nor provided against a recurrence of similar disputes. In the replies it was contended that Spain had done all that we had a right to expect, by her disavowal of the act complained of; that the first affront had been given by our people, in warning the Spaniards from an island which they considered as their own; and that the title to these islands had always been a matter of dispute, the claims on each side being so equivocal and uncertain that they were incapable of decision. In the end, addresses to the king were carried in both houses, expressing satisfaction in the redress obtained, and assurances of their zealous support on every future occasion. It may be presumed, that all will at present agree, that it would have been great folly on either part to have gone to war about a group of barren islands, in a miserable climate, which have since been abandoned by both nations, and left to the occupation of seals and penguins.

The principles upon which the Middlesex election had been decided, being still regarded as bringing into question points very important to the constitution, a member of opposition, high in character and consequence, moved, on February 7th, for leave to bring in a bill for ascertaining the rights of electors in respect to the eligibility of persons to serve in parliament. The points which he affirmed had by that decision been unconstitutionally determined, were, 1. that the House of Commons could by its own power make law; 2. that one determination of the house was such law; 3. that incapacity was the consequence of expulsion. On these heads he argued with much acuteness; and a debate between the different parties ensued, which terminated in a division that negatived the motion by a majority of 167 against 103.

A remarkable circumstance brought before the house in which it acted with laudable unanimity, was the detection of gross corruption in the borough of New Shoreham. The consequence was a bill for the incapacitation of 81 of the freemen from voting at elections for representatives and an address to the crown for a public prosecution of the committee which managed the nefarious traffic.

This session of parliament was distinguished by some singular occurrences, materially affecting the privileges and prerogatives of the House of Commons. It had become the practice of newspaper writers to take a liberty, not before ventured upon, of printing the alleged speeches of members of parliament under their names, some of which in the whole, and others in essential parts, were spurious productions and in any case contrary to the standing orders of the house. A complaint on this ground having been made by a member against two of these printers, an order was issued for their attendance at the bar of the house, with which they did not comply. A final order being sent with no better success, a motion was made and carried by a great majority, that they should be taken into the custody of the serjeant at arms for contempt. This officer having reported that they were not to be found, a royal proclamation was obtained, offering a reward for their apprehension; and six more printers were included in the order for attendance. Soon after, one of the printers named in the proclamation was apprehended in the city, and carried before Alderman Wilkes, who, regarding the caption as illegal, no crime having been proved or charged against him, and also as contrary to the privileges of the city of London, not only discharged the man, but bound him over to prosecute the captor for an assault and false imprisonment, whom likewise he obliged to give bail for his appearance to answer for the offence. Another printer, who was apprehended and carried before Alderman Oliver, was liberated exactly in the same manner. A third, being apprehended at his own house by a messenger of the House of Commons, sent for a constable, who took them both before the Lord Mayor, Crosby, at the Mansion-house, where at the same time were the Aldermen Wilkes and Oliver. The deputy serjeant at arms also attended, and the Speaker's warrant being produced, it was adjudged illegal, as not being backed by a city magistrate. The printer was accordingly discharged; and upon his making a complaint against the messenger for an assault, a warrant for his commitment to prison was signed by the three magistrates, which would have been put in execution, had not the serjeant at arms at length given bail for him.

The account of these transactions was received with high indignation by the House of Commons, and an order for the Lord Mayor's attendance in his place, as a member of parliament, was carried by a great majority. His lordship justified his conduct by his oath of office to preserve inviolate the franchises of the city, and he desired to be heard by counsel, which was refused. His clerk was also ordered to attend with the minute book of recognizances, when he was obliged to erase that of the messenger; most of the opposition members quitting the house during this proceeding, with the declaration that they would not witness an act so arbitrary and subversive of justice. Alderman Oliver, also a member of parliament, was ordered to attend, and was committed to the Tower upon the ground of breach of privilege: and the lord mayor, whom illness had hitherto prevented from appearing before the house in person, on his attendance two days after, was likewise committed to the Tower on the same charge. Meantime the city of London had not been remiss in taking up the cause of its magistrates. A court of common council had voted thanks to the lord mayor and the two aldermen for their assertion of the privileges of the city; and a committee was appointed to assist them in their defence, with power to draw for money on the chamber of London. The populace displayed their zeal in favour of persons whom they regarded as sufferers for the public liberty, by accompanying them in crowds with loud acclamations when they went to, and returned from, the House of Commons; and on one of these occasions they grossly insulted several obnoxious members, and Lord North was brought into imminent danger of his life.

The house had the advantage, in their contest with the Lord Mayor and Alderman Oliver, of employing their authority over their own members; but with respect to Alderman Wilkes, they lay under an embarrassment which for some time prevented any proceedings against him. To an order for his attendance at the house, he had sent a letter to the Speaker, in which he observed that no notice had been taken of his being a member, and he had not been desired to attend in his place, both which circumstances were essential; and that he now, in the name of his constituents, demanded his seat in parliament where he would give a full detail of his conduct in the transaction. This letter being offered to the house by the Speaker, a long debate ensued, which ended in the refusal of its reception; and other orders were issued for his attendance, of which he took no notice. At length, a few days before the recess, the house finding they had got into a difficulty, and doubtful of the extent of their privileges, made an order for the alderman's attendance on a certain day, and then adjourned to the day after; a mode of escape which certainly could not tend to raise their character in the nation. The other two magistrates, who had been brought up by writ of before the court of Common Pleas, after long pleadings were remanded to the Tower, here they remained in custody till the end of the session, when their liberation was celebrated with great rejoicings. A committee of the House of Commons, which had long sat on the matter of privilege, on bringing in its report, only recommended to the house, that Miller, the printer of the London Evening Post, should be taken into custody; and thus ended a contest, in which passion seems to have greatly predominated over wisdom. From that period, the proceedings of parliament, and the speeches of the members, have been published in the newspapers without obstacle.

Whatever credit might have been lost by the ministry in some of these disputes, they never were firmer in their seats than in the present year. The great majorities by which everything was carried in parliament, and the defection of Mr. Grenville's party, reduced opposition for the most part to a state of apathy; and the public at large little interested itself in political concerns. The city of London, indeed, remained in ill-humour on account of the treatment of its magistrates; and a farther topic of complaint was afforded by a bill for the embankment of Durham Yard, which was regarded as a gross violation of the city's right of conservancy and property in the bed of the river Thames, and was imputed to the court favour acquired by two builders.

In June, the death of the Earl of Halifax made a vacancy in the northern secretaryship of state; which was filled by the Earl of Suffolk, whose place of lord privy seal was taken by the Duke of Grafton.

In the beginning of the year a spirited attempt was made by a number of the Scotch peers to liberate their elections from the dictation of the ministers. On the vacancy among the sixteen chosen to sit in the House of Lords, occasioned by the death of the Duke of Argyle, the Earl of Dysart was first recommended by a circular letter from Lord North; but objections arising to him, the Earl of Stair was proposed in his stead in a letter from Lord Sandwich. The independent party determining to support the Earl of Breadalbane, at the election at Holyrood House on January 2d, a majority of the peers present voted for that nobleman, but the signed lists of those who were absent were so much in favour of the Earl of Stair, that he was returned by a majority of nine. The Earl of Selkirk thereupon entered a protest against the return, upon the ground of the open interference of the ministers of state by their circular letters, which, though couched in terms of simple good wishes for the approved candidate, were in fact meant to be compulsory on all who expected favours from the administration. This protest was concurred in by thirteen other noblemen, the Duke of Buccleugh at the head.

The war between the Turks and Russians was attended in the early part of the campaign with few important events, both parties appearing to feel the exhaustion consequent upon a long drain of blood and treasure. Various actions, however, occurred between the troops posted on each side of the Danube, in most of which the Russians were the victors; and in March a considerable body of Turks was driven out of Giurgewo on the Walachian side of that river, where they were strongly entrenched. The principal object of the Russians in this year was the conquest of Krim Tartary, to which the operations on the Danube were only secondary. The army destined for this enterprize was commanded by Prince Dolgoruki, who in the month of June came in view of the lines of Precop, the main defence of that peninsula, which were occupied by the Khan Selim Gueray, at the head of a numerous army of Turks and Tartars. On the 25th an attack was made by the Russians, which was completely successful, and on the following day the garrison of Precop surrendered prisoners of war. The whole peninsula was in a short time over-run by the conquerors; its capital, Kaffa, was taken, after a defeat given to the Turks under its walls; several other fortresses were abandoned without resistance, and the Tartar inhabitants every where submitted and entered into conditions with their new masters. In less than a month only one fortress in the Krimea remained unsubdued. On the side of the Danube, success for a time attended the Turkish arms; Giurgewo being recovered by a sudden assault, and an attack of the Turkish entrenchments being repulsed with considerable loss. Later in the campaign, however, the Turks, who had a design of establishing their winter quarters on the Walachian side of the Danube, were defeated in various encounters; the grand vizier in his fortified camp, was forced by General Weisman, with the loss of his artillery, and his whole army was put to the rout; and Giurgewo again came into the possession of the Russians.

The naval transactions in the Mediterranean were of little importance. The Russian fleet, though much out of condition, had no antagonist to contend with, and spread terror and desolation through the islands and coasts of the Turkish empire. The Greeks, deterred by the bad success of their revolt, remained quiet, or only employed themselves in piratical enterprizes.

In the midst of the triumphs of Russia, one of the capitals of the empire became a prey to an enemy from which no military prowess could protect it. Among the horrors of a Turkish war, that of the communication of pestilential contagion is not the least; and in the summer of this year, by some unknown means, the plague was conveyed, probably from the Polish frontier, to the distant city of Moscow. It appears to have existed there for some months, concealed under the disguise of a malignant fever; but in the autumn it shewed itself under its true colours, and made a dreadful havoc. Fanaticism augmented the mischief, by inspiring a faith in the power of the effigy of a certain saint to dispel the disease, and the vast crowds brought together through that persuasion, served to propagate the infection beyond the possibility of restraint. The venerable Archbishop Ambrosius having ordered the removal of the picture, an infuriated mob pursued him to a monastery in which he had taken shelter, dragged him from the altar, and murdered him in the most barbarous manner. To quell the savage tumult, a body of troops fired into the midst of the crowd, and killed a great number. Many more were apprehended and punished; and thus evils of every kind were let loose upon the wretched inhabitants of Moscow.

The confederacies of Poland, which had appeared almost extinguished, broke out again in the course of this year with renewed vigour, privately supported, it was imagined, by the court of France. A number of French officers entered among them as volunteers, and better discipline being introduced into their troops, war was carried on with the Russians in many parts with balanced success. One of the most remarkable circumstances attending this scattered warfare was an atrocious attempt to carry off the king, whom the malcontents never regarded as the choice of the nation, but as one imposed upon it by a foreign force. One Pulawski, a confederate general, was the planner of this conspiracy, for the execution of which about forty persons were engaged under three chiefs. On the night of September 3d, having obtained admission into Warsaw under disguise, they stopped the king, who was returning in a coach to his palace, and dispersing his attendants, dragged him forcibly out of the carriage, in which violence he received a deep cut with a sabre on the head, and conveyed him on horseback out of the city. The night being extremely dark, the conspirators, of whom only a few were left with the king, wandered in the meadows, and perceiving the difficulty of carrying him off, repeatedly asked their leader, Kosinsky, if they should not kill him. He diverted them from their purpose, and at length was left quite alone with his royal captive, who by discourse made such an impression on his feelings, that he threw himself at the king's feet, implored forgiveness, and swore to protect him from farther outrage. After some delay they obtained admission into a mill, whence the king sent a note to the commander of his guards at Warsaw, who brought him back with an escort, amid the unbounded rejoicings of the court and people. Such was the termination of an enterprize, of which the circumstances were still more romantic, than the design was atrocious. The fate of Poland was now drawing to a conclusion. The Russian troops were reinforced, while those of Austria and Prussia advanced into the country from different sides, and any effectual resistance became impossible.

In many parts of Germany great distress was undergone from a scarcity of the necessaries of life, inclement seasons, and extraordinary inundations.

The King of Sweden died suddenly on February 12th, and was succeeded by his son Gustavus III who was then at Paris. The new king immediately sent a declaration to the senate, in which he solemnly promised to govern according to the laws and the constitution, and protested that he should regard as his enemies, and as traitors to their country, all who should attempt again to introduce a *sovereignty*, or unlimited authority. Having on his return passed some days with the King of Prussia, his uncle, he arrived at Stockholm in May, where he was received with the greatest demonstrations of joy. He adopted popular manners, was easy of access, and familiar in his address to the lower orders, whose affections he was studious to gain. A general election taking place for members to the diet, the majority returned were of the country party, or *caps,* who were in opposition to the court party, or *hats*. At the opening of this assembly, June 25th, the king made a much admired speech, in which he renewed his professions of attachment to his country and its free constitution, and strongly recommended concord and unanimity. He was not able, however, to obtain from the diet a relaxation of those capitulations, or articles of agreement with the people, in limitation of the regal authority, which every King of Sweden is obliged to subscribe at his coronation.

The disputes between the crown and the parliaments in France were in this year brought to a crisis. The king in person having caused an edict to be registered by the parliament of Paris, which recognized as a law of the state the obligation of all the sovereign courts to register royal edicts, though in opposition to their own remonstrances, the parliament, which had previously entered protests against all that they should be compelled to do at a bed of justice, sent a deputation to the king, with a tender of the resignation of their offices should he refuse to withdraw the obnoxious edict. The king, in return, commanded the parliament to resume their functions on pain of loss of their employments, declaring at the same time that they must not hope for the revocation of his edict; to which it was answered that they could not obey, but would wait with submission his Majesty's pleasure. On January 19th, a party of musquetaires went at night to the houses of most of the members, and presented to each a lettre de cachet requiring them to declare immediately, by signing Yes or No, whether they would or would not resume their usual duties; to which the greater part returned No, while some refused any explanation, as being a general not a private concern. Two days after, about forty members who had not been served with these letters went, with the first president at their head, and passed an act against what had been done, merely that they might put themselves in the same situation with their brethren. The result was, that the members were all banished to villages near to, or distant from, Paris. The patriotism which dictated this sacrifice was the more meritorious, as the places in parliament are all purchased, some of them at a very high rate, and the possession of them is entirely at the will of the court. To supply the place of these distinguished magistrates, a temporary tribunal was erected at which the King's council were obliged to act; but this measure was so unpopular, that it was necessary to place a guard of soldiers for their protection. On February 22d, the King held a bed of justice, at which an edict was passed declaring, that as the jurisdiction of the parliament was too extensive, it was thought proper to divide it into six parts, under the denomination of superior courts, each of which was to possess a similar jurisdiction; and a number of regulations were specified, plainly implying that this arrangement was intended to be permanent. Against this abolition of the most illustrious judicial court in France, protests and remonstrances were made by other parliaments, and by many of the peers and princes of the blood, which were very ill received by the king. The Chancellor Maupeau had in the meantime framed a new code of laws which was approved at court, and measures were taken for carrying it into execution; and for the purpose of establishing this code and the new tribunals, another bed of justice was held on April 15th. The princes of the blood testified their dissatisfaction at the system adopted, by refusing their attendance, which was so much resented by the king, that letters were sent to them forbidding them to appear in his presence. The parliament of Rouen, acting with the intrepidity which had always distinguished it, issued an arret by which the members of the new parliament were declared intruders and usurpers, and the acknowledgment of their decrees was strictly forbidden. This bold proceeding highly irritated the court, and violent measures were said to have been designed, but that the Duke of Harcourt refused to take the command of the troops in Normandy for carrying them into execution. In other parts of France the arbitrary plans of the court were fully brought to effect, and during this year the parliaments of Besançon, Bourdeaux, Aix, Toulouse, and Britany were totally suppressed, most of their members sent into banishment, and new courts erected in their room. So little did the court fear the consequences of these acts of violence, that a considerable reduction was made of the French forces, both infantry and cavalry.

Corsica was still in a state of resistance to its new yoke, and the mountaineers waged a war with the French troops, attended with every circumstance of cruelty on each side. Count de Marbœuf having marched up the country at the head of several battalions was attacked with so much fury in the passes of the mountains, that he incurred a very serious loss; and a large detachment under the command of a colonel was attacked near Bastia, and almost totally destroyed. The French could not stir out of their garrisons without danger of massacre, and found it necessary to discontinue the works they were carrying on in different parts of the island.

In the month of November the incessant rains occasioned unusual floods in various parts of England, especially in the northern counties, where great damages were sustained. One of the most remarkable occurrences was the bursting of Solway Moss in Cumberland on the border of Scotland, the contents of which rushed like a torrent over the adjacent low tracts, sweeping away houses and trees, and converting many acres of arable land into a black bog.

1772

12th & 13th Year of the Reign

THE session of parliament opened on January 21st, with a speech from the throne, in which satisfaction was expressed that the state of affairs, foreign and domestic, was such as had not called for an earlier attendance of that assembly; and the performance of the King of Spain's engagement relative to the Falkland Islands was considered as promising the continuance of peace. An intimation was however given of the expediency of maintaining a respectable naval establishment; and hints were thrown out of a necessity for the interference of the legislature for remedying abuses or defects in the administration of remote possessions, which were understood to point at the East Indies.

The first public business in parliament was a motion from the ministry in the House of Commons for voting 25,000 seamen for the service of the current year. It was advanced as a reason for this augmentation, that the French having sent a considerable fleet to the East Indies, it was necessary to increase our naval force in that quarter in order to preserve a superiority; that on account of the late differences with Spain a larger squadron than usual was employed for the protection of the West India Islands; and that the war between the Turks and

Russians had caused a greater number of ships to be occupied in protecting our trade in the Mediterranean than had been customary in time of peace. A farther argument was derived from the very improved state in which the establishment of guard-ships had been placed, which was now such that twenty of the best ships in the navy were kept in complete condition, and so nearly manned, that a slight press would at enable them to put to sea in a few days. The motion was opposed, but it was carried without a division.

A petition was brought to be presented to the House of Commons on February 6th, involving a topic which, more than any other, has been found fertile of debate, and liable to agitate men's minds. In the progress of free discussion relative to religious opinion, it was not surprizing that systems established at the early periods of the reformation, should appear to many later enquirers tinctured with error and inconsistency; and the fundamental principle of protestantism being the right of private judgment, and a reference to the authority of scripture exclusively, the members of established churches would naturally in time feel a desire to be liberated from declarations of belief respecting points which the controversies of learned men had rendered dubious. In no protestant church had such controversies been carried on with more freedom and intelligence than in that of England, whence it had long been manifest that among its clergy, differences of opinion subsisted on important articles. A number of clergymen, and some members of the professions of law and physic, who found themselves compelled to dissent from many of the doctrines of the thirty-nine articles, which every clerical person, and every graduate of the English universities, is obliged subscribe, had held frequent meetings at the Feathers tavern in London, for the purpose of obtaining a relaxation in the matter of subscription; and at length about 250 of them signed the petition to parliament, which was now offered. In the statement of their arguments, it has been remarked, that they weakened their cause by directing them more against establishments in general, and the requisition of declarations of faith, than against the particular points to which they objected; so that they met with opponents in some who, though perfectly tolerant of diversities in religious opinion, thought it essential to an established church to have some criterion by which the profession of a common faith among its clergy might be secured. They who adhered more rigorously to the peculiar doctrines of the thirty-nine articles, were of course decidedly adverse to any alteration in the terms of subscription, which, they contended, would endanger the existence of christianity itself, and would be an infringement of the king's oath at his coronation. After an animated debate, the motion for receiving the petition was rejected by the great majority of 217 against 71.

Another debate, in which the church was concerned, though in a very different way, occurred on a motion made February 17th, for leave to bring in a bill for quieting the possessions of the subject against dormant claims of the church. It was argued, that as the *Nullum Tempus* of the crown had been given up in favour of the people, there was no reason why some limitation should not be made to the claims of the church, the revival of which had in several instances proved a heavy grievance. The arguments on the other side went to shew that the power of revival was absolutely necessary to protect the church from those encroachments which the laity have always been ready to practise upon her. The ministers exerted all their influence to defeat the motion, which was rejected by a majority of 141 to 117.

On February 20th a message from the king was brought to both houses of parliament, stating, that his Majesty being desirous that the right of approving all marriages in the royal family, which has ever belonged to the kings of this realm, may be made effectual, recommends to both houses to take into their serious consideration, whether it may not be expedient to supply the defects of the laws in being, and by some new provision, to guard the descendants of his late Majesty (other than the issue of princesses married into foreign families), from marrying without the approbation of his Majesty and his successors. The immediate occasion of this message was supposed to be the recent marriage of the Duke of Cumberland, the king's brother, to Mrs. Norton, a widow lady; following that which had been contracted some time before by the Duke of Gloucester, his elder brother, with Lady Waldegrave, neither of which had been recognized at court. A bill was accordingly introduced in the House of Lords, which began with a declaration of the legality of the power claimed by the crown in this respect, and proceeded to enact the incapability of contracting marriage by the persons specified in the message, without the royal consent declared in council, and signified under the great seal. A proviso was, however, inserted, that such persons, being above the age of twenty-five, after giving twelve months' previous notice to the privy council, might marry without the royal consent, unless both houses of parliament should declare their disapprobation of the union. In the progress of the bill, the opinion of the judges was taken, how far by the laws of the kingdom the king is entrusted with the care and approbation of the marriages of the royal family; and the answer returned was, that such power belonged to the Kings of England as far as to their children and grand-children, but how much farther, they did not take upon themselves to determine. Scarcely any bill in this reign underwent a more vigorous opposition, which was continued in both houses during every stage, and appeared in a variety of motions for amendments, all of which were negatived. The closest division occurred in the House of Commons on a motion for omitting the words in the preamble, acknowledging the prerogative of the crown asserted in the king's message: this was rejected by no greater majority than

200 to 164. The bill was carried through with considerable rapidity. Two strong protests were entered against it in the House of Lords.

The debates respecting the petitioning clergy having given rise to some observations with regard to the hardships undergone by dissenting ministers, in being obliged to subscribe the doctrinal articles of the established church, from which they derived no emolument, and an inclination appearing in many members to afford them relief, the body of those ministers in London were induced to appoint a committee for preparing a bill to that purpose. Their case was, that by the act of toleration in the reign of William and Mary, while a right was granted to the dissenters of exercising their public worship without restraint, their ministers and school-masters were laid under the obligation of subscribing all the doctrinal articles of the church of England, under heavy penalties for the omission. As at that period the dissenters in general agreed with the established church in point of doctrine, this obligation probably was not felt as a grievance; but the spirit of enquiry, still less shackled among them, than among the establishment, had effected such a change of opinion, that only a small proportion of ministers had complied with the requisition for subscription, and the greater number were therefore obnoxious to the penalties, though from the tolerant spirit of the time they had not been enforced. The bill for relieving them in this point, was brought in by Sir George Saville; and so reasonable did its principle appear to the house in general, that it passed the third reading with a very inconsiderable opposition, many members who had objected to the petition of the clergy, concurring in this. Its reception in the House of Lords was, however, very different, and it was thrown out at the second reading by a majority, including proxies, of 102 to 29.

Two other circumstances, connected with religion, may deserve recording. A Dr. Nowell having preached before the

House of Commons a sermon on the 30th of January, containing passages unfavourable to liberty, the thanks given him as a matter of course were, upon consideration, voted without a division to be expunged. Shortly after, Mr. Montague made a motion for a repeal of the act enjoining the observance of that anniversary, which was negatived.

On March 30th a motion was made in the House of Commons by the deputy chairman of the East India Company for leave to bring in a bill for the better regulation of the company's servants and concerns in India. Its object went to restraining the governor and council from engaging in trade, and to a total alteration of the judicature in Bengal, as well as to other changes, which obviously could not receive a full consideration so late in the session; it was therefore laid aside after the second reading. Such, however, was the impression of the necessity of strict examination into the subject, that a motion passed without a division, for the appointment of a select committee of members to enquire into the nature and state of the East India Company and of the affairs in the East Indies. Nothing further of importance passed in parliament to the close of the session in the month of June.

On February 8th, died her Royal Highness the Princess Dowager of Wales, in the 53d year of her age.

In the autumn, the Earl of Hillsborough resigned the post of secretary of state for the colonies, in which he was succeeded by the Earl of Dartmouth, a nobleman supposed favourably affected to the American colonists, as he had acted with those who repealed the stamp tax, and had opposed all other modes of taxing them. Other changes afterwards took place. Earl Harcourt was appointed to the viceroyalty of Ireland, in the room of Lord Townshend, who was placed at the head of the ordnance. Among the promotions was that of the Honourable Charles Fox to a seat at the Treasury board. The strength of the ministry was in no respect impaired by these alterations.

The East India Company, alarmed at the parliamentary enquiry into their affairs, and conscious of the prevalence of great abuses, resolved to send out a new commission of supervision in the place of that which had so unfortunately miscarried; but the publication of the report of the select committee having excited general indignation, and the king's speech at the opening of the autumnal session particularly pointing out the situation of the company to the consideration of parliament, the subject was directly taken up by government. Lord North moved for the appointment of a committee of *secrecy*, consisting of thirteen persons, to be chosen by ballot, for taking into consideration the affairs of the East India Company. This motion, though opposed as unconstitutional in a case where there was no criminal charge, passed without a division; and the ballot took place, by which a committee was nominated, principally consisting of men in office, or such as were known to be entirely devoted to the ministry. In a short time after its appointment, the secret committee laid a report before the house, stating that although the Company were much distressed in their finances, they were going to send out an expensive commission of supervision; and recommending that a bill should be brought in to restrain them for a limited time from executing such a measure. A very warm debate ensued, in which all the arguments were touched upon — on one side relative to the violence and injustice of interfering with chartered rights; on the other, to the misconduct of the Company, and the necessity of putting their affairs under other management — which in many subsequent debates were repeated in the most varied and diffuse forms. The bill however passed in both houses by great majorities. A second report in the meantime had been published by the *select* committee, which also subsisted, giving a very unfavourable view of the Company's finances, notwithstanding the great addition to their territorial revenues.

The Caribbs or aboriginal natives of the West Indian Island of St. Vincent's, ceded to Great Britain at the peace, having been for some years at variance with the English settlers, who wished to dispossess them of their lands, took up arms, resisted a proposed exchange of lands, and boldly asserted the rights of an independent people. As it appeared impossible for the European inhabitants to hold their settlements in safety under such a divided occupation, orders were sent in April from government, for two regiments in North America to join about an equal number already in the island, for the purpose of reducing the Caribbs to submission. This proved to be a service of difficulty and danger, and the troops, in the middle of November, had not been able to penetrate more than four miles into the country, after undergoing considerable losses. The business was brought before parliament in December, but the proceedings upon it were deferred till after the Christmas recess.

The disturbances between the native and negro population and the European, in the southern part of America, during this year, extended to the possessions of other powers and were much more serious and alarming than those above-mentioned. In the Dutch colony of Surinam a formidable insurrection of the negro slaves, who have always been treated by the settlers of that nation with great severity, for several months spread terror throughout the country, and caused many of the most valuable settlements to be abandoned. The insurgents were so well provided with arms and ammunition, and so expert in the use of them, that it was found necessary to send ships and troops from Holland, and act against them as a regular foe. In Brazil, the negro and Indian slaves united, assembling in great numbers, advanced against the Portuguese, and various actions ensued attended with much bloodshed. The free natives of Chili, resenting an attempt of the Spaniards to re-establish their settlement at Castro in the island of Chiloe, rose in arms, and destroyed a great part of the cities of Baldivia and St. Jago.

So dangerous did this insurrection appear, that the Viceroy of Peru ordered a body of troops to be assembled at Lima for its suppression, and an armament was sent from Spain for the same purpose.

The war between the Turks and Russians was this year in a state of suspension. Negotiations had been carrying on during the winter under the mediation of the courts of Vienna and Berlin, but the demands of Russia were so high that the Porte absolutely refused to accede to the proposed conditions. An armistice however, was signed on May 30th, between the two opposite commanders on the Danube, the Grand Vizier and General Romanzow, and a congress for settling the articles of peace was agreed on, which opened on July 15th at Foczani in Walachia, in presence of the Austrian and Prussian ministers. Nothing effectual being done at the conferences, the congress broke up in September; but before the resumption of hostilities, the Grand Vizier sent to Romanzow to propose a renewal of it, which was acceded to, and the suspension of arms was prolonged to the following March. The Russians in this interval concluded a treaty with the Tartars of the Krimea, in which these people renounced the Ottoman sovereignty, and were declared independent under the protection of Russia.

The Porte, however, received some compensation for this loss in the recovery of its dominion over Egypt. Ali Bey having in consequence of some jealousy banished from his court his brother-in-law, Aboudaab, and some other Beys, they retired to Upper Egypt, and formed a conspiracy against him. In April he sent forces to oppose them, which were entirely defeated; on which event Ali Bey fled from Cairo with his treasures, and took refuge with his friend and ally, Chiek Daher, a distinguished aged chief in Syria. Upon this intelligence, the Ottoman government sent Aboudaab a firman constituting him its commander in Egypt, which thus again submitted to its authority.

This year will be memorable in history as the commencement of that partition of Poland between three contiguous powers, which has served as an example and apology for all those shameless violations of public right and justice that have stained the modern annals of Europe. It has been already mentioned that the troops of the three powers had entered Poland from different sides, and were conjoined in the design of suppressing those confederacies which were ruining their country; and such a purpose would have been laudable had its ends been fair and disinterested. The original intention of Russia, however, in intermeddling with the Polish affairs, was that of rendering the republic entirely dependent upon her. Prussia, from the first entrance of her troops, displayed that boundless rapacity and unfeeling tyranny which always marked the conduct of the Great Frederic towards weaker neighbours; and besides immoderate pecuniary exactions, the transportation of numbers of Polish families to people the barren sands of his hereditary dominions was a characteristic trait of his despotic policy. Austria, under the rule of the empress-queen appears long to have held back from the projects of guilt, but at length, in February 1772, the fatal treaty of partition was signed. At this time the confederacies were in a state of vigour inspired by despair, and they gained possession by surprize of the citadel of Cracow, and frequently skirmished with the Russian detachments and Polish crown troops. Shortly however, all their remaining fortresses being taken or under siege, their principal leader entered into terms with the Russian command. The foreign armies successively occupied the districts near them, and in September, the treaty of partition which had hitherto been kept secret, was declared to Poland and Europe. After expressing the kindest intentions towards Poland, the allied powers mention, that "having respectively very considerable claims on the possessions of the republics they will not expose them to the hazard of future contingencies, and have therefore determined among themselves to assert those rights and claims, which each of them will hereafter be ready to justify in time and place, by authentic records and solid reasons." The specifications are then given of the countries they mean to take as equivalents to their rights, to which, however, they did not adhere when they had agreed among themselves on a more commodious partition. Promises were lavished in profusion, of paying regard to the liberties, privileges, and property of the acquired subjects, provided they submit quietly to the new order of things. The unfortunate King of Poland, with his little senate, issued a spirited counter-declaration to that of the powers, and solemnly protested against the injustice of dismembering the country; which had no other effect than that of exciting their indignation, and producing menaces. At length, in December, the king found it expedient to consent to their demand of convoking a diet of the nation, for the next year, in order to enter upon a negotiation for settling all differences. Before this extremity was acquiesced in, the king and senate had not neglected to make applications to the courts of Great Britain, France, and Spain, and the States General of Holland, for the fulfilment of their ancient treaties, and their protection against violence and spoliation; but it does not appear that any attention was paid to them.

Sweden, in this year, was the theatre of an extraordinary political revolution. The new king signed, in February, the capitulation with the States of the kingdom in the accustomed form, adding, on his own motion, an article absolving them from their oath of allegiance, should he premeditatedly infringe the terms of the capitulation. He was crowned in May with unusual magnificence, and in a subsequent speech expressed the most patriotic attachment to the country and its freedom. The diet was still sitting, when in August, an insurrection took place in the garrison of Christianstadt, in which a captain at the head of the soldiery, having seized the magazines and fortifications, issued a manifesto representing the States of the kingdom as usurpers of an authority despotic towards the nation, and subversive of the legal rights of the crown, and calling upon all true Swedes to join with them in liberating their country.

The king's next brother, Prince Charles, who was at this time at Carlescroon, availed himself of the occasion to assemble all the troops in the neighbourhood, and take the command; and having published a mysterious manifesto, and put a garrison in Carlescroon, he marched towards Christianstadt, as if to suppress the insurrection. Intelligence of these transactions being brought to Stockholm by General Rudbeck, a senator, measures were taken for assembling troops; and as the regiments quartered in the capital were suspected on account of their attachment to the royal family, orders were sent to the regiments of Upland and Sudermania to march thither with the utmost expedition. The king, in the meantime, who was not consulted with respect to any of the resolutions of the senate, affected perfect satisfaction with all that was going forward, and even visited the posts and patroles of the burghers, who had been ordered to assemble in arms, as if all had been done by his direction. The diet, to whom the senate and the secret committee had communicated their measures and resolutions, approved and confirmed them. This was the state of things, till the king, having received dispatches from his brother Prince Charles, summoned a meeting of the senators, August 19th, when he expostulated severely with them on the orders they had issued without his consent. The senators taking no notice of his complaints, insisted that he should shew them the letters which he had received from his brother; and on his refusal, it is affirmed that an attempt was made to secure his person, which he resisted by drawing his sword, and that retiring, he locked the door of the senate chamber, and put the key in his pocket. Another account says, that the dispatches from Prince Charles had been intercepted by the prime minister, Count Kaling, who privately assembled the senate, before whom they were opened and read; and knowledge being thereby obtained of a scheme for overthrowing the government; after a night spent in consultation, it was resolved to send for the king next morning and put him under arrest. Whichsoever of these accounts be the true one, it is certain that his Majesty went to the grand guard, and having assembled the officers, made a speech to them, complaining of the aristocratical tyranny under which he and the nation groaned, and demanded of them whether they would assist him in throwing off the yoke. To this proposal the officers in general, and all the soldiers, assented; and the king, marching at their head, proceeded to the arsenal and admiralty, where he received the same assurance from the rest of the military. Without entering into farther particulars, it is sufficient here to mention, that oaths of allegiance being administered to all ranks, and the few who refused being committed to custody, the revolution in the capital was accomplished without a drop of bloodshed. On August 21st, the king assembled the states, with cannon planted in the court of their hall, and troops posted all around. Entering the hall in his regalia, with the silver hammer of Gustavus Adolphus in his hand, he made them a long address full of accusation against the senate, and justification of his own conduct, and then ordered the new form of government to be read, consisting of 57 articles. Of these, the most material were such as gave to the crown the whole executive power, the nomination of the senate, the right of convening and dissolving the states at his pleasure, the nomination and removal of the judges, the appointment to all employments civil and military, the imposition of taxes in case of actual invasion, and the disposal of the public money. The assembly was then asked if they would give their oaths to observe this form of government; and under such circumstances, it is no wonder that there was not a single dissentient voice. The work being completed, the king rose, and taking a psalter out of his pocket, began to sing a *Te Deum,* in which the whole audience joined. On the next day the old senators were dismissed, and new ones were appointed by the king. The states were afterwards re-assembled, when they displayed abundant loyalty. On their dismission, they were told by the king, that he hoped to meet them again at the end of *six years*. Rewards and distinctions were bestowed on the principal agents in this revolution, and every precaution was taken for its security. The king himself is universally allowed to have displayed on this important occasion, great talents, firm resolution, and profound dissimulation.

The neighbouring court of Denmark was also the scene of a revolution, which if of less political consequence than that of Sweden, was more interesting with respect to its effect on individuals. The king, whose mental imbecility threw him entirely into the power of favourites, had given all his confidence to Struensee, who from his physician became his prime minister, and to Count Brandt. These favourites were closely connected with the queen, sister of the king of England, whilst the queen dowager, sister of the Duke of Brunswick Wolfenbuttle, and mother to the king's half-brother Frederic, headed an opposite party. Struensee, a man of ambition and enterprize, and fond of novelty, introduced many changes in the internal administration of Denmark, which created him numerous enemies, and the arts of the queen dowager inflamed the discontents which his conduct and measures had occasioned. A plot being at length arranged for effecting his downfall, early in the morning after a masked ball given at court, on January 16th the queen dowager, her son, and two nobles, entered the king's bed-chamber, and having terrified him with the information that the queen and Struensee had resolved to compel him to sign a renunciation of the crown, obtained from him an order for the arrest of her Majesty and her accomplices. This was put in execution, and Struensee, from being the most powerful man in Denmark, saw himself chained in a dungeon, whilst the populace plundered or demolished the houses of his adherents. A commission was appointed for the trial of the alleged criminals, who brought in Struensee and Brandt guilty of high treason, for which they were executed with circumstances of great severity. The queen, who had been confined in the castle of Cronenburg, was charged with a criminal connection with Struensee; and it is thought that a design was entertained against her life, but that apprehension of the resentment of the English court caused it to be abandoned. She was afterwards conveyed by an English squadron to Stade, and took up her residence at Zell, where she formed a small court.

The opposition to the arbitrary measures of the crown in France was nearly terminated in this year. The princes of the blood, unable to bear exclusion from the court, made overtures for accommodation, which were gladly accepted.

A hurricane of uncommon violence occurred in the beginning of September, in the West India Islands, by which those of St. Christopher, Antigua, St. Croix, and St. Eustatia, suffered very severely in their buildings and plantations.

1773

13th & 14th Year of the Reign

O NE of the first subjects brought under discussion in parliament after the recess was the expedition against the Caribbs of St.Vincent, and motions were made in the House of Commons, calling into question both its justice and policy, and requesting his Majesty to acquaint the house by whose advice it was undertaken. A long debate ensued, after which the motions were negatived by a great majority. In the meantime hostilities were terminated in the island by a treaty concluded on February 17th, between Major General Dalrymple and the Caribbs, by which the latter acknowledged the sovereignty of the King of Great Britain, and agreed to submit to the laws of the island as far as regarded their transactions with the white inhabitants, while they were to retain their own customs and usages with respect to their intercourse with each other. The Caribbs also ceded a large tract of land to the crown, but were secured in the full possession of the part which they still retained.

A petition presented to the house by the captains of the navy for a small addition to their half-pay was opposed by the minister on the principle of economy, and the danger that the admission of this claim would open the way to many others of a similar kind. Such however, was the sense of the house of the merits of the petitioners, and the reasonableness of their request, that upon a division the petition was received by a majority of 154 to 145; and a committee being appointed to examine into the allegations, an address was presented to the throne for an addition of two shillings a day to the captains' pay.

The partial success which had attended the bill for the relief of the dissenters in the last year, encouraged them to bring in one of the same tenor in March. The most remarkable circumstance attending it was, that petitions against the bill were presented from several congregations of protestant dissenters of the calvinistic class, who apparently could not endure that others should be relieved from shackles which were not felt by themselves. The fate of the bill was exactly the same with that of the preceding year: it passed in the House of Commons by a great majority and was rejected in the House of Lords by one as great.

A farther attempt for relief with respect to the subscriptions enjoined by the established church, was made by a motion for a committee of the whole House of Commons to consider of the subscription to the 39 articles or any other tests required of persons in the universities. It produced a considerable debate, but was rejected by a majority of 159 to 64.

The principal business which occupied the attention of parliament in this session related to the East India Company. A petition was presented to the House of Commons from the Company, in March, containing a request for a loan from the public of £1,500,000 for four years at four per cent interest, to be repaid by instalments of £300,000 with a restriction of the Company's dividend to six per cent until half the debt was discharged, after which they might be raised to eight per cent. Other proposals were annexed, one of which was that the Company might be freed from their annual payment of

£400,000 to the public for the remainder of the five years specified in the contract. After this petition had been read, Lord North, having first observed that granting relief to the Company was a matter of necessary policy, but by no means a claim of right or justice, moved two resolutions which were, in substance, that the affairs of the East India Company are in a state to require parliamentary assistance; and that a loan of £1,400,000 be granted to it, with the proviso of adopting such regulations as may prevent the recurrence of the like exigence: which were agreed to. In the same month the minister proposed two other resolutions, namely, that supposing the loan above-mentioned be granted to the Company, its dividends shall be restricted to six per cent, till the re-payment of the whole sum; and that the Company shall not be permitted to divide more than seven per cent till its bond debt be reduced to £1,500,000: and these also passed without a division. On April 5th, he moved the following resolutions: That it will be more beneficial to the public and the Company to let the territorial acquisitions remain in the Company's possession for a time not exceeding six years, (which was the term of its charter): That no participation of profits between the public and the Company shall take place till the repayment of the loan, and the reduction of the bond debt as above specified: and that after such period, three fourths of the Company's net profit at home above eight pet cent on its capital stock shall be paid into the exchequer for the public use, and the remaining fourth be set apart, either for reducing the Company's bond debt, or for answering any other exigences. In these resolutions, the right of the state to the territorial possessions was directly asserted, which was exclaimed against by the opposition, as an extraordinary assumption without any legal hearing or decision. They were however agreed to; and as a favour to the Company, it was allowed to export teas duty free. The resolutions being considered by the Company as highly unjust and injurious, a strong petition was presented to the house against them, in which the Company absolutely refused to acquiesce in the proposed allotment of the surplus profits.

On May 3d, the minister moved a string of resolutions as the foundation of a bill "for establishing certain regulations for the better management of the East India Company's affairs, as well in India, as in Europe." By these, the court of directors was to be elected for four years; the stock for qualification of electors to be raised from £500 to £1000 and to have been possessed twelve months previous to election; the mayor's court of Calcutta to be confined to mercantile causes; a new court to be established consisting of a chief justice and three puisne judges, appointed by the crown; and a superiority to be given to the presidency of Bengal over the other presidencies. Every one of these clauses was a topic of warm debate; and the disfranchisement of the £500 stockholders, above 1200 in number, was the subject of strong petitions from the stockholders themselves, the East India Company, and the City of London. The questions, however, were all carried by great majorities; and on June 10th, the bill framed upon the resolutions was passed through the House of Commons by a majority of more than six to one. It encountered no less opposition in the House of Lords, where a petition from the Company against it was delivered, and council was heard; but in fine, it passed that house by a large majority. From this era the East India Company has been regarded as entirely in the hands of the ministry.

The close enquiries into East India transactions carried on by the select committee had laid open scenes of rapacity and treachery which deeply involved several of the principal civil and military officers of the Company in India, and were productive of a resolution of the committee, importing that great sums of money and other property had been acquired in Bengal from princes and others of that country, by persons entrusted with the civil and military powers of the state, which had been appropriated by them to their private use. As Lord Clive appeared to be the principal delinquent, it was thought that justice required, notwithstanding his great and brilliant services, that he should first be brought to account; and a motion was put and carried in the House of Commons: That Lord Clive, about the time of deposing Serajah Dowlah, and the establishing of Meer Jaffier (1756) did possess himself of several sums under the denomination of private donation, of the value of £234,000 sterling. It was added in the original motion "To the dishonour and detriment of the state," but after long debates, these words were rejected, the minister dividing with the minority. His lordship defended his conduct with great ability, by the assistance of the solicitor-general, whilst the attorney- general led the attack; and the court members voted on different sides, but the opposition, chiefly in his favour. A motion, "That Lord Clive, in so doing, abused the power with which he was entrusted, to the evil example of the servants of the public;" was made and negatived; and another motion, "That Lord C. did at the same time render great and meritorious services to this country," was carried, and put an end to the enquiry. It may be observed, however, that his lordship's character never recovered from some of the wounds inflicted upon it by facts which were brought out in the course of this examination.

Whilst the East India regulation bill was under discussion in the House of Lords, and the loan bill in the House of Commons, a petition was presented by the Company to the latter, containing a refusal to accept the loan on the conditions annexed to it; but this was regarded by the ministry as an act of insanity, and no attention was paid to it. In fact, the Company had no longer a choice left.

The farther negotiations between the Russians and Turks having proved ineffectual, the war was renewed in the spring, and the banks of the Danube became the theatre of a great number of desultory actions attended with much bloodshed, but with no decisive results to either party. The Russian army under Count Romanzow crossed the Danube in June with the intention of carrying the war into Bulgaria, and advanced to Silistria. That town was defended by a large body of troops encamped on an adjoining eminence, who being attacked by the Russians, were forced, after a vigorous resistance, to retire into the place. Preparations were then made for a general assault; but advice having been received that a powerful Turkish army was coming to its assistance, and that the Grand Vizier was taking measures for cutting off the retreat of the Russians, it was thought advisable to march back to the Danube. This was not effected without considerable loss; and the sickly season following, obliged Romanzow to retire from the banks of the river to the neighbourhood of Jassy. In October, the Russians again crossed the Danube, and while one division renewed the siege of Silistria, another pushed on to Varna, a port of the Black sea, which they attempted to carry by assault. In both these enterprizes however, they were unsuccessful, and on the approach of winter they recrossed the Danube and concluded the campaign. Their efforts in this quarter were impeded by an insurrection which broke out in the Krimea, among the Cossacks, joined by the Tartars and Turks, whereby the whole peninsula, except one or two fortresses on the coast, was for a time withdrawn from the Russian authority. Several bodies of Russian troops were sent for its suppression, but the country continued in a very disordered state during the whole year. Another deduction from the force of Russia was made by a rebellion under one Pugatcheff, which broke out towards the close of the year in the kingdom of Casan, and which in the event proved of very serious consequence.

A considerable Russian fleet was in this year maintained in the Levant seas, which made predatory descents upon different islands, and took a number of prizes, conducing more to the detriment of the European trade in that quarter, than to any material advantage with respect to the war. The Russian commander held a close correspondence with Chiek Daher and Ali Bey, and promised the latter every assistance in his enterprizes against the Porte. This adventurer having collected a body of forces in Syria, marched for the recovery of Egypt, and had approached Cairo, when he was met, on May 7th, by a much superior army under Aboudaab, which, after an obstinate resistance, cut in pieces almost the whole of Ali Bey's troops, and took himself prisoner. He died soon after, either in consequence of his wounds, or of an order from Constantinople for his execution.

The Grand Duke of Russia in October married a Princess of Hesse Darmstadt. He afterwards made a cession of his patrimonial right to the Duchy of Holstein to the King of Denmark, receiving in exchange the county of Oldenburg, and Delmenhorst with its territory.

The Polish diet opened at Warsaw on April 13th, and although that city was surrounded by the lines of the allied powers, it was found impossible to suppress the ferment in that assembly arising from the indignant feelings of freemen convoked for the purpose of giving sanction to a forcible dismemberment of their country. As a confederacy of nobles had been formed at Cracow in opposition to the diet, another was formed under the influence of the allied powers to support its decisions, to which the unhappy King adhered. The debates in the assembly continuing with great violence, the Austrian and Prussian hussars entered Warsaw, and were quartered in the houses of the principal inhabitants, and the ministers of the three powers declared that no further delays would be permitted, nor any mitigation made of the terms prescribed. The cession however, was finally passed with no greater majority than that of 52 to 50; and several dissentients, who had found means to escape from Warsaw, assembled at Cracow and published a manifesto, protesting against the acts of the diet as illegal. Such opposition however, could be of no avail against the preponderating force. The territories seized by the partitioning powers were more than a third of Poland.

The change of government in Sweden, though effected in a violent and arbitrary manner, was quietly acquiesced in by the body of the nation, which was probably little attached to the former aristocracy, and was now suffering under a dreadful scarcity of food, followed by a mortal epidemic. The King took every measure to alleviate the calamity; and at the same time employed his newly acquired prerogatives in putting his army and navy in the best condition, and making a variety of military preparations, which indicated an enterprizing spirit, and inspired no small jealousy in his neighbours, Russia and Denmark.

Another young sovereign, the Emperor Joseph, also exhibited tokens of that restless activity and fondness for change, which so much distinguished his subsequent reign. He recruited his armies, formed encampments in remote parts which he was constantly visiting, so that during this summer he was computed to have travelled on horseback more than 3000 English miles, generally contenting himself with the simplest fare and humblest lodging. He also made a commencement of that inroad on the Papal authority, which gave so much uneasiness to the court of Rome, by claiming the investiture of all the bishoprics in his hereditary dominions, and appointing successors in four or five vacant sees in Hungary and Bohemia.

The Pope, after long procrastination, found himself at length obliged to comply with the instances of the Bourbon courts, and on July 21st, issued a bull for the total suppression of the order of Jesuits. A great number of charges against the order were contained in this writing, but chiefly of a vague and general nature, and among the causes for its dissolution are mentioned "other motives reserved in the breast of the sovereign Pontiff." In consequence of the bull, ten bishops, attended by a detachment of soldiers, went by night to all the colleges and houses of the Jesuits in Rome, of which they took possession, requiring from the fathers all their keys, and sealing up their archives. Eight days were allowed them to find new dwellings and quit the habit of the order. The general, Father Ricci, was nominated to a bishopric; such of them as were in holy orders, were permitted to become secular clergymen, or to enter into other orders; and several regulations were made, as indulgent to their persons as was compatible with the purpose of entirely annulling their vocation as members of the suppressed society. The effect of the Pope's compliance was a thorough reconciliation of the court of Rome with the house of Bourbon. The Italian states, however, persisted in curtailing the ecclesiastical authority in their dominions; and the Venetians refused to receive the Pope's bull, conferring two abbeys upon Cardinal Rezzonico, having resolved that no ecclesiastic should possess a benefice in their dominions, who did not reside in them.

The King of Sardinia died on February 20th, in his 72d year, after a prosperous reign of more than 40 years.

Towards the latter part of the year, a violent insurrection broke out at Palermo, occasioned by monopolies, which raised the price of the necessaries of life, in which the populace took possession of the fortifications, and obliged the viceroy, after running great hazard of his life, to retire to Messina.

The discontents which had never ceased to prevail in the American colonies against the rule and policy of the mother country, broke out during this year into a flame, that spreading into a general conflagration, finally dissolved all the ties by which an union, in its nature so delicate, had been held together. The unfortunate measure of retaining the trifling duty on tea as an assertion of the right inherent in the British parliament to tax the colonies, was a source of perpetual irritation, which displayed itself in associations in various parts, for the encouragement of home products and manufactures, to the exclusion of foreign articles, and tea itself was prohibited in several colonies, though it was clandestinely imported. In most of the colonies, the governors and people were at open variance, and used every means to thwart each other's measures;

and the late regulation that the salaries of governors and judges should be paid by the crown, by which they were removable, aggravated the public jealousy and disaffection. The tendency to riot was first displayed by an outrage committed on a King's schooner, posted at Providence in Rhode-island for the prevention of smuggling. It was boarded on the night of June 10th, by a number of armed men; the captain and crew were obliged to go on shore, and the vessel was burnt; and though a large reward was offered for discovering the perpetrators, they remained concealed.

Another circumstance productive of great animosity, was the discovery and subsequent publication of a number of confidential letters during the former disputes between the colony of Massachusets and the mother country, written by the governor and deputy-governor to persons in office in England, in which a very unfavourable view was given of the disposition of the people, and of the purposes of their leaders in that province, and measures of coercion, with changes in the colonial constitution, were represented as necessary. These letters coming into the hands of Mr. Franklin, agent for the colony in London, were transmitted by him to the assembly of the province, in which they excited the highest indignation, and produced a petition to the King, charging their governor and his second, with being betrayers of their trust, and enemies to the colony, and praying for their removal.

It has already been noticed, that a permission had been given to the East India Company, to export tea duty-free. As they had a large quantity in their warehouses, a plan was adopted of exporting tea to the colonies on the Company's own account, consigned to particular venders. This scheme was particularly obnoxious to those who considered the import-tax left on that article, as meant to enforce the claim of a right to tax America, and as a probable prelude to future taxation; and it was the more grating, as it threw a monopoly of trade in tea into the hands of particular persons, who were nominated on account of their attachment to the English ministry, and their connection with the governors. Strong measures were therefore taken in most of the colonies to frustrate the plan. Popular committees were appointed with powers to inspect merchants' books, and propose tests; and in some places the consignees were compelled by the threats of tumultuous assemblies to relinquish their appointments. In this state of things, three ships laden with tea having arrived at the port of Boston, the captains were induced by menaces to promise that if they were permitted by the consignees, the board of customs, and the fort, they would sail back with their cargoes to England. This permission they could not obtain; and the Bostonians being sensible that if the vessels continued in the harbour, means would be found of landing the cargoes by detail, an effectual mode of prevention was resolved upon. On December 18th, a number of armed men, in the disguise of Mohawk Indians, boarded the ships, and threw the whole cargoes into the sea, without any other damage, or offering injury to the crews. Some smaller quantities of tea afterwards were treated in the same manner at Boston and its vicinity, and also in South Carolina. A cargo was landed at New York under the guns of a man of war, but the officers of government were obliged to consent to its being locked up from use. In the colonies in general, no persons venturing to act as consignees, the masters of the tea-ships returned with the article to England, without making any entry at the custom-houses. Such was the perturbed and, it may be said, the lawless condition of the American colonies at the close of the year.

At home, commercial credit was greatly injured by some capital bankruptcies which occurred in England and Holland. The great diminution of the weight of gold coin, by wear or fraudulent practices, was a cause of much inconvenience to the circulation, and the loss upon it being by an act of parliament thrown upon the holders, heavy complaints were made by the monied men and bankers, of this addition to the distress of the commercial class.

1774

14th & 15th Year of the Reign

THE session of parliament opened on January 13th, when the speech from the throne particularly recommended to its consideration the state of the gold coin. In the debates concerning the supplies, complaints were made by the opposition, of the great increase of expence in the naval and ordnance departments, and of a general want of economy in the application of the public money, which the minister appeared under some embarrassment to answer.

A renewed motion was made in February by Sir G. Saville, relative to the Middlesex election, and leave was desired to bring in a bill for more effectually securing the rights of electors, and the eligibility of persons to serve in parliament. A considerable debate ensued, in which former arguments on the topic were recapitulated; and upon a division, the motion was rejected by a less majority than might have been expected, the numbers being 206 to 147. Soon after, a motion being made for rendering perpetual Mr. Grenville's bill for the trial of controverted elections, its utility had so strongly impressed the house, that not withstanding the opposition of the minister, it was carried by a majority of more than two to one, and a bill for the purpose passed into a law.

The news of the outrages committed at Boston arrived in the beginning of March, when the whole transactions were laid before both houses in a message from the king, in which a confidence was expressed that parliament would not only enable his Majesty to adopt such measures as might put an immediate stop to those disorders, but would take into their consideration what further regulations might be necessary for better securing the execution of the laws, and the just dependence of the colonies upon the crown and parliament of Great Britain. A motion being made in the House of Commons for a corresponding address to the throne, it brought on a discussion relative to American affairs, in which the opposition recommended a retrospect of the measures that had provoked the violence of the colonies, whilst the ministry argued for keeping to the present point, that of reducing them to obedience. In pursuance of this purpose, Lord North opened his plan, the first part of which was to inflict a punishment on the town of Boston, for the heinous act perpetrated in it; and this was to consist, not only in obliging it to pay for the tea destroyed, but in taking from it the privilege of a port, until his Majesty in council should declare himself satisfied with the security given, that in future, property should be protected in it, laws obeyed, and duties regularly paid. In consequence, on March 14th, he moved for leave to bring in a bill for the immediate removal of the custom-house officers from Boston, and the discontinuance of the landing, discharging, and shipping of goods in its port. The bill being introduced, it underwent a strong opposition during its progress, and its justice was particularly attacked in a very able petition from some North Americans, then in London, presented to the house by the Lord Mayor. No division, however, was called for, the opposers being conscious of the weakness of their numbers; and its passage through both houses was so speedy, that it received the royal assent on March 31st.

An attempt made by some friends to conciliation, for a repeal of the tea duty, gave occasion for a review of the policy which had been pursued with regard to the colonies for some past years, but was otherwise ineffectual; and the minister proceeded in the development of his coercive plan. The next measure was a bill for "the better regulating government in the province of Massachusets' Bay;" the purpose of which was to alter the constitution of that province as framed by the charter of King William; to take the whole executive power out of the hands of the democratic part, and to vest the nomination of counsellors, judges and magistrates of every kind in the crown, and in some cases in the governor, all of whom were to be removable at the pleasure of the crown. The opposition to this bill in both houses was by so much the more keen and active than that to the Boston port bill, as its provisions appeared to strike a severer blow against the fundamental principles of free government, by abolishing chartered rights, and placing the administration of justice entirely under the influence of the crown. The same Americans who petitioned against the former bill, stated with great energy various objections to the present, and foreboded the effects that it would produce on the minds of their countrymen. The bill, however, passed in both houses by great majorities.

The third step in this hazardous progress was the bringing in of a bill "for the impartial administration of justice in the case of persons questioned for any acts done by them in the execution of the laws, or for the suppression of riots and tumults in the province of Massachusets' Bay." By its tenor, any person indicted for murder or any other capital offence, under the circumstances above-mentioned, might, if the govenor should think that a fair trial could not be obtained in that province, be sent to any other colony, or to Great Britain, to be tried. This was likewise strongly opposed, and the case of Captain Preston was adduced, to show that it was not necessary for the purposes of justice, which would be much more violated by the obligation of sending the witnesses against a murderer, to give evidence at three thousand miles distance. It, however, passed by the same majorities as the preceding. Such was the temper of the nation at this time, that an old member of the House of Commons, after a vaticination of the ruinous consequences of these measures, lamented that not only the house had fallen into error, but the people approved what was done. As a means of enforcing the determinations of the ministry, four regiments were sent to Boston under General Gage, as governor of the province and commander in chief.

Near the close of the session, another American bill was introduced, which was a source of more national discontent than any of the former: it was "for making more effectual provision for the government of the province of Quebec." In the House of Lords, where it was first introduced, it passed with scarcely a remark; but in the House of Commons a disposition appeared to canvass it with severity, which gave some uneasiness to the ministry, knowing how liable it would be to excite the passions of the people. Its principal objects were to ascertain the limits of the province; to form a legislative council appointed by the crown, in which the Canadian Roman Catholics were to have a place; to establish the French laws, without a jury in civil causes; and to secure to the Roman Catholic clergy, regulars excepted, the enjoyment of their estates, and of tythes from those of their own communion. Though it was thought that the introduction of this bill at the present time, was for the purpose of attaching the Canadians to the British government, in opposition to the English colonies, yet arguments were not wanting to prove the justice of its provisions, as being suited to the habits and sentiments of the people, and to the expectations given them at the conquest. It was, however, vehemently arraigned in the House of Commons, as establishing a civil government under the British dominion, on principles incompatible with the English Constitution, and particularly as containing an establishment of the Roman Catholic religion. These objections, particularly the latter, were so conformable to popular feelings, that a great clamour was raised respecting the bill, and an address and petition against it from the corporation of London, was presented to his Majesty. In its progress it underwent various amendments, which rendered it less exceptionable, and it passed both houses by large majorities.

Parliament broke up on June 22d, with a full persuasion, on the part of ministers and their supporters, that the measures carried could not fail of ensuring the submission of the colonies, which was likewise expressed in the speech from the throne.

The temper prevalent in the province of Massachusets at the early part of the year, was manifested by a petition to the governor from the house of representatives, for the removal of Peter Oliver, Esq. chief justice of the superior court of judicature; and this not being complied with, articles of impeachment of high crimes and misdemeanours were drawn up against him, on the ground of having betrayed his trust by accepting a salary from the crown, instead of the customary grant from the house. The resolution for carrying these up to the council board, was carried by a majority of 92 to 8. The governor refused to receive the articles, and dissolved the assembly.

The Boston-port bill being received in May at Boston, a town meeting was taking it into consideration just at the time that General Gage arrived in the harbour. Nothing could exceed the mixed consternation and rage which this decree against the trade and prosperity of a whole town excited, and violent resolutions were immediately entered upon in retaliation. The bill was printed and rapidly conveyed through the whole continent, and every where kindled a flame of resentment. Provincial or town meetings were held in all parts, at which an abhorrence was expressed of the act and its principles.

Days of prayer and humiliation were appointed, and letters were addressed to the town of Boston, expressive of sympathy, and declaring that its cause was regarded as that of America. The assembly of Massachusets, which, according to the act, had been removed by General Gage to Salem, whither also the port business of Boston had been transferred, passed a resolution, declaring the expediency of a general meeting of committees from the several colonies, and appointed five persons to act for that province, with a sum of money to defray their expences. The governor refusing his assent to this appropriation, various altercations followed, which terminated in the dissolution of the assembly on June 17th. On the following day, an address from the merchants and freeholders of Salem was presented to the governor, containing sentiments certainly very different from those which had been expected to prevail in the minds of persons to whom such an opportunity had been granted of rising upon the ruin of a neighbour. They expressed a deep sense of the public calamities, and particular commiseration of their brethren in the capital, the evils pressing upon which they implored his excellency's endeavours to alleviate. They affirmed that nature had not made their harbour to be a rival to that of Boston; and that even were the case otherwise, they could not be so dead to the feelings of justice and humanity, as to indulge a thought of acquiring wealth at the expence of their suffering neighbours. The inhabitants of the port of Marblehead even made an offer of their stores and wharfs to the Bostonian merchants, with that of transacting their business without expence.

The arrival of the other bills levelled against the province of Massachusets, filled up the measures of the indignation and apprehensions of the colonists; and though there was a more moderate, as well as a violent party among them, all, except the individuals particularly connected with the English government, concurred in determinations to support the general cause. The committee of correspondence at Boston entered into a *solemn league and covenant* for suspending all commercial intercourse with Great Britain till the repeal of the obnoxious acts; and similar agreements were adopted in various other parts of the continent. Meantime steps were taken for the more alarming measure of holding a *general congress* of the American colonies; and Philadelphia, as a central spot, was fixed upon for the place, and the beginning of September for the time of this meeting. Popular assemblies were held for electing deputies to the congress, at which strong declarations passed against the Boston-port bill and the other acts. The proceedings at Boston itself were continually assuming a more hostile aspect. Several British regiments had arrived from different parts, which were encamped on the common of the peninsula, in which the town is seated. A guard was placed on the neck of the peninsula; and upon a report that this was intended to starve the town into compliance, messengers were received from the inhabitants of the county of Worcester, signifying that there were several thousand men ready to march to their assistance. The governor having received a list of 36 new counsellors appointed by the crown conformably to the new regulations, about 24 of them accepted the office, but being declared enemies to their country, and threatened by the populace, most of them renounced the appointment. The new judges in like manner were prevented from holding their courts, and a state of general anarchy prevailed. Appearances were so alarming, that General Gage thought it necessary to fortify Boston neck; and the season for a militia muster approaching, he seized upon the ammunition and stores lodged in the provincial arsenal at Cambridge, and conveyed them to Boston. These acts excited a violent ferment; and an assembly of delegates from all the towns in the county, in which Boston is situated, being held, a number of resolutions passed, directly oppugning the authority of the new legislature.

The congress, consisting of representatives from the twelve old colonies, 51 in number, opened at Philadelphia on September

5th. The instructions given to them disclaimed every idea of independence, recognized the constitutional authority of the mother country, and acknowledged the prerogatives of the crown; but unanimously declared that they would never give up the rights and liberties derived to them from their ancestors as British subjects, and pronounced the late acts relative to the colony of Massachuset's Bay to be unconstitutional, oppressive, and dangerous. The first public act of the congress was a resolution declarative of their favourable disposition towards the colony above-mentioned; and by subsequent resolutions, they formally approved the opposition it had given to the obnoxious acts, and declared that if an attempt was made to carry them into execution by force, the colony should be supported by all America. After these and other resolutions had passed, they wrote a letter to General Gage, expostulating with him upon the appearance of hostility in his proceedings towards the colony of which he was the governor, and intreating him to discontinue the fortifications at Boston, and allow its communications with the country to be free and open. They published a declaration of the rights of the North American colonies, both natural and constitutional, and the privileges resulting from them; they enumerated the grievances for which they expected redress, recommending as the means of obtaining it, a non-importation, non-exportation, and non-consumption agreement, the articles of which they specified, and to which they bound themselves and their constituents. In fine, they drew up a petition to the king, a memorial to the people of Great Britain, an address to the colonies in general, and an address to the inhabitants of the province of Quebec, all which were composed with an energy of language, and strength of argument, which proved that no common men took the lead in the assembly. After performing these offices, the congress terminated its session on October 26th, having first passed a resolution that another such assembly should meet on the 10th of May next.

The British parliament was unexpectedly dissolved on September 30th, and although some of the elections were warmly contested, and many old members lost their seats, the general complexion of that body seemed to be little altered. Mr. Wilkes was returned for the county of Middlesex without the least opposition from the court, which prudently avoided at such a time renewing those contests which had been a source of so much vexation. The speech from the throne, after noticing in strong terms the spirit of resistance to the law, which still subsisted in the province of Massachuset's Bay, and which had been countenanced in the other colonies, gave assurance of his Majesty's steadfast resolution to withstand every attempt to impair the authority of the legislature over all the dominions of the British crown. The motion for the usual corresponding address was warmly debated in both houses, but was carried in both by great majorities. A strong and pointed protest was, however, entered against it in the journals of the lords. Little of importance was brought forward before the Christmas recess. Ministers appeared desirous of encouraging the hope that affairs would terminate amicably in America, and the naval establishment for the ensuing year was reduced.

The rebellion of Pugatcheff in Russia, was one of the remarkable foreign incidents of the present year. This man, a Cossack by birth, assumed the name of the Emperor Peter III, pretending that he had providentially escaped from those who designed to murder him. His marvellous tale, with the sanctified air which he assumed, procured him a great number of adherents in the remote government of Orenburg, which was the first theatre of his imposture, among whom were several of the nobility, a class not in general favourable to the empress. So serious an aspect did the insurrection assume towards the end of 1773, that a manifesto had been published against Pugatcheff, and several bodies of troops had been sent for its suppression. The superiority of numbers possessed by the rebels, rendered them successful in several encounters on which occasions they usually massacred all the officers who fell into their hands. They became masters of several places in the province of Orenburg, and laid siege to its capital. Prince Gallitzin having marched to its relief, a bloody engagement ensued on March 25th, in which the rebels were defeated with great loss. Pugatcheff found means, however, to assemble fresh forces; and though he underwent several successive defeats, at least as they were represented at the court of Petersburgh, he was able still to maintain himself on the borders of the Wolga, the Yaik, and the Ilik, exciting terror by his devastations and cruelties. He even made a sudden assault upon the city of Kasan, the fortress of which was with difficulty saved by the arrival of a detachment of Count Panin's army. At length, after another entire defeat, the rebels were totally dispersed, and Pugatcheff, crossing the Wolga almost alone, wandered in the deserts nearly in want of common necessaries. In this condition he was betrayed by some Cossacks who had been made prisoners by the Russians, and was brought bound hand and foot to Count Panin's quarters. The relics of the rebellion were then quelled and it is to the honour of the empress's humanity that the punishments were not numerous, and that even the leader simply suffered death without any of its aggravations.

Whilst the Russian empire was labouring under this dangerous internal commotion, its contest with the Ottoman arms was drawing to a triumphant conclusion. In the month of January, the Turkish Emperor, Mustapha III, closed his unfortunate life, having nominated for his successor his brother Abdul Hamet. The new sovereign exerted himself with vigour in recruiting his armies, though interrupted by a mutiny among the Janissaries at Adrianople, who were desirous of placing on the throne his nephew, the young Prince Selim. A great force was at length assembled under the Grand Vizier on the banks of the Danube, which was opposed by the Russians commanded by Marshal Romanzow. After various movements, the whole of the Russian troops were transported across the Danube, and Romanzow encamped near Silistria. On June 20th, General Soltikow was attacked with so much vigour by the pashaw of Rudshuck at the head of a body of Arnauts and other Europeans, that he was obliged to quit the field; but this was the concluding honour of the Turkish arms. On the same day, the Reis Effendi leading 40,000 men against the Generals Kamenski and Suwarow, was so ill supported, that both cavalry and infantry deserting their colours, he lost his camp and all his artillery. Thenceforth nothing but disorder and dismay appeared in the Turkish armies; large bodies after plundering their baggage, and massacring their officers, disbanded and marched back towards the Hellespont, committing every kind of outrage in their way. The Grand Vizier shut himself up in his camp at Scliumla, where he was at length entirely invested by the Russian divisions. In this situation he was obliged to enter into a negotiation with Romanzow, which, after two short conferences, terminated in signing a peace on July 21st. It was ratified at Constantinople, the Mufti giving his reluctant consent with these words: "Since our troops will no longer fight with the Russians, it is necessary to conclude a peace." Among its principal articles were the independency of the Krimea; the absolute cession to Russia of Kinburn, Kerche, and Yenicala, and of all the district between the Bog and the Dnieper; and a free navigation in all the Turkish seas, including the passage of the Dardanelles. Russia restored her conquests, with the exception of Azof and Taganrok. Stipulations were made in favour of the inhabitants of Moldavia and Walachia, and of some of the Greek islands. A short time previous to this treaty the Capitan Pashaw had landed Dowlet Gherai with an army on the Krimea, where they were proceeding with success when they were stopped by a cessation of arms.

The unfortunate country of Poland, notwithstanding its sacrifices, was still smarting under the rule of foreign force.

Encroachments on the stipulated limits were made by Austria and Prussia; and those of the latter power were so galling, that they were resisted by the Poles, and blood was shed on both sides in the contest. The establishment of a new constitution under the name of the Permanent Council was an object in which the allied powers took much interest, and it was decided upon in August. The number of the council was fixed at forty, including the three estates, of the king, the senate, and the equestrian order: the king to be chief; the senate to comprehend the great officers of the state; members of the senate and the equestrian order to be chosen at the diets, and the majority to be decided by ballot; their power to continue only from one diet to another. It had been proposed that the dissidents should be eligible to this council, but the proposal was almost universally rejected; a conclusion that proves the unquenchable hostility of an established religion towards sects, and which in this case was extraordinary, since two of the allied powers first interfered in the Polish affairs on the sole pretext of seeing justice done to the dissidents. It was remarked, that of the three powers Russia was by much the most just and moderate in its conduct towards Poland, as Prussia was the least so.

The republic of Venice was thrown into a state of alarm by the entrance of some Austrian troops into the Venetian Dalmatia, where they took possession of several towns and districts, and compelled the people to take an oath of fidelity to their imperial Majesties. This violence was justified by claims advanced relative to these countries, and the republic had no other way of defending its rights than by negotiation.

The King of France, Louis XV, died of the smallpox on May 10th, in the 64th year of his age, and 59th of his reign. The gross debauchery, equally unworthy of his age and station, into which he had sunk, with the despotic measures he had been led to adopt with respect to the parliaments in his latter years, had entirely rendered inapplicable his early appellation of the *well-beloved*, and few French sovereigns have left a less respected memory. He was succeeded by his grandson, Louis XVI, who began his reign with various popular acts. He recalled the Count Maurepas, formerly minister of the marine, who had been 23 years banished from court; and he dismissed from their posts the Duke d'Aiguillon, prime-minister, the Chancellor Maupeon, and the Abbé Terray, comptroller-general of the finances. The restoration of the ancient parliaments was now looked for as a consequence of the changes in the throne and ministry, and the delay of this measure produced a refusal of the Duke of Orleans to attend the solemn service for the late king, on which account he was forbidden to appear at court. To the manifest dissatisfaction of the people on this occasion is imputed the king's determination of recalling the duke, and reinstating the parliaments; and accordingly, on November 12th he made an entry into Paris, accompanied by his family and the princes of the blood, and followed by the exiled members of the parliament of Paris, amidst the joyful acclamations of innumerable spectators. The conditions however, on which the parliament was restored, greatly abridged the prerogatives which it had assumed during the minority of Louis XV; and the king in his speech to the members explicitly informed them that he would not suffer the smallest infringement of the regal authority. The ordinance issued as a code of regulation for the parliament particularly prohibited any union with the other parliaments, as composing one general body in the nation. It was permitted, before the registry of edicts or letters patent, to make such representations or remonstrances as it should judge for the public benefit, but on condition of registering such edicts, &c. within a month from their publication; and the prohibition of issuing any arrets which might excite trouble, or retard the execution of the edicts. The Chatelet and other tribunals connected with the parliament were also reinstated. Something of the former spirit having been shewn by the restored members in disputes relative to registering and remonstrating, they were silenced by the king's declaration "that he must be obeyed!" Such were the auspices with which the reign began.

In Corsica, the continued inveteracy of the natives against the French yoke having displayed itself in acts of fierce hostility and, as asserted, in a plot to cut off all the French in the island on an appointed day, measures of extraordinary rigour were adopted against them and cruelties were practised derogatory to the character of a humane and civilized nation.

A war broke out in this year between Spain and Morocco, the pretext for which, in the sovereign of the latter country, was a compliance with the injunctions of the Koran. The Emperor of Morocco, in a letter to the King of Spain, September 19th, informed him, that he and the Algerines had determined to fulfil the command of their religion, not to suffer Christians to hold territorial possessions in Mahometan countries. In consequence, he intended to attack the Spanish settlements in Africa, but hoped that this would not occasion a breach between the nations elsewhere. This extraordinary declaration was followed by hostilities against the garrison of Ceuta, which produced a declaration of war from Spain. In December, the Emperor of Morocco appeared at the head of a numerous army before Melila on the coast of Fez, which he began to cannonade, but the unskilfulness of his officers, and the bravery of the commander, prevented any considerable progress. An attempt upon Penon de Velez was not more successful.

The internal government of Spain was at this time distinguished by an extraordinary attention to new manufactures, but upon the bad system of establishing them under the immediate direction of the crown. An important advance in liberality was displayed by taking from the court of inquisition those powers and modes of procedure which rendered it so terrific, and restricting it nearly to the functions of a court of enquiry into religious matters.

The troubles in Sicily were in this year tranquilized by a prudent mixture of firmness and compliance. Palermo underwent no other punishment for its insurrection, than a transfer of the seat of government to Messina. A general pardon was published; the commander in chief of the forces in Sicily was removed to make way for the popular prince of Villa Franca; and though the obnoxious viceroy was for a time continued, to assert the dignity of the court, it was not long before a successor was appointed.

The Pope died on September 21st; and although natural infirmities, age, and anxiety, were obvious causes for bringing his life to a close in his 70th year, an opinion generally prevailed, that he was poisoned by the Jesuits. It is certain that his spirits drooped after he had consented to the abolition of that order, and he is said to have predicted that he should not long survive the event; but there seems no ground to charge that body with a crime which would have been merely vindictive. In the conclave for electing a new pontiff, parties were so balanced, and the usual intrigues were carried to such a length, that no decision was made before the expiration of the year.

1775

15th & 16th Year of the Reign

THE American colonies were now the point on which all the political interest of the British nation was centered; and during the recess of parliament, meetings had been held of the merchants trading to them, who were deeply alarmed for the consequences of the measures lately adopted. On the first day of the re-assembling of parliament, January 20th, the papers relative to America, having been laid before the House of Lords, Lord Chatham moved for an address to his Majesty, for the purpose of re-calling the troops from Boston. In his introductory speech, he dwelt with great force on the immediate necessity of allaying the ferment in America, as a short delay would probably cut off the possibility of a reconciliation. The subsequent debate gave scope to much severe censure of the measures which had brought on the present extremity; but on a division, the majority against the motion numbered a high as 68 to 18, a presage of the fate of all other attempts to procure a relinquishment of the coercive system.

A petition of the London merchants being presented to the House of Commons on January 23d, by an alderman who was a member, and a motion made for taking it into consideration, a suggestion was advanced by the ministry, that the American business being regarded in a political, not in a commercial light, there was little connection between the views of the house, and those of the merchants; it was therefore proposed to appoint a separate committee for its consideration, to meet on the day after that on which the American papers were to be considered. This was carried as an amendment to the motion by a majority of 197 to 81; and all the other petitions from commercial towns being treated in the same manner, they were in effect made of no weight in the question. A second and stronger petition from the London merchants, arguing against this determination, and praying to be heard in support of their former petition, produced a motion for rescinding the resolution of the house respecting it, which was rejected by a great majority.

The petition from the American congress to his Majesty having been referred by him to parliament, three American agents, of whom Dr. Franklin was one, petitioned the House of Commons to be heard at the bar in its support, stating that they were enabled to throw great light on the subject. This was opposed by the ministers, on the ground that the congress was no legal body; and after a keen debate, the petition was rejected by 218 votes against 68.

Lord Chatham, not discouraged by the fate of his former motion, and resolved to omit no effort for effecting a reconciliation which he thought absolutely necessary for preserving the British empire from ruin, brought, on February 1st, before the House of Lords, the outlines of a bill, under the title of "A provisional act for settling the troubles in America, and for asserting the supreme legislative authority, and superintending power of Great Britain over the colonies." In his argument, he shewed that the act contained a full acknowledgment of the supremacy of the British legislature; and though it did not absolutely decide on the right of taxation, it declared in the way of concession, which seemed to imply the right, that no tax should be levied in America, except by common consent in their provincial assemblies. A long and pointed debate ensued, after which the bill was rejected by 61 to 32. On the following day, a petition was presented to the House of Commons from the West India sugar-planters residing in London, setting forth the great difficulties that would accrue to the plantations were their intercourse with North America to be interrupted by hostilities with the colonies; but the only notice this petition obtained, was referring it, like the others, to what was termed the committee of oblivion.

The prime-minister then opened his plan of measures which he intended to propose with respect to America, which consisted in sending a larger force to that country, and in bringing in a temporary act for putting a stop to all the foreign trade of the New England colonies, and especially to their fishery on the banks of Newfoundland; at the same time declaring, that whenever they should acknowledge the supremacy of the British legislature, pay obedience to the laws of this realm, and make due submission to the king, their real grievances should be redressed. He then moved a long address to his Majesty, in which it was declared that there now actually existed a rebellion in the province of Massachuset's Bay, countenanced by unlawful combinations in several of the other colonies and his Majesty was intreated to take the most effectual measures for enforcing obedience to the authority of the supreme legislature, with a promise to stand by him at the hazard of their lives and properties. In the debate which ensued, whilst on the part of opposition such a violent step as declaring a rebellion was strongly deprecated, on the ministerial side, great contempt was expressed of any resistance that could be made by the colonists to a serious effort for bringing them to submission. The question for the address passed by a majority of 296 to 106. A conference was then held with the House of Lords, to propose their joining in the address, which occasioned a long and warm debate in that house, introduced by a motion from the Marquis of Rockingham, to take into consideration the petitions which he presented from the American merchants, and the West India planters and merchants, in London. The debate was rendered remarkable from the open disavowal of three lords who had been cabinet counsellors and great officers of state, of any share in imposing the American duties in 1767, which were the primary cause of the disagreement. The address was voted in the House of Lords by the majority of 104 to 29. With the answer from the throne was joined a message for an augmentation of the forces by sea and land, which was referred to the committee of supply.

On February 10th the minister moved the bill for restraining the trade and fisheries of the New England colonies, according to his proposed plan. In its progress, a petition was presented from the London traders to America, in which the mischief's likely to arise from it in a commercial view were dwelt upon, and evidence on the subject was heard at the bar. Among other matters adduced was a petition from the quaker whale-fishers of Nantucket, the most extraordinary patterns of industry and sobriety perhaps existing, who pleaded that their ruin must be the consequence of such restriction. In the debates on the bill many forcible objections were made to the sweeping severity of its provisions; but coercion in its utmost rigour being the principle now adopted by government and its supporters, it passed by still increasing majorities. During the discussion in the House of Lords an amendment was moved for including the colonies of New Jersey, Pennsylvania, Maryland, Virginia, and South Carolina, in its restrictions; as by the last accounts they appeared to be equally contumacious with those of New England; and on a division, this amendment was carried. When the bill however, was returned to the Commons, the amendment was rejected by them, as apparently at variance with the title of the bill; and the objection appearing valid, the bill passed in its original form. Another act, however, soon afterwards passed for restraining the trade of the above-mentioned colonies.

The augmentation of the forces, naval and military, had just been voted, when Lord North equally surprized both sides of the house by a conciliatory motion to the following effect: That when the governor and assembly or general court of his Majesty's colonies shall propose to make provision according to their circumstances for contributing their proportion to the common defence, such proportion to be raised under their own authority, and disposable by parliament, and shall also engage to provide for the support of the civil government, and the proposal shall be approved by the King in parliament, the forbearance shall be exercised with respect to such colony, of levying or imposing any further tax or duty, except such as may be expedient for the regulation of commerce, the proceeds of which last are to be carried to the account of the colony. After the wonder excited by this motion had in some degree subsided, the opposition to it began from the Minister's own party, who regarded it as a contradiction to all the acts and declarations of parliament which he himself had promoted. Great pains however, being taken by a friend of government and himself, to show that it secured all the essential rights of taxation, and the minister acknowledging that he did not expect that the proposal would be generally received by the Americans, and that he intended it to separate the best affected from the worst, the motion was carried by the customary majority. Soon after, upon an enquiry from the opposition concerning a petition and memorial to his Majesty in council from the assembly in Jamaica, it was laid before the house. It contained a very free argumentative discussion of the question between the colonies and the mother country, explicitly asserting the rights of the former, and denying that the colonists are subjects to the people of England, though bound to all due allegiance to the crown; and it concluded with imploring his Majesty to become a mediator between his European and American subjects.

On March 22d, Mr. Burke, in a very celebrated speech, introduced his conciliatory propositions. Laying a deep foundation in acute observations respecting government in general, and that of colonies in particular, he framed a set of resolutions for the purpose of establishing the justice of taxing America by grant, and not by imposition; the legal competence of the colonial assemblies for the support of their government in time of peace, and for raising aids in time of war; and the benefits arising from the exercise of such a competence. The debate was then opened with the first resolution, which was an affirmation that the colonies in North America, containing upwards of two millions of free inhabitants, are not represented in parliament. The previous question being moved, after a long debate upon this proposition, it was carried by 270 to 78, and of course the whole fell to the ground. Shortly after, Mr. Hartley introduced a conciliatory plan, the basis of which was that moved by Lord North, but with various alterations in favour of the colonies. It was rejected without a division.

While the second restraining bill was passing the house, the minister moved for adding the Delaware counties to those colonies which were included in the commercial prohibitions of the act, which was carried, upon the general assertion that they were as criminal as the rest, without any particular enquiry into the fact.

At this time the usual party contest of petitions and counter-petitions was actively carrying on in the nation; and the city of London, on April 10th, again addressed the throne with a remonstrance and petition, expressing the strongest abhorrence of the measures that had been adopted against the Americans, justifying their resistance, and beseeching his Majesty to dismiss his ministers for ever from his councils. It was officially presented by Mr. Wilkes, now lord mayor, who was informed by the lord in waiting that the King expected that he should not speak to him (as Mr. Beckford had done on a former occasion of the like kind). The royal answer displayed great displeasure; and the lord mayor afterwards received a letter from the Lord Chamberlain, acquainting him that the King would not receive on the throne any address, remonstrance, or petition from the lord mayor and aldermen, but in their corporate capacity.

For the purpose of attaching Ireland, and supplying the place of the abolished American fisheries, a committee of the whole House of Commons was formed to consider of the encouragement proper to be given to the fisheries of Great Britain and Ireland, which granted bounties to the ships of both countries engaging in the Newfoundland fishery, and also gave advantages to other branches of the Irish trade.

The province of New York had hitherto acted with a moderation which had shielded it from the restrictions and prohibitions laid on the other colonies; but in principle it coincided with them as far as concerned the great cause of America. On May 15th Mr. Burke informed the House of Commons that he had received a paper of great importance from the general assembly of the province of New York, which was a complaint, in the form of remonstrance, of several acts of parliament, the principles and regulations of which were, as they affirmed, subversive of the rights of British subjects; and though he did not know that the house would approve every opinion contained in the paper, yet as the whole tenor and language of it were decent and respectful, he trusted it would be received and attended to. He then moved that it might be brought up. This was opposed by the minister in a motion by way of amendment, which in effect negatived it; and the amendment being carried, the motion so amended was rejected without a division. The same assembly also transmitted a memorial to the Lords, and a petition to the King, for the reading of the first of which a motion was made by the Duke of Manchester, but it was rejected. Thus terminated all the attempts for bringing this fatal quarrel to an amicable conclusion.

Petitions against the Quebec bill, from the British inhabitants of that province, were presented to both houses. In the

House of Lords a bill for the repeal of that act was proposed by Lord Camden, but was rejected on a division; and the same fate attended a motion of a similar kind in the House of Commons by Sir G. Saville. The session of parliament closed on May 26th.

Whilst the momentous contest was carried on by debates, petitions, and bills, on this side the Atlantic, warfare of a different kind was commenced on the field of action. Before the close of the year, the seizure of military stores by the governor of Massachusets had been retaliated by two petty acts of violence in Rhode Island and New Hampshire, in the first of which the people had carried off all the crown ordnance which lay upon the batteries raised for the defence of the harbour; and in the second, had attacked and taken (apparently without resistance), a small fort, in which was contained a quantity of powder, the object of the assault. Resolutions were formed in the conventions of Maryland and Pennsylvania for the providing of arms and ammunition, and the manufacturing of gunpowder; and a firm determination of resistance was universally diffused, which became the more animated on the receipt of every act and declaration from England intended to intimidate. The circular letter from the American secretary, forbidding in the King's name the electing of members for the ensuing congress, was entirely without effect; and such elections took place even in the province of New York, in which the assembly had passed, though by a small majority, a resolution against them.

The new provincial congress of Massachusets published an address to the people, in which, having informed them that there was reason to apprehend hostile measures from the large reinforcement of troops expected in the colony, they strongly urged the disciplining and arming of the militia, and particularly that the select part of that body called *minute men*, should be held in readiness for service at the shortest notice. It was not long before the certain result of the state of irritation between two parties, who had now only the sword for their umpire, displayed itself, and the first blood was spilt in this unhappy difference. The Americans having collected a considerable quantity of military stores at the town of Concord, at which the provincial congress was held, General Gage detached the light infantry and grenadiers of the army, to the number of about 900, for the purpose of destroying them. The party, embarking in boats at Boston, proceeded to some distance up Charles's river, and landing on the morning of April 19th, marched in silence towards Concord. The country, however, was soon alarmed, and people began to assemble on all sides; so that when the soldiers reached Lexington, they found a body of militia drawn up on a green near the road side. An officer in the van ordered the provincials, under the appellation of rebels, to throw down their arms and disperse; and the soldiers rushing on with huzzas, some scattering shots were fired, (by which party first is a matter in dispute), and a volley succeeding, eight of the militia were killed, and several were wounded. The detachment then marched forward to Concord, preceded by some companies of light infantry, which took possession of two bridges, a body of militia retiring at their approach. The main body, on their arrival, spiked three pieces of cannon, destroyed some gun-carriages, and threw into the river some barrels of flour, powder, and ball. In the meantime the country assembled, and attacking the troops on all sides, they commenced a retreat to Lexington, which was a continued skirmish. General Gage had providently sent a strong reinforcement to meet them at that place, which was of essential service during the remainder of the march, as the Americans continued the pursuit in still increasing numbers. The party reached Charlestown near Boston at sunset, exhausted by fatigue, and having sustained a loss in killed, wounded, and prisoners, of 273 men and officers. The loss on the opposite side was stated at only 60.

This affair summoned the whole province to arms, and a body of militia, said to exceed 20,000 men, invested the king's troops in Boston. The provincial congress drew up an address to the people of Great Britain, the object of which was to shew that the hostilities on this occasion began from the regular soldiers. They also passed votes for the array and maintenance of an army, and a resolution, that General Gage by his conduct had entirely disqualified himself for the office of governor, and was no longer entitled to obedience. The highest indignation was excited in the other colonies by the occurrences at Lexington and Concord, and preparation for war was the general cry. Magazines were in some places seized upon; a stop was put to the exportation of provisions; and Lord North's conciliatory plan when it arrived was rejected with disdain.

The continental congress met a second time at Philadelphia on May 10th, and their first measures were resolutions for raising an army, and for the issue of a paper currency for its payment, on the security of the United Colonies. They also prohibited the supplying of the British fishery with provisions, in consequence of which, several ships at Newfoundland were obliged to return empty. The province of New York, which had hitherto held back, now imbibed the general spirit, and elected a provincial congress. Some private persons in the back parts of Connecticut, Massachusets, and New York, fitted out an expedition at their own expence, for obtaining possession of the fortresses on the lakes, which command the passes to Canada, and a few men, under the orders of Colonels Warren and Allen, surprized Ticonderoga and Crown Point, which they took without loss on either side; making prize of a quantity of artillery and military stores, and of two vessels on Lake Champlain.

Near the end of May, three generals, Howe, Burgoyne, and Clinton, arrived at Boston with troops to supply the vacancies, and were followed by several regiments from Ireland, the whole composing a very considerable force. The harbour of Boston was likewise filled with British ships of war, so that little danger could be apprehended from any attack by the provincials. The continental congress passed a resolution in June, that the compact between the crown and the people of Massachusets' Bay having been dissolved by the violation of their charter, it should be recommended to them to proceed to the establishment of a new government, by the election of a governor, assistants, and house of assembly. About the same time General Gage issued a proclamation, offering in the King's name a pardon to all who should immediately lay down their arms and return to their occupation, with the exception of Samuel Adams and John Hancock, and declaring that all who should not accept of this proffered mercy, would be treated as traitors and rebels. It also proclaimed martial law till the laws were restored to their due efficacy. So little was this paper regarded, that Mr. Hancock was chosen president of the continental congress.

Further hostilities being now mutually expected, the possession of the post of Charlestown, separated from Boston only by Charles river, was thought important, for which purpose the Americans sent a party of men at night to throw up works upon Bunker's Hill, commanding the isthmus which joins the peninsula to the continent. This was effected with so much silence and expedition, that before day-break a small redoubt with intrenchments and a breast-work were nearly finished. As soon as these operations were discovered, a heavy cannonade began from the ships upon the works, and about noon a strong body of troops under Major-General Howe and Brigadier-General Pigot was sent to attack them. They slowly advanced, supported by a severe fire of artillery, which was borne by the provincials with great steadiness; and as the troops approached the works, so hot a fire was opened upon them, that they were thrown into confusion, and for a short time General Howe was left nearly alone. They were, however, soon rallied, and furiously attacking the American works with fixed bayonets, they forced them in every quarter. The provincials, after an obstinate resistance, retreated over Charlestown neck. In this affair, which is said to have been conducted with more spirit than military skill, the loss of the British in killed and wounded amounted to 1054, about half their number, among whom was an unusual proportion of officers. That of the provincials was returned by themselves at 450. In the conflict, Charlestown, which had been occupied by a party of the Americans, was set on fire and burnt to the ground.

Immediately after this action the provincials threw up works on another hill on their own side of Charlestown neck; and securing their posts with strong redoubts, whilst they advanced their lines to the fortifications on Boston neck, they held the British troops closely invested in the peninsula, and rendered their situation very uncomfortable. The troops suffered much from sickness and scarcity of provisions, which last could only be supplied from England, whence, at a vast expence, great quantities were sent, of which a small proportion arrived safe. The blockade continued through the year, and nothing more of importance occurred in this quarter. General Gage returning to England in October, the chief command of the troops devolved on General Howe.

Although the north was the earliest and principal seat of hostile operations between the British government and the colonists in this year, yet the flame was kindled throughout the whole extent of North America, and in various parts was disclosing itself in acts of mutual enmity. The colony of Virginia had been among the most zealous in promoting the common cause by the assembling of the general congress, and entering into private associations; but internal order and tranquillity had been preserved, a state particularly desirable in a community where the slaves greatly out-numbered the free citizens. The want of a legal assembly, however, and the expiration of the militia laws, put the Virginians in an uneasy situation, which they endeavoured to remedy by convoking a provincial congress in the month of March, which immediately took measures for arraying the militia, and also recommended to each county the raising of a volunteer company for the better defence of the country. This proceeding gave an alarm to the Governor, Lord Dunmore, who thought it necessary to get into his possession the public magazine of powder in Williamsburgh; and by his direction, the captain of an armed vessel in the river went with a detachment of marines by night, and conveyed the powder on board of his ship. As soon as this act was discovered, the mayor and corporation of the city sent an address to the governor, reclaiming the powder as the property of the colony, and representing the danger to which they should be exposed for want of it in case of an insurrection of their slaves. This requisition was not complied with by the governor, who, irritated by some violences of the populace, even threatened to set up the royal standard, and enfranchise the negroes. The colonists were now greatly exasperated, and a number of the inhabitants in the adjacent counties taking arms, marched towards Williamsburgh with the avowed purpose of obtaining the restitution of the gunpowder by force, and securing the public treasury. Through the intervention of the magistrates, a compromise was entered into: but in the meantime Lord Dunmore had sent his family on board a man of war, and fortifying his palace, issued a proclamation in which he charged the insurgents with rebellion. While affairs were in this state of commotion, the governor, on receiving dispatches from England, convoked the general assembly of the province, in order to lay before it Lord North's conciliatory proposals; but the first business entered upon was an enquiry into the causes of the late disturbances, and an examination of the state of the magazines. Meantime the governor thought he saw such indications of evil designs against him, that he privately quitted his palace, and with his family retired on board the Fowey man of war. Various negotiations passed between his lordship and the assembly, in which the latter in vain urged his return on shore; and as they equally refused to attend him upon business in a king's ship, they finally broke up the session. Lord Dunmore, joined by some persons attached to government, and resorted to by a number of runaway negroes, fitted out a marine force, which during the summer and autumn carried on a predatory war on the coast of Virginia; and being foiled in an attempt to burn the town of Hampton, he issued a proclamation declaring martial law throughout the colony, and proclaiming freedom to all indented servants and negroes belonging to rebels, who should join the king's forces — a measure which more perhaps than any other during the war excited general horror and indignation, as breaking all the bands of society. To conclude the unpleasing narrative of the transactions in this province, the year terminated with the total conflagration of the town of Norfolk, the most considerable for commerce in the colony.

In North and South Carolina the differences between the governors and the people ran equally high, and in the same manner ended in the secession of the former on board ships of war, and the governments falling into the hands of councils and committees of safety.

The general congress published, on July 6th, a declaration setting forth the causes and the necessity of their taking up arms, among which were mentioned the attempts made to induce the Canadians and Indians to attack them. They mentioned foreign aid as a thing attainable, but affirmed that they had no intention of dissolving the union which had so long subsisted between them and their fellow-subjects, and which they sincerely wished to see restored. This was followed by an address to the inhabitants of Great Britain; another to the people of Ireland; and a petition to his Majesty. They afterwards took into consideration the proposition of Lord North, which they condemned as unreasonable and insidious, complaining that its purpose was to divide the colonies, and to inculcate a belief that there was nothing more in dispute than the *mode* of levying taxes, which being given up, the colonies ought to be perfectly satisfied. In this month, Georgia joined in the continental alliance, and sent its delegates to congress, which now assumed the appellation of that of the thirteen united colonies. In compliance with the general wishes, congress appointed George Washington, a gentleman of fortune in Virginia, who had acquired experience in the command of different bodies of provincials in the French war, to be commander in chief of the American forces, and they nominated four major-generals and an adjutant-general.

The success which had attended the expedition to the Lakes, joined with the apprehension of a meditated war against the northern colonies from the Canadian border, induced the congress to undertake the bold enterprize of an invasion of Canada whilst the main British force was cooped up in Boston. For this purpose Generals Schuyler and Montgomery were placed at the head of near 3000 men raised in New York and New England, who were to be conveyed along Lake Champlain to the river Sorel which discharges itself into the St. Laurence. Montgomery, in the latter end of August, proceeded with the force under his command to Isle aux Noix; and Schuyler having been foiled in an attempt to carry Fort St. John, and obliged to retreat to Albany, the whole weight of the expedition fell upon the former. He took St. John's after a vigorous defence, and advancing to Montreal, it was surrendered to him by capitulation. In the meantime a separate expedition against Quebec was undertaken by Colonel Arnold with about 1100 men from the camp near Boston. After a most toilsome march, he arrived at Point Levy, opposite to Quebec, on November 9th. At this time that capital was in a state very ill calculated for defence; the British inhabitants much discontented with the Quebec bill against which they had fruitlessly petitioned; many of the Canadians little attached to the government; scarcely any troops in the place, and General Carleton, governor of the province, absent. The inhabitants, however, in dread of pillage, united to protect their property; and Arnold, disappointed in his expectation of a rising in his favour, withdrew his men to quarters of refreshment. About the same time, General Carleton arrived, and immediately adopted the most efficacious measures for defence. Montgomery on December 5th, appeared before Quebec, and sent a summons to the governor, who refused to admit his flag, or to allow of any communication. A battery was then opened against the place, which produced little effect; and the provincial soldiers were suffering extremely from the inclemency of the weather. Their leader now founded all his hopes upon the success of an escalade, which he put in execution on the last day of the year, himself and Arnold conducting attacks against the upper and lower town. The event was that Montgomery, with several officers, and most of the men near his person, were killed on the spot; and Arnold's division after making considerable progress, being deprived of their commander, whose leg was shattered, was repulsed and obliged to surrender. General Carleton treated his prisoners with great humanity; and honourably interred Montgomery, who, for his qualities as a man and a soldier, was admired and beloved both by friend and foe. The expedition was completely defeated, though Arnold, with the relics of the forces, kept Quebec in a state of blockade for some months longer.

We now revert to the remaining home transactions of the year. The city of London persisted in its opposition to the measures of government by various public acts, some of which could not fail of being extremely displeasing at court. Several mercantile places and commercial bodies also expressed their disapprobation of the coercive plan which had been adopted with respect to the colonies; but on the other hand, many addresses to the crown expressed entire satisfaction with the determination not to abate the least of the authority of the mother country, and made zealous declarations of their readiness to support the cause with their lives and fortunes. By the remaining friends to conciliation something was hoped from the petition of the American congress to the King, which was presented by Mr. Penn, proprietary governor of Pennsylvania; but no answer was returned to it. The question was now become rather one of party than of political expedience; the votaries of high principles in government uniformly supporting the measures of authority, while those who have usually borne the title of whigs were in great part, though by no means universally, favourable to the cause of the colonies, as connected with that of liberty in general.

An extraordinary report of a conspiracy for seizing his Majesty's person and conveying him out of the kingdom, raised by one Richardson, an adjutant in the guards, occasioned the apprehension of Mr. Sayre, an American by birth, and a banker in London, and his commitment to close custody in the Tower for high treason, by warrant from Lord Rochford, secretary of state. Being brought by *habeas corpus* before Lord Mansfield, the charge appeared so absurd that he was admitted to bail, and the recognizance was afterwards discharged. Mr. Sayre then brought an action against Lord Rochford for false imprisonment, and was awarded £1000 damages.

On October 26th the parliament assembled, and was opened by a speech from the throne, in which the prominent topic, as might be expected, was the war commenced in America. It being assumed in the speech, that the view of the colonial leaders was to establish independence, when the usual echoing address was moved in each house, very long debates ensued, and amendments were repeatedly moved, which were rejected, and the original addresses passed by nearly the usual majorities. On this occasion the ministerial party was deserted by two distinguished characters, the Duke of Grafton and General Conway, both of whom spoke in strong language against the principles which had brought on the catastrophe. One of the measures of administration having been the sending of Hanoverian troops to garrison Gibraltar and Port Mahon, in place of British regiments ordered for America, the Duke of Manchester moved a resolution, "That bringing into any part of the dominions of Great Britain the electoral troops of his Majesty, or any other foreign troops, without the previous consent of parliament, is dangerous and unconstitutional." This motion occasioned warm debates, but was disposed of by the previous question; and the same fate attended a similar motion by Sir James Lowther in the House of Commons. The introduction of a new militia bill produced a debate in the House of Commons on account of the additional power vested by it in the crown, of calling out the militia in case of a rebellion existing in any part of the empire; it was however carried by a very large majority. For the military service of the coming year were voted 28,000 seamen, and 55,000 landmen.

The Duke of Grafton, after his declaration against the American measures, resigned his place of lord privy seal, in which he was succeeded by the Earl of Dartmouth, who quitted the colonial secretaryship, which post was taken by Lord G. Germain (late Sackville). The Earl of Rochford retiring from public business, Lord Weymouth succeeded to the office of secretary for the southern department.

On November 10th, on motion from the Duke of Richmond, Mr. Penn was examined at the bar of the House of Lords, after which the Duke moved "That the petition of the continental congress to the king was ground for a conciliation of the unhappy differences subsisting between Great Britain and America." This produced an animated debate, but the motion was rejected by 86 votes to 83. On November 13th, Lord North moved an advance of the land-tax to four shillings in the pound in the year 1776. This proposal was ill received by some of the country gentlemen who had supported the plans of American taxation with the sole view of alleviating their own burdens; it was, however, carried by a great majority.

Mr. Burke, on November 16th renewed his conciliatory attempt by moving a bill "For composing the present troubles, and for quieting the minds of his Majesty's subjects in America." The ground-work of the bill was a renunciation of the exercise of taxation by this country, without interfering with the question of abstract right; to which was added the power of levying duties for commercial regulation, and of convening at the pleasure of the crown general meetings of deputies from the colonies, whose acts were to be binding on all; and also an amnesty for the past. The motion was discussed by all the eloquence of the house, and was rejected by a majority of just two to one, which was less than that in former divisions. Mr. Hartley afterwards moved to bring in a conciliatory bill upon principles similar to that which he had before offered, but it excited very little attention.

On November 20th Lord North proceeded to the crowning measure of hostility against America, that of bringing in a bill to interdict all trade and intercourse with the thirteen united colonies, and to declare all property of Americans taken on the high seas or in harbour, prize of the captors, being his Majesty's ships of war. It repealed all the former restraining acts, as short of the present purpose; and it enabled the crown to appoint commissioners, vested with powers not only to grant pardons to individuals, but to determine whether a part or the whole of a colony were returned to a state of obedience which might entitle it to be received into the king's peace. This bill was opposed with great vigour in both houses of parliament; Mr. Fox, who had now for some time quitted the treasury board, and joined the ranks of opposition, particularly distinguishing himself on the occasion. A clause which compelled all who were taken on board American vessels to serve as common sailors in British ships of war, was especially noticed in the House of Lords, as "a refinement in tyranny." The bill, however, passed by the usual majorities.

The occurrences in other parts during this year were not in general of much importance.

The Emperor of Morocco abandoned as ingloriously, as he had undertaken rashly, the siege of the Spanish fortresses Melilla and Penon de Velez; he still, however, persisted in refusing an accommodation with the Dutch, against whom he had declared war.

The court of Spain having determined upon chastising the Barbary powers for their hostility, made great preparations for an expedition against Algiers, and in the summer a force consisting of seven sail of the line and a great number of frigates, with 400 transports, conveying an army of 22,000 infantry and 4000 cavalry, and an immense train of artillery, sailed from Carthagena. It arrived in the beginning of July in the Bay of Algiers, which place had been well prepared for a defence. About 8000 of the Spanish troops being landed, an engagement was brought on with the Moors, which continued with great fury for many hours, when the Spaniards were obliged to retreat with a severe loss to their ships. This was the end of the expedition, and the fleet returned, to the great dissatisfaction of the Spanish nation, whose clamours against the General O'Reilly, could only be appeased by his dismission.

The Roman conclave was terminated in February by the election of Cardinal Braschi, a native of Cesena, who assumed the name of Pius VI. In the Duchy of Tuscany a law passed for regulating the age and terms of admission into the monastic orders, the object of which was to reduce the number of votaries. The tribunal of the inquisition was perpetually abolished in the Duchy of Milan; and the policy of abridging the prerogatives of the see of Rome was still persisted in by the other Italian states.

In France great distress was undergone from a scarcity of corn, which was the occasion of riots in the provinces. The king was crowned at Rheims in the month of June.

The oppressed peasantry in Bohemia and Moravia broke out into insurrection in the spring; assembling in great bodies to demand the abolition of the corvees, by which almost their whole time and labour were consumed; and committing great violence on the property and dwellings of their lords. They were so much inflamed with rage and desperation, that they ventured to encounter the troops which were sent to quell them. A grand commission was at length appointed to examine their grievances, which restored tranquillity by procuring them relief from some of the most burdensome of the duties required.

The British government in this year influenced Holland, Denmark, and some other states, to prohibit their subjects from exporting military stores, in order that they might not be obtained by the Americans.

The exiled Queen of Denmark died at Zell on the 10th of May.

The pashaw of Egypt, Aboudaab, in this year marched a large army into Syria against Chiek Daher, and took several places, when his advance was stopped by death. The captain pashaw however, arriving on the coast with a considerable force, completed the enterprize, and becoming master of the Chiek's person, put him to death and seized his treasures.

1776

16th & 17th Year of the Reign

THE first important discussion in parliament after the Christmas recess arose from the following circumstance. The Earl of Harcourt, Lord Lieutenant of Ireland, had sent to the House of Commons in that country a message containing a requisition in the king's name of 4000 troops of its establishment for the American service, with a promise, that they should not, during their absence, be a charge upon that establishment, and also an offer to replace them, if desired, by an equal number of foreign protestants, the charge of which should be defrayed without expence to Ireland. The troops were granted according to this requisition; but notwithstanding the efforts of government, the offer of the foreign troops was rejected by a considerable majority. This transaction, in which the disposal of the public money was engaged for without consulting the British House of Commons, was introduced on February 15th into parliament by way of complaint of a breach of privilege, by Mr. Thomas Townshend, who moved for a committee to enquire into the matter. A considerable debate ensued, in which the ministers and their friends were somewhat embarrassed for a consistent defence of the measure: the motion was however quashed by a majority of 224 to 106. Another motion relative to the subject was got rid of by the previous question.

A motion by Mr. Fox for a committee to enquire into the causes of the ill success of his Majesty's arms in North America, and of the defection of the people of the province of Quebec, gave scope to much severe censure of the measures of ministry, in which some of the friends of government joined, but was rejected by a large majority.

The treaties entered into with the Landgrave of Hesse Cassel, the Duke of Brunswick, and the Hereditary Prince of Hesse Cassel, for the hire of troops for the American service to the amount of about 17,000 men, were laid before the House of Commons on February 19th, and a motion was made by the minister for referring them to a committee of supply. In the debate which followed, the measure of engaging foreign troops was defended from the experienced impossibility of raising a sufficient number of recruits in these kingdoms for the reduction of America, and the advantage of employing well disciplined instead of raw troops. These reasons were warmly combated by the opposition, but the motion was carried by 241 to 88. In the House of Lords a similar debate took place on the subject, with the like event.

One more effort towards conciliation was made in a motion by the Duke of Grafton for an address to his Majesty, requesting that a proclamation might be issued to declare that if, within a reasonable time before or after the arrival of troops in America, the colonies shall present a petition to the commander in chief or the commissioners under the late act, setting forth what they consider to be their just rights and real grievances; his Majesty will consent to a suspension of arms, and will assure them that their petition shall be received and answered. This motion was productive of a long and vigorous debate, in which the ministers and their friends held, in firmer language than before, the doctrine of unconditional submission on the part of the Americans. The motion was rejected by a majority of nearly three to one.

A bill for the establishment of a militia in Scotland had been brought in by Lord Mount Stewart in the preceding December, but for want of attendance had not obtained due discussion. The second reading of it having been ordered for March 20th, the measure was fully argued; the advocates for it, among which were included all the Scotch members, reasoning upon the utility of a militia, as a national defence, and the injustice of refusing to Scotland its share in this institution; and the opposers objecting the expence and the addition it would make to the already excessive power of the crown. On a division it was thrown out by 112 votes to 95, the minister being in the minority.

The other business of the session was of no material importance; and a vote of credit for a million having been obtained, it was concluded on May 23.

At Boston, the troops and the remaining inhabitants were reduced to much distress during the winter-season, for want of provision and fuel, many vessels with articles for their relief being taken in the very entrance of the harbour, and the attempts for procuring them elsewhere being attended with small success. The armies had been inactive on both sides till the beginning of March, when the Americans opened a battery near the water-side, from which they carried on a cannonade and bombardment against the town. Shortly after, some works were raised on the heights on the opposite side of the town, whence other batteries were opened. It now became evident, that the British troops must either quit Boston, or dislodge the enemy; and General Howe, conceiving that a regard for the reputation of the army required an attempt for the latter, however hazardous, made preparations for the purpose. A strong detachment was destined for embarkation in the evening, but the design was rendered impracticable by a violent storm; and when, on the next day it was resumed, a new and stronger work was found to have been thrown up by the Americans, which took away all hope of success. Nothing then remained, but to abandon the town, and convey on ship-board the troops, artillery, stores, and portable effects, not only of the soldiers, but of all the inhabitants who had attached themselves to the royal party, and were to accompany the army in its removal. This business occupied ten days, during which no molestation was given by the Americans. On the 17th of March, as the rear embarked, General Washington marched triumphantly into Boston on the other side. The king's troops were obliged to leave behind them a considerable quantity of stores and some cannon. They blew up the fortification of Castle William before their departure. Thus terminated the attempts for reducing that colony, which was the first and principal object of resentment to the British cabinet.

The blockade of Quebec had in the meantime been continued by Arnold, notwithstanding all the hardships and difficulties attending it. On the approach of the season in which supplies from England might be expected, the siege was renewed, and attempts were made to set the town on fire, but with no other success than that of burning the suburbs. At length, a man of war and two frigates having made their way up the St. Laurence through the ice, and landed their marines and a small detachment of soldiers, General Carleton, on March 6th, made an attack upon the American camp, where every thing was in great confusion, a retreat being already begun. The besiegers immediately betook themselves to a precipitate flight, leaving behind them their artillery and military stores, and some sick, who were made prisoners; and Quebec was thus liberated after an investment of five months. In the latter part of May, several British regiments, and the Brunswick succours, arrived in Canada, making a total of about 13,000 men in that province, the general rendezvous of which was appointed at Three Rivers (Trois Riviéres.) The provincials continued their retreat to the banks of the Sorel, where they were joined by some reinforcements; but they suffered much from the small-pox which spread through their quarters. They failed in an attempt to surprise a division of the royal forces; and having abandoned Montreal, and burnt St. John's and the vessels which they were unable to drag across the rapids, they embarked on Lake Champlain, and reached Crown Point without further loss.

Governor Martin of South Carolina, who had taken refuge on board a man of war, kept up a correspondence with the Regulators in the back settlements, and the Highland emigrants, and engaged a number of them in the king's service, under the command of a Mr. M'Donald, to whom he gave the commission of General. This leader erected the royal standard in February, and advanced against General Moore, the commander of a provincial regiment, who had taken a strong post at Rockfish-bridge. Whilst they were parleying, other bodies of provincials collected, so that M'Donald, in fear of being surrounded, commenced a retreat. He was pursued, and brought to action on February 27th, by Colonel Caswell, at the head of an inferior body of militia and minute-men, the result of which was, that M'Donald's corps was entirely dispersed, and himself, with most of his officers, taken prisoners.

A squadron of five frigates was sent out by the Congress early in the year under Commodore Hopkins, who sailed to the Bahamas, and plundered the island of Providence of a quantity of artillery and stores, carrying off the governor and other public officers. They made several captures on their return, and the Glasgow frigate escaped from them with difficulty after a sharp engagement.

Lord Dunmore, with his flotilla of negroes and fugitives, rowed during the greatest part of the year along the coasts, and in the rivers of Virginia, repulsed in every attempt to land, as strict guard was kept in all accessible places. The heat, bad provisions, and filth of the crowded vessels, produced an infectious distemper which made great havoc in the crews; and the survivors were obliged to take refuge in Florida, Bermuda, and the West Indies.

A squadron under the command of Sir Peter Parker, which sailed from Portsmouth at the close of the year, was so much retarded by unfavourable weather, that it did not reach Cape Fear in South Carolina, till the beginning of May. General Clinton was there waiting for it with a small force; and these commanders, with Lord Cornwallis, agreed to make an attempt upon Charleston, the capital of the province. The fleet anchored off that place in the beginning of June, consisting of three 50 gun ships, four frigates, and some smaller armed vessels. The first object of the expedition, after passing the bar, was the attack of a fort upon Sullivan's Island, which commanded the access to Charleston. The troops were landed on another island, separated from Sullivan's by a small creek, which was represented as fordable at low water, but which was defended by works erected by the Americans; and General Lee, who had gone over from the British service to that of the Americans, lay encamped with a considerable force on the continent. It was not till the 28th, that the attack of the fort on Sullivan's Island by the men of war took place; and its result was the repulse of the assailants with great loss, after a gallant and long continued action. From some circumstance, they were unaided by co-operation from the land forces. One of the frigates which got aground was burnt to prevent her from falling into the hands of the enemy.

The state of war was now so decided, and the hope of accommodation without absolute submission so entirely cut off, that the congress began to entertain the idea of declaring for independence; and in order to sound the public feelings on this head, they sent to each colony a kind of manifesto, stating the causes which in their opinion rendered it necessary that all authority under the British crown should be abrogated, and the powers of government assumed respectively by themselves; and they recommended it to those colonies, whose govern-

ment was not already sufficient for the present exigency, to proceed to the establishment of such a form as should answer the
purposes of internal peace and external defence. Pennsylvania
and Maryland alone opposed the plan of independence. In the
former, after much discussion, it was carried by great majorities
that their delegates should concur in the determination of the
congress. In the latter, the delegates having been instructed by
a majority to oppose the question of independency in congress,
which they did, retiring at the same time from the assembly,
the idea of standing alone had such an effect on the province
that they were directed to return and act as they thought best
for the interest of America. Thus all were united in the measure. On July 4th, the thirteen colonies declared themselves
independent, abjured their allegiance to the crown of Great
Britain, and renounced all political connection with her. Their
declaration began with an assertion of the general rights of
men, of the purposes for which governments were instituted,
and of the right of changing them when they no longer answer
those purposes. It then proceeded to a long enumeration of
the wrongs affirmed to have been sustained from the King of
Great Britain, and for the redress of which, all their petitions
had been fruitless; and concluded with a solemn appeal to
the Almighty for the rectitude of their intentions, and with
asserting, in the name, and by the authority, of the people of
North America, that "these United Colonies are, and of right
ought to be, Free and Independent States."

The British army embarked at Boston was conveyed to
Halifax, where it was detained above two months waiting
for reinforcements. At length, General Howe impatient of
further delay, sailed with the troops under convoy of Admiral
Shuldham, and near the close of June arrived off Sandy Hook
on the coast of New Jersey. He landed his men on Staten Island,
where he was joined by his brother, Admiral Lord Howe, who
arrived with the fleet after touching at Halifax. On July 14th
he sent by a flag, a circular letter to the late governors of the

several colonies, acquainting them with the civil and military powers with which he was invested, and desiring them to make public an enclosed declaration. The purpose of this was, to give information of the powers entrusted to him and his brother under the late act of parliament, of granting general and particular pardons to all who should return to their allegiance. These papers being forwarded by General Washington to the congress, were published by that body in all the newspapers, introduced by a preface in the way of comment. A letter was about this time sent ashore by Lord Howe, directed to George Washington, Esq. which the general refused to receive, as not being addressed with the title belonging to the rank held by him under the United States; a conduct which was highly approved by congress. An adjutant afterwards waiting on General Washington, from General Howe, on a message relative to prisoners, great politeness was observed on both sides. The officer having mentioned the great powers with which the commissioners were furnished for effecting an accommodation, the general remarked, that as far as appeared, their powers were only to grant pardons, which those did not want who had committed no crime, and that they were only defending their indisputable rights. Such appeared to be the general sentiment of the colonies, though in some of them were many individuals attached to the royal cause, or at least averse to the declaration of independence.

Almost all the forces destined for General Howe's command being now arrived, which, according to the original estimate, should have amounted to about 35,000 men, of the first military quality and abundantly provided with every warlike necessary, an attack was planned against the provincials who were encamped in force upon Long Island. A landing being made without opposition on August 22d, under General Clinton, Lord Cornwallis, and Earl Percy, an engagement was brought on with a part of the provincial troops on the 27th, in which the latter incurred a severe loss, stated at 3000, including 1000 prisoners, among the latter of whom were three generals; that of the combined British and Hessians not amounting to 350. The remainder of the provincials, still occupying their lines, were withdrawn on the night of the 29th across the channel, separating the island from New York, without being perceived and brought away their baggage, stores, and part of their artillery. The attempt to defend this island against such a superior force was afterwards much censured; and the loss would probably have been much greater had the conquering troops been permitted in the ardour of victory, to storm the American lines. Soon after this event, at the request of Lord Howe, a committee from the congress waited upon him to confer on terms of conciliation; but their report of the conference was the same in effect with the opinion above-mentioned as entertained by General Washington, respecting the powers of the commissioners.

No hope remaining of an accommodation, the British commanders resolved to push their success; and on September 15th, the troops were landed on the island on which New York is situated. That city was immediately abandoned by the provincials, who displayed evident tokens of the effect of the late action on their spirits, and in their hasty retreat left behind them their artillery and military stores. Possession of New York was taken by a brigade of the British army; and soon after, it was set on fire in different parts by some incendiaries, and nearly a third of the city was reduced to ashes.

The provincials still occupied strong works at Kingsbridge and on the northern side of the island, which were turned by General Howe, who, embarking the greatest part of his troops, landed them on that part of the continent of New York which adjoins to Connecticut. He then advanced to the high grounds called the White Plains, which obliged General Washington to make a movement, which placed him opposite to the line of march of the King's troops, the river Brunx being between them. Commanding an inferior and dispirited army, it was by no means his design to hazard an engagement. When, therefore, the British army had forced a passage across the river, after a desultory combat, in which the provincials were driven from their posts, Washington on the night of November 1st quitted his camp and retired farther back, and the British took possession of his entrenchments. Fort Washington, on the North river, was then attacked by a detachment of British and Hessians, and was taken with a garrison of near 3000 men, and Fort Lee, on the opposite side of the river, was deserted. The Jerseys were thus left entirely open to the King's troops, which at length extended their cantonments from New Brunswick to the Delaware.

During these successes, General Clinton, with a force of British and Hessians, and Sir Peter Parker with a squadron of men of war, were sent to make an attempt on Rhode Island in the colony of that name. The island being abandoned on their approach, it was taken possession of without resistance on December 8th; and Hopkins's squadron was blocked up in the harbour of Providence by the British ships, which, with the troops, passed the winter on this station.

The British commanders in Canada having succeeded in freeing that province from the colonial invaders, determined to carry their arms into the enemy's quarters, and for this purpose under the conduct of Captain Pringle, and headed by General Carleton in person, they came on October 11th in sight of the American fleet commanded by Arnold, but much inferior in strength. After a spirited combat of two successful days, the American flotilla was almost entirely destroyed, only a galley and three small vessels escaping to Ticonderoga; and in their flight they evacuated Crown Point, setting fire to the houses, and destroying every thing which they were unable to carry away. General Carleton afterwards returned to Canada.

Among incidents which threw a gloom on the American cause, was the capture of General Lee. This officer being on his march with the few men he could keep together to join

General Washington, took up his quarters in New Jersey at some distance from his main body. Intelligence of his situation being communicated to Colonel Harcourt, he pushed on with a party of light horse, and eluding the guard, seized the sentries, and carried off the General with a rapidity that prevented any rescue. As Lee was not only regarded as an able commander, but was peculiarly obnoxious to government in the light of a deserter from the King's service, (the resignation of his commission not having been accepted) great was the triumph on his capture. An offer made by General Washington to exchange six field officers for him was refused. He was committed to close custody, and there can be little doubt that a resolution had been taken in England to make him undergo the utmost rigour of martial law; but it was determined by congress that full retaliation should be made on the persons of prisoners in their hands, for any violence that should be practised against him.

At this time, the American army, reduced by losses of every kind, had dwindled to a small number, and at the expiration of their year of service, few men were prevailed on to continue in the field. Congress however in the midst of these discouragements retained an unsubmitting spirit. On October 4th they signed a treaty of perpetual union and confederacy between the thirteen colonies, which laid down rules for their government in all cases respecting their mutual relations in peace and war. They also assiduously employed themselves in devising means for levying a new army, and negotiating a loan. On December 10th they published an address to the people in general, and especially to those of Pennsylvania and the adjacent states, in which, for the purpose of animating them to resistance, they expatiated on the relentless and inhuman manner in which, they said, war was carried on by the British and their auxiliaries. The ill success of the American arms began, however, to produce those internal effects on a cause founded only on opinion which were as much to be dreaded as external force.

After the taking of New York, a petition signed by a large number of the inhabitants of the city and island was presented to the Howes, declaring their acknowledgment of the constitutional supremacy of Great Britain over the colonies, and requesting to be received into the King's peace and protection; and it was followed by another of the like kind from the people of Long Island. The vicinity of Philadelphia to the royal troops having induced the congress to remove to Baltimore, dissentions arose in that city, in which a strong opposition to the declaration of independency had before existed. On this occasion several of the leading men both in Pennsylvania and the Jerseys went over to the commissioners at New York; and of those who staid in Philadelphia, the quakers, uniting with those called loyalists or Tories, impeded the execution of an order for fortifying the city. These proceedings induced General Washington to detach three regiments to the place, which measure gave a check to the movements of the disaffected.

On the approach of winter, the British army went into cantonments, forming an extensive chain from Brunswick on the Rariton to the Delaware. Among these posts, Trenton, the highest of those on the latter river, was occupied by Colonel Rall, with three battalions of Hessians, and some British light-horse and chasseurs. Their detached situation led General Washington to form the design of making an attempt to surprise them; for which purpose, pushing a corps across the Delaware, on December 26th he made a sudden attack on their picquets, which brought Rall to their assistance. He soon received a mortal wound; and the Hessians being repulsed in their endeavour to retreat, were obliged to surrender prisoners of war, to the number of 918. This success greatly raised the spirits of the Americans, not only as a change of fortune in their favour, but because it was a triumph over foes, who, on account of their ferocity and rapacity, were equally dreaded and detested. One of its effects was the return to their colours of many provincial soldiers who had deserted them.

In another quarter, and against a very different enemy, the exertions of the colonists were crowned with success. The British agents had been active in instigating the Indian tribes at the back of the southern colonies to make an inroad on the frontiers, holding out to them the prospect of being aided by a British force from West Florida. The Creeks and Cherokees were thereby induced to take up arms; but the former, finding that the expected succour did not arrive, stopped short in the enterprize. The Cherokees, however, fell with fury upon the adjacent settlements; carrying ravage and massacre through them during great part of the summer. At length the neighbouring militias of Virginia and the Carolinas assembling, not only drove back the savages, but pursuing them into their own country, inflicted so severe a chastisement upon them, that the nation was nearly exterminated, and the survivors were obliged humbly to sue for peace.

Whilst the American cause was undergoing these difficulties and vicissitudes at home, it was in general looked upon with favour among the European nations, not so much, it may be supposed, through approbation of its principles, as in consequence of a jealousy of that high rank in power and prosperity, which Great Britain had attained by its successes in the late war. The Bourbon courts were particularly sensible of a superiority which directly tended to their comparative depression; and the maritime states viewed, in the independence of the Anglo-American colonies, a source of traffic hitherto interdicted to them. The French and Spanish ports were freely opened to American ships, notwithstanding the remonstrances of the British ministers; and the prizes, which a retaliatory declaration of congress, authorizing the capture of all British property on the high seas, now rendered frequent, were allowed to be disposed of in them. Artillery and military stores were also sent, either as gifts or objects of sale, to the Americans, and several French engineers and officers entered into their service.

The great increase of American privateers, some of which, in the West Indies, were French ships which had taken out American commissions, with few or no American seamen on board, together with the large armaments fitting out in the French and Spanish ports, occasioned the British ministry, shortly before the termination of the parliamentary recess, to put 16 more men of war of the line into commission, and to issue proclamations augmenting the bounty for entering the navy, recalling seamen who were in foreign service, and laying an embargo on the exportation of provisions.

On October 31st, the meeting of parliament was opened by a speech from the throne, in which great indignation was expressed at the renunciation of allegiance, and the claim of independence, by the rebellious colonies; one advantage arising from which, would however be a clear disclosure of their object, and a consequent unanimity at home, founded on a conviction of the justice and necessity of our measures. Mention was made of amicable assurances received from other courts; but though a continuance of the general tranquillity was to be hoped for, it had been thought expedient that we should be placed in a respectable state of defence at home. On the usual motions for an applauding address, the opposition in both houses made warm attacks on the policy which had been pursued in this unfortunate contest, but the motions in each were carried by great majorities. Soon after, the proclamation issued by the Howes on their entrance into New York, having appeared in a common newspaper, though it had not been noticed in the Gazette, Lord John Cavendish in the House of Commons, called upon the ministers to declare whether it was or was not authentic. Its authenticity being avowed, his lordship expressed great astonishment, as well at the manner in which it was suffered to come to the knowledge of the public, as at the contents of the paper, which acquainted the Americans that his Majesty had directed a revision of such of his instructions as might be construed to lay an improper restraint upon the freedom of legislation in the colonies. This, he contended, was a high indignity offered to parliament by ministers, in engaging its sanction to their propositions; and he made a motion for the purpose of taking into its hands the revisal alluded to. The motion was however rejected by a majority of 109 to 47. After this decision, a number of the opposition members, especially those of the Rockingham party, seceded from the public business of parliament, on the ground that all discussion of ministerial measures was entirely unavailing. Others, however, not only refused to adopt, but loudly condemned this conduct; and this disagreement would have strengthened, had it been necessary, the government party.

Europe in general, during this year, enjoyed a state of tranquillity. The augmentation of the Spanish forces, which occasioned some disquiet in the British cabinet, had a cause, or at least a pretext, in a dispute with Portugal, respecting the limits of the two crowns on the Rio de la Plata in South America. Troops had been gradually sent to the Brazils, and warlike preparations had been made, which preceded acts of hostility in which several Spanish forts were taken. In consequence, large bodies of Spanish troops had been advanced towards the frontiers of Portugal; and France had been called upon by Spain to afford the stipulated aid in case of a war with that power. The mediation of England and France, however, prevented the difference from coming to extremities, and a temporary, but imperfect accommodation took place.

In the Austrian dominions, the spirit of improvement inherent in the Emperor Joseph was operating in the most laudable manner by the abolition of torture, and the introduction of a liberal religious toleration; and also by releasing the peasants of the imperial demesnes in Bohemia from the state of villanage, and granting them allotments of land at easy rents. He likewise adopted the scheme of an East India trading company.

In Asia a war had for some time been subsisting between the Regent of Persia and the Ottoman Porte, in which the former had laid siege to the city of Bassora. This had continued above twelve months under the usual oriental management, when, on April 16th, the place was compelled by sickness and famine to surrender. In a subsequent attempt to reduce the city and province of Bagdad, the Persian troops were routed with great slaughter.

A very extraordinary incident took place in this year in the British East Indies. The Nabob of Arcot, Mahommed Ally Cawn, had found means to obtain a preponderating influence over the governing powers at Madras, which produced a junction of the Company's troops with his, in an expedition planned by him against the Hindoo Rajah of Tanjore who had long been, and then was, in alliance with both. Its result was the capture of Tanjore with its district, which were seized by the Nabob, who applied the Rajah's treasures to defray the expence of the war, and left that unfortunate prince stript of every thing but his life. The intelligence of this event, and of the manner in which it had been brought about, excited the greatest indignation in the Company, and the restoration of the deposed prince was decided on, as a measure equally necessary for their reputations and for their political interest. For the effecting it, Lord Pigot was looked to, who had formerly, by his defence and government of Madras, established a high character civil and military, and who was much esteemed in his private capacity. The Nabob, foreseeing the probability of such a consequence had prepared against it by borrowing great sums of money from several members of the council of Madras, and mortgaging to them the revenues of Tanjore as a security. Lord Pigot arrived in his government at the latter end of 1775, and notwithstanding the opposition he met with, he succeeded in restoring the Rajah. Finding afterwards that all his measures were thwarted by a majority of the council, he took the strong step of carrying the suspension of two

of them by his own casting vote, and he put under arrest
Sir Robert Fletcher, commander in chief of the forces. These
acts occasioned a conspiracy to seize his person, in which
Colonel Stuart, who succeeded to the military command,
though apparently in intimate friendship with Lord Pigot,
took a part; and on August 24th, the colonel having by
stratagem drawn him out of the garrison to a villa, whither
he himself accompanied him, caused him to he surrounded
by a party of Sepoys, and carried prisoner to a place called
the Mount, where he was strictly confined under guard. The
prevailing party then issued a declaration, that the governor
had forfeited all legal claim to authority; and taking possession
of all the powers of government, they appointed their leader
to act in his place. The governor and council of Bengal gave
their approbation to this act of violence; and both parties sent
home their own representation of the transaction.

1777

17th & 18th Year of the Reign

On the meeting of parliament after the recess, a bill was passed in the House of Commons February 6th, for enabling the Admiralty to grant letters of marque to private ships against all vessels belonging to the revolted American colonies: it afterwards went through the House of Lords, and in both without opposition.

On the same day, Lord North moved for a bill "to enable his Majesty to secure and detain persons charged with, or suspected of, the crime of high treason committed in America, or on the high seas, or the crime of piracy." On the second reading of this bill it appeared, that by its enactments, anyone under the charge or suspicion abovementioned, was liable to be committed to any place of confinement appointed by the King's sign manual, *within any part of his dominions*, and detained without bail or trial during the continuance of the law. Mr. Dunning thereupon expressed high astonishment that a bill which struck directly at the great constitutional security of British liberty, the *habeas corpus* law, should be brought in without notice, and in so thin a house; and he moved for the printing of the bill, which was granted. The alarm thus sounded brought on a severe discussion of the measure, which however did not prevent the commitment of the bill from being carried by a majority of more than four to one; but the ministry finding that some of the objections were strongly supported in argument, an amendment was proposed by a person in office, consisting in the omission of the words "in any part of his Majesty's dominions," and the substitution of "within the realm." This amendment by no means satisfied the opposition, and during the farther progress of the bill the city of London presented a petition against it. In every stage it was combated, and amendments were proposed by the minority, which were rejected; at length, the minister declaring that he had no purpose of extending the operation of the bill beyond its open and avowed objects, and that it was intended for America, and not for Great Britain, and an amendment to that effect being agreed to, it passed into a law.

Some warm debates arose when the accounts of the unprovided war expences were laid before the committee, of supply, several of the items being reprobated by the minority, as lavish and enormous; and censures were particularly passed on an unexpected demand by the Landgrave of Hesse, for levy-money, on account of his hired troops. The minister's task was rendered more embarrassing, by the necessity he was under of introducing to the House of Commons a message from his Majesty, desiring that he might be enabled to discharge a second debt of the civil list, amounting to upwards of £600,000. When the message was taken into consideration, copious debates ensued, in which all the accounts of the civil list expenditure presented to the House were severally canvassed; such, however, was the prevailing sentiment of loyalty, that not only the deficient sum was voted, but an addition of £100,000 was made to the former grant of £800,000 a year. The patience of the House was still farther tried by the Landgrave of Hesse, who brought forward a dormant claim of £40,000 for the expence of foreign hospitals in the last war. This instance of rapacity proved so galling, that the resolution for discharging it was carried only by 50 to 42.

A singular circumstance was the occasion of a hot debate in the House of Commons, in which the ministers found themselves embarrassed by one of their own friends. The speaker (Sir Fletcher Norton) on presenting for the royal assent the bill for the augmentation of the civil list, had used some expressions of an unusual kind. In displaying the liberality of the grant, he had said that his Majesty's faithful Commons had granted him not only a large present supply, but a very great additional revenue, "great beyond example; great beyond your Majesty's highest expence: and this they have done in a well grounded confidence, that you will apply wisely, what they have granted liberally." He had also, by way of enhancing the grant, observed, that it was made at a time "full of difficulty and danger," and when their constituents were labouring under burdens "almost too heavy to be borne." For this speech the thanks of the House were immediately and unanimously voted; but on reflection, its tenor was by no means agreeable to that part of the House which bore the appellation of the King's friend and on a debate upon another topic, a member high in office took the occasion of censuring the speaker with great vehemence, accusing him of having uttered sentiments at variance with those of the majority of the House. The speaker appealing to the thanks of the House in his defence, the attack upon him was repeated with still greater acrimony, till the ministers, fearing lest the matter should go too far, wished to put it to rest. Mr. Fox, however, asserting that a direct charge had been made against the speaker, which it was necessary for his reputation and that of the House to bring to a decision, made a motion for approving the manner in which he had expressed himself. This, after an attempt to get rid of it by an adjournment, was carried without opposition.

When the transactions in India relative to Lord Pigot were brought under the consideration of the Court of East India

Directors, many of that body, though not undertaking entirely to justify the violent proceedings with respect to his lordship, yet loudly condemned his conduct in various points, and held that the restoration of the Rajah of Tanjore was an imprudent and unwise measure. About an equal number maintained the opposite opinion; and the case being laid before a court of proprietors, a resolution was agreed on, by a majority of 382 to 140, for restoring Lord Pigot to his full powers, and enquiring into the conduct of those who had been instrumental in his imprisonment. The court of directors afterwards passed resolutions conformable to this determination, to which, however, was annexed a vote of censure on Lord Pigot's conduct, as in several instances reprehensible; and at length, through the influence, it was said, of administration, a vote was carried at a court of proprietors, by a majority of 414 to 317, for the recall of Lord Pigot, his friends, and his enemies. The matter was brought into the House of Commons on May 22d by Governor Johnstone, in a motion for several resolutions, on which he proposed to found a bill for the better securing of our settlements in the East Indies. Their tenor was a strong approbation of Lord Pigot's conduct as governor, and a confirmation of the acts of the company in his favour, with the annulling of the resolution for his recall. This was the occasion of a vigorous debate, in which the ministers opposed, and the opposition supported, the motion. On a division, it was rejected by 90 votes against 67. During this contest Lord Pigot died still under confinement, at the Garden-house, Fort St. George, on May 11th.

The Earl of Chatham, notwithstanding his advanced years and bodily infirmities, determined to make one more effort for delivering the country from the dangers which, in his opinion, were immediately impending over it. On May 30th, he made a motion in the House of Lords for an address to his Majesty, requesting that the most speedy and effectual measures might be taken for putting a stop to the hostilities carrying on against the American colonies, upon the only just and solid foundation, that of "the removal of accumulated grievances." In his explanation of the motion he said, that by these words he meant every thing which had passed in parliament relative to the colonies since the year 1763. He insisted upon the immediate necessity of adopting an effectual plan of conciliation, from the certainty that a treaty would be entered into between America and France, in case of the continuance of the war. "America," said he, "is contending with Great Britain under a masked battery of France, which will open upon this country as soon as she perceives us to be sufficiently weakened, and finds herself sufficiently prepared." The ministers, in reply, denied this danger; and opposed the motion principally on the assumption, that independency was the primary, and is now the determined, object of the Americans, which would render all concessions fruitless as well as degrading. The principal speakers in opposition warmly supported the motion, which was negatived by 99 to 28.

Nothing further of importance occurred in this session of parliament, which broke up on June 6th.

In the principal theatre of American warfare, after the disaster which had happened to the Hessians, the British and auxiliary troops assembled with the purpose of advancing to Princetown, and Lord Cornwallis moved to attack Washington, who was posted on Trenton creek. On January 2d, the two armies cannonaded each other, and withdrawing for the night, three British regiments, under Lieutenant-colonel Mawhood, were posted at Princetown. Washington, in the dead of night, keeping up the fires of his camp, marched with the greater part of his troops towards Princetown, and fell in with Mawhood at sunrise, as he was beginning his march at the head of the 17th regiment. By great exertions of courage and discipline, the regiment forced its way through the American ranks, and pursued its march without further molestation. The 55th was also attacked, and made good its retreat to Brunswick. The

40th was less engaged than the others, and retired by another road to the same place. A considerable loss was sustained by the whole, though less than might have been expected; and Washington, contented with this success, made no further attempt. Soon after, however, the Americans overran both Jerseys, and became masters of the coast opposite Staten Island. During the remainder of the winter and the spring, Lord Cornwallis, leaving the Delaware, continued, much straitened in quarters, at Brunswick and Amboy.

In April, expeditions were sent from New York to destroy some magazines of provisions and ammunition, which proved successful. Washington now considerably reinforced advanced, and took a strong position in the Jerseys, not far from Brunswick. In the month of June, General Howe took the field, and used all his endeavours to bring his antagonist to an engagement. After a variety of manœuvres for this purpose, which the caution of Washington rendered ineffectual, Howe, changing his plan, passed his army over to Staten Island, and made preparations for an embarkation. In July an incident occurred which probably had a considerable influence on the fate of General Lee. Colonel Barton, a provincial officer, with a corps of volunteers, crossing by night from Providence to Rhode Island, surprized General Prescott in his quarters, and brought him and his aide-de-camp prisoners to the continent, thus securing a pledge of equal value for the safety of the Anglo-American captive.

Meantime events of great importance were taking place in a different quarter. A plan had been laid, of which General Burgoyne was said to be the author, of penetrating by the lakes of Canada to the North of Hudson's river as far as Albany, and by forming a communication with the British army in the middle colonies, to cut off all intercourse between the northern and southern portions of North America. The most sanguine expectations from this scheme were entertained by the ministers, especially by the colonial secretary of state, and it was resolved to afford every facility for its execution. The command was given to General Burgoyne, in whose abilities and enterprize much confidence was placed; and the regular force assigned to him consisted of about 7200 men, British and German, exclusive of artillery. A number of Canadians were also engaged to assist by various military services; and several tribes of savages, a kind of auxiliary force, against the employment of which scruples appear hitherto to have subsisted, were induced by liberal presents to take a part in the expedition. A lesser armament was fitted out to proceed from the upper part of Canada by the way of Oswego to the Mohawk river, under the command of Colonel St. Leger.

General Burgoyne encamped his army on the west side of Lake Champlain in June, whence he issued a manifesto in lofty language, apprizing the colonists of the dangers impending over them should they resist his Majesty's arms, and rhetorically amplifying the terrors of a savage foe let loose upon them — a style of address which, if it failed to deter, would infallibly add force and animosity to opposition. In the beginning of July the army advanced to the attack of Ticonderoga, which had been strengthened by many additional works by the Americans since the last unsuccessful attempt against it. These however, inspired no confidence; and as soon as the defenders found that the investment was on the point of being completed, they determined upon evacuating the place. This was effected on the night of the 5th; and their flight being descried in the morning, a keen pursuit was commenced by land and water. The result was highly disastrous to the fugitives, their rear being overtaken and routed with the loss of a number of men, and all their baggage. They afterwards abandoned Fort Edward on the Hudson's, and at the approach of the royal army retired to Saratoga.

It was the end of July before General Burgoyne was able, from the difficulties of the country, to reach Hudson's river. His troops were full of spirits and confidence, whilst dismay spread through the provincials, who saw themselves laid open without resistance to a dreaded enemy. The New England States, however, manifested not the least disposition to submit, but actively employed themselves in collecting forces for more effectual defence. Arnold was sent to reinforce the routed northern army, with a train of artillery which he received from Washington; and on his arrival, he drew back the army to Still-water, in order to keep in check Colonel St. Leger, who was advancing along the Mohawk river. The American army was daily increased by the very cause which was intended to deter from resistance — the ferocity of the savages, who could not be restrained from perpetrating their accustomed cruelties, and which obliged every inhabitant to arm for his own protection. The royal army encamped at Saratoga now began to suffer from the want of provisions, for the procuring of which a detachment was sent to gain possession of a deposit of stores which the provincials had collected at Bennington, guarded by a body of militia. This proved a very unfortunate enterprize, almost the whole party being killed, or taken prisoners, with the effect of reviving the depressed spirits of the provincials. At this time Colonel St. Leger was engaged in an attempt against Fort Stanwix, since named Fort Schuyler, which at first promised to be successful, a body of militia coming to its relief being defeated with great slaughter. But the commander of the fort holding out with exemplary firmness, and a report of Arnold's approach having alarmed the Indian auxiliaries, who threatened to quit the besieging army if a retreat was not immediately commenced, the colonel, on August 22d found himself obliged to raise the siege, leaving behind him his tents and most of his artillery and stores.

During this interval a large force of provincials had been collected under General Gates, an officer of English birth, on whom the congress placed great reliance. Burgoyne, who still lay opposite to Saratoga, having at length procured a supply of provisions, sufficient for thirty days consumption, now determined to cross the Hudson's river, a measure which afterwards underwent much discussion, as his chance of ultimate success had been greatly diminished. In fact, his retreat to Canada, or his advance to Albany for the purpose of joining Sir H. Clinton, the British commander at New York, was almost equally hazardous, whilst the latter hazard appeared to him preferable, as an attempt, at least, to fulfil the original object of the expedition. He put his design in execution about the middle of September, and on the 19th arrived in front of the American army at Still-water. A severe but indecisive action ensued, attended with considerable loss on both sides, and each army entrenched itself in its position. The Americans, however, were daily acquiring strength by reinforcements; while desertions were taking place in the royal army among the Canadians and British provincials; and the savages, finding no more plunder was to be expected, left their friends when their services would have been most useful. In the early part of October, Burgoyne, whose provisions were beginning to fall short, and who no longer could indulge the hope of effectual co-operation from the central army, made a movement with part of his force, as well for the purpose of a reconnissance, as to cover a foraging party. An action was thence brought on, in which the British underwent a severe loss, and the pursuing enemy forced their way into a part of their entrenchments. Nothing now remained but an immediate retreat to Saratoga with the melancholy necessity of abandoning the sick and wounded. In this post, hemmed in on all sides by an enemy so situated as to fire into his camp, without the possibility of forcing his way, and reduced to three days provision, General Burgoyne was obliged to submit to the only means of preserving the remains of an army which had merited every praise of bravery, patience, and discipline, by entering into a convention, with the American commander, signed on October 17th. By its terms, the troops were to march out of camp with all the honours of war, and after depositing their arms, to be allowed to embark for Europe at Boston, under condition of not serving again in America during the war, the army not to be separated, private property to be held sacred, and no baggage searched, and the Canadians to be sent to their own country on similar conditions. General Gates, who had behaved with great honour and humanity during the whole transaction, fulfilled all these conditions with entire punctuality as far as depended upon himself, and had the delicacy not to suffer an American soldier to be a spectator of the humiliating circumstance of piling the British arms. The whole number of military of all sorts comprized in this surrender, was stated by the Americans at 5752 men.

We now revert to the events that were passing in the central part of this continent. General Sir W. Howe, having embarked 36 British and Hessian battalions, with a powerful artillery, sailed from Sandy Hook on July 23d, leaving 17 battalions and a regiment of light horse at New York and its vicinity, under General Clinton, and 7 battalions at Rhode Island. After a tedious navigation, he arrived on August 25th at the head of Chesapeak bay, where the troops were disembarked. General Washington in the meantime had left the Jerseys, and marched with his army to defend Philadelphia, the object of the British commander's enterprize. The royal forces began their march towards that city on September 3d, whilst the provincial army had advanced from the Brandy-wine creek. After several skirmishes, the latter fell back to the same position, and on the 11th a partial but warm action was brought on, in which the Americans were routed with considerable loss and in consequence retreated, first to Chester, and then to Philadelphia. In this battle several foreigners fought in the American ranks, among whom was the Marquis de la Fayette, a French nobleman of high rank, induced by his enthusiasm for liberty to cross the Atlantic. This apprenticeship to republicanism as it may be termed, had serious consequences at a later period. Washington, not venturing a general action for the rescue of Philadelphia, it was entered without resistance by Lord Cornwallis, on September 26th. Some quakers and other principal inhabitants who had refused to give any security for their submission to the American independent government, were carried away by the retreating army, and sent to Virginia. The main body of the British lying at German-town, a short distance from Philadelphia, in a widely spread encampment, was attacked by surprize on October 4th by the Americans, and a severe action ensued, attended with loss on both sides, but in the end the assailants were repulsed.

Lord Howe was now engaged in bringing round his fleet from the Chesapeak to the Delaware, with the intention of approaching up the latter as near as possible to Philadelphia. The Americans had opposed a variety of obstacles to this attempt, and had constructed works and batteries upon different points. Against one of these, named Red Bank, a Hessian detachment was sent to make an attack by land, whilst the ships were to batter the fort on Mud Island on the opposite side. The Hessian attack failed with the loss of the commander, Colonel Donop, and many men; but Mud Island was taken, and Red Bank was afterwards evacuated. At length, all the forts being demolished, and the obstacles removed, the American shipping which lay in the Delaware, ran up above Philadelphia for safety; but being pursued thither, they were abandoned and set on fire by their crews. Washington, who had now received a reinforcement from the northern army, encamped at White Marsh, 14 miles distant from Philadelphia, where General Howe in vain attempted to bring him to action. The British army then returned to the city, and Washington removing to a stronger position upon the Schuylkill, called Valley Forge, both armies went into winter quarters.

General Clinton, the commander at New York, in the beginning of October, conducted an expedition up Hudson's river, assisted by a naval force under Commodore Hotham, the first object of which was the reduction of the forts

Montgomery and Clinton. This was effected by a coup de main, the Americans undergoing considerable loss. Another fort was taken soon after, and a large quantity of artillery and stores was the prize of the victors. Two new frigates and some other vessels were also destroyed, and other damage to a large amount was sustained by the Americans. A flying squadron and a detachment of light troops under Sir James Wallace and General Vaughan proceeded farther up the river, carrying terror and devastation wherever they went. The conflagration of the flourishing town of Esopus was a circumstance which, occurring at the very time when Burgoyne's army was receiving favourable terms of surrender, produced a severe letter of remonstrance from General Gates. At the approach of this commander the expedition returned to New York, having dismantled the captured forts. So far its intention was answered; but the secondary purpose of making a diversion in favour of Burgoyne entirely failed.

Parliament opened again on November 20th, with a speech from the throne, in which, after intimation was given of the necessity of large supplies for the various requisite services, one of which was a considerable augmentation of the naval force, on account of the armaments still going on in the ports of France and Spain, a resolution was declared of steadily pursuing the present measures for the re-establishment of that constitutional subordination which his Majesty was determined to maintain through the several parts of his dominions. The accustomed addresses and debates upon them in both houses, terminated in the usual manner.

The bill passed last session for the suspension, in certain cases, of the Habeas Corpus law, being now near expiration, the attorney-general moved on November 26th for its renewal during a certain limited term. Although the bill was warmly opposed, it passed by a majority of nearly two to one. Sixty thousand seamen, and such other supplies as the ministers thought necessary for the support of the war, were voted, and the enquiries into the state of affairs, and the management of particular departments, which the opposition occasionally called for, were got rid of by the usual majorities. The debates, however, assumed a tone of increased acrimony; and the news of Burgoyne's surrender, while it struck the ministers with equal surprise and dismay, gave a keener edge to the sarcasms of the minority. The employment of the savages, in particular, excited the severest reproaches, and Lord Chatham, who moved for an address for farther information on the subject, branded the measure with all the fire of his eloquence. An adjournment for six weeks was soon after (December 11th) moved by the ministers, which was violently opposed in both houses, but was carried in both by great majorities.

European affairs presented little matter of interest during the present year. The death of Joseph I, King of Portugal, in February, effected a change in the politics of that kingdom, which tended to compose its differences with Spain. He was succeeded by his daughter, who was married to her own uncle. One of the first acts of the new government was the dismission of the Marquis of Pombal from the post of prime minister, which he had long held with almost unlimited authority. This change was extremely grateful to the nation, all ranks of which he had displeased, by a system of measures opposed to the general prejudices, and conducted with arbitrary severity, but many of them enlightened and patriotic. The court of Madrid, immediately upon this event, relinquished all hostile purposes against Portugal, and orders were sent for the cessation of hostilities in South America. Before their arrival, however, a Spanish fleet appeared off the island of St. Catharine's on the coast of Brazil, which was strongly fortified, and defended by a numerous Portuguese garrison; but the Spaniards having landed, the whole island was evacuated without resistance, and the garrison surrendered prisoners of war. The Spanish force then proceeding to Rio de la Plata, obtained possession of the colony of St. Sacrament and other places. Preliminaries of peace were at length agreed on by the two courts, and a treaty of limits was concluded, by which all differences were terminated; and the final result was, that the closest alliance was formed between the royal families of Spain and Portugal.

As nothing but necessity could have compelled the Ottoman Porte to submit to the terms of the late peace with Russia, its stipulations soon became a subject of dispute between the two courts. The permission given to the Russian vessels of passing the Dardanelles, being particularly galling to the Turks, pretexts were found for stopping at Constantinople all ships of that nation proceeding from the Mediterranean. The independence of the Krimea produced two parties in that peninsula, one attached to the Turks, the other to the Russians; and on the election of a Khan, each returned its own candidate. A civil war was the consequence, in which several of the neighbouring Tartar tribes took part.

War still continued between the Turks and Persians, but without any important event.

1778

18th & 19th Year of the Reign

THE difficulty of levying troops to supply the losses sustained in America, began to be strongly felt at the commencement of this year, and the influence of ministry was employed to induce that party which from the first had been zealous in support of coercive measures against the colonies, to use their voluntary efforts in aid of the ordinary public means resorted to for this purpose. The great trading towns of Manchester and Liverpool took the lead in this display of loyalty, and offers were sent to court by each of them, of raising at their own expence a regiment of a thousand men. The proposal was thankfully accepted, and the friends to the cause in each town, with the neighbouring country gentlemen, engaged in the business with the greatest ardour. It was much desired that the city of London would follow the example, and a motion was made in a meeting of the corporation for that purpose; but while it was supported by a majority of 11 to 9 in the court of aldermen, it was thrown out by a majority of at least three to one in the common council. The prevalent temper of the city was farther shewn by the notice of a motion for address to his Majesty, that he would be pleased "to offer such terms to our American brethren, as would put a stop to the present calamitous war." The monied interest of London, however, showed its attachment to the king and administration, by opening a subscription for raising men for his Majesty's service, "in such manner as his Majesty shall think fit;" — words that were afterwards much commented upon. An attempt to obtain a vote for the same purpose from the corporation of Bristol failed. In Scotland the measure of raising new regiments was adopted with great alacrity. Edinburgh and Glasgow levied regiments of their own, and several gentlemen in the Highlands raised corps in that martial district. One incentive to zeal on these occasions, was the privilege granted of nominating the officers, which, with other advantages, made it in some places a very gainful concern. The benefit which accrued to government from the subscriptions, was not so much in a pecuniary view, as in the revival of that spirit for subjugating the colonies, which the late events had in some measure repressed. The satisfaction derived to the ministers from this testimony of approbation of their policy, became apparent on the discussion, consequent upon a motion of Sir P.J. Clerke, in the House of Commons, immediately after the recess, for an address, that an account of the number of troops raised during the adjournment, with a specification of the corps, the names of the officers, &c. should be laid before them. This being agreed to, Lord North expressed himself in terms of cordial self congratulation, at such a display of general concurrence in the plans of administration. The opposition, however, charged the measure adopted with being illegal and unconstitutional; and some warm debates on the question were brought on, when a sum was moved for in the committee of supply, for clothing the new troops. The majority by which this was carried, was less than had been usual, being 223 to 130. In the House of Lords, two motions were made by the Earl of Abingdon, in direct reprobation of the levies and subscriptions, which were rejected by a majority of three to one. The leaders of opposition in both houses afterwards introduced a variety of motions, which had for their purpose enquiry into the transactions of the war, and the conduct of ministers, but which it is at present unimportant to specify, their result being the same as that on former occasions.

On February 17th Lord North, who appears always to have had conciliation in view, though he had been so unfortunate as always to be too late with his proposals, brought into the house two bills, one, for declaring the intentions of the parliament concerning the exercise of the right of imposing taxes on the colonies; the other, to enable his Majesty to appoint commissioners with powers to treat upon the means for quieting the disorders now subsisting in America. In his preliminary speech he said he had always known that American taxation could never produce a beneficial revenue, and that he had never proposed any taxes on the colonies, but unfortunately found them taxed when he came into office. He justified the coercive acts as apparently necessary at the time, though they had produced effects which he never intended; and he expressed his disappointment at the military failures that had occurred, observing that Sir W. Howe had always been superior, not only in the goodness and appointment of his troops, but in their number to those opposed to him. With respect to the proposed commission, it was to be enabled to treat with the congress by name, as if it were a legal body; to order a suspension of arms; to suspend all restrictive laws, and grant all sorts of pardons and immunities; to restore to any of the colonies their ancient form of constitution; and where the King nominated governors, council, &c. to nominate others, till his pleasure were known. The minister's motion excited strong expressions of disapprobation from the strenuous supporters of the national sovereignty and the royal prerogative, and some of the country gentlemen warmly complained of the deception practised on them relative to American taxation. On the other hand, the propositions were in general approved by the opposition, but not without some severe remarks on the fruitlessness of a war, the objects of which appeared never to have been understood, and were now entirely renounced. The bills, however, passed with some amendments, one of which was a clause for the express repeal of the tea tax.

During the progress of these bills in the House of Lords, the Duke of Grafton, on March 5th, informed the house that he had received intelligence from an unquestionable source, that a treaty had been actually signed between the court of France and the deputies of America, and put the question to the ministers present whether this were the fact. The secretary of state in reply affirmed that he knew nothing of such treaty, nor had received any authentic information of its being either in existence or contemplation. On March 16th Lord North gave notice to the House of Commons that he should have occasion upon the following day to present to it a message from the throne; accordingly, on the 17th, the French declaration was laid before both houses, with a message purporting that his Majesty, relying upon the support of his people, was determined to exert, if necessary, all the force of his kingdom, to repel every attack, and uphold the power and reputation of this country. The French treaty of defensive alliance with the American colonies, which was concluded at Paris on February 6th, avowed its essential and direct end to be "the effectual maintaining of the liberty, sovereignty, and independence, absolute and unlimited, of the thirteen United States of America, as well in matters of government as of commerce." The French declaration signed by M. de Noailles, the ambassador to England from that court, stated the actual independence of the Americans, proclaimed by them, in July 1776, as a justification for beginning to form a connection between France and the new nation, and for consolidating it by treaty of friendship and commerce. It proceeded to profess a desire of cultivating a good understanding with Great Britain; but concluded with intimating, that the King of France, determined to protect the lawful commerce of his subjects, and to maintain the dignity of his flag, had taken measures for the purpose, in concert with the United States.

Lord North, having acquainted the house that in consequence of this offensive communication his Majesty had sent orders to his ambassador to withdraw from the court of France; moved an address to the throne, in which the highest indignation was expressed at the unjust and unprovoked conduct of France, and the strongest assurance was given of the zealous support of that house, and of its confidence that the loyalty of the people would lead them to sustain with firmness any extraordinary burdens that might be found necessary to enable his Majesty to vindicate the honour of his crown, and to protect the rights and interests of these kingdoms. An amendment to this motion was moved by an opposition member, consisting in the insertion of words expressing the hope and trust of the house that his Majesty would remove from his counsels those ministers on whom, from the experience of their past conduct, the public could place no confidence in the present situation of affairs. This brought on a severe attack on the ministers, particularly with regard to incapacity or negligence in not obtaining intelligence of the designs of France till they were put in execution, or, if they were known, in not providing against them. The amendment was, however, rejected and the original address was carried by 263 to 113. Similar motions were made in the House of Lords with the like event.

The present parliamentary session was rendered in some degree memorable, as making the commencement of those acts of justice towards the sister-island, with respect to its commerce, which have terminated in a great melioration of its condition. On April 2d Earl Nugent moved for a committee of the whole House of Commons to consider of the trade of Ireland. This being granted, he introduced motions for the purpose of taking off the subsisting restrictions on the Irish commerce, under the head of direct exportation to the British plantations and settlements; of direct importation from the same; of exportation of glass manufactured in Ireland to all places except Great Britain; and of the importation of cotton yarn manufactured there, into Great Britain: to which Mr. Burke added the importation of Irish cotton yarn and cordage. Although apprehensions were expressed that these permissions would prove detrimental to the manufactures of Great Britain, the motions were for the present agreed to, and bills were framed upon them. The consequence was a prodigious alarm throughout most of the manufacturing and trading districts of the kingdom, the inhabitants of which betrayed a jealousy of any participation of the Irish in the advantages enjoyed by themselves, little to the credit of their liberality. The city of London remained uninfluenced by such considerations: from the others numerous petitions and instructions to representatives were sent up, which, on the motion for the second reading of the bills, occasioned a motion for deferring it to that day three months. The great advocate for Ireland on this occasion was Mr. Burke, and on a division, the motion was rejected, and the bills were committed. In the farther progress, counsel and evidence were heard on different matters relative to them; and in consequence of a compromise between the supporters and opposers of the bills, a great part of the advantages proposed for the Irish trade were for the present given up. Some enlargement of the linen trade was however granted, and some new access was opened to the African and West India commerce.

In consequence of a message from the throne on April 8th, a bill was brought into the House of Commons to enable his Majesty to make suitable provision for his younger children out of the hereditary revenues of the crown. It proposed to settle an annuity of £60,000 on the six younger princes, and of £30,000 on the five princesses; and also of £12,000 upon the son and daughter of the Duke of Gloucester; the same only to take effect on the demise of the king in the first instance, and of the duke in the second. The bill passed into a law without impediment.

On April 13th, Sir Philip Jennings Clerke introduced a bill for restraining any member of the House of Commons from being concerned in any government contract; the motion for which was carried by a majority of 71 to 50. The second reading of the bill was also carried by 72 to 61; but the opposition to it still increasing, when the motion was brought on for its commitment, a majority against it appeared of two only, the numbers being 115 to 113.

A committee on the state of the nation had been a considerable time sitting in the House of Lords, in which many subjects had been warmly debated, when, on April 7th, the Duke of Richmond closed it by moving a long address to his Majesty, in which the necessity of admitting the independence of America was insinuated. Lord Chatham, who was present, though in a very debilitated condition, rose and expressed in strong terms his indignation at the idea of a dismemberment of the empire. He was replied to with great deference by the duke; when eagerly attempting to rise again, he fell back in a convulsive fit, and was carried out of the house of which an immediate adjournment took place. He recovered for a time, but the powers of life were exhausted, and he expired in the following month. His remains were honoured with a public funeral; his debts were paid by the nation; and an annuity of £4000 out of the civil list was settled upon the Earldom of Chatham.

The liberality of the times with respect to religious differences was laudably displayed by the reception given to a bill moved in the House of Commons on May 14th, by Sir George Saville, for the repeal of certain penalties and disabilities imposed in an act of William III for preventing the further growth of popery. These penalties included the punishment of officiating popish priests as felons or traitors; the forfeiture of popish heirs educated abroad; the power given to a son or nearest relation, being a protestant of taking possession of a father's or other relation's estate; and the depriving papists of the power of acquiring landed property by purchase. Although the lenity of the times had in practice mitigated the rigour of these intolerant provisions, yet it was justly observed, that the liability to incur such penalties at the pleasure of an informer, or an unnatural child or kinsman, was of itself a severe hardship. The motion was received with universal approbation and a bill framed upon it passed into a law without the least opposition.

General Burgoyne arriving from America, a court of enquiry into his conduct was appointed, but the general officers of which it was composed reported, that in his then situation of prisoner of war to the congress no cognizance could be taken of it. He then demanded a court martial, which on the same grounds was refused. Bringing his case before parliament, motions were made in both houses by himself and his friends for an enquiry into the causes and circumstances of his surrender, but they were defeated by the influence of the ministry. The general afterwards refusing to return to his captive army, was by the king deprived of all his military commands.

The state and management of the navy was a subject of much warm discussion in both houses of parliament, and various enquiries were moved, which were negatived by the usual ministerial majorities. Parliament was prorogued on June 3d.

The militia was embodied in the spring, and several camps were formed. For the purpose of animating the spirit of loyalty and patriotism, his Majesty, on the 24th of April, attended by the Earl of Sandwich, paid a visit to Chatham. He afterwards visited Portsmouth, where he reviewed the fleet at Spithead under the command of Admiral Keppel. At a later period of the year he reviewed the troops at Winchester, Salisbury, Warley, and Coxheath.

In America, the main armies passed the winter near each other in a state of inaction; the royal army in quarters at Philadelphia; the Americans hutted at Valley Forge. The congress, desirous of preventing the troops comprised in the Saratoga convention from returning to Europe, raised captious objections to their embarkation according to the terms agreed on, and at length passed a resolution for suspending it till the ratification should arrive from England. Some predatory expeditions into the Jerseys and on the Delaware were under-taken in the spring from Philadelphia, and others from Rhode Island, which succeeded in the pillage and destruction of American property to a great value. In some of these instances, the severities practised gave occasion to great complaints from the Americans as being acts of cruelty and wanton mischief.

In the beginning of May the congress received, by an agent conveyed in a French frigate, copies of the treaties of alliance and commerce concluded between France and the United States. This intelligence, immediately published in a gazette with comments on the most favourable articles, and flattering encomiums on the French King, was received with great public rejoicings, and raised the spirits of the Americans to the highest pitch. Soon after, Sir Henry Clinton arrived at Philadelphia to take the command of the army in the room of Sir William Howe, who embarked for England.

In the beginning of June the three commissioners appointed by Lord North's conciliatory bills, who were the Earl of Carlisle, Mr. Eden, and Governor Johnstone, arrived in the Delaware. A sketch of the proposals, of which they were the bearers, had been received a considerable time before by Governor Tryon at New York, who had used every means to give it circulation; which being regarded as an insidious attempt to break the colonial union, the congress shewed how little they apprehended its effects by publishing the paper in their gazettes. The commissioners immediately dispatched a letter to the president of congress, with the late acts of parliament, and a copy of their commission: their secretary, Dr. Ferguson, was intended to have been the bearer of these documents, but was refused a passport. The concessions now offered were so large, that at an earlier period they could scarcely have failed of acceptance. Indeed, they produced considerable debates in congress till the 17th of June, when an answer was returned by the president. In this it was observed, that the acts of parliament and other papers supposed the people of the United States to be subjects of the crown of Great Britain, which could not be admitted. It was farther said, that they would be ready to enter upon the consideration of a treaty of peace and commerce not inconsistent with treaties already subsisting, when the King of Great Britain should demonstrate a sincere disposition for that purpose; the only proof of which, however, would be the explicit acknowledgement of their independence, or the withdrawing of his fleets and armies.

A determination was now made of removing the British army from Philadelphia, and on June 18th the whole was transported across the Delaware without loss or molestation. Washington having obtained notice of this intention, sent a reinforcement to the Jersey militia, in order to enable it to impede the progress of the troops till he should bring up his own force. The British were encumbered with such a quantity of baggage, including provisions, which it was necessary to carry with them, that their line of march extended twelve miles, and the extreme heat of the weather rendered their advance still more slow and toilsome. Their course was directed to Sandy Hook; but when they had arrived at a place called Freehold, they were overtaken by some detachments of the American army, and brought to a partial action on June 28th. The valour and good conduct of the British troops and their commanders extricated them with a moderate loss from their dangerous situation, after fatigues, the severity of which may be estimated from the extraordinary circumstance of the death of 59 soldiers without a wound, merely through the joint effects of toil and burning heat. According to the American account, their loss would have been much greater had it not been for the mistake or misconduct of General Lee, now exchanged and restored to his military station, who, having been entrusted with the command of the American advanced corps of 5000 men, gave them orders to retreat just as Washington was marching in haste to their support. For this behaviour he was tried by a court martial, found guilty, and suspended from command during a year. The British army reached Sandy Hook on the last day of June, whither Lord Howe's fleet from the Delaware had arrived on the preceding day, and they were conveyed by a part of it in safety to New York.

It will now be proper to turn to the British channel, in order to take up the narrative of naval occurrences which occupy an important place in the military history of the year. The French court, as soon as the effect of the declaration delivered by their ambassador in England was known, gave orders for the seizure of all British vessels found in the ports of France. A similar retaliatory order was given on this side, but few seizures were made in consequence, on either part. It was now the great object to fit out a fleet for the channel service, able to cope with that which the long preparations of the French were likely to send out from their harbours, and this, at the present juncture, appeared to be a matter of difficult execution. Admiral Keppel, who was destined to the command, found at Portsmouth only six sail of the line fit for immediate service; by the 13th of June, however, he was enabled to put to sea with twenty sail, and the promise of a speedy addition. Proceeding to the Bay of Biscay, two French frigates, with two smaller vessels, were descried, taking a survey of the fleet. War not having yet been declared, it was a matter of delicacy to determine how to act on the occasion; the admiral, however, thought it his duty to stop the frigates. One of these, the Licorne, having been brought into the fleet, a shot was fired across her way as a signal to keep her course, which she returned by a whole broad-side into a 74 gun ship, and then struck her colours. Not withstanding this provocation, not a shot was returned. The other frigate, the Belle Poule, being overtaken by an English frigate, a desperate engagement ensued, in which the English ship was so much disabled in her masts and rigging, that she was unable to prevent her antagonist from escaping to her own coast. Another frigate was detained by the admiral, who, however, suffered several French merchantmen to pass through the fleet unmolested. From the captured ships he obtained the alarming intelligence, that the French fleet lying in Brest roads consisted of 32 ships of the line and 10 or 12 frigates, which great superiority induced him to avoid so unequal a contest, and return to Portsmouth. Party was at this time prevalent in the navy as well as every where else, and Admiral Keppel was not looked upon with favour by the nobleman at the head of the navy-board; to which circumstance may be attributed the mortification he underwent at receiving no official approbation of his conduct, either in stopping the frigates, or returning into port: for the latter he was treated with much obloquy in the papers regarded as being under ministerial influence. The arrival of the West India and Levant trading fleets produced a supply of seamen which enabled the admiral to put to sea again with 24 ships of the line, on July 9th, and on his way he was joined by six more. The French fleet about the same time sailed from Brest in three divisions, under the Count D'Orvilliers, commander in chief, the Count Duchaffault, and the Duke de Chartres, son of the Duke of Orleans. The English fleet was also disposed in three divisions, the van commanded by Sir Robert Harland, vice-admiral of the red; the rear by Sir Hugh Palliser, vice-admiral of the blue; and the centre by Admiral Keppel. The two fleets, the English of 30, and the French of 32 ships of the line, and the latter much superior in frigates, came in sight of each other on July 23d. After the manœuvres of several days, during which two of the French line of battle ships had been separated from the fleet, an action was brought on upon the 27th, which proved wholly indecisive, both fleets being much shattered, but without the loss of a ship on either side. That of men was the greatest on the part of the French. Its particulars were afterwards a matter of much discussion and controversy; but upon the whole, it is certain, that the nation was greatly disappointed in the result. The French, on the contrary, seemed to regard it as a triumph that they came off on equal terms from a contest with the British navy. The latter, however, in the consequences, displayed its usual superiority; Keppel, after refitting, riding for the remainder of the season in the channel, and effectually protecting the English commerce; whilst that of the French suffered much from captures, their fleet keeping far to the southward, out of the way of another action.

Considerably before the appearance of the hostile fleets in the channel, a French squadron had been fitting out at Toulon, which sailed thence in April, under the command of the Count D'Estaign. Its destination was America, and it was seen on the coast of Virginia, on the very day that the British army arrived for embarkation at Sandy Hook. By good fortune the weather prevented it from coming up time enough to impede the transportation of the troops to New York; and it was July 11th, when it appeared in sight of Lord Howe's fleet at Sandy Hook. The French force consisted of 12 ships of the line, several being of high rates, and three large frigates; that of the English, was six of 64 guns, three of 50, two of 40, and some smaller vessels, most of them in bad condition, and weakly manned: they had, however, the advantage of being in possession of the harbour formed by the Hook. D'Estaign anchored his fleet without the Hook, where he continued eleven days, not venturing to make any attempt upon Lord Howe, who had disposed his force with admirable skill, and was seconded by the most ardent zeal not only of his own crews, but of the masters and mates of the merchant-men lying at New York. At length, on July 22d, the French sailed away for

Rhode Island, and here again, the point of time was singularly favourable to the British; for immediately after their departure, single ships from the squadron sent out under Admiral Byron, which had encountered many storms in its passage, began to drop in at Sandy Hook, in a very shattered condition.

The purpose at Rhode Island was a joint attack upon the British fleet and army lying there, by the French from the sea, and the Americans from the land. D'Estaign arrived there on July 29th, and cast anchor not far from Newport; and afterwards entering the harbour, the danger of capture produced the necessity of burning four British frigates, and sinking two others, by their crews. The commander of the troops, General Sir Robert Pigot, meantime exerted himself in making every possible preparation for defence against the expected attack by the American General Sullivan. When the danger of Rhode Island was made known to Lord Howe, he sailed with his squadron, which was re-inforced, and arrived there on August 9th. On the following day, D'Estaign stood out to sea, and Lord Howe endeavoured to gain the weather-gage in order to bring him to action: but before this was effected, a violent tempest came on, which separated and damaged the two fleets so much, that an engagement was impracticable. The French, who were the greatest sufferers, bore away for Boston to refit. Lord Howe, having repaired his damages, followed them, and entered the bay of Boston; but he found D'Estaing so advantageously situated, under the protection of land batteries, that no prospect appeared of a successful attack. General Sullivan, on the day when the French sailed from Newport harbour, landed on Rhode Island from the continent, and on the 17th broke ground against the British works; but the appearance of Lord Howe, and the departure of the French fleet, so much diminished his chance of success, that he was deserted by the volunteers, of whom half his force was composed, and found it necessary to retreat. Thus a scheme was frustrated on which sanguine hopes were founded by the Americans, who loudly complained of the conduct of their French allies. Lord Howe, who returned from Boston to Rhode Island, finding the danger there at an end, proceeded to New York, where he resigned his command, and sailed for England.

In other parts of America, military transactions were taking place, some of which may deserve a brief commemoration. A strong party of the American loyalists, called Tories, with some Indians, under the command of one Colonel Butler, appeared in July on the Susquehanna, and proceeded to attack Wyoming, an extremely beautiful and prosperous settlement of eight townships, situated on that river. They defeated in the field the garrison of the principal fort, slaughtered all the rest, with the women and children, and carried fire and sword through the settlement, committing the most shocking cruelties. On the other hand, an expedition was undertaken by some Americans from the back part of Virginia, against the Canadian settlements on the Mississippi, which they reduced, exacting from the inhabitants an oath of allegiance to the United States; and other parties of them retaliated upon the Indians their barbarities at Wyoming.

Major General Grey was dispatched by Sir H. Clinton, in the beginning of September, with a fleet of transports and troops, to destroy some nests of privateers in the part of New England called the Plymouth colony, which service was effectually performed; and a large booty of sheep and oxen was afterwards made at the island named Martha's Vineyard. He likewise surprized and put to the sword a body of American light-horse; and some other successes were obtained by the British in this desultory warfare.

Admiral Montague, who commanded on the Newfoundland station, on being informed of the hostilities commenced by D'Estaign, sent some frigates to take possession of the small islands of St. Pierre and Miquelon, which had been ceded to the French for carrying on their fishery; and no resistance being made, all the inhabitants were, by agreement, transported to France.

The southern states had for a considerable time partaken little in the ravages of war, and Georgia, the most remote from the scene of action, was carrying on its traffic nearly as in peace, when towards the close of the year, an expedition was planned against it by the commander in chief. For this purpose, a force of British and Hessians under Colonel Campbell, escorted by a small squadron of ships of war commanded by Commodore Hyde Parker, sailed from Sandy Hook on November 27th, which arrived at the mouth of the river Savannah on December 23d. The troops on landing proceeded with little opposition to the town of Savannah, the capital of the colony, and having completely defeated the American force under a General Howe drawn up for its defence, they obtained possession of the fort with its garrison, the town, and the shipping of the river, without farther resistance. The American general withdrew with the remains of his army to South Carolina, and in less than a fortnight, the whole province was reduced to submission to the British Government, with the exception of the town of Sunbury, which afterwards fell to a body of troops brought against it by General Prevost, governor of East Florida.

Notice has already been taken of the difficulties which met the commissioners who were the bearers of those conciliatory proposals that had been sent to America from the British ministry. As the congress refused to open any negotiation without a previous acknowledgement of independency, or the removal of all the British military force, one of the commissioners, Governor Johnstone, who by a former residence had made many connections in the colonies, endeavoured to renew a correspondence with some private friends who were members of the congress. A lady was employed as the medium, and money was offered as a reward for those who should exert their influence in promoting the object of the commission. This secret practice being made known to the congress, they passed a declaration on the subject, and sent it by a flag to the commissioners at New York, in which they expressed high indignation at an attempt to corrupt their integrity, and declared "that it was incompatible with the honour of Congress to hold any manner of correspondence or intercourse with George Johnstone, Esq. especially to negotiate with him upon affairs in which the cause of liberty and virtue is interested." This personal attack drew forth an exceedingly angry reply from that gentleman, who absolutely disowned the most objectionable transaction imputed to him; and a paper war ensued between the commissioners and the congress, carried on with great acrimony on both sides. At length, on October 3d, the commissioners, on the eve of departure, issued a manifesto, some of the declarations of which were afterwards the subject of parliamentary discussion. Affirming that the whole question between the colonies and the mother country was changed since their alliance with France, they say, "under such circumstances the laws of self-preservation must direct the conduct, of Great Britain; and if the British colonies are to become an accession to France, will direct her to render that accession of as little avail as possible to her enemy." This menace, as it was understood, of a war of absolute destruction, was returned by a counter manifesto of the congress, in which they threatened the most complete retaliatory vengeance; and thus the final attempt at conciliation had no other effect than to aggravate the mutual exasperation of the parties.

The new war commenced with France soon disclosed itself by the usual hostilities in the West India Islands, the unprotected state of the British part of which had been long a subject of complaint to government. Dominica, which by its situation between Martinico and Guadaloupe, is particularly exposed to danger, had indeed been strengthened with fortifications at a great expence since its cession to England, but its garrison was much too weak for their defence. On September 7th the Marquis de Bouillé landed 2000 men upon this island, and all resistance to such a force being unavailing, a surrender by capitulation was almost immediately negotiated by Lieutenant-Governor Stuart, and the terms granted were extremely liberal. From some causes, the conveyance of intelligence from England to the West Indies had been so defective, that Admiral Barrington, who lay with a naval force at Barbadoes, was first informed of hostilities between the two nations by a document from Paris published at Martinico in the middle of August.

In the beginning of November, D'Estaign quitted Boston with his fleet and sailed for the West Indies. On the day of his departure, a detachment of about 5000 men under Major-General Grant, which was dispatched by Sir Henry Clinton for the protection of the West India Islands, sailed from Sandy Hook under the convoy of Commodore Hotham; and the fleets might probably have fallen in with each other on the passage, had not that of D'Estaign been dispersed by a violent gale. Hotham, having kept his ships better together, reached Barbadoes, on December 10th, where he joined Admiral Barrington; and an expedition was immediately undertaken against the French island of St. Lucia, the troops employed in it being placed under the command of Brigadier-General Meadows. They were landed upon the island on the 13th, and immediately took possession of some heights occupied by the Chevalier de Micoud, the commandant, with the regulars and militia of the island. General Prescot in the meantime landed five regiments in the same bay, and on the next day the small capital of Morne Fortune was entered by the British. General Meadows pushed on against the retreating French, and had carried several important posts when D'Estaign's fleet came in sight, which, besides his original force of twelve ships of the line, consisted of a great number of frigates and transports, conveying troops estimated at 9000 men. Admiral Barrington was lying in Cul de Sac bay with a force of no more than four ships of the line, two of 50 guns, and three frigates, and with this disproportion he prepared to receive the enemy's attack.

This was made in two separate attempts, both of which were unsuccessful, and D'Estaign afterwards bore away to another part of the island and landed his troops. He then led 5000 of his best men against General Meadows, who, with about 1300, was entrenched on a peninsula, the approach to which was enfiladed by a chain of batteries. The onset was desperate, and thrice repeated; but at length the French were obliged to give up the contest, after a loss in killed and wounded greater than the whole number of their opponents. D'Estaign remained ten days longer on the island, without any farther attempt either by land or sea. At length he re-embarked his troops, leaving St. Lucia to its fate, which capitulated before he was out of sight.

Whilst the war was thus commencing in the Western Indies, it had been opened with great effect in the eastern possessions of the contending powers. The English East India Company, soon after the delivery of the French declaration, not doubting that hostilities must be the consequence, sent instructions to Madras for immediate undertaking the siege of Pondicherry. Fortunately they were conveyed with unusual expedition, and early in August Major-General Monro had assembled a body of troops in the vicinity of that town. Sir Edward Vernon, the British naval commander in those seas, had previously sailed with his small squadron to block up the port of Pondicherry, where he encountered a French squadron of somewhat superior force under M. de Tronjoly. An indecisive action ensued, after which the French went into Pondicherry to refit. Sir Edward returning to his station some days after, the French commander came out, as if for the purpose of engaging; but during the night he made off to sea, leaving the English to their blockade without molestation. The place was at this time closely invested by land, and batteries were opened against it. The gallantry of the commander and garrison prolonged the defence to October 17th, when an intended assault was prevented by an offer to capitulate. This was accepted, and honourable terms were granted to the garrison. The reduction of Pondicherry, with the previous capture of several French factories and settlements by the Company's forces in Bengal and elsewhere, entirely annihilated the power of that nation in the East Indies.

Parliament was opened on November 25th by a speech from the throne, the leading topic of which was complaint against the court of France for its unprovoked acts of hostility. Notice was then taken of the measures which had been employed for disappointing the malignant designs of the enemy, and making reprisals; and it was observed, that "although our efforts had not been attended with all the success which the justice of our cause and the vigour of our exertions seemed to promise," yet that the commerce of the nation had been protected, and large reprisals had been made upon the aggressors. The failure of the conciliatory measures adopted with respect to America was then regretted; and a confidence was finally expressed in the concurrence and support of parliament for those exertions which would maintain the honour of the crown and the interests of the people. Some parts of this speech offered matter to the opposition for objecting to the usual respond-ing addresses, and amendments were moved which occasioned vigorous debates. In the House of Commons an amendment of this kind was rejected by a majority of 226 to 107. In the House of Lords no specific amendment was proposed, but a division occurred on the address, which was carried by 67 to 35. A copy of the manifesto of the commissioners in America being laid before parliament, Mr. Coke, in the House of Commons, and the Marquis of Rockingham in the House of Lords, made motions for addresses to his Majesty to express the displeasure of parliament at those passages which announced a new principle of conducting the war; and very strong censures were passed in the subsequent debates by the opposition, on a declaration of a nature, as they represented it, so repugnant to humanity. The motions were negatived in both houses by majorities, which in the House of Commons were considerably less than two to one.

The parties and discontents which had long prevailed in the navy broke out into a flame towards the close of the year, and engaged the notice of parliament as well as of the nation at large. Admiral Keppel, in his public dispatch after the battle of July 27th with the French fleet, had bestowed encomiums on the conduct of the other commanders, and had imputed his not renewing the engagement late in the evening solely to an expectation that the enemy might be brought to fair action on the next morning. The result, however, being such as occasioned a general disappointment, the circumstances of the battle were canvassed in the fleet, and blame was imputed according as party or favour directed. At length a letter appeared in a newspaper, which was attributed to an officer who had been present in the engagement, directly charging the escape of the French fleet to the disobedience of signals by the vice-admiral of the blue, Sir Hugh Palliser. The latter thereupon applied to Admiral Keppel, requiring him to sign and publish a paper asserting that his calling into his wake on the evening of July 27th, the two vice-admirals, was not for the purpose of then renewing the battle, but of being in readiness for the next day. The admiral refusing to do this, Sir Hugh published under his own name, in one of the morning papers, a long statement of particulars of the action, containing much direct or implied censure of the conduct of the commander in chief; in consequence of which proceeding, Admiral Keppel declared to the first Lord of the Admiralty, that without a satisfactory explanation he could never again go to sea with the vice-admiral of the blue. In this state the affair stood at the meeting of parliament, when, on the first day of the session, the Earl of Bristol called upon the first Lord of the Admiralty for an enquiry into the conduct of the naval officers on July 27th. That minister expressed the warmest disapprobation of such an enquiry, and declared his conviction that both the officers in question had honourably performed their duty. The matter was brought on in the House of Commons in a debate on the voting 70,000 seamen for the ensuing year, by Mr. Luttrell, who said that the case demanded an immediate investigation; and both the admirals being then present each gave his own statement of the occurrences. That of Admiral Keppel containing a direct assertion that the signal for coming into his wake had been flying from three in the afternoon till eight in the evening without being obeyed, Mr. Luttrell immediately moved for an address to his Majesty for an order to bring Sir Hugh Palliser to a trial. A very warm speech followed from Sir Hugh, in which he informed the house, that finding no other mode of obtaining redress for the attacks on his honour, he had already demanded from the admiralty a court martial on Admiral Keppel, which had been granted. This declaration occasioned great surprize in the house, and many severe censures were passed on the conduct of the admiralty on the occasion. A general sympathy was shewn for Admiral Keppel, a man much beloved, who made a pathetic speech, which concluded with his thanking God that he was the *accused* and not the *accuser*; after which he left the house. The debate ended by moving for the order of the day, which set aside Mr. Luttrell's motion. On December 16th, Admiral Pigot moved for a bill to enable the admiralty to hold the trial of Admiral Keppel in some place on shore, instead of on ship-board, on account of his state of health, which was carried. The sequel of this unpleasant business belongs to the following year.

This year witnessed the commencement of a war in Europe between two powers, the magnitude and martial character of whose forces seemed likely to renew those scenes of sanguinary contest which had devastated Germany in the late conflict of seven years. The extinction of the Guillelmine line of Bavaria, by the death of the Elector Joseph Maximilian in December 1777, had assigned the succession of his estates to the Elector Palatine of the Rhine, who took peaceable possession of them. He found, however, a formidable competitor in the house of Austria, which, reviving some obsolete claims, enforced them by marching an army into the country. The elector, unable to oppose an effectual resistance, entered into a convention, by which he ceded the better half of Bavaria to the empress-queen. Against this agreement, the next heir, the Duke of Deux Ponts, together with some other German princes, entered a protest; and the King of Prussia, jealous of the aggrandisement of Austria, declared himself a supporter of the rights of the Germanic body. Negotiations were set on foot, but the court of Vienna haughtily persevered in its claims. The Elector of Saxony united himself with Frederic, who resolved upon an appeal to the sword. He took the field in person, as did the Emperor Joseph on the other side; and perhaps more numerous troops, better appointed, and more ably commanded, had never been assembled to decide a political contest. The King of Prussia in July marched to the borders of Bohemia, whilst another army invaded Austrian Silesia. The emperor was opposed to the king, and each was attended by the most distinguished generals in his service. The plan of the Austrians was defensive; and a campaign of marches and counter-marches ensued, in which all the resources of military science were exhausted. So equally was the great game played, that not one considerable action was brought on, though sharp skirmishes were frequent. At length, Frederic, unable to penetrate into Bohemia, withdrew in September from the frontiers, and returned to his own dominions, having, as well as the Austrians, incurred great loss among his troops by sickness and desertion.

1779

19th & 20th Year of the Reign

THE public attention was very generally engaged at the beginning of the year by the trial of Admiral Keppel, which commenced at Portsmouth on January 7th. Some days before, a memorial had been presented to the king, signed by twelve admirals, Lord Hawke being at the head of the list, strongly condemning the conduct of the accuser, and stating with great energy the mischievous consequences which would result to the naval service and discipline from establishing the precedent and principle now introduced. No effect was, however, produced by it. The court martial, after employing 30 days in examining the evidence on both sides, gave a full and honourable acquittal of the admiral, of every accusation brought against him, and declared that the charge was malicious and ill founded. On the subsequent day, February 12th, a motion was made in the House of Commons to present thanks to Admiral Keppel for his conduct during the course of the last summer, and particularly "for his having gloriously upheld the honour of the British flag on the 27th and 28th of July last," which was carried with only one dissentient voice. A similar motion passed unanimously in the House of Lords. As the conduct of the admiralty in this business was supposed to have been influenced by party, and the admiral was regarded as an intended sacrifice, extraordinary rejoicings celebrated his acquittal, especially in the cities of London and Westminster, attended with violent marks of popular odium towards the persons who were conceived to have had a share in the prosecution. The resignation by Sir Hugh Palliser of his seat at the admiralty board, of his lieutenant-generalship of marines, and his government of Scarborough castle, and also of his seat in parliament, attested his consciousness of the weight of public opinion against him, though he was universally considered as a brave and skilful officer, and in the very action in question, had behaved, when engaged, with distinguished valour.

The blame attached to Lord Sandwich in this affair brought upon him, in the House of Commons, three motions of censure relative to the state and disposition of the navy, and one for his removal from his Majesty's service. The first of these, made by Mr. Fox on March 3d, related to the inadequate force with which Admiral Keppel was for the first time sent to cruise off the French coast; and the charge was brought so home, that the motion was negatived by no greater majority than 204 to 170. Administration having afterwards rallied its forces, the subsequent divisions were more in its favour. The discontents in the navy, however, continued to augment, and several officers of high rank and reputation either relinquished the service altogether, or declined acting under the present admiralty board.

The bill for prohibiting members of parliament from being concerned in government contracts, was again introduced in this session, but was rejected on the motion for a second reading, by 164 to 124.

The liberal spirit displayed in the relief granted in the last session to the Roman Catholics, encouraged the dissenters to apply for a further exemption to their ministers and schoolmasters, from the penalties to which they still by law remained liable. A bill for the purpose was moved in the House of Commons by Sir Henry Hoghton, and seconded by Mr. Frederic Montague; and the opposition to it was so inconsiderable, that a motion by the representative of the university of Oxford, for putting it off for four months, was supported by only 6 votes against 77. It passed without difficulty through the Lords, and received the royal assent in the course of the session.

The distressed condition of Ireland, owing to the American war, and the embargo upon the exportation of provisions, occasioned a notice to be given in the House of Commons of an intention to move for one or more bills for affording commercial relief to that country; and that an alarm might not be excited among the British manufacturers, the first attempt was a motion by Lord Newhaven, on March 10th, for a committee of the house to take into consideration the acts of parliament relating to the importation of sugars from the West Indies into Ireland; the object of which was a repeal of that clause in the act of navigation, which obliged every ship laden with sugar to bring its cargo directly to England, whence the necessary quantity for the consumption of Ireland might afterwards be re-exported. The motion was carried by a majority of 47 to 42, the minister not interfering in the question; but petitions being received against the intended measures from Glasgow and Manchester, in which towns the friends of administration began to accuse Lord North of duplicity, he exerted his influence, so that the motion for the Speaker's quitting the chair, in order that the committee might be formed, was lost on a division by 62 to 58.

The unprecedented amount of the army extraordinaries, exceeding two millions, occasioning a motion from a member in opposition, that the estimates should be printed for the use of the members, it was opposed by the minister as a matter improper to be submitted to the discussion of coffee-house politicians, and on a division, was rejected by 130 to 104.

Admiral Pigot, on April 16th, having entered into a detail of the circumstances attending the government of his late brother, Lord Pigot, moved for an address to his Majesty, praying that he would give directions to the attorney-general, for prosecuting four persons by name, on account of their arrest and confinement of their governor and commander in chief, Lord Pigot. One of these gentlemen, Mr. Stratton, who was present, spoke in justification of his conduct and that of his colleagues, but the motion was carried without opposition.

The ill success of the principal military operations in America having caused much public dissatisfaction, and blame having been loudly imputed either to the commanders or the ministry as party feelings suggested, the two brothers, Admiral and General Howe, strongly insisted upon the necessity of an enquiry into the conduct of the war, particularly as far as they were immediately concerned in it; and after long and warm debates, a committee for this purpose was appointed by the House of Commons, which began to act on May 6th. The officers called upon for examination, were Earl Cornwallis, Major-General Grey, Sir Andrew Snape Hammond, Major Montresor, and Sir George Osborne, whose united testimony went to establish the facts, that the force sent to America was at no time adequate to the subjugation of the country, and that the difficulties proceeded in great measure from the almost unanimous aversion of the people to the British government, added to the nature of the country, which was particularly unfavourable to military operations. They also concurred in many points of detail, in justification of the commanders on particular occasions for which they had undergone censure. On the other side, Major-General Robertson, and Mr. Galloway, a member of the first congress, who had come over after General Howe's first successes, were examined, and gave evidence contradictory to the opinions advanced by the officers above-mentioned. During the sitting of the committee, General Burgoyne, whose character had been very severely treated, procured an enquiry into his conduct which was attended with many respectable testimonials in its favour. After a great deal of time spent in these different examinations, which elicited much curious and important matter, the committee on some pretext of delay was suddenly dissolved, without having come to any determination.

The House of Lords had in the meantime been much occupied in discussions and debates relative to the state of the navy, the conduct of the first lord of the admiralty, and the abuses in Greenwich hospital, which it is unnecessary to specify as the motions brought on by the opposition were all defeated by large majorities.

On June 16th the Spanish ambassador to the court of Great Britain, presented a manifesto amounting to a declaration of war, and notified his immediate departure from this country. The document contained a great number of lax and general charges against the conduct of England, the insults and injuries inflicted by which were said to have lately amounted to just one hundred. One piece of information, hitherto kept secret, which it communicated was, that Spain had been applied to as a mediator in the quarrel between England and France, and had actually been negotiating a treaty of peace between them for the last eight months. This manifesto being communicated by a message from the crown to both houses of parliament, the usual addresses, assuring his Majesty of an unshaken resolution to support the crown and the country with their lives and fortunes, were moved. In the House of Commons the address was unanimously voted, though, not without some severe strictures on the blindness of ministers, in not foreseeing this event. In the House of Lords amendments were proposed, but were negatived. As the addition of a new enemy required additional force for defence, a proposal of doubling the militia was introduced by Lord North, which was carried in the House of Commons, after a clause had been added on the motion of

Lord Beauchamp, for allowing volunteer companies to be raised and attached to the militia regiments of the county or district. Its fate was different in the House of Lords, where the compulsory part of it was strongly objected to, not only by the opposition, but by the lord president of the council, and the two secretaries of state, and upon a division it was rejected by a majority of 39 to 22. Being sent back to the Commons with no other effective part than Lord Beauchamp's clause, it passed by 63 votes to 45. At the same time with this bill, another was introduced for taking away for a limited time the legal exemptions from being pressed into the navy, which, after a considerable opposition, and an amendment in favour of the colliers, was carried through both houses. Parliament was prorogued on July 3d.

Among the domestic occurrences of the year, the manifestation of a fanatical spirit in Scotland deserves particular notice, on account of the very serious consequences of which it was the fore-runner.

The passing of the bill in favour of the oppressed English Roman Catholics induced some gentlemen in Scotland to form a design of proposing its extension to that country in the ensuing session of parliament; to which they were encouraged by the circumstance, that the general assembly being sitting at the time that the act was first in agitation, a motion for remonstrating against it was rejected by a majority of more than a hundred voices. A spirit, however, was rising among the zealots, unfavourable to such an indulgence to the professors of a religion long the object of peculiar abhorrence; and its effects, fostered by the circulation of a virulent pamphlet, soon appeared in some of the provincial synods, where resolutions were passed and published expressive of a determination to resist every attempt for the relief of the catholics. At the same time, some bigots, chiefly of the lower class, in Edinburgh and Glasgow, formed an association for the like purpose, which assumed the appellation of friends to the protestant interest. These persons, by their activity in diffusing pamphlets, hand-bills, and newspaper letters, kindled a flame throughout the country, by which such an odium was excited against the catholics, that, dreading the consequences, they requested that the intention of applying for a bill in their favour might be laid aside; and accordingly it was made publicly known that this had been done. Fanaticism, however, was not thus to be appeased; and letters were dropt in the streets of Edinburgh, calling upon the people to pull down a "pillar of popery" lately erected. A mob was, in consequence assembled on the night of February 2d, which proceeded to attack a building occupied by the catholic clergyman or bishop and some other families of that persuasion, and containing a room meant to serve as a chapel, but not yet used for that purpose. The building was pillaged and set on fire; and a party of the mob was then detached against the old catholic chapel, the inside of which, and of the house containing it, were demolished with all their furniture, and a considerable library belonging to the bishop was destroyed or carried away. The rioters then committed outrages on the property and habitations of some catholic tradesmen; and their threats obliged two ladies of fashion of that communion to take refuge in the castle.

These disorders continued with no effectual check from the magistrates, for some days; and at length the rioters, carrying their designs further, attacked the house of Principal Robertson and Mr. Crosbie an eminent advocate, who they considered as promoters of the intended bill, but they found them so well defended, that they withdrew after breaking some windows. Some dragoons were now called in for the protection of the town but peace was not restored till the Lord Provost issued a proclamation in which he took upon himself to assure the *well-meaning* people that no repeal of the penal statutes against papists should take place. Similar riots occurred at Glasgow, and the house and manufactory of a catholic potter were destroyed; but the exertions of the magistrates and principal inhabitants soon restored tranquillity.

The opposition made by the manufacturing interest in Great Britain to the removal of the severe restrictions imposed on the Irish commerce, occasioned a meeting at the Tholsel of Dublin, April 16th, in which resolutions were entered into against the importation and use of goods of British manufacture or product, which could be made or produced in Ireland.

In America, the possession of Georgia by the British forces excited hope on the one part, and apprehension on the other, respecting the two Carolinas. The loyalists, or Tories, as they were called, in the back settlements of North Carolina, began to move in consequence of this event, and assembled to the number of about 700. They were, however, entirely defeated by the militia of the neighbourhood, and only about 300 of them were able to make their way to the royal army in Georgia. General Prevost, now the British commander in chief in that quarter, found it advisable to concentrate his force in the vicinity of Savannah; and in the meantime the American General Lincoln arrived with a reinforcement of continental troops for the protection of South Carolina, and took post on the opposite side of the border river about twenty miles above Savannah. Higher up the river was posted a body of provincials and militia under General Ashe, who was directed by Lincoln to cross over into Georgia, and take a strong position on Briar Creek. This being done, Lieutenant-Colonel Prevost, who commanded a detachment of the British army, formed a plan of surprizing Ashe, which he effected on March 2d, putting to flight the whole body with great loss, and clearing the province of the enemy. A subsequent movement of Lincoln with the greatest part of his forces leaving the passage of the river into South Carolina guarded only by a body of militia, General Prevost determined to make a push for Charleston, where he was led by the loyalists to expect a friendly reception; accordingly, marching with about 3000 men, he readily dispersed the militia, and on May 11th took post nearly within cannon shot of Charleston. On the next day he summoned the town to surrender, but the negotiation for the purpose proved fruitless, and preparations were made for a vigorous defence, in the expectation of an immediate attack. Prevost, however, finding himself entirely disappointed in the hopes held out to him, and expecting the speedy approach of Lincoln with a superior army, thought it most prudent to break up his camp without loss of time. He crossed Ashley river during the night, and led his troops to the islands which lie to the southward of Charleston harbour, where he lay waiting for supplies of ammunition and necessaries from New York. On receiving them, he moved the army to the island of Port Royal between Charleston and Savannah. An attack made by General Lincoln on a detachment under Lieutenant-Colonel Maitland, posted at Stono ferry on June 20th, was repulsed with considerable loss to the assailants.

In the beginning of May, an expedition from New York was sent to the Chesapeak, under Sir G. Collier and Major-General Mathew, which proceeding up Elizabeth river in Virginia, took possession of the towns of Portsmouth, Norfolk, and Suffolk, burned and captured a great number of vessels, and destroyed a vast quantity of provisions and stores destined for Washington's army. Having demolished the fort which defended Portsmouth, and set fire to the buildings of the dock-yard, they returned before the expiration of the month.

A more important object which at this time engaged the attention of Sir Henry Clinton, was the possession of two strong works on the Hudson's river in the Highlands, called Verplanks and Stoney-point, and commanding the communication between the eastern and western colonies, which the Americans had nearly completed, but not yet rendered defensible. The troops for this service were placed under the command of General Vaughan, and the naval armament under that of Sir G. Collier; and the expedition proceeded up the river on May 30th. No effectual resistance could be made to such a force, and the forts were occupied by the British troops, and put in a complete state of defence. Several desultory attacks were afterwards made on the coast of Connecticut, by which a number of the small privateers which swarmed in its harbours were destroyed, and some towns were consumed, with much merchandize and other effects. Washington, on the intelligence of the capture of the forts upon Hudson's river, removed his army from the Jerseys to the mountainous country in their neighbourhood, but without abandoning his cautious plan of avoiding a general engagement. Whilst the hostile armies were occupied in watching each other's motions, the American General Wayne was employed to surprise the fort of Stoney-point, which he very gallantly effected on July 15th, carrying the strong works at the bayonet's point, and making the garrison prisoners of war. Measures being immediately taken by the commander in chief for its recovery, the fort was abandoned by the Americans, after destroying the works and carrying off the artillery and stores.

Early in the year, a French squadron under the Marquis de Vaudreuil, on its way to join D'Estaign, made a sweep of all the English forts and settlements at Senegal, in the river Gambia, and at other parts of the African coast, which were incapable of any resistance.

Admiral Byron arrived in the West Indies soon after the surrender of St. Lucia, and took the chief command of the fleet, which, by his junction with Admiral Barrington's squadrons was become superior to that of the French. Many fruitless attempts were made to draw out D'Estaign to an action and in the meantime the British troops at St. Lucia were suffering a dreadful mortality from the unhealthiness of that island. In June, Byron having sailed with his whole squadron to convoy the trade of the West India islands part of the way to England, the French sent out a small equipment from Martinico which, landing in St. Vincent's, gained possession of that island without a shot fired, the hostility of the Caribbs, who joined the invaders immediately upon their landing, having apparently been the cause of this easy conquest. D'Estaign, being joined by a reinforcement under La Motte Piquet, now put to sea, and in the beginning of July arrived with a numerous fleet, and a large body of land forces off the island of Grenada, which was very slenderly garrisoned. He landed two or three thousand men under Count Dillon, who invested the fortified hill on which the governor, Lord Macartney, was posted. The French were repulsed on the first attack, but they afterwards made a lodgement which obliged the governor to propose terms of capitulation. These were haughtily rejected by D'Estaign, and it became necessary to surrender at discretion. Byron now returned, and being unacquainted with the strength of the French fleet, he sailed to the relief of Grenada. On July 6th the fleets were in sight of each other, the British consisting of 21 ships of the line and one frigate; the French of 25 or 26 of the line and 12 frigates. The action which ensued was irregular, and some ships of the English fleet were much more engaged than others. The result was, that the island having been discovered to be already in the possession of the enemy, and some disabled vessels being obliged to quit the line, Admiral Byron returned to St. Christopher's, and D'Estaign remained at Grenada. The loss of men by the French was much more considerable than that of the English and though the former claimed the victory, no further attempt was made upon the British islands.

In the month of August, Don Galvez, the Spanish governor of Louisiana, having collected his force at New Orleans, marched against the British settlements on the Mississippi, which he captured, with the few troops by which they were protected.

A naval occurrence of some importance took place about this time in the northern part of the American continent. A British detachment from Halifax having established a post on the river Penobscot, the alarm excited by it at Boston caused a considerable armament to be fitted out under Commodore

Saltonstall, with some land forces on board, for dispossessing them. It arrived, to the number of 37 sail, in the river on July 25th, and began to batter the fort, and three British sloops of war, which assisted in the defence. The attack was persisted in for a fortnight, when Sir G. Collier with his squadron from New York, who had been dispatched for the relief of the place, came in sight. The Americans immediately abandoned their works, and their shipping ran up the river. Being pursued they set fire to their own vessels, the whole of which were destroyed, with the exception of two ships of 20 and 18 guns which were taken. Those blown up amounted to 17 armed vessels, from a frigate of 32 guns downwards, and more than 20 transports, and nothing could be more complete than the success of the British.

The Americans finding little occupation for their arms in the vicinity of New York, determined to take a severe vengeance in the autumn on the hostile Indians for their cruelties on the frontiers. For this purpose a force was prepared under the command of General Sullivan, which marched against the tribes called the confederacy of the five nations. The Indians, headed by Butler, Brandt, and other chiefs, and joined by some hundreds of Tories, advanced to meet the invaders, and posted themselves behind a strong breast-work at a pass in the woods. They were here attacked, and so completely defeated that they never again ventured to make a stand; and Sullivan penetrating into the interior of the country which he found well cultivated and inhabited, utterly destroyed a great number of their towns and settlements, cutting down their fruit trees, and laying waste all the products of the fields.

D'Estaign, in the beginning of September, with 22 ships of the line, arrived on the American coast, where an English 50 gun ship and two frigates fell into his hands; and on the 9th he anchored off Savannah. General Prevost was at this time in Savannah, but the greater part of his force was at the isle of Port Royal. The French commander disembarked his troops, and being joined by the Americans under General Lincoln, invested Prevost in his lines, who had now been reinforced by Colonel Maitland with the troops from Port Royal. A severe cannonade and bombardment being carried on against the town, the general wrote a letter to D'Estaign, requesting permission to put the women and children on board ships in the river, under the protection of a French man of war, which was brutally refused. On October 9th a furious assault was made by the allied army, which was resisted with so much gallantry and skill, that after a long combat the assailants were repulsed with great slaughter. They soon after abandoned their camp; and D'Estaign returning to his fleet, quitted the American coast, and proceeded with part of his ships to France, sending the rest to the West Indies. Although this commander had effected much less than was expected from the force entrusted to him, yet his appearance on the American coast had excited great alarm at New York, where it was supposed that he was to make a junction with Washington and attack the British army. It was therefore thought expedient to draw the troops from Rhode Island, and suffer that place to revert to the possession of the Americans.

After the departure of D'Estaign from the West Indies, the Admirals Parker and Rowley preserved a decided superiority over the French Fleet under La Motte Piquet, which enabled them greatly to distress the trade of that nation. They took a great part of a convoy within his view at Fort Royal, and he himself only escaped falling into their hands by good seamanship. Three large French frigates were captured on their return from Savannah to Martinico.

The Spaniards having molested the English logwood cutters on the Mosquito and Honduras shores, a force was sent from Jamaica for their succour; and a squadron of frigates was detached from Admiral Parker's fleet to cruise in the bay of Honduras, in order to intercept the Spanish register ships. Some of these having taken shelter in the harbour of

Fort Omoa, an expedition was undertaken for the reduction of that strong fortress. On October 16th it was assaulted by a small combined force of soldiers and sailors, and carried after extraordinary exertions of valour. A very rich booty was obtained from the vessels in the port, and a garrison was left in the castle, which was afterwards so much diminished by the unhealthiness of the climate, that the place was recovered by the Spaniards.

The war in Europe, being only subordinate to that beyond the Atlantic, afforded few memorable events during the present year. An attempt upon the Isle of Jersey, by a French armament under the command of a titular Prince of Nassau, was repulsed with little loss on either side.

A great plan was formed by the united powers of France and Spain for an expedition to the English coasts, probably with the purpose of a partial invasion should a favourable opportunity occur. The French fleet of about 28 sail of the line commanded by M. d'Orvilliers sailed from Brest on June 4th, and forming a junction with that of Spain off Cadiz, they bent their course northwards, to the formidable amount of between 60 and 70 line of battle ships, with a vast attendance of frigates and smaller armed vessels. They entered the British channel about the middle of August, having passed unobserved the English fleet of about 38 sail, cruizing under Sir Charles Hardy in the Bay of Biscay. The combined fleets appeared for two or three days before Plymouth, where they excited a great and well-founded alarm, as the means of defence in that important place were shamefully deficient. No attempt against it was however made, and the fleets for some time after ranged about the Land's-end and the Scilly Isles. On the 31st of August Sir Charles Hardy came in sight, entering the channel. He was pursued by the combined fleets as far as Plymouth; but the equinox now approaching, and the fleets being in an extremely sickly state, with many ships greatly out of condition, they returned to Brest, having performed nothing in the least worthy of one of the most powerful armaments ever seen in those seas.

The celebrated siege of Gibraltar had its commencement in the present summer, the reduction of that fortress being apparently a principal object of the court of Spain in entering into the war.

Whilst Great Britain was thus urged by perils from foreign force, discontents were prevailing in the empire itself, which greatly added to the hazard of her situation, and the embarrassment of her rulers. Notice has already been taken of the measures adopted in Ireland to obtain redress for the restrictions under which the commerce of that country was still permitted to labour. Something more effectual was however determined upon, and for this, the present unprotected state of that island, from which the military force had been continually drained by the exigencies of the American war, afforded a plausible pretext. Under the necessity, as it was represented, of providing for self-defence, associations were entered into for raising volunteer corps, which soon became universal, comprising all ranks and parties. To enter into them was regarded as an act of patriotism which it would be highly disgraceful to decline, and men of the first fortune served in the ranks. All this was done with admirable order, and the internal tranquillity of the country was never better preserved. Government, however, could not fail to look with some apprehension upon a state of things which seemed to take the island out of their controul; and they made some attempts to bring this newly-created force under the regulation and authority of the crown; but their aim being entirely frustrated, they prudently seemed to concur in a scheme now beyond their power to defeat, and furnished a supply of arms to the volunteers. The nation, feeling its strength, now began to consider of its rights; and a free and unlimited commerce with all the world was an object which it resolved to pursue. The Irish parliament, which met in October, declared in their

addresses to the throne, that nothing short of such a concession could save the country from ruin; and in order that their
farther proceedings might not be intercepted by a prorogation,
they passed a money bill of six months only.

Some changes in the English ministry, though of no
political importance, took place in November. Earl Gower
resigned the place of lord president of the council, in which
he was succeeded by Earl Bathurst. The northern secretaryship, which had been some months vacant in consequence
of the death of the Earl of Suffolk, was assigned to Lord
Stormont, late ambassador to the court of France; and the
Earl of Hillsborough was appointed to that of the southern
department in the room of Lord Weymouth who resigned.

Parliament met on November 25th, when the King's speech,
and the addresses upon it, afforded matter for very warm
debates in both houses. The ministers were attacked with
more than usual severity on the dangerous state into which the
country was brought under their direction; they were however
supported by majorities sufficiently efficient, though less than
those of the earlier periods of the war.

The affairs of Ireland were brought into immediate
consideration by a motion of the Earl of Shelburne for a
resolution declaring the ministers highly criminal in having
neglected to take measures for the relief of Ireland in
consequence of the address of the House of Lords to his Majesty
in May last. The subsequent debate was rendered remarkable
by the declaration of the late president of the council, that
he was fully convinced that the charge brought against the
ministers was strictly true; that if nothing had been effected
for the relief of Ireland, it was not his fault; he had done
every thing in his power to keep the promise he had given
for this purpose, but his efforts had been totally fruitless. The
motion, however, was rejected by a majority of more than two
to one. After a similar motion had be made and rejected in the
House of Commons, Lord North, on December 13th, brought

forward his own propositions for affording relief to Ireland. They consisted in, first, a repeal of the laws prohibiting the export of the Irish woollen manufactures from Ireland to any part of Europe: second, a repeal of the prohibition of importing glass except of British manufacture into Ireland, and of exporting glass from thence: third, permission to the Irish to carry on a direct export and import trade with the British colonies in America, and the West Indies, and on the coast of Africa, under regulations to be imposed by the parliament of Ireland. Such was the present temper of the houses, that these propositions were agreed to without the least opposition, and bills were brought in on the two former, before the recess.

Motions were made by the Duke of Richmond and the Earl of Shelburne respecting the enormous expenditure of the public money, especially under the head of army extraordinaries; and though they were defeated by majorities, they made a great impression on the public at large; and the necessity of strict economy in the arduous contest in which the nation was engaged, appeared to be admitted by all parties.

The war between the Austrian Emperor and the King of Prussia was renewed in the spring; but both sides were now fully sensible of the seriousness of the contest in which they were involved, while the other continental powers exerted their influence to put an end to a dispute which endangered the tranquillity of all Europe. An armistice being therefore agreed upon in March, a congress was held at Teschen in Silesia, under the mediation of France and Russia, which was productive of a treaty of peace signed on May 13th. By its conditions, the convention between the court of Vienna and the Elector Palatine was annulled, and the former restored all the places and districts seized by it in Bavaria, except a part which was ceded to Austria as an indemnification for her claims. Cessions and indemnifications were granted to the house of Saxony, and other matters in dispute were adjusted upon equitable principles. On the whole, the emperor's ambitious views were defeated, and Frederic gained the honour of being the champion of the Germanic body.

Some disputes which occurred between Russia and the Porte relative to the fulfilment of the articles of the late peace, and which threatened a renewal of hostilities, were accommodated by the interposition of France.

1780

20th & 21st Year of the Reign

THE general ill success of the war, the alarming circumstances in which the nation was placed, and the loud complaints against ministers, often rather refuted by votes than by reasonings, had now widely diffused a spirit of discontent which, at the commencement of this year, manifested itself by the meetings of a great number of counties for the purpose of framing petitions to parliament for the redress of grievances. The county of York took the lead, and in a petition signed by persons of the first consequence, both clergy and laity, stated in strong terms the evils arising from the war, the wastefulness of expenditure, the unconstitutional influence acquired by the crown in consequence of the increase of places and pensions, and the absolute necessity of correcting these abuses before new burdens were imposed on the people. The county of Middlesex succeeded, and the example was followed by a number of other counties and towns, some with greater, some with less unanimity. In some associations were entered into, and committees were named to further the objects in view, a measure which was objected to in others, as too close an imitation of America and Ireland. After the Christmas recess these petitions were presented to the House of Commons, Sir George Saville leading the way with that of Yorkshire. A petition was about the same time presented from Jamaica, complaining in very strong language of the negligence of ministers in providing for the safety of that important island.

On February 11th, Mr. Burke, in a speech, regarded as one of the greatest efforts of that celebrated orator and statesman, introduced to the House of Commons his plan, "For the better security of the independence of parliament, and the economic reformation of the civil and other establishments." It consisted of five separate bills, of which the objects were the abolition of useless places, the sale of crown lands and forests, and the union to the crown of the detached jurisdiction of Wales, and the Duchies of Lancaster and Cornwall. The extensive information and comprehensive views displayed in these bills, and in the introductory matter, commanded general admiration, and no opposition was made to the motion for bringing them in, except with regard to that relative to the duchy of Cornwall, which was objected to on account of the minority of the Prince of Wales, and was therefore withdrawn. Various motions for the controul of the expenditure were made by other members, some of which were lost, and others carried. Among the latter was a proposition by Colonel Barré, for the appointment of a commission of accounts, which was adopted by the minister. A motion by Sir George Saville, for an account of all subsisting pensions granted by the crown, with their amount, and the times when, and the persons to whom, they were granted, was strongly opposed by the minister, who proposed some restrictive amendments upon it. These were carried by a majority of two only, the numbers being 188 to 186, in which division it was remarked, that among the county members of England and Wales, 11 only voted for the amendments, while 57 supported the original motion. Economy and care of the public money were now, indeed, the most popular of all topics. The dismission of two lord-lieutenants of counties from their posts, on account of votes given against the administration, occasioned a motion for enquiry, in the House of Lords, by the Earl of Shelburne, which, after a warm debate, was negatived by a majority of 92 to 39.

The discussions on Mr Burke's bill occupied much of the attention of the House of Commons in March; and one of the clauses, that for the abolition of the board of trade, an institution which had long served scarcely any other purpose than that of providing places for the friends of ministers, was carried against the efforts of the administration, by 207 votes to 199. Clauses were then added for the abolition of various places about the royal household, and a division being called on the first of them, it was thrown out by the majority of 211 to 158. The subsequent clauses were all negatived without a division. The contractor's bill being again introduced, it passed without opposition in the House of Commons, but was thrown out by the Lords. Lord North afterwards having moved, that as the East India Company had not made such proposals for the renewal of their charter as were deemed satisfactory, the three years' notice should be given them from the Speaker, ordained by parliament previous to the dissolution of their charter, that the debt due to them by the public should be paid in April 1783, the motion was warmly opposed by Mr. Fox and Mr. Burke, as an impotent menace; the previous question moved upon it was, however, rejected by a large majority, and the motion passed.

On April 6th, the day for taking into consideration the petitions for reform, Mr. Dunning moved his famous resolution, "That the influence of the crown has increased, is increasing, and ought to be diminished." In the debate which it produced, the Lord Advocate of Scotland, by way of defeating the motion, moved as an amendment to prefix the words, "That it is now necessary to declare;" to which the opposition readily agreed; and the question being put with this addition, it was carried in a very full house by 233 votes against 215. Mr. Dunning followed up his victory with moving a resolution, "That it is competent to this House to examine into, and to correct abuses in the expenditure of the civil list revenues, as well as in every other branch of the public revenue," which was carried without a division. Another resolution, from Mr. T. Pitt, declaring it to be the duty of the house, to provide an immediate and effectual redress of the abuses complained of in the petitions presented to it, was also carried in the affirmative; as was likewise Mr. Fox's motion, that these resolutions be immediately reported. When, however, a motion was introduced by Mr. Dunning, for an address to his Majesty, requesting that he would not dissolve the parliament, or prorogue the present session, until measures should be taken by the House to diminish the influence of the crown, and correct the evils complained of in the petition, the recovered influence of the ministry was rendered apparent by a majority of 51 for its rejection, the numbers being 254 to 203.

Mr. Burke's reform bill, after having for some time lain dormant, was brought on again on April 28th, and several clauses for the abolition of offices about the court were successively moved and rejected. Lord North's bill for a commission of accounts was carried through the house, and the commissioners were appointed, members of parliament being excluded from the number.

A motion being made by Mr. Dunning in a committee of the whole house on the consideration of the petitions which had been presented, that their own two resolutions of April 10th should be then reported, warm debates ensued, and a motion on the other side was made for the chairman to quit the chair, which was carried by 177 to 134. The committee was thus dissolved, and the petitions and resolutions were alike consigned to disregard.

Before we proceed to the narrative of the most remarkable incident in the internal history of the year, it will be proper to relate the military occurrences which took place in the early part of it.

Sir George Rodney, who had been appointed to the chief naval command in the West Indies, was ordered, in his way thither, with a strong squadron to proceed for the relief of Gibraltar, then under close blockade by the Spaniards. He had been only a few days at sea, when on January 8, he fell in with a convoy bound from St. Sebastian to Cadiz, consisting of 15 merchant men, guarded by a 64 gun ship, four frigates, and two smaller vessels, the whole of which he captured. Their lading was in great part of flour and other provisions, which were much wanted at Gibraltar, whither he sent the prizes, except some that were laden with naval stores, which he dispatched for England. This was only a prelude to more important success. On January 16th, off Cape St. Vincent, he came in sight of a Spanish squadron of 11 ships of the line commanded by Don Juan Langara. The great inferiority of the Spaniards led them to use their efforts to avoid an engagement, but they were brought to action on that evening; and soon after its commencement, a Spanish ship of 70 guns blew up, and all on board perished. In the sequel, the Spanish admiral-ship of 80 guns, and three of 70 guns, were taken and sent into port. Another of 70 was taken, and 70 English seamen were put on board, but the night being dark and tempestuous, she ran on shore. Another ship of the same force was captured, but afterwards ran on the breakers, and was totally lost. The remainder escaped into Cadiz. Sir G. Rodney proceeding to Gibraltar, executed his commission there, and about the middle of February, set sail for the West Indies, leaving the bulk of the fleet under Rear-admiral Digby, to convoy the Spanish prizes to England. In their way, the latter met with a French convoy for the Mauritius, under the protection of two ships of the line. Chase being made, one of the men of war and two or three vessels laden with military stores were captured.

From the beginning of the war with France, differences had subsisted between Holland and Great Britain, on account of the seizure and detention of Dutch ships bound to French ports; and, the merchants, insurers, &c. of Amsterdam, Rotterdam, and other maritime towns in Holland, had made strong remonstrances to the States respecting the injury they had sustained from this practice. These disputes were in some measure compromised, when, upon the declaration of war against Spain, a demand was made by the British court on the States General, to contribute the aid to which they were bound by treaty in such a case as that which now occurred. To this no answer was obtained; and it was evident that the French interest in that country was preponderant. During this state of things, the English government having received intelligence, that a number of ships laden with timber and naval stores for the French service, not directly protected by the States, intended to elude the British cruizers, by accompanying Count Byland, who with a small squadron, was to escort a convoy to the Mediterranean, Captain Fielding was sent out with a suitable force to examine the convoy, and seize such vessels as were laden with contraband articles. The fleets having met Captain Fielding's boats, which he sent for the purpose of search, were fired at, upon which he fired a shot ahead of the Dutch Admiral, who answered it with a broadside. This being returned by the English ship, Count Byland struck his colours, and in the meantime, most of the merchantmen keeping close to the shore, made their way to French ports. A few with naval stores were stopt, and the Dutch admiral was told, that he was at liberty to prosecute his voyage. This he declined doing, and with the rest of his fleet accompanied the British squadron to Spithead, where he remained till he should receive instructions from his government. On April 17th, a proclamation was issued at London, in which the non-performance by the States General of the stipulation in the treaty respecting succours being represented as a dereliction of the alliance between the two countries, the subjects of the United Provinces were placed upon the footing of other neutrals, not privileged by treaty.

A more formidable attack upon the maritime claims of Great Britain was made by the *armed neutrality* entered into by the northern powers, which was announced in a manifesto from the court of Petersburgh, issued on February 26th. Its leading principle was, that "free bottoms make free goods;" which was applied to the authorising of neutral states to carry on without interruption their usual commerce with belligerent powers, and even to convey from one port to another of a belligerent state, all goods, except such as could be deemed contraband, in consequence of the stipulations of former treaties. Although the principle was laid down generally, yet its operation was especially directed against Great Britain, which possesses the means of intercepting the supply of naval stores from the north of Europe to the ports of France and Spain, if not permitted to be conveyed under the protection of neutral flags. These powers therefore expressed great approbation of the new system; but the British court expostulated with that of Russia on the occasion.

Sir Henry Clinton, with the forces under his command, embarked at New York near the close of the year, and after a rough and tedious passage, arrived in February off Savannah, whence he proceeded to Edisto in South Carolina, where the troops were landed. He took possession of the islands to the south of Charleston harbour, and on April 1st, broke ground before the town. Soon after, the fleet under Admiral Arbuthnot forced its way into the harbour, and proved of great service in the operations of the siege. The defence was conducted by General Lincoln; and some bodies of militia, infantry, and cavalry assembled in the neighbourhood to impede the progress of the besiegers. Against these, a detachment was sent under Lieutenant-Colonel Webster; and here it was, that the daring and active services of Lieutenant-Colonel Tarleton, as a cavalry partizan, first became conspicuous. During the siege, a strong reinforcement arrived from New York, which enabled the British to extend themselves in the interior, and induced

Lord Cornwallis to take a separate command on Cooper's river. The works being now advanced close to the town, and a storm in preparation, Lincoln signed a capitulation on May 11th, by which the continental troops and the sailors were to remain prisoners of war till exchanged, and the militia to return home as prisoners on parole, and private property, both of the military and citizens, to be untouched. The whole number of men in arms included in this surrender, amounted to 5611, exclusive of near 1000 seamen. Lincoln's return to congress of continental troops, was somewhat less than 2500. A very numerous artillery, with three American and one French frigate, and a French polacre, were among the fruits of victory.

Lord Cornwallis, on marching up the north side of the Santee river, having received intelligence, that the remaining American force was collected near the borders of North Carolina, dispatched Colonel Tarleton, at the head of a body of cavalry and mounted light infantry, who, after a long and very rapid march, surprised the enemy at a place named Waxsaw, and upon their refusal to accept conditions of surrender, attacked, and entirely defeated them, with great loss of men, and that of their baggage and artillery. Nothing was now left able to resist the British arms; and at the time of Sir H. Clinton's departure in the beginning of June, to return to New York, there were scarcely any men through the colony of South Carolina in arms against the British government, and a number of persons had come from every quarter to declare their allegiance to his Majesty.

Early in the spring, Don Galvez, the Spanish governor of Louisiana, fitted out an expedition at New Orleans against the fort of Mobille, which surrendered on March 12th, just as a force from Pensacola under Major-General Campbell, was come in sight for its relief.

Towards the end of March, Admiral Rodney arrived in the West Indies, and proceeded to cruise off Fort Royal in

Martinique, where Guichen lay with a superior fleet. Not being able to draw the French admiral out to an engagement, he sailed to St. Lucie, leaving some swift sailing vessels to watch the enemy. In the middle of April, Guichen put to sea, and was immediately pursued by Rodney, who came in sight of him on the following day. The English fleet consisted of 20 sail of the line and a 50 gun ship; the French of 23 of the line and a 50 gun ship. The engagement which ensued was indecisive, and Admiral Rodney's public account of it contained much implied censure of his officers; the French, however, were cut off from Fort Royal, and were obliged to bear away for Guadaloupe. The fleets coming again in sight of each other, after much manœuvring another partial engagement took place on May 15th, and at length both fleets returned to their respective harbours to refit. A plan having been formed early in the year of such a junction of force between the French and Spaniards, as should render them decidedly superior in the West Indies, Admiral Solano sailed from Cadiz in April, with 12 sail of the line and a large fleet of transports, conveying a land force which amounted to 11,460 men. An English frigate falling in with the Spanish fleet, conveyed the intelligence to Admiral Rodney, who was lying at Barbadoes, upon which he immediately put to sea, in order to intercept Solano before he should join the French; in this attempt, however, he was frustrated, and the fleets formed a junction, when the whole number amounted to 36 sail of the line. Jamaica and the other leeward islands now appeared to be in great danger; but a sickness had broken out in the crowded Spanish ships, which rendered them incapable of any considerable effort, and they withdrew to the Havanna. The French admiral, in fine, was induced by the bad condition of his fleet, to sail for Europe; and thus was defeated, not only the scheme of a powerful co-operation with the Spaniards in the West India islands, but a concerted plan of joining with the Americans in an attack upon the British force at New York.

On the central coasts of America a destructive predatory war was carried on between the associated loyalists at New York, and the independent party, attended with all the rancour and animosity of civil hostility, but with no events tending to a decision of the contest. Early in June a body of 5 or 6000 men was carried over from Staten Island to Elizabeth Town in New Jersey, under Generals Knyphausen, Tryon, and Robertson, for the purpose of attacking some of Washington's advanced posts, and they marched up the country with the intention of attacking the town of Springfield. This, however, appeared to be so well protected by an American force under General Maxwell, that the army returned to Elizabeth Town. On the arrival of Sir H. Clinton from Carolina, the design was resumed, and a demonstration was made of an expedition up the North river, which called Washington with the greater part of his troops to the defence of that quarter. The forces at Elizabeth Town then advanced again to Springfield, near which the American General Greene was posted. The suddenness of the attack prevented him from impeding the burning of that place by the British, after which they retreated to Elizabeth Town, and on the same night passed back to Staten Island; and thus terminated the short campaign in the Jerseys.

We now revert to the British metropolis, which, in the month of June, was the scene of riots more dangerous to its safety, and disgraceful to its police, than it has witnessed in modern times.

At the head of the Scotch associations against any relaxation of the penal laws respecting the catholics, was Lord George Gordon, brother of the Duke of Gordon, a man of a singular character, compounded of enthusiasm, artifice, and folly. Chiefly through his exertions, the same fanatical spirit was roused in London; and as early as January 4th a deputation from a body called the Protestant Association, of which he was the patron, waited on Lord North to request him to present a petition to parliament against the law which had passed in favour of the catholics, which his lordship absolutely refused to do. During the subsequent session of parliament, Lord G. Gordon, who was a member of the House of Commons, frequently interrupted its business by bringing in topics relative to religion and the danger from popery, and by dividing the house on questions in which he stood entirely or almost alone. His dress and manner were equally singular with his language, but he was rather an object of amusement to the house than of any serious apprehensions. The association in London meantime appears to have been secretly increasing in numbers; and on May 29th a meeting called by public advertisement having been held at Coachmakers' hall, Lord G. Gordon took the chair, and made a vehement and inflammatory harangue, in which he endeavoured to persuade his auditors of the rapid progress of popery in the kingdom; and concluded with moving a resolution, that the whole body of the Protestant Association should on the next Friday accompany him to the House of Commons for the delivery of their petition. He declared that he would not present it if attended by fewer than 20,000 persons, and moved that they should be arranged in four divisions, one of them composed of the Scotch residents in London, and all distinguished by blue cockades. These motions were all carried with great applause. In addition to this public procedure, Lord G. Gordon gave notice to the House of Commons of the intended delivery of the petition, and of the day and manner of it.

On June 2d the associators to the number of many thousands assembled in St. George's Fields, and marshalling themselves as directed, proceeded in great order to the Houses of Parliament. Although their demeanour was at first peaceable, they soon inflamed each other so far as to commit violent outrages on the persons of such members of both houses as came in their way, especially such as were connected with administration, or were regarded as promoters of the obnoxious bill. Within the House of Commons, Lord G. Gordon having brought up the petition, moved to have it taken into immediate consideration. This occasioned some debate, during which Lord G. Gordon often went out to inform the mob what was passing, and who were the principal opponents of their cause. His motion was negatived by 192 votes to 6. After a length of time spent in much alarm and confusion, a party of horse and foot guards arrived, with a magistrate at their head, who assured the mob that the soldiers should be ordered away if they would disperse. This they generally did from the environs of the parliament house, but it was for the purpose of demolishing two Romish chapels, in Lincoln's-inn Fields, and Golden Square, which they effected without opposition, but some of the rioters were afterwards apprehended. On the following day the tumult appeared to have nearly subsided, but this calm was only a prelude to a much more furious storm. In a capital like London, whatever be the cause that first collects a riotous assembly, it will soon be joined by a crowd of turbulent banditti whose sole view is pillage and mischief. In the present case, it cannot be doubted that the petitioners mustered in St. George's Fields were actuated by religious fanaticism, and to them may be attributed the outrages of the first day before the houses of parliament, and the demolition of the catholic chapels. But it is probable that they had in general withdrawn before the subsequent widely-extended scenes of destruction, and that in fine, all the scum and dregs of the metropolis overflowed its streets, fired with a blind and indiscriminate rage for devastation.

For the particulars of the following dreadful days the periodical publications of the time may be consulted. It is sufficient here to relate, that not only many more Romish chapels and dwelling houses of catholics were destroyed, but prisons were set on fire, and the prisoners liberated, and many houses of supposed friends to the catholics were burnt and pillaged. On the 7th these disorders were at their height: thirty-six fires were seen blazing at once in different parts, and two attempts were made to force the Bank. It was now time to think seriously of preserving the capital from utter ruin, and even the frame of government from dissolution. Hitherto the magistrates of London and Westminster had shewn little but timidity and supineness, the ministers of state had appeared irresolute, and even the military, when called in, had either of themselves acted faintly, or had been cramped in their exertions for want of sufficient authority from the civil power. But troops now poured into London from all quarters, and an order was issued from his Majesty that they should use their arms against the rioters without waiting for directions from the civil magistrates. This was indeed very effectually done, for the return of killed and wounded amounted to 458, besides a number who were supposed to have perished in the ruins of the demolished houses, mostly in consequence of inebriation. From these exertions tranquillity was soon restored, and nowhere was any resistance of consequence attempted by the rioters, — a proof how easily all this mischief and disgrace might have been prevented by a timely application of spirited measures. In fact, the populace of London, as they are less sanguinary, are also less daring than those of many other capitals. The former part of their character was strikingly displayed by the circumstance, that amidst all this unbridled destruction of property, no personal injury was offered to any of the owners. The author of this memorable calamity, Lord G. Gordon, was apprehended, and sent with a very strong escort to the tower. He was afterwards tried on a charge of high treason, and acquitted, his crime appearing to the jury not to answer that description. A special commission was issued for the trial of a great number of the apprehended rioters, many of whom underwent the full rigour of the law.

The meeting of parliament after the recess on occasion of the riots was opened by a speech from the throne which met with general approbation. In the House of Commons some resolutions were carried for quieting the apprehensions of

ill-informed persons relative to the act for relieving the
catholics; and a bill passed that house for affording security to
the protestant religion from the encroachments of popery, by
more effectually restraining papists from taking upon themselves the education of protestant children. This was a kind of
concession to the spirit that had produced so many lamentable
effects, which the lords considered as unworthy the dignity
of parliament; and a motion was carried in their house for
deferring the third reading of the bill to a day beyond the
intended prorogation. A letter which had been written
during the late disturbances by the commander in chief, Lord
Amherst, in which an order was given for the disarming of
all persons who took up arms without the royal authority,
produced motions in both houses for resolutions to declare
such an order unconstitutional, as it in fact had interfered with
the purpose of some of the most respectable inhabitants in the
city of London, to arm for mutual defence under the conduct
of their magistrates. The motions were, however, negatived,
without a division. Parliament rose on July 8th.

Government was eventually a great gainer by this dreadful
tumult for it so strongly impressed the minds of the public
with the danger arising from popular assemblies for political
purposes, that the county associations for promoting reform
fell into some discredit, and were deserted by many persons
who had at first encouraged and joined them.

Admiral Geary, who had succeeded to the command of
the channel fleet on the death of Sir Ch. Hardy, sailed early
in June with 23 ships of the line, and was afterwards joined
by five or six more. In the beginning of July he fell in with
a homeward-bound fleet from the French West Indies, of
which he captured twelve merchantmen, the rest, with the
convoying ships of war, escaping in a fog. He then proceeded
southward as far as Cape Finisterre, in the hope of intercepting a detached squadron of French and Spanish ships of
war. About the end of the month, a rich and numerous fleet

bound for the East and West Indies, under convoy of a man of war and two or three frigates, which sailed from Portsmouth, unfortunately came in the way of the combined fleets under Don Cordova, and five East-Indiamen and above fifty West-Indiamen were taken. Besides the usual commodities, the East-Indiamen had on board, arms, artillery, ammunition, and naval stores, which were greatly wanted in that quarter, as well as a considerable supply of soldiers. In addition to this disaster, intelligence arrived that a great part of a valuable outward-bound Quebec fleet had fallen a prey on the banks of Newfoundland to some American privateers.

Admiral Geary, on the return of his fleet to port, resigned his command, which, after being refused by Admiral Barrington, was accepted by Admiral Darby. The channel fleet sailed again in September, and in November fell in with a French fleet much superior in number, but greatly out of condition. Neither party being eager to engage, the rencounter was without consequences.

After the departure of Sir G. Rodney from Gibraltar, the Spaniards redoubled their vigilance to cut off all relief to the garrison from sea; and for that purpose they made an attempt to destroy a small British squadron which lay in the bay, by sending down upon it a number of fire ships supported by row-boats and gallies, and covered by a squadron of men of war. The enterprize was however entirely defeated by the dexterity and intrepidity of the British officers and sailors, and the fire from the batteries.

Several events of importance occurred in America, during the latter half of the year. A French squadron of 7 sail of the line and 5 frigates arrived at Rhode Island on July 11th, convoying a land force of five regiments of infantry and a battalion of artillery, consisting in all of about 6000 men, under the command of the Count de Rochambeau. They were received with many expressions of esteem and gratitude by the Americans, while their commander announced them as only the vanguard of greater intended succours. In the same month Admiral Graves arriving at New York with a reinforcement to the ships of Admiral Arbuthnot, the British fleet being now superior, sailed to Rhode Island, where it blocked up the French squadron, and meditated an attack upon the town. It was found, however, that the fortifications had been put in such condition, and were so well manned, that an attack by sea was impracticable. General Clinton proposing a joint attempt by sea and land, embarked 6000 of his best troops, with which he proceeded to Long Island; but a difference in opinion between him and the naval commanders induced him to renounce the expedition, and re-land his men. During his absence, General Washington, crossing the north river and marching towards Kingsbridge, gave an alarm to New York; the return of Clinton, however, prevented any attempt against the place. Washington's army was afterwards augmented to 20,000 men, and the congress were full of hopes of getting New York into their possession with the aid of the French allies; but the plan, as already mentioned, was rendered abortive by the departure of Guichen for Europe.

Lord Cornwallis who, after the capture of Charleston, and his other successes in South Carolina carried his views to North Carolina, held a correspondence with the loyalists in that colony, who eagerly urged him to advance. In their impatience of a necessary delay, they broke out into insurrections against the American government, which were suppressed without difficulty; about 800 of them however escaped and joined the royal army. Lord Rawdon had in the meantime been sent towards the frontiers, and fixed his post at Camden, which Lord Cornwallis intended to make the place of arms and military repository of his forces. The Americans collected a powerful force for the defence of North Carolina, which they placed under the command of General Gates, who advanced with 5 or 6000 men towards Camden. The intelligence of this circumstance drew Lord Cornwallis to the spot, at the head of about 2000 men, one fourth of whom were militia and refugees. Learning that Gates was encamped in an unfavourable situation, at some miles from Camden, he proceeded by night with an intention of surprizing him, and in his way fell in with Gates, who was making a forward movement. At day light, August 15th, an action was brought on, at the very commencement of which almost the whole of the American militia, which constituted the greatest part of Gates's force, took to flight and dispersed. The remaining continental troops long stood firm, but in the end the British obtained a complete victory, taking all the American artillery with other trophies of war, and pursuing them above twenty miles from the field of battle. The vanquished had 8 or 900 men killed, and 1000 taken prisoners, while the whole loss of the victors little exceeded 300. In addition to this misfortune, the American partizan Sumpter was surprized at the Catawba fords by Colonel Tarleton with his legion, and utterly routed, with a considerable loss in killed and prisoners. On the other hand, Colonel Ferguson, who had been dispatched by Lord Cornwallis with a corps of light infantry and a body of militia of his own training (for he was an excellent partizan officer) to make incursions on the borders of North Carolina, was pursued on his return by a large force of militia cavalry, and being overtaken, was killed with 150 of his men, and 800 more were taken prisoners.

Whilst the British and American armies in and near New York were keeping each other in check, an incident occurred which formed an interesting topic at the time, and is one of the memorable events of the war. General Arnold has stood conspicuous for his daring courage and enterprize at the beginning of the contest; and he appears to have been one of those whom nature marks out for situations to which they are called by fortune. Retiring from active service in consequence of the severe wounds he had received, he was rewarded by his countrymen with the place of governor of the city of

Philadelphia, as soon as it was relinquished by the British troops. His moral qualities, however, did not support the character which his military talents had acquired. He incurred the charges of oppression and extortion, and of applying the public money to his own use; and appealing from the commissioners who were appointed to inspect his accounts, to the congress, their report was not only confirmed, but it was adjudged that they had allowed him more than he had a right to demand. He had further to undergo the ordeal of a court martial, which was appointed to enquire into various charges against him for malversation in office; and by this court his conduct was found so culpable that he was sentenced to be reprimanded by the commander in chief. These prosecutions he met by violent complaints of injustice and ingratitude; and although his past merits caused him again to be taken into favour by General Washington, and he was placed in a situation of considerable rank and trust in his army, yet his affections appear from the sequel to have been entirely alienated from his country. He opened a secret negotiation with Sir H. Clinton, the object of which was his delivering up the post and the division of troops which he commanded, to the British general. The person employed by the latter for the purpose of conferring with Arnold and settling the plan of operations, was Major André, adjutant-general, a very amiable and estimable officer, whose open and candid disposition perhaps rendered him less fit for such an office than one more practised in artifice would have been. Arnold's command was at the important post of West Point, on the North of Hudson's river, the loss of which, with the troops attached to it, would have been a very severe blow to the American army in that quarter. On September 21st, André was landed by night from a British sloop of war, and was received by Arnold, who conducted him to his camp, where he remained on that night and the following day. During that time he changed the British uniform which he had worn under his surtout for a common dress; and Arnold not being able to convey him back by the way he came, he was sent on the second night through a remote part of the camp, provided with a horse and passport, and under the name of Anderson, to find his way back to New York. He passed the out posts of the army in safety, but on the following morning he was stopped by three young volunteers, who examined his passport. With this they were at first satisfied, but suspicions occurring to the mind of one of them, he was examined more strictly. Unused as he was to deception, he disclosed himself by offering to his captors a considerable reward to be set free, which, though in an humble rank of life, they honourably refused. Being led to quarters, papers were found on him containing exact returns, in Arnold's hand-writing, of the forces, ordnance, &c. at West Point, as well as information of what had passed at a council of war; but nothing could be obtained from him respecting the writer, till Arnold, on information of his danger, had time to escape. The British commanders reclaimed André on different grounds; but Washington having assembled a board of general officers to judge of the case, André's own confession was sufficient to fix upon him the character of a spy; and the dangerous extent of the attempted treachery prohibited, in their opinion, any relaxation of the punishment annexed to it by the laws of war. The unfortunate officer only deprecated the ignominious mode in which he was to forfeit his life, but though he was treated in every other respect with humane sympathy, no remission in that point could be obtained. He died like a man and a soldier, and his memory was honoured with a monument in Westminster Abbey. Arnold, who now declared the most violent hostility to the independent government, was made a brigadier-general in the British army.

Admiral Rodney, apprized of the danger of New York, sailed thither in September, and although he found, on arriving, that his aid was not required, his departure from the West Indies was fortunate, as the means of escaping the effects of one of the most dreadful hurricanes which these islands ever experienced. It began at Jamaica on October 3d, where, by an irruption of the sea, the town of Savanna la Mar was utterly swept away, with 300 of its inhabitants; and four parishes on that side of the island, by a succeeding hurricane and earthquake, underwent terrible devastation of property and loss of lives. At Barbadoes it did not occur till the 10th, when the capital, Bridgetown, was almost levelled to the ground, with the death of some thousands of people. St. Lucie, Grenada, Dominica, and St. Vincent's were also great sufferers; from the former most of the ships of war were driven out to sea and greatly damaged. The French islands at least equally partook of this calamity, and their shores were covered with wrecks of ships of different countries, which were totally lost, with the crews of many of them. It deserves to be recorded, that the Marquis de Bouillé sent a flag of truce to Commodore Hotham, with a message, accompanying some English sailors, declaring that he could not consider as enemies, men who had escaped on his coast from the rage of the elements, and whom humanity entitled to every relief, which in such a season of general calamity could be afforded. The squadron under Admiral Rowley, convoying the Jamaica trade to Europe, also suffered severely from the hurricane, several of the ships, with that of the admiral, being obliged to put back disabled, and a 64 and 74 gun ship being totally lost. Several frigates and other armed vessels were likewise wrecked on the different coasts.

The capture of Mr. Laurens, late president of the American congress, on his passage to Holland, was a circumstance which proved of much political importance. That gentleman being brought to England on October 6th, was committed to close confinement in the Tower, under a charge of high treason, as a British subject. Though, on his examination, he declined answering questions, his papers gave full information of a projected treaty of friendship and commerce between the American States and Holland, which he was proceeding to bring to a conclusion. From the draught of the treaty, the States General do not appear to have been consulted upon it, the city of Amsterdam, by its pensionary, M. Van Berkel, being the ostensible party on that side. These papers were laid before the States General by Sir Joseph Yorke, with a strong memorial of complaint respecting such a correspondence carried on with his Majesty's rebellious subjects, and the demand of a formal disavowal of the proceeding on the part of the States, and the punishment of Van Berkel, and the other persons concerned in it. No immediate answer was given to this memorial; and soon after, a counter remonstrance was made by Count Welderen, the Dutch minister at London, respecting a violence committed at the Dutch West India island of St. Martin, in seizing some American vessels under the cannon of the fort. A second memorial was presented to the States by Sir Joseph Yorke in December, requiring a categorical answer, and no other being given, than that the States had taken the matter *ad referendum,* the British ambassador was ordered to withdraw from the Hague, and hostilities were declared against Holland on December 20th. Thus Great Britain was engaged with a fourth enemy, without a single ally.

Parliament was unexpectedly dissolved on September 1st, and a general election ensued, in which there were fewer expensive contests than almost ever known. The temper of the nation was such that many of the opposition members were thrown out; it being the general effect of accumulated danger and alarm, to strengthen the influence of authority. On the meeting of parliament, October 31st, the late speaker of the House of Commons, Sir Fletcher Norton, who had incurred the displeasure of the court, and the personal enmity of the prime minister, lost by a considerable majority the reappointment to that post, on a competition with Mr. Cornwall. No public business of consequence was transacted before the Christmas recess, which took place at an unusually early period.

Europe in general during this year enjoyed a state of tranquillity. The King of France honoured himself by the abolition of the inhuman and irrational practice of putting the question, or enforcing confession and evidence in criminal cases, by torture. He also, under the influence of M. Necker, his first minister of finance, made a great economical reform in his household, 406 officers in that department being abolished by a single edict. It was another gain to the cause of humanity, that the Duke of Modena abolished the court of inquisition in his dominions. An interview, as it was supposed for political purposes, took place at Mohilow in Poland, in the month of June, between those great potentates, the Empress of Russia, and the Emperor of Germany.

The court of Vienna in this year brought to effect a scheme for the aggrandisement of the house of Austria, by procuring the election of the Archduke Maximilian, the emperor's brother, to the coadjutorship to the bishopricks of Cologne and Munster, with the consequent reversion to the electorate attached to the former, although the measure was opposed by the King of Prussia.

Maria Theresa, Empress of Germany, and Queen of Hungary and Bohemia, died on November 29th, in the 63d year of her age. She possessed many amiable and estimable qualities, though somewhat tinged by bigotry and love of power; and will rank in history among the illustrious sovereigns of her time.

In the East Indies events took place, for the full comprehension of which, with respect to their origin and causes, a distinct narrative of the state of that country for several years past, and of the intricate politics of the different native powers and the English Company, would be requisite. All that can be here attempted is a summary of the events themselves, as far as they concern the British empire in part of the world.

The different presidencies of the Company appear to have entered deeply into the intrigues and quarrels of the natives, for the purpose of making their own advantage out of them; and they are charged with having by turns deceived and injured most of those with whom they had to do. The consequence at length was a confederacy between Hyder Ally, the Nizam, the Mahrattas, and some other princes or tribes, for the purpose of effecting the expulsion of the British from India. Their intentions being discovered, it was resolved to anticipate them; and the Bombay government placing its whole disposable force under the command of General Goddard, he marched in the month of February against Ahmedabad, the capital of Guzerat, which he took by storm within five days of his arrival before it. The Mahratta chiefs Scindia and Holkar then approaching with an army towards Surat, Goddard attacked their camp, on April 5th, and obliged them to abandon their ground with great loss. Other partial actions followed, in which the Mahrattas underwent defeats which brought the campaign to a close in this quarter. On the side of Bengal they were likewise worsted, and the supposed impregnable fortress of Gualier was taken from them by a force under Major Popham.

The fortune of the Company was very different on the Coromandel coast. Towards the close of 1779 the presidency of Madras was apprized by the Nabob of Arcot of the peace concluded between Hyder and the Mahrattas, and of the intended alliance against the English, to which last they were unwilling to give credit, but a letter from Hyder to the president in March appeared to Admiral Sir Edward Hughes to contain such manifest indications of hostility, that he dispatched a copy of it to England. The presidency had been more employed in disputes among themselves, than in active measures of preparation, when in July, Hyder having made way through the Ghauts, burst like a torrent with a numerous army into the Carnatic. His son, Tippoo Saib, at the same time advanced with a great body of cavalry upon the northern Circars; whilst at the opposite side other parties were approaching to Madura and the Tinevelly district. Terror was now universally spread, and Madras itself was alarmed with an attack upon the adjacent villages by some of Hyder's horse. On August 21st Hyder invested Arcot, the garrison of which had been previously reinforced by a detachment of the Company's troops from Vellore. Colonel Baillie was now at the head of a body of men in the Guntoor Circar, with which it was intended that he should invade Hyder's territories in that quarter, but upon the present emergency orders were sent to him to march towards Madras. In the meantime the commander in chief, Sir Hector Monro, made a forward movement to Conjeveram, for the purpose of drawing Hyder from Arcot, and directions were sent to Baillie to change his route, and join him at that place. This movement had the expected effect on Hyder, but he took a position with his army to prevent Baillie's junction with Sir Hector. He detached Tippoo with a large body of the best troops in his army to make an attack on Baillie, which, after a severe action, the latter repelled. He was, however, unable to make way with his small force through Hyder's whole army to reach the British camp; and having conveyed intelligence of his situation to the commander in chief, Colonel Fletcher was dispatched to his relief with the flower of the army. He effected a junction with Baillie's troops, and they advanced together towards Conjeveram. On September 10th they were suddenly attacked by Hyder's whole force, consisting of 25,000 cavalry, 30 disciplined regiments of native infantry, a corps of European auxiliaries, and a numerous artillery. By prodigies of valour they repulsed with great slaughter the attacks made upon them, and victory was about to declare for the British, when an unfortunate explosion of the tumbrils with ammunition laid open their center, and Tippoo rushing in with the cavalry, followed by the French and other infantry, it was no longer a battle but a carnage. Colonel Baillie with about 200 Europeans were made prisoners: the rest were left slain on the field, to the number, according to different estimates, of from 3300 to 5000 Sepoys, and from 500 to 700 Europeans. This disaster was followed by mutinies of the native troops in different places, and other disorders. Arcot was taken by storm sometime after, and its citadel, from the defection of all the sepoys in its garrison, was under the necessity of surrendering. Intelligence of these events being received at Calcutta, the presidency of which had strongly disapproved of the conduct of that of Madras, it was thought necessary to request Sir Eyre Coote, commander in chief of all the forces in India, to repair thither, and take upon himself the command of the army in the Carnatic, with the direction of all the means they should furnish, for retrieving affairs in that quarter. He accordingly sailed to Madras, where he arrived on November 5th, bringing with him a reinforcement of European artillery and infantry, and a body of Lascars; and at the close of the year he encamped at the Mount near Madras with a force of about 7000 men.

1781

21st & 22^d Year of the Reign

O<small>N</small> the re-assembling of parliament, January 25th, a message from the throne, with the papers relative to the rupture with Holland, having been presented to the House of Commons by the minister, Mr. Burke rose to make observations on the *prudence* and *policy* of the new war in which we had engaged, the *justice* of it, he said, being a topic which could not be fully discussed for want of sufficient information. Lord North having replied to his remarks, moved an address of thanks to his Majesty for the communication, with assurances of support in the prosecution of this *just* and *necessary* war. These terms gave rise to a debate, in which amendments were proposed by some opposition members, but rejected, and the address passed in the original form. Similar debates occurred on the delivery of the same message to the House of Lords, and a motion of the Duke of Richmond for an address to the throne for farther information on the being put to the vote, was rejected by the great majority of 84 to 19.

Certain petitions to parliament transmitted from India brought the affairs of the British dominion in that country before the consideration of the House of Commons. By the new regulations adopted in 1773, Bengal had been made the principal seat of government, and two supreme jurisdictions had been there established. One of these possessed all the political and executive powers of government, and, under the name of governor-general and council, extended its controul over the other presidencies of Madras and Bombay. The other, composed of judges from England, and named the supreme court of judicature, was entirely independent of the former. The judicial business of the country had hitherto been transacted in its provincial courts, in which litigated causes were decided according to the known laws and customs of India; but their authority was not only denied by the new judicature, but their members were severely punished for the discharge of their functions pursuant to the laws and constitution of their country, which had hitherto been acknowledged by all its conquerors. The natives of Bengal now beheld with terror English bailiffs, accompanied by bodies of armed men, traversing the country, at a great distance from Calcutta, in order to execute decrees founded upon laws and regulations perfectly incomprehensible to those who were subjected to their authority, and even on the persons of the Zemindars, or hereditary great landholders, who were venerated by the people as their natural princes. In these instances, force was often opposed to force, and blood was shed in the quarrel; whilst the religion and domestic privacy of the natives were often exposed to rude violation. The governor-general and council, regarding these practices as an invasion of their authority, and apprehending dangerous consequences from the odium excited by them, employed the Company's military force to restrain the violences of the civil power; and in one instance about fourscore bailiffs and their assistants were disarmed and sent prisoners to Calcutta. This state of things produced two petitions to parliament; one, from the governor-general and council, giving a minute account of all these transactions, and requesting an indemnity from the penalties they had incurred by their interference; the other, from a number of British subjects in the provinces of Bengal, Bahar, and Orissa, complaining of the many oppressions and injuries they had sustained, under the authority of the supreme court of judicature, and the extraordinary assumptions of power by that court. The matter of the petitions was amply discussed by General Smith, who moved that they might be referred to a select committee of fifteen members chosen by ballot. No objection was made on the part of the minister to the motion, and the committee was accordingly appointed.

Mr. Burke was not deterred by the fate of his reform bill in the former session, from again introducing it to parliament; and accordingly made a motion for that purpose on February 15th. The bill was suffered to be read for the first time, but the motion for its second reading was the occasion of a vigorous debate, memorable for the early display of ability and eloquence exhibited in its support by William Pitt, second son of the Earl of Chatham. On a division the motion was rejected by a majority of 233 to 190; and by a subsequent resolution, the bill was postponed for six months.

A loan for 12 millions negotiated by Lord North, which in a short time rose to a premium of from 9 to 11 per cent was the occasion of some severer censures of his ministerial conduct at this time, than almost any that he had encountered. Mr. Fox opened the attack on March 7th, the day of bringing forward the budget, in a speech replete with financial knowledge, in which he not only endeavoured to prove that the bargain was a most improvident one for the public, but argued that the power of disposing of such profit at the pleasure of a minister was a very dangerous source of political corruption. He particularly objected to the lottery annexed to the other douceurs of the loan, both as adding to advantages already sufficiently great, and as exceedingly prejudicial to the morals of the people; and he moved for omitting the clause in the loan bill containing it. This amendment was however rejected by a majority of 169 to 111. The contest did not end here; and in the progress of the bill, various other attacks were made on the minister, especially with regard to the use of the loan for corrupt purposes. These were defeated by majorities; but, that great abuses did at that time prevail in this matter, seems to be acknowledged by the improvements which have since taken place in negotiations of that kind.

Sir P.J. Clerke's renewed motion for bringing in the contractor's bill, and Mr. Crewe's bill for restraining revenue officers from voting in elections for members of parliament, were both thrown out on divisions of the house.

The unfavourable intelligence concerning the war in the Carnatic being received in England, it was communicated to the House of Commons by the minister, who moved for the appointment of a committee of secrecy to enquire into the causes of that war, and the present state of the British possessions in that part of India. Objections were made to the motion on the ground of the proposed secrecy of the enquiry, and Mr. Fox moved as an amendment, the omission of the word "secrecy," in which he was seconded by Mr. Burke; but the amendment was rejected, and the original motion was carried. The fifteen members of the committee chosen by ballot proved to be, in the majority of four to one, particular friends of the minister.

The committee for examining the petitions from Bengal, having delivered their report, a bill for new modelling the supreme court of judicature at Calcutta, and for indemnifying the governor and council for their resistance to the decree of that court, and for directing the future operation of that jurisdiction, was brought in by General Smith, and after some opposition, passed both houses, and received the royal assent.

In order to bring the East India Company to submit to the terms for a renewal of their charter which the minister had proposed, but which they had rejected, as incompatible with their interests, he had, as mentioned in the last year, carried a vote for giving them notice for the re-payment of the sum due to them by the public, which implied the dissolution of the charter. To augment the intimidation, he now brought before the House of Commons several propositions for its consideration, of so much severity to the Company, that they were reprobated by the opposition in the most reproachful terms. The discussions on this topic continued through the greater part of the session, when at length, the news from India having put an end to the view of obtaining a large sum for the renewal of the charter, and the parliament becoming thin from the retreat of the members, Lord North, on June 1st, brought in a temporary bill for continuing to the Company the benefit of their exclusive trade and territorial possessions during a limited term, but at the same time charging them with the sum of £630,000 by way of participation in their past profits. This condition was strongly opposed as a measure of violence and injustice, and the sum was reduced to £402,000 in which state the bill passed into a law.

Various motions of a popular kind were introduced in this session by opposition members, which met with their usual fate, the influence of the minister appearing down to this period not in the least inferior upon the present parliament, to what it had been upon the former. One more effort was made to bring the American war to a conclusion in a motion by Mr. Fox, June 12th, founded upon the latest gazette intelligence from that country, for a resolution "that his Majesty's ministers ought immediately to take every possible measure for concluding peace with our American colonies," which was negatived. The session of parliament was concluded on July 18th.

Of the military occurrences of the year, the first to be mentioned was a renewed attempt by the French on the isle of Jersey. The Baron de Rullecourt landed about 800 men upon the island on the 6th of January, and leaving a part of them in a redoubt in Grouville-bay which he had surprised, proceeded with the rest before day-break to the town of St. Hellier. This he entered without noise, and took possession of the market place; and having made prisoners of the lieutenant-governor, the magistrates, and principal inhabitants, he dictated a capitulation of the whole island, with the threat of instant destruction to the town should it be refused. The capitulation being signed by the lieutenant-governor who seems to have lost all presence of mind on the occasion, Elizabeth Castle was summoned by the French commander, but the officers in it refused to pay any regard to a surrender made under such circumstances, and fired on the French troops on their advance. In the meantime the militia and other force in the neighbourhood was collected by Major Pierson, a spirited and intelligent young officer, who formed them advantageously on the heights above the town; and to a message from Rullecourt requiring him to comply with the terms of the capitulation, he replied by saying that if he and his troops did not surrender themselves prisoners of war within twenty minutes, they should be attacked. This event followed: the French were driven from street to street to the market-place, where the commander, who obliged the lieutenant-governor to stand close by his side, fell under several mortal wounds. Major Pierson, in the instant of victory, received a shot through the heart, and his death was a circumstance which threw a damp upon a success which was rendered complete by the capture or destruction of the whole of the invading party.

In America, the year opened with a circumstance which appeared to promise great advantage to the royal cause. The very embarrassed state of the American finances had subjected their army to great hardships and privations: long arrears of pay had been accumulated; and from the failure of several of the States in sending recruits, many of the soldiers had been obliged to serve beyond the term of their enlistment. These hardships had occasioned much murmuring and discontent; and at length, on January 1st, the division called the Pennsylvania line, which was hutted at Morris-town in the Jerseys, turned out to the number of 1300 and declared that they would serve no longer till their grievances were redressed. After a fruitless attempt to quell the meeting, they collected the stores and artillery belonging to their division, marched out of camp, and chose a favourable position for an encampment. They elected officers and a commander from their own body, and then advanced to Prince-town. As soon as Sir H. Clinton received intelligence of this defection, he sent emissaries to the mutineers, with great offers to induce them to lay down their arms, and return to their allegiance to the King. He also passed over to Staten Island with a large body of troops, to be ready for action on any emergency. The mutineers, however, were so far from lending an ear to his proposals, that they removed farther from the British quarters, to Trenton, and gave up two of his emissaries, who were immediately hanged. A committee of congress was at length deputed to treat with them, which, upon an engagement of indemnity, and the redress of their grievances, brought them back to their duty. A similar disturbance which took place in the Jersey line, was accommodated in the same manner. It was remarkable that Washington did not make the smallest movement on this occasion; being probably conscious, that the troops had just ground for their complaints, and not unwilling that congress should be made to feel the necessity of redressing them.

Lord Cornwallis, towards the close of the former year, had been making preparations for an active inroad into North Carolina; and on the other hand, Washington had sent General Greene, an officer of high reputation, to take the command in that quarter, which had been resigned by General Gates. He was accompanied by Colonel Morgan, who had acquired distinction as a partizan in the northern war. Lord Cornwallis, in January, advanced to the borders between the Broad and the Catawba rivers, whilst Greene, who was not strong enough to oppose him in the field, made a diversion by an attack on

Fort Ninety-Six. Morgan at the same time, with a force of
Virginia regulars and militia, advanced upon the Pacolet river.
Tarleton, who was on that side with his legion of cavalry and
light infantry, and other troops, was directed to strike a blow
at Morgan. He accordingly advanced upon that leader, who
retreated, till finding himself unable, without great danger, to
cross the Broad river, the waters of which were much out, he
took his ground for an engagement, January 18th. Posting his
men with great judgment, he received the impetuous attack
of Tarleton, in such a manner, that the forces of the latter, by
an unexpected charge were thrown into irretrievable disorder,
and were totally defeated with great loss. Tarleton rallied a part
of his cavalry, and repelling an attack of that of the enemy,
brought them away. Lord Cornwallis, on the news of this defeat,
dispatched a part of his army to intercept Morgan, but without
success. Afterwards, divesting himself of every incumbrance, he
hastened after Greene, who retreated before him. A very long
and fatiguing march ensued, in which hardships of every kind
were undergone by the British army, and sustained with the
greatest courage and perseverance, whilst in all the skirmishes
with hostile parties on the rout, they proved victorious. At
length, on March 15th, Lord Cornwallis came in view of
Greene's army, drawn up in line of battle, near Guilford Court-
house, in number much exceeding his own. The action which
followed was long, greatly diversified, and well contested. It
ended in the rout and retreat of the Americans, whom, however,
the royal army was not in condition to pursue; and the British
commander found it necessary to draw back his fatigued
troops to the vicinity of Wilmington in North Carolina,
which town had previously been reduced by an expedition
from Charleston.

This movement of Lord Cornwallis having left South
Carolina open, Greene marched against Lord Rawdon, who
had been left at Camden. He came in view on April 19th,
and made demonstrations of an intended attack of the British

posts; but Lord Rawdon obtaining information of his having detached a part of his force, determined to take the occasion for anticipating him. Arming every man in his corps who was able to use a musket, he attacked the Americans by surprize, and routed them with considerable loss. His deficiency of strength, however, and the revolt of the country at his back, rendered it expedient for him to abandon the post of Camden, and crossing the Santee, to move towards Charleston, which now began to be exposed to danger. Fort Ninety-six, in the meantime, was invested by Greene, who met with a resistance, which obliged him to lay formal siege to it. The arrival of three regiments from Ireland, enabled Lord Rawdon to march for its relief; but before he could reach the place, an attempt was made by Greene to carry it by storm. He was, however, resisted with so much courage, that after the slaughter of many of the assailants, he drew off the remainder, and commenced a retreat. He was closely pursued, but without effect; and in the sequel, Ninety-six was evacuated by the British, and Rawdon, after undergoing much hazard, returned to Charleston. The result of the campaign in this quarter, was, that Greene recovered the greater part of Georgia and of the two Carolinas.

Early in the year, Arnold was placed at the head of a body of troops amounting to about 1700 men, and conveyed by a naval force to the Chesapeak, for an expedition to Virginia. Ascending the rivers, and traversing the coasts of that country, he spread ravage and destruction wherever he went, acting at once as a public foe, and a personal enemy. The evils which he inflicted upon the Virginians at length attracted the attention both of the Americans, and the French at Rhode Island; and while Washington sent to their relief 2000 of his best troops under the Marquis de la Fayette, the French embarked the same number commanded by Count Rochambeau, on board the fleet of M. de Ternay. This squadron, on March 16th, fell in off Cape Henry with the English fleet under Admirals Arbuthnot and Graves, and an engagement was brought on which proved indecisive; it had however the effect of cutting off the French from the Chesapeak, and obliging them to return without landing their troops, or effecting any other purpose. Soon after, Major-General Phillips arrived under convoy from New York, with about 2000 select troops, and took the chief command in Virginia. In conjunction with Arnold, he defeated all the bodies of militia which were brought to oppose them, and sailing up James river, they did incalculable mischief on its banks, destroying a great quantity of tobacco ready for exportation, and other commodities, with shipping, dock yards, buildings of various kinds, timber, stores, &c. to a vast amount. Such were the principal occurrences in North America, during the first half of the year.

Don Galvez, early in the year, fitted out an expedition from the Havanna, intended against Pensacola; but a violent hurricane, in which four capital ships with several others were lost, obliged him to return to port. The fleet was, however, refitted, and on March 9th appeared with between 7 and 8000 land forces before Pensacola. After a gallant defence by General Campbell, with a motley and very inferior garrison, the place was obliged to capitulate on May 9th, and with it fell the province of West Florida, one of the principal acquisitions of the treaty of Paris.

Admiral Rodney, who had returned at the end of the year from New York to St. Lucia, concerted with General Vaughan an expedition for the recovery of St. Vincent; but after landing on the island, they found it, notwithstanding the effects of the late hurricane, in such a state of defence, that they re-imbarked the troops without hazarding an attack. They afterwards, in consequence of instructions from England, proceeded against the Dutch island of St. Eustatius, which, though small and sterile, was rendered of great commercial importance, as a free port and general magazine of West Indian and American commodities belonging to different nations. They appeared with a great land and sea force before this island on February 3d, and summoned the governor, who had not yet heard of hostilities between the two countries: He replied, that being utterly incapable of resisting such a force, he must necessarily surrender, only recommending the town and inhabitants to the well-known clemency of British commanders. The riches found in the island were immense, and at a loose computation, were estimated at more than three millions sterling. Besides this booty, above 250 vessels, many of them richly laden, were taken in the port; and information having been obtained that a fleet of 30 West Indiamen, under convoy of a 60 gun ship, had shortly before departed for Holland, Admiral Rodney sent two men of war and a frigate after them, which captured the whole. The small islands of St. Martin and Saba, also partook of the fate of St. Eustatius. The Dutch colours being kept flying at St. Eustatius, the island for sometime served as a decoy to French, Dutch, and American vessels, many of which ran in, and were taken without trouble. A squadron of privateers hearing of the rupture with Holland, though unprovided with letters of marque against this new enemy, boldly entered the rivers of Demarary and Essequibo, in Guiana, on which the Dutch possessed colonies; and captured almost all the vessels lying in them, which were prizes of considerable value. The settlers, feeling their defenceless situation, and dreading to become the prey of corsairs, made a tender of submission to the governor of Barbadoes upon the same terms which had been granted to St. Eustatius, and of which they were then ignorant.

It soon appeared that the confidence of the governor of St. Eustatius in British clemency had not the foundation which he expected. The inhabitants having incurred the charge of perfidiousness and perjury, were regarded as unworthy of protection, and an indiscriminate confiscation of private property took place. The Jews, who were considerable in number and wealth, were peculiarly the objects of rigorous treatment. Several of them, being first stript of their property, were condemned to banishment, and were transported to St. Christopher's, where, to the honour of that island, they were received with kindness and liberality. All other strangers were subsequently sent away in a similar condition. A great share of the property taken in St. Eustatius belonged to British merchants in the East Indies and at home, particularly those of St. Christopher's; and being of consequence severe sufferers from the confiscation, they made many remonstrances to Admiral Rodney on the subject, which were treated by him with contempt. His final answer was, "that the island was Dutch, every thing in it was Dutch, was under the protection of the Dutch flag, and as Dutch it should be treated." In the meantime, public sales were advertised of the captured goods, and one of the greatest auctions ever known was opened at St, Eustatius, where great bargains were bought, the French, it is said, being the chief purchasers. It may further be mentioned, with regard to this unpleasant topic, that the captors were afterwards involved in troublesome and expensive law suits; and that a great part of the plunder was taken by the French near the English coast, on its conveyance home.

Towards the end of March, M. de Grasse sailed from Brest with 25 sail of the line, 6000 land forces, and a convoy of between 2 and 300 ships, and parting during the voyage with M. de Suffrein with five sail of the line and part of the land forces destined for the East Indies, proceeded with the remainder for Fort Royal bay in Martinique. For the purpose of intercepting him, Sir G. Rodney detached Sir Samuel Hood and Drake to cruize off Fort Royal bay with 17 sail of the line, himself remaining at St. Eustatius, with his own and another ship of the line. On April 29th De Grasse's fleet came in sight, and the British commanders were unable to prevent four sail of the line and a fifty gun ship from coming out of Fort Royal harbour and joining him. Sir Samuel Hood was also joined by a man of war from St. Lucia, but the French were still superior by six sail of the line. A partial action ensued, the consequence of which was that the English bore away in the night for Antigua. This result gave an opportunity to the Marquis de Bouillé of landing on St. Lucia, May 10th, with a body of troops, but after an ineffectual attempt on the English posts, he quitted the island, the French giving out that this was only a feint to cover an attempt on Tobago. In fact, a small French squadron, with a considerable body of land forces, appeared off that island on May 23d, and having effected a landing, laid siege to the strongest post in the island, which was bravely defended by Governor Ferguson; but an attempt for relief by sea having failed, he was obliged to capitulate.

The Channel fleet under Admiral Darby sailed on March 13th for the relief of Gibraltar, which, from its close block-ade, was suffering considerably under the want of wholesome provision. The French at this time were so eager in their schemes respecting America and the West Indies, that they were not inclined to join the Brest fleet with that of the Spaniards which was cruizing about Cadiz, with the avowed purpose of preventing any succour to Gibraltar; and the latter, though of the force of 30 sail of the line, not choosing alone to encounter the English of 27 sail, Admiral Darby found no impediment in effecting his purpose. After this was done, he cruized some time off the Straits mouth, to watch the motions of the Spaniards, who were lying quietly in Cadiz harbour, where they remained till his departure. By this time, the siege of Gibraltar was so far advanced, that prodigious works were erected before it, filled with an artillery of greater number and power than had almost ever been brought against a fortress; and it was employed in a cannonade and bombardment, which entirely ruined the town of Gibraltar, and reduced its inhabitants to the greatest distress, but did little damage to the fortifications.

The grand fleet, on setting sail from England, was accompanied by a small squadron commanded by Commodore Johnstone, consisting of a 74, a 64, and three 50 gun ships, with several frigates and smaller vessels, and convoying some outward bound East Indiamen: on board the fleet were three new regiments of 1000 men each, under the command of General Meadows. The object of this expedition was the reduction of the Dutch settlement at the Cape of Good Hope. The commodore on his voyage put in for refreshments at Port Praya in St. Jago, one of the Cape de Verd islands; where, on April 16th, he was overtaken by Suffrein who, as already mentioned, parted from De Grasse's fleet, with the express purpose of following Johnstone's armament, of which the French had obtained accurate information. Suffrein with his five sail of the line steered directly into the midst of the English fleet, which was taken at a great disadvantage, not having entertained any suspicion of an attack. The French commenced the action with great spirit, and for a time their fire was very powerful; at length, several of the India ships getting into action, they began to find their situation too hot, and one by one withdrew, till a single ship, which had anchored, was left to sustain the whole fury of the contest. She escaped with great difficulty with the loss of all her masts, and no ship was lost on either side. Suffrein sailed away, and on June 21st, arrived at False bay, near the Cape, whilst several Dutch East Indiamen were anchored in Saldanha bay. Of these circumstances Commodore Johnstone was informed by a captured vessel; and finding that the landing of the French troops had rendered the Cape-town secure, he resolved to make an attempt on the Dutch ships in Saldanha bay. This enterprize was perfectly successful. The Dutch, on the entrance of the English ships, ran their vessels on shore and set fire to them. By the activity of the British sailors, however, four large ships were saved from the flames; a fifth blew up soon after she was abandoned. The commodore, with his own ship and the frigates, convoyed his prizes to England, leaving the rest of the fleet with General Meadows to proceed to India.

The war in America during this summer took a turn which, in the event, proved to be of the highest importance. Lord

Cornwallis, finding his situation at Wilmington very distressing and insecure, formed the resolution of marching to Virginia to effect a junction with General Phillips. He commenced his march near the close of April, and in something less than a month arrived at Petersburgh in Virginia. He there found that Phillips was dead, and Arnold had succeeded him in the command, who had been strengthened by a reinforcement of from 1500 to 2000 men sent by Sir H. Clinton. The Marquis La Fayette, with a very inferior force of Americans, was acting on the defensive on the north side of James river. Lord Cornwallis advancing from Petersburgh crossed James river, and proceeded up the country, followed, but at a distance, by Fayette. Detaching Colonels Tarleton and Simcoe to scour the interior, they were able to do great mischief in a tract hitherto exempt from the ravages of war, and the depository of large quantities of military and other stores. Cornwallis on their return, fell back to Richmond, whence he moved nearer the sea, and at the latter end of June arrived at Williamsburg, the capital of Virginia. At this time, Fayette had been reinforced by General Wayne with the Pennsylvanian succours, and by the junction of a corps under Baron Steuben, and some of the Virginian militia, so that the British army was restricted from distant operations. It had been a favourite idea in the English cabinet since the news of the victory at Guilford, and Arnold's successes in Virginia, to make that colony the seat of war, and establish a permanent station on its coast, by means of which, enterprizes might be carried on by sea and land as occasion demanded. For this purpose, Lord Cornwallis examined different situations near the mouth of the Chesapeak, and fixed upon Yorktown, situated on the peninsula between the rivers York and James, as the most suitable. There he took post in August with a force of about 7000 choice troops; and applied himself with great diligence to fortify both it, and Gloucester point on the opposite side of York river, which together entirely command its navigation.

In the meantime Washington was using his endeavours to propagate the idea that New York was the object of an intended attack by himself in conjunction with the French, and that he had given up all intention of proceeding to the succour of Virginia; and as the British had intercepted and published dispatches taken from the Americans, which gave a very unfavourable account of their affairs, he employed the stratagem of sending fictitious letters announcing the intention above-mentioned, which he took care to throw in the way of the British scouts. Forming a junction in the beginning of July with the French troops from Rhode Island under Rochambeau, in order to carry on the deception, they advanced to the neighbourhood of King's-bridge, and gave a hot alarm to New York. After making demonstrations for some time of a serious purpose against that city, the combined forces suddenly crossed the North river and marched through the Jerseys to Trenton, whence on September 3d they reached Philadelphia. Their next progress was to the head of the river Elk, at the upper end of the Chesapeak. Here, being destitute of shipping for their conveyance down the bay, the light troops alone were embarked, and Washington, with the main body, pursued his march through Baltimore to Annapolis in Maryland.

Sir Samuel Hood, on August 25th, arrived off the Chesapeak from the West Indies with 14 sail of the line and some frigates, and not meeting with Admiral Graves with the squadron from New York, who had received damage in a cruize off Boston, he proceeded to Sandy Hook. There Admiral Graves arrived on the 31st with five sail of the line and a 50 gun ship, and took the command. De Grasse came with his fleet from the West Indies to the Chesapeak on August 28th, and sent the welcome news of his arrival to the combined French and American army. He then blocked up York river, and occupied James river to a considerable extent with his armed vessels, in order to prevent Lord Cornwallis from attempting a retreat to Carolina. On September 5th, a partial and indecisive engagement took place off the mouth of the Chesapeak between the French and English fleets, the former of 24 sail of the line, the latter of 19. The fleets continued in sight of each other, repairing their damages, for some days after, when the French having been reinforced by the squadron from Rhode Island, the English returned to New York. De Grasse from that time remained master of the Chesapeak, and thus all hope of the relief of Lord Cornwallis by sea was brought to a close.

That gallant commander was now completely invested in Yorktown by an army of 8000 French and about as many American continentals, and 5000 militia, and had no other cover than earthen works hastily thrown up. The trenches were opened against him on October 6th and 7th with near 100 pieces of heavy ordnance, which in a few days almost silenced the British batteries and ruined their defences. A determination had been formed at New York to attempt, under every disadvantage, the relief of the besieged army, and Sir H. Clinton had embarked with 7000 of his best troops on board of the men of war lying there; but the delay or difficulty of getting to sea precluded all possibility of bringing any succour previously to the final decision. The storming of two redoubts in advance of the British position was a circumstance that removed all doubt of the event, and the success of a spirited sortie from the British lines could only for a short time retard the necessary surrender. This took place on October 19th, and by its terms between five and six thousand men, a large proportion of whom were sick or wounded, and 1500 sailors, became prisoners of war. The General, with all the civil and military officers, except such of the latter as were necessary for the care of the soldiers, were set at liberty on their parole, and all their baggage was to be retained by them, unless containing property taken from the country. Lord Cornwallis in his public letter acknowledged that he and the army had received the most liberal treatment after the surrender, and particularly extolled the kindness and generosity of the French officers. It was a singular circumstance that the American commissioner who drew up the articles of capitulation was the son of Mr. Laurens, at that time a close prisoner in the tower of London. The British fleet and army from New York arrived off the Chesapeak five days after the surrender, which event being made known to them, they sailed back, no movement being made on the part of the French to molest them.

During these transactions an expedition from New York had been sent into Connecticut under the command of Arnold, who was a native of that colony. It was directed against the port town of New London, and succeeded in becoming master of it, after carrying by storm its principal defence, Fort Griswold. The town was committed to the flames, and great quantities of property and commodities of various kinds were destroyed.

In South Carolina there had been an interval of tranquillity for some time, till at length, General Greene having received some reinforcements, made an advance to attack Colonel Stewart who commanded a British force on the Congaree river, and who found it expedient to draw back to the Eutaw Springs, about 60 miles to the north of Charleston. He was followed thither by Greene, and a severe action was brought on, September 8th, attended with various success, and in which both parties claimed the victory. The final result, however, was that the British decamped on the following evening, and withdrew to the vicinity of Charleston, which for the remainder of the year became the theatre of a petty and exasperating warfare.

An expedition for the recovery of the island of St. Eustatius from its British captors was undertaken by the Marquis de Bouillé in November. Embarking with 2000 men in small vessels at Martinique, he attempted a landing on the island, in which, on account of the surf, he succeeded only with 400 of them at day break on the 26th. Sensible that his only chance for safety was a bold advance, he pushed forward and surprized the garrison of the town, nearly 700 in number, so effectually, that the whole island was in his power in a few minutes without the loss of a man on his part. A considerable spoil, the remainder of the produce of the late sales, became the prize of the victors.

The addition of Holland to the number of the enemies of Great Britain had for some months afforded only a new source of booty to the latter, to such a state of weakness had its once formidable navy been reduced. By great exertions, however, about the middle of July, a force of eight ships of the line, from 54 to 74 guns, ten frigates, and five sloops, under Admiral Zoutman, sailed from the Texel, with a large convoy. Admiral Hyde Parker was at this time returning from Elsineur, with a great convoy under his protection, for which purpose he had sailed from Portsmouth in June with four ships of the line, and one of 50 guns. He had been joined at sea by several frigates, and very fortunately, off the coast of Scotland, was reinforced by a 74 gun ship commanded by Commodore Keith Stewart. The two fleets, nearly equal in effective force, came in sight of each other on the Dogger Bank early in the morning of August 5th, when Admiral Parker, detaching his frigates with the convoy, made the signal for a chase. The Dutch admiral also sent away his convoy, and steadily awaited the attack in line of battle. The engagement which ensued resembled the old contests between the fleets of the two nations. It was a continued cannonade, without any manœuvring, for three hours and forty minutes, at the end of which the hostile squadrons lay like logs upon the water, incapable of farther efforts. The carnage was great on both sides, but chiefly on that of the Dutch. No ship was taken or sunk during the action; but the Hollandia, a Dutch ship of 68 guns, sunk in the night before reaching port, her wounded men going down with her. The Dutch convoy was obliged to return without prosecuting its voyage, which was for the important purpose of procuring naval stores from the north.

The combined fleets of France and Spain having convoyed the Duke De Crillon with a large body of troops to the island of Minorca, they were landed without opposition on August 20th, and the siege of Fort St. Philip immediately commenced, the garrison of which consisted only of two British and two Hanoverian regiments, at that time extremely sickly. This service performed, the fleets, consisting of 49 ships of the line, sailed to the mouth of the English channel, the entrance of which they barred, by forming a line from Ushant to the Scilly isles. So defective was the English intelligence, that Admiral Darby, who was at sea with no more than 21 ships of the line, had nearly fallen in with them, when being informed of their position and number by a neutral vessel, he returned to Torbay, and moored his ships across the entrance. He was there reinforced, so that his fleet amounted to 30 sail, with which he was ordered to proceed to sea at all hazards, in order to protect an expected West India convoy. Contrary winds detained him in Torbay till September 14th; and in the meantime the commanders of the combined fleets held a council on the question of attacking him. This measure was strongly recommended by M. De Guichen, supported by the third Spanish Admiral, but being opposed by M. De Beausset and Don Cordova with all the other Spanish flag officers, it was over-ruled; which determination was justified by the bad condition of the combined fleets, and the sickness raging among them. Each of them returned to their respective ports soon after, and Admiral Darby kept the sea till November.

Guichen having been refitted at Brest, set sail in the beginning of December with 19 ships of the line, several of them first rates, and a large fleet of transport and store ships, for the East and West Indies, under his convoy. For the purpose of intercepting this fleet, Admiral Kempenfelt was sent out, but, apparently from ignorance of the enemy's strength, with no more than 12 sail of the line, one 50 gun ship, and four frigates. He fell in with the French on December 12th, in a hard gale of wind, when they were considerably dispersed, and the convoy had fallen astern of the men of war. This gave him an opportunity of capturing about 20 of the former, laden chiefly with ammunition and with implements of every kind, a prize of great importance; with which were also taken near 1100 land-forces, and between 6 and 700 seamen. The admiral then drew up his squadron in line of battle for the purpose of engaging the enemy; but discovering him to be so much stronger than himself, he changed his purpose, and they parted as it were by mutual consent.

The arrival of General Coote in the Carnatic, infused a vigour and unanimity into the proceedings of the East India Company's servants, to which they had long been strangers; and although Hyder's successes had augmented his forces to a very formidable amount, a resolution was formed to encounter him in the field. He had at this time laid siege to several important places at once. Of these, Wandewash being reduced to the most imminent danger, Coote marched to its relief on January 17th. On his approach, Hyder not only relinquished the siege of this fortress with precipitation, but abandoned those of all the others, and withdrew with his whole force to a cautious distance. For some time, this caution on his part, and want of strength on that of the English, rendered the campaign barren of events; but at length, Hyder having made preparations for the siege of Tritchinopoly, Sir E. Coote marched to frustrate his design. Having encamped his army at Porto Novo, near Cuddalore, on July 1st, he brought to action the vast force of Hyder, and, after an obstinate conflict, obtained a complete victory, of which, however, he was unable to make the desired advantage for want of cavalry. Hyder withdrew to the neighbourhood of Arcot, whilst Coote marched northwards to form a junction with an expected reinforcement from Bengal, which he effected in the beginning of August. He then, having taken Trepassore, advanced to meet Hyder, who was marching to its relief, and on August 27th fought another pitched battle with him, which, after the hard contest of a whole day, terminated in driving him from all his strong posts; and obliging him to quit the field. On that day month Coote again attacked Hyder, and after a short action routed him with great loss; after which, he relieved Vellore, which had been reduced to the last extremity. These successes closed the year with a great improvement of the Company's affairs, occasioned by the military talents and energy of the commander in chief and his able coadjutors.

During this summer, transactions of importance to the Company took place at Benares. That fine district, which had been a dependency of the Nabob Vizier of Oude, had, upon the treaty with Sujah Ul Dowlah in 1765, been secured to its possessor the Rajah Bulwant Sing; on whose death in 1770, the presidency of Bengal caused the investiture to be conveyed to his son Cheit Sing. Disputes arising between this Rajah and his superior the Nabob Vizier, Mr. Hastings, then president of the council of Calcutta, took a journey in 1773, to the court of the latter, for the purpose of settling them, when he acted as the protector of the young Rajah. On the death of the Nabob Vizier, in 1775, an arrangement took place with his son and successor, by which the sovereignty of Benares was transferred to the Company, and from that time they stood in the same relation of superior to Cheit Sing that the Nabob had done. No complaint appears to have been made against the Rajah, till, in 1778, war having broken out between England and France, he was required to contribute an extraordinary subsidy towards its expences. A long series of differences then arose, the representations of which by the opposite parties are naturally discordant; but, on the whole, it may be concluded that the demands augmented on one side, and the repugnance to comply with them on the other, and that the Rajah became more and more disaffected to the Company, especially as he found their affairs brought into a hazardous state by the invasion of Hyder Ally. Such was their reciprocal situation when Mr. Hastings, now governor-general in India, set out from Calcutta, in July 1781, on a progress for the purpose of restoring order in the dominions of the Nabob Vizier and calling to account the Rajah of Benares, who was suspected of a design entirely to throw off the Company's authority, and to render himself independent. Proceeding up the Ganges, Mr. Hastings reached Buxar, where he had a conference with the Rajah, of which very different accounts have been given. The Rajah being at length, after various negotiations, placed under arrest, he was rescued, with the massacre of his guard, and fled to the fortress of Luttefpoor. The governor learning that there was a design of attacking his quarters near Benares by night, retired to Chunar. Repeated applications from the Rajah for an accommodation were ineffectual and after reinforcements had been received at Chunar, several of the Rajah's strong holds were attacked and taken, and he himself fled to Bidjeygur, and all his troops dispersed. The governor-general returning to Benares, settled the government, and appointed a new Rajah, with whom he made an agreement, by which the tribute paid to the Company was augmented. Their affairs in this part of India were now so successful, that a treaty of alliance and friendship was concluded with Madajee Scindia, by Colonel Muir. Major Popham then advancing in pursuit of Cheit Sing, to Bidjeygur, an almost impregnable fortress, in which his treasures were deposited, he abandoned the place and his country, carrying with him all the property he was able to convey; and the fortress afterward capitulating, a great booty was divided among the captors. Such was the issue of the transactions relative to Benares.

Intelligence of the Dutch war having reached India in August, the arrival of five of the Company's ships from China at Fort Marlborough on the coast of Sumatra, stimulated the gentlemen of that factory to undertake with their assistance an enterprize against the Dutch settlements in that island. By little more than intimidation this attempt completely succeeded. An undertaking of greater importance was the reduction of the Dutch port and fortress of Negapatam in the Tanjore country, which Sir Edward Hughes had blockaded by sea, from the time of his first knowledge of the rupture with Holland. Sir Hector Monro being appointed to act by land in conjunction with him, the troops destined for this service were landed at Nagore October 21st, and being joined by the marines of the fleet and a detachment of sailors, broke ground before the fort on November 3d. The advances were so vigorous, that the place capitulated on the 12th, although the garrison, reinforced by some of Hyder's men, much surpassed the besiegers in number. The result of its capture was the evacuation by Hyder's troops of all the places which they held in Tanjore and its borders.

The autumnal session of parliament was opened on November 27th, by a speech from the throne, the language of which was not less determinate than it had ever been in maintaining the necessity of continuing the most vigorous exertions for the preservation of the essential rights and permanent interests of the country. Very different, however, were the feelings of the nation in general since the intelligence of Lord Cornwallis's surrender, which was considered as decisive of the impracticability of recovering by force the American colonies; and on the usual motion for the answering address in the House of Commons, Mr. Fox exerted all the power of his eloquence to prevent any pledge from being given for a perseverance in so hopeless a contest. His proposed amendment was however rejected by a large majority; as was likewise a similar one moved in the House of Lords. The ministers on this occasion declared strongly that no such pledge was intended, and the tone of some of them was remarkably moderate. The change in public opinion was rendered more apparent on a motion made by Sir James Lowther, on the day appointed for voting the army supplies, for a declara-

tion against all farther attempts to reduce the Americans to
obedience by force. After a long debate, in which the nature
and objects of any future war on that continent were closely
canvassed, the motion was negatived by no greater majority
than 220 to 179.

Mr. Burke having made a motion for an enquiry into
the confiscations and other proceedings at St. Eustatius, Sir
George Rodney, who was present, defended his conduct by an
invective against the perfidy of the Dutch, and their attachment to the enemies of Great Britain, and also replied to the
attacks on his military character relative to his remaining inactive at that island. In his defence he was followed by his fellow-
commander General Vaughan, and the motion was finally
quashed on a division.

Notice being given by Mr. Burke of an intention after the
recess to move for a bill for regulating the mode of exchanging
prisoners with America, he took occasion to inveigh against the
cruelty, injustice, and impolicy of the treatment of Mr. Laurens
during his confinement in the Tower; and he delivered a representation and prayer from that gentleman, addressed to the
House of Commons, written by him with a black lead pencil,
as he had refused the indulgence *lately* offered him of the use of
pen and ink, from which he had been long debarred — with so
much augmented acrimony had the contest with America been
carried on near its period. Some severe attacks on the conduct
of the Admiralty were the most interesting occurrences in the
remainder of the session previous to the recess.

1782

22^d & 23^d Year of the Reign

THE first business brought before the House of Commons after the Christmas recess, was an enquiry into the conduct of the first lord of the Admiralty, opened by Mr. Fox in a motion, January 23d, for a committee to be appointed for that purpose. The motion being assented to, Mr. Fox, on February 7th, having stated at length what he represented as instances of gross and criminal neglect in that nobleman, moved for the resolution "that there has been gross mismanagement in the administration of the naval affairs of Great Britain during the course of the year 1781." The defence of the Earl of Sandwich was undertaken by Lord Mulgrave, who endeavoured to refute all the particular charges adduced. Lord Howe supported the accusations; and after a long debate, a division took place, in which the motion was negatived by 205 against 183. The same question being brought afterwards before the house, it was rejected by 236 against 217.

The time now arrived in which the sense of the public with respect to the continuance of the American war was to be rendered so apparent, that no secret wish for a farther prosecution of it should induce the ministers to take any measures for retarding a final agreement. On February 22d,

General Conway moved in the House of Commons that an address should be presented to his Majesty, imploring him to listen to the advice of his commons, that the war in America might be no longer pursued for the impracticable purpose of reducing the inhabitants of that country to obedience by force, and to express their hopes that a happy reconciliation might be effected with the revolted colonies. A long debate ensued, in which the ministers continued to speak on the subject in a vague and indeterminate manner. On the division, the numbers were, for the address 193, against it 194. A ministerial victory by one vote was not likely to deter the opposition from pursuing their point; and on February 27th General Conway moved a resolution similar to that which had been rejected before the recess, and containing a declaration against an *offensive war* with America. An attempt was made by the attorney-general to elude the motion by moving an adjournment of the debate, which was negatived by 234 votes against 215, after which, the original motion, and an address to the king formed upon the resolution, were carried without a division. His Majesty's answer reported to the house was to the effect that such measures should be taken as should appear to him most conducive to the restoration of harmony between Great Britain and the revolted colonies; and that his efforts should be directed in the most effectual manner against our European enemies, until a peace should be procured consistent with the interest and welfare of these kingdoms. For this answer the thanks of the house were unanimously voted; after which, General Conway moved a resolution that the house would consider as enemies to his Majesty and the country all who should advise or attempt the prosecution of offensive war in North America, which passed without a division.

It was now expected that the prime minister, conformably to the manly language he had held in the debate, would have resigned a post in which he was no longer supported by the confidence of parliament; but some secret reasons induced him still to linger in his seat, and he even defeated by small majorities some motions of opposition members for strong censures on the past conduct of the administration. At length, a renewed motion of this kind being brought forwards, Lord North rose and declared *that the administration was no more*; and in order to give time for the new arrangement which his Majesty had determined to make, he moved an adjournment, which was agreed to.

In the administration now formed, under the auspices of the Marquis of Rockingham, that nobleman took the post of first lord of the treasury; the Earl of Shelburne and Mr. Fox were secretaries of state; Lord Camden, president of the council; the Duke of Grafton, lord privy seal; Lord John Cavendish, chancellor of the exchequer; Admiral Keppel (created a viscount), first lord of the admiralty; General Conway, commander in chief of the forces; the Duke of Richmond, master-general of the ordnance; the Duke of Portland, Lord Lieutenant of Ireland. Lord Thurlow was continued in the office of lord-chancellor. This arrangement was announced to parliament, which further adjourned for the Easter holidays.

On April 8th, Mr. Eden, secretary to Lord Carlisle in his vice-royalty of Ireland, having just arrived from that country with his lordship's resignation, moved in the House of Commons for leave to bring in a bill for the repeal of that clause in the act of George I which asserted a right in the parliament of Great Britain to make laws binding upon the kingdom of Ireland. The precipitation with which so important a matter was introduced without any communication with the ministers, was much censured; and the mover being with difficulty induced to withdraw his motion, Mr. Fox, on the following day, brought a message from the king, informing the house, that discontents and jealousies prevailing amongst his subjects in Ireland respecting matters of great moment, he recommended to it to take them into serious consideration, in order that a final adjustment might be made which should prove satisfactory to both kingdoms. A similar message was delivered to the House of Lords, and correspondent addresses were voted by both houses. A message to the same purpose being transmitted to the Irish House of Commons, Mr. Grattan moved an address which, after an explicit declaration of the independent rights of Ireland, proceeded to state the causes of the subsisting discontents, namely, the act of George I above-mentioned, the power of suppressing or altering bills, lodged in the privy council, and the perpetual mutiny bill. On the ground of this address, the secretaries of state on May 17th moved in each house of parliament the repeal of the obnox-ious act, to which, in the House of Commons, was added the motion for a resolution declaring the necessity of establishing a firm and solid connection between the two countries by the consent of both: which motions passed without opposition. The Irish parliament being informed by the Duke of Portland of the steps that had been taken by the British legislature, and of the farther intention of passing acts for preventing the suppression or alteration of bills in the privy council, and for limiting the duration of the mutiny act to two years, that parliament voted a second address to his Majesty expressing their perfect satisfaction with the measures proposed; and they farther testified their gratitude by voting £100,000 for the raising of 20,000 Irish seamen. They also voted £50,000, for the purchase of an estate to be settled on Mr. Grattan, "as a testimony of their gratitude for the unequalled benefits conferred by him on that kingdom."

The temper of the new ministry was shewn by the introduction of several bills for promoting economy and reform, which had failed in the late administration. Those for disqualifying revenue officers from voting in elections for members of parliament, and rendering contractors incapable of a seat in the House of Commons, passed through both houses; and received the royal assent. Mr. Burke's plan of reform in the civil list expenditure was again brought before parliament, introduced by a recommendation from the King, expressed in the most gracious and popular language. In consequence, a committee of the House of Commons was appointed to take the matter into consideration, and a bill was framed which went to the abolition of a number of offices usually held by members of parliament, and the salaries of which amounted to more than £72,000. It being objected that this bill was not so extensive as the original plan, Mr. Burke gave reasons for the omissions, which had been made, either from a compliance with the opinions of others, or from a maturer consideration of the particular cases. He displayed his personal disinterestedness by a bill for the regulation of his own office, that of paymaster of the forces, the principal object of which was to prevent the accumulation of any balance in the hands of the paymaster, which had often amounted to an enormous sum.

Mr. Wilkes took advantage of the change in the times by a motion for expunging the resolution of the house in 1769 relative to the Middlesex election, which was now carried by the majority of 115 to 47. Mr. Fox and Lord North both spoke and voted against the motion.

Mr. Pitt, who began his political career with the ardour for melioration characteristic of ingenuous youth, brought again before the House of Commons the topic of reform in the constitution of parliament; and desirous of avoiding the difficulties which have always occurred in procuring agreement to specific propositions, he moved, May 7th, "that a committee be appointed to enquire into the state of the representation in parliament, and to report to the house their sentiments thereon." The point was ably debated, but on a division, the motion was rejected by 161 votes to 141.

The new ministry were still engaged in their plans of improvement and correction, and a number of resolutions had passed to bind parliament to an early consideration in the next sessions of various specified subjects, which there was not time at present to discuss, when it received a fatal blow by the death of the Marquis of Rockingham on July 1st. This event was immediately succeeded by the appointment of the Earl of Shelburne to his vacant place at the head of the treasury; and this was followed by the resignation of some of the most distinguished persons in the administration, among whom were the Duke of Portland, Lord John Cavendish, Mr. Fox, Mr. Burke, Lord Althorpe, and Mr. J. Townshend. In the new arrangement, Mr. Pitt was made Chancellor of the Exchequer, Mr. T. Townshend and Lord Grantham secretaries of state, and the Earl of Temple Lord Lieutenant of Ireland, besides several minor changes. Such a sudden and radical alteration in the frame of ministry, necessarily occasioned much speculation in the public as to its causes; and the conversations respecting it in both houses of parliament only partially gratified curiosity. It appeared that great differences had existed in the cabinet during the illness of the deceased marquis, which Mr. Fox affirmed to be on points of the most essential importance; and he said, that even whilst the recovery of that person was confidently hoped, he had in a full cabinet declared his intention of resigning, if certain measures were not adopted, and that being outvoted on that occasion, he had determined no longer to act in a situation in which he could not act without renouncing his principles. Lord John Cavendish made a declaration to the same effect. On the other hand, Lord Shelburne declared it as his opinion that there was no other cause for the secession of Mr. Fox, than that his Majesty had been pleased to appoint him (Lord Shelburne) first lord of the treasury. The conversation in the House of Commons on this topic came on during a debate relative to a pension granted to Colonel Barré, which was severely reflected on by a member of the old administration.

During the whole of this session of parliament the two committees on East India affairs in the House of Commons sat with unremitting diligence and drew up extremely voluminous and able reports on the matters under their investigation. The secret committee, of which the Lord Advocate of Scotland was chairman, moved no fewer than III resolutions, some of which severely censured the conduct of certain individuals, and a bill of pains and penalties was brought in against Messrs. Rumbold, Whitehill, and Perring. The select committee strongly inculpated Mr. Sullivan, and moved an address to the King for the recall of Sir Elijah Impey, who had been appointed by Mr. Hastings to an office held at the pleasure of the governor-general, contrary to the intent of an act of parliament.

The prorogation of parliament took place on July 11th.

The West Indies were in this year the theatre of much active warfare. In January the settlements of Demarary and Essequibo were retaken by the French, and restored to Holland.

In the same month, the Marquis de Bouillé landed a force of 8000 men upon St. Christopher's, supported by De Grasse with 32 ships of the line. General Frazer with a garrison of 600 men retired to the almost inaccessible post of Brimstone-hill which was closely invested by the French. The English fleet of 22 ships of the line was then at Barbadoes, commanded by Sir Samuel Hood, who, though so much inferior in force, resolved to make an attempt for the relief of St. Christopher's. By a skilful manœuvre he gained possession of the enemy's anchoring ground, where he repulsed two severe attacks from De Grasse. An attempt was afterwards made to succour the garrison on Brimstone-hill, by landing General Prescot with a body of men upon the island; but this proved ineffectual, and the fortress with the whole island capitulated on February 13th, on favourable conditions. The English fleet slipt its cables and put to sea; and the islands of Nevis and Montserrat followed the fate of St. Christopher's. Jamaica now appeared to be brought into greater danger than ever, for whilst De Grasse was riding superior among these islands, the Spaniards were in great strength at Cuba and Hispaniola; and the fleets of the two nations, if combined would have consisted of 60 ships of the line, while their land forces would have constituted a powerful army. In this state of things, Sir George Rodney arrived at Barbadoes on February 19th with 12 sail of the line, and made junction with Sir S. Hood's squadron. He was soon after reinforced by three ships of the line from England, and his fleet now consisted of 36 of the line. It was fortunate that Guichen's squadron, which had been encountered by Kempenfelt, was afterwards so much shattered by storms, that only two men of war, with a few vessels of the convoy could reach the West Indies, the remainder being obliged to put back to France. Rodney, after being disappointed in an attempt to intercept a French convoy, put into St. Lucia; while De Grasse was lying at Martinique with 34 ships of the line, his object being to avoid an engagement till he had made a junction with the Spaniards. For that purpose he sailed from Port Royal bay on April 8th, with a great convoy, keeping close under the islands. Intelligence of this movement being directly conveyed to the English admiral, a pursuit was instantly begun, and the fleets were in sight of each other off Dominica on that night. An action in which the van chiefly of the English fleet was engaged with the main body of the French, took place on the next day, and two French ships were so much disabled, that they were obliged to quit the fleet and put into Guadaloupe: some of the English ships suffered greatly, but still kept in the line.

On the 11th, the French fleet had gained such a distance that its body only could be descried from the mast heads of the English centre, when two of their damaged ships were observed to fall off from the rest to leeward. The pursuit now became so vigorous that they would necessarily have been cut off had not De Grasse borne down with his whole fleet to their rescue. The result was to bring on that general engagement which had been the object of the English commander, and it commenced about seven o'clock on the following morning, April 12th. In this action, which continued till sun-set, Rodney

was the first who practised the manœuvre, since attended with
such signal success, of breaking the enemy's line. The most
determined courage was displayed on both sides; and it was
not till the crew of De Grasse's ship, the Ville de Paris of 112
guns, had suffered prodigious carnage from several successive
antagonists, that he struck his flag to Sir Samuel Hood in the
Barfleur. With her were taken four others of the line, one of
which afterwards blew up; and one more was sunk by a single
broadside in the engagement. Not a ship was lost in the English
fleet, and its whole loss of men computed to be less than that
on board the Ville de Paris alone. Of the vanquished ships,
some were scattered, but the greater part, under Bougainville
and Vaudreuil, bore away in a body for St. Domingo. In the
pursuit, Sir Samuel Hood's division, after some days, came
up with and captured two ships of the line and two frigates in
the Mona passage. This decisive victory put an end to all the
projects against Jamaica, and Admiral Rodney, after enjoying
his triumph at that island as its saviour, returned to England,
where he was rewarded by a peerage.

In North America, the armies on both sides being nearly
balanced in strength, remained almost inactive in and about
New York; and the intelligence of the resolutions in parliament
against offensive war farther confirmed this disposition.

Some enterprizes upon a small scale fill up the history of the
trans-atlantic warfare of this year.

In May, the governor of Cuba, with an armament of
much greater force than the occasion required, undertook an
expedition against the Bahama islands, the whole military
defence of which consisted of a few invalids under Governor
Maxwell at the town of Providence. Resistance being hopeless, a
capitulation was obtained on honourable conditions, and that
group of islands passed under the dominion of Spain.

To the losses already sustained by the Dutch, was added that
of their settlements on the African coast, which were reduced
chiefly by an inconsiderable naval force under Captain Shirley

of the Leander. Their principal fort, named Commenda, was carried by some land forces of the African company, assisted by a detachment of sailors from the Argo frigate.

A French squadron under M. de la Perouse, consisting of a 74 gun ship and two frigates, with soldiers and artillery on board, sailed from Cape François on May 31st, against the settlements and possessions of the Hudson's Bay Company. They did not arrive at the entrance of Hudson's Bay till July 17th, and even at that season, experienced great difficulties in their advance on account of the ice. At length, on August 8th, they arrived at Fort Prince of Wales, upon the Churchill river, which being like the other forts of the Company, little more than strong factories, with no other garrison than clerks and storekeepers, not the least resistance was attempted. The invaders had no other trouble in making the conquest of this and the other forts than what arose from the approach; and having blown up and destroyed all the buildings, with the exception of one magazine, which the commander humanely left furnished with provisions and stores for the winter sustenance of the English who had fled to the woods, they returned at the close of August. Two of the Company's ships and a sloop had the good fortune to escape.

The recovery of Fort Omoa, and the failure of an expedition from Jamaica to the river St. Juan on the Spanish main, had caused the Spaniards to press closely upon the British settlers and the Indians in the bay of Honduras, and on the Mosquito shore, and they had possessed themselves of Fort Dalling on Cape river, and of other posts in that country. A plan being formed for their expulsion, Captain Campbell at the head of a body of negroes, after several other successes against them during this summer, carried Fort Dalling in a nocturnal assault. A small army was afterwards formed of shore-men, Indians, and American rangers, who, appointing Lieutenant-Colonel Despard their commander, marched to attack the Spaniards in their posts at Black river, consisting of 7 or 800 men.

These were soon brought to a surrender, and the forts with a considerable booty were the prize of the victors.

The siege of Fort St. Philip in Minorca rendered memorable by the gallantry of its defenders, under the pressure of a scorbutic malady, which at length diminished their originally insufficient numbers, to a remnant incapable of manning the works, terminated on February 5th by a capitulation, by which the garrison was made prisoners of war. They were, however, treated with the most humane sympathy by the victors, whose admiration they had strongly excited.

The home fleet of Great Britain, much inferior to the united force of its enemies, was obliged in this year to act chiefly on the defensive, yet the enterprize of its commanders found occasions for spirited service. In April, Admiral Barrington sailed with 12 ships of the line for the Bay of Biscay, where, on the 20th, he gave chase to a fleet laden with warlike stores, and conveying a considerable body of troops for the supply of the French in the East Indies, under the protection of two men of war of the line, a large ship armed *en flute*, and a frigate. The result was the capture of the Pegase man of war, and the ship *en flute*, and about 12 of the convoy, with several hundred soldiers, and many valuable stores.

In May, intelligence having been received, that the Dutch were preparing to come out of the Texel with all their force in order to convoy a fleet of merchantmen, and afterwards to join the French and Spanish fleets, Lord Howe was dispatched with 12 sail of the line to intercept them. The Dutch had already set sail; but so low was at that time their spirit of enterprize, that they returned to the Texel; and Lord Howe, after cruizing upon their coast for a month, finding his men become sickly, and the Dutch lying quiet, returned to port.

De Guichen, in the beginning of June, sailed from Cadiz with Don Cordova, and a combined fleet of 25 ships of the line, and proceeding northwards, fell in with the outward-bound Newfoundland and Quebec fleets, of which he captured 18, the armed vessels who were their convoy escaping. Being afterwards joined by the Brest fleet, they rode masters of the sea from the Straits mouth to Ushant. Great apprehension being excised for the homeward Jamaica fleet, convoyed by only three men of war, under Sir Peter Parker, Lord Howe sailed early in July, with Admirals Barrington, Ross, and Kempenfelt, to afford them assistance, having only 22 sail of the line, while the combined fleet were in the chops of the channel, with more than double that force. By skilful management, however, the whole convoy was brought in safe, and the fleet returned to Portsmouth. It was there that a memorable disaster happened to the finest ship in the navy. As the Royal George of 108 guns was receiving a slight careen at anchor, with her commander, Admiral Kempenfelt, her officers and crew on board, and a number of women and children from shore, being laid somewhat on one side to examine her lower works, a sudden squall threw her off the balance, and her ports being open, she took in so much water, that she instantly went to the bottom, with 8 or 900 people. The loss of so many lives was aggravated by that of the admiral, one of the bravest and ablest commanders in the service.

A still heavier calamity befel a portion of the British navy in the course of this year. Near the close of July, Admiral Graves took his departure from Jamaica, with seven ships of the line, and about 100 sail of merchantmen. Part of the convoy being bound for New York, the fleet took a more northerly course than usual, which probably brought them into worse weather than they would otherwise have experienced; several of the men of war, likewise, were French prizes taken in the battle of April 12th, and the damages they sustained had been only imperfectly repaired. On September 8th, a heavy gale came on, in which the Caton and a frigate became leaky, and were sent to Halifax. On the 16th, the fleet being off the banks of Newfoundland, a storm of uncommon violence occurred which lasted through the night, and was succeeded by a sudden squall in an opposite direction, the joint effect of which, brought the fleet into the most distressed condition. The Ramillies, the Admiral's ship, suffered so much, that it being impossible any longer to keep her above water, she was set on fire on the 21st, after the crew had been shifted to the merchantmen which still kept company. The Centaur, Captain Inglefleld, was kept from sinking till the 23d, when she was alone in the midst of the Atlantic. Being now just on the point of going down, the captain and ten of the crew got into the pinnace, and determined to take a wretched chance for life. With difficulty they pushed clear of the ship, and committing themselves to the wide and stormy ocean, with no other sail than a blanket, with a miserable pittance of provision, and very thin clothing, after 16 days of struggles which rendered their deliverance one of the most remarkable instances of the kind upon record, they all arrived safe at the harbour of Fayal. The fate of the Ville de Paris, the pride of the French navy, and of the English victory, was only known from one man who was taken up at sea floating on a piece of wreck, and who could just recollect his quitting her as she was going to pieces, and also that he had seen another prize, the Glorieux, founder on the preceding day. The fortune of the Hector was in some respects still more calamitous, since in a most distressed condition, she was attacked by two French frigates, and had many of her crew killed and wounded. The assailants failed in an attempt to board the Hector, and at length quitted her, but in a state which exposed the remainder to dreadful sufferings from fatigue and want. In fine, the survivors were taken on board a ship bound to Newfoundland, leaving the vessel to founder. Such was the end of five out of the seven men of war in this unfortunate fleet; many merchantmen also perished, but their number bore a small proportion to the loss in the former class.

The most interesting scene of military action which the present year afforded was the siege of Gibraltar. Although there was scarcely any sacrifice which the court of Spain was not

ready to make for the possession of this fortress, and each year
of the siege had augmented the assailing force, and the annoyance offered to the town and garrison, yet no real advance
had been made towards overpowering the terrific defences of
the place; and a formidable sally directed by the active and
vigilant commander, General Elliot, at the close of the preceding November, had spread ruin through the nearest works of
the besiegers. It was now resolved to make trial of the utmost
that force and skill could effect in vanquishing the impediments that both nature and art had lavished to render Gibraltar
impregnable. The aid of twelve thousand French troops was
procured to diffuse a spirit of enterprize in the Spanish army.
The supreme command was conferred on the conqueror of
Fort St. Philip, the Duke de Crillon; and the plan of attack was
confided to the Chevalier d'Arcon, a French engineer of high
reputation. The preparations by land and water were prodigious, and the accumulation of artillery and warlike materials
of every kind was beyond all former example. Volunteers and
spectators of the first rank assembled from almost every part
of Europe to witness and assist in the expected conflict; and
at the head of the list were two French princes of the blood,
the Count d'Artois and the Duke de Bourbon. The grand
project of d'Arcon was founded on the construction of floating
batteries so contrived that they could be neither sunk nor set
on fire; for this effect, besides having timbers of extraordinary
thickness, they were fortified on the exposed side with a wall
of cork and soaked timber, between the layers of which wet
sand was interposed, while a circulation of water was provided
through the whole mass. The vessels thus fitted up were ten
ships from 600 to 1400 tons burden, cut down to the requisite
height for the intended superstructure, and furnished with
new brass cannon of great weight. At the same time new and
powerful batteries were opened on the land side, and a fleet
of 48 sail of the line with many smaller vessels was brought
to co-operate.

In the morning of September 13th, the ten battering ships were skilfully moored in a line from the old to the new mole at about 900 yards distance from the rock of Gibraltar, and a cannonade and bombardment from all quarters of the attack and defence, more tremendous than imagination can conceive, instantly commenced. The fire of the floating batteries equalled all that could have been expected from it, and for many hours was maintained without intermission, whilst the contrivances for their protection seemed fully to answer their purpose. But the showers of red-hot shot from the fortress were at length not to be resisted by any efforts of human art. Smoke began to appear from the admiral's ship soon in the afternoon, and gradually the rest of the line exhibited the same alarming symptom. Confusion and distress hourly augmented, flames broke out from stem to stern; and not to dwell on a scene which would afford scope for a narrative of tragical grandeur suited to the poet or orator, all the vessels in succession blew up, and not a vestige was left on the following day of an apparatus of war so novel and formidable. The number of men lost on this occasion must have been very considerable, notwithstanding the efforts made not only by the Spaniards, but after the affair was decided, by their generous foe, to save the men crying for help from the midst of the flames. Of these near 400 were brought away by the English gun-boats under the direction of Captain Curtis. The loss in the garrison upon this day of peril was very moderate; and the damage sustained by the works was not such, as to afford any cause of apprehension for future security.

The only remaining chance for the reduction of Gibraltar was the prevention of that annual relief from England which was necessary for the health and sustenance of the garrison; and the vast naval force collected for this purpose was thought fully equal to the object. The attempt, however, was resolved upon; and history affords few examples of national magnanimity superior to that now exhibited by Great Britain, which, confiding in the skill and courage of its navy, collected the whole force remaining for the defence of its coasts, and sent it for the succour of a distant fortress, with the certainty of having to confront a hostile fleet at least one-fourth superior in strength, on its own seas. Lord Howe, with 34 ships of the line, several frigates and fire-ships, and a fleet of store-ships with troops on board, sailed from Portsmouth in September; and after encountering much unfavourable weather, entered the mouth of the Straits of Gibraltar on October 11th. A storm the preceding night had thrown the combined fleet at Algeziras into great confusion, so that an opportunity was offered to the store-ships of running in to the port of Gibraltar without molestation. Of this, however, but a small number could avail themselves: the rest were driven through the straits into the Mediterranean, and were followed by Lord Howe. The combined fleet sailed from Algeziras on the 13th, and entering the Mediterranean, bore down, in the number of 42 ships of the line, to the English fleet, now of 32 sail, drawn up to receive them. Changing their mind, they tacked and stood in for the shore; and Lord Howe being enabled by a favourable wind to return to the straits, employed himself in sending in the store vessels, and landing the supplies of troops for the garrison. On the 20th he repassed the straits, followed by the enemy; and on the next day a partial action was brought on in which they made attempt to cut off a part of the British rear. This being frustrated, and battle fairly offered by Lord Howe, but refused, he pursued his way to England, having with admirable seamanship performed the arduous task assigned to him.

The East Indies were a scene of busy action in this year. Towards the close of the preceding year, Sir Edward Hughes sailed upon an expedition against the Dutch settlement of Trincomalee in the Island of Ceylon, and on January 5th anchored in its bay, bringing with him, besides the marine forces, about 500 volunteer sepoys, and a company of artillery.

The troops immediately on landing pushed on to Trincomalee Fort, which they carried with little resistance; and the principal defence, Fort Ostenburg, being held out by the commander, it was stormed and taken on the 11th, on which occasion the victors honoured themselves by their clemency towards the prostrate foe. The fine harbour of this place rendered it a very valuable capture.

M. de Suffrein, after he had left some French troops to strengthen the garrison of the Cape of Good Hope, proceeded to Mauritius, where he made a junction with the squadron of M. d'Orves. The united fleet, consisting of 10 sail of the line, a 50 gun ship, and several large frigates, then sailed for the coast of Coromandel, accompanied by a number of store-ships and transports, with a considerable body of land forces. The news of their arrival reached Sir E. Hughes, on February 8th in Madras roads, whither he had returned from Trincomalee with only six sail of the line. He was however joined on the following day, by Captain Alms with his own and another ship of the line, and a 50 gun ship, another of the same force having unfortunately fallen into the power of Suffrein's fleet on the passage from the Cape. On the 15th the French appeared in sight, and after some manœuvres during two days, a partial action was brought on, in which some of the English ships, being engaged with a superior number of the enemy, suffered great damage. Sir E. Hughes then repaired to Trincomalee to refit, and about the middle of March returned to Madras.

While this was passing at sea, Major Abingdon, arriving from Bombay, with a considerable reinforcement, at Tellicherry, which continued to be invested by Hyder's troops, resolved upon an attempt to dislodge them.

Having taken to his assistance a part of the garrison, he surprized and carried their forts in the morning of January 8th, and pushing his success, stormed their fortified camp, and completely routed their main body. A great spoil was the fruit of victory; and the coast for some miles on each side of Tellicherry was entirely cleared of the enemy. This blow inflicted upon Hyder was, however, more than retaliated shortly after. Colonel Braithwaite was lying on the banks of the Coleroon, a river which forms the northern boundary of Tanjore, with a detachment consisting of 2000 Sepoy infantry and 250 cavalry, with some field pieces. On February 16, Tippoo Saib with 20,000 native troops and 400 French under M. Lally, having suddenly surrounded the English force, began an attack which was gallantly resisted for two days, but terminated on the third, with the slaughter or captivity of the whole. This success was followed by the siege of Cuddalore by a body of French from Pondicherry, joined by some of Hyder's troops, which place capitulated on April 8th. The victors then advanced to Permacoil, of which they also made themselves masters.

The securing of Trincomalee, and the protection of an expected convoy, re-called Sir Ed. Hughes to Ceylon, and on his way thither he was joined by two men of war, who had made a tedious passage from England which had rendered their crews very sickly. Soon after, Suffrein's fleet appeared in sight, and accompanying the English squadron to the coast of Ceylon, gained the wind as the latter was steering for Trincomalee. On April 12th Sir E. Hughes, forming his line of battle a-head, was attacked by Suffrein, and a very severe engagement ensued, which ended in both fleets drawing off to refit. They continued for several days in this position, when on the 19th the French bore down as if with an intent to renew the combat; but when arrived within two miles of their adversaries, they suddenly tacked, and by evening were entirely out of sight. Hughes then proceeded to Trincomalee, having sustained a loss of 137 killed and 430 wounded, a share of which fell upon the Monmouth, which was almost entirely disabled. The French acknowledged to a somewhat inferior loss: no ship was taken or sunk on either side.

After the capture of Cuddalore and Permacoil, the French
and Hyder planned an attack upon Wandewash, but Sir Eyre
Coote advancing for its protection, Hyder retired, and took
a strong position among the hills. In order to bring him to
action, the English general marched towards Arnee, where
Hyder's principal magazines were deposited, and encamped
within five miles of the place. As he was afterwards advancing
to a nearer approach, Hyder's army in full force was descried
coming to its defence and on June 2d a general action was
brought on, which terminated in Hyder's total rout. The want
of cavalry, however, prevented a pursuit; and on the next day
intelligence was received that Hyder was again encamped on
strong ground. The approach of the British induced him to
make a precipitate retreat; but nothing could be gained in
such a war against an enemy so numerous and so quick in his
movements; and the fatigue of his troops and want of
provision, soon after induced Sir E. Coote to fall back nearer
to his supplies. That distinguished commander was rendered
incapable through ill health of continuing much longer in the
field. He was succeeded in the command by Major-General
Stuart, and the remainder of the campaign was spent in long
and toilsome marches for relieving particular places and
counteracting the enemy's designs, without any event of great
importance.

Suffrein, having returned to the coast of Coromandel, and
revictualled and fully manned his ships, appeared on July 5th,
before Negapatam, where Sir Edward Hughes was lying with
his squadron after a repair at Trincomalee. The English admiral
immediately stood out to sea; and on the following day brought
the French to close action. The latter after a time appeared to
have suffered so much, that nothing but a sudden shift of
wind could have prevented them from undergoing a decided
defeat. The engagement afterwards was partial and irregular,
and ended with the retreat of the French to Cuddalore. One
of their ships of 64 guns having become ungovernable, fell

alongside of an English ship and struck her colours, but finding an opportunity to escape, she availed herself of it, according to a not uncommon practice of the French; and the English admiral's demand of her was answered by the excuse that her striking had been accidental. In this action the acknowledged loss of men in Suffrein's fleet much exceeded that of the English. Unfortunately, however, the French so much sooner repaired their damages, that Suffrein, being informed of the arrival of two French men of war and a reinforcement of troops and artillery at Point de Galle in Ceylon, sailed thither, and in conjunction with them, attacked Trincomalee, which in a short time capitulated. Sir E. Hughes, informed too late of its danger, did not arrive off the port till the French flag was flying in the forts. Suffrein sailing out to meet him, a fourth action ensued between these habitual antagonists, on September 3d, which was disputed with extraordinary spirit, but proved indecisive, and like the other three was not attended with the loss of a single ship. One of the French ships of the line, however, on the return of the fleet to Trincomalee, was lost on getting into the harbour. Hughes went to refit at Madras, where he narrowly escaped a dreadful hurricane on October 15th, which caused the wreck of several English traders, and a great many coasting vessels laden with rice, and eventually produced a shocking famine among the natives. Sir Richard Bickerton arrived at Madras in that month with five ships of the line, and a considerable reinforcement of troops.

The Mahratta war having been concluded by a treaty, the presidency of Bombay dispatched Colonel Humberstone with a considerable detachment of troops to the Malabar coast. He made himself master of the cities of Calicut and Paniany and all the intermediate places on the coast; and quitting the sea-coast in September, he advanced to the interior against the town of Palicancherry. At this place he found the enemy so strong, that he made a hasty retreat to Mangarry Cottah, a fortress which he had taken, losing some men and his baggage in the pursuit. His perilous situation caused the government of Bombay to send General Matthews to his relief; and in the meantime Tippoo, having collected a body of troops, marched from the Carnatic in order to intercept Humberstone. The latter, informed of his approach, fell back to Paniany, where he arrived without farther loss. Colonel Macleod who superseded him in the command at that place, was soon invested by Tippoo and Lally with a formidable combined force, which he resisted with great gallantry; and a general attack being made on his lines, it was repulsed with considerable loss to the assailants. Tippoo in December broke up his camp, and by rapid marches returned to the Carnatic, where Hyder, his father, was lying at the point of death. This extraordinary person died about the close of the year, leaving a territory of his own acquisition to his son Tippoo, which rendered him one of the most powerful princes in the south of India.

In Europe, one of the most remarkable events of this year, was a visit paid by the Pope in the month of March to the Emperor Joseph at Vienna, for the purpose of dissuading him from that suppression of religious houses, and other measures hostile to the church of Rome, which, among his multifarious plans of reform, he was actively pursuing. The pontifical zeal of Pius VI led him, notwithstanding his age and infirmities, and the inclemency of the season, to set out from Rome at the close of February, for a personal interview with this refractory son; and nothing could afford a more striking contrast to ancient times than such a reverse in the relative situations of a pope and an emperor of Germany. The latter, however, paid every mark of external respect to the holy father, going to meet him, in company with his brother the Archduke Maximilian, as far as Neukirchen, and conducting him to Vienna in his own coach. Frequent conferences took place between them with apparent mutual satisfaction during the month of his stay; but no intermission afterwards took place in the emperor's ecclesiastical reforms.

The inquisition was in this year abolished in the dominions of the Grand Duke of Tuscany.

Constantinople suffered under two dreadful conflagrations, in July and August, by which it was supposed that two thirds of the city were laid in ashes, and more than 40,000 houses were destroyed, and their inhabitants left without shelter. The deposition of the Grand Vizer, by way of an offering to the popular discontent, was one of the consequences.

The conclusion of a destructive war, now without any specific object, was a point to which as well the belligerent powers themselves, as the other European potentates, turned their serious attention; and the Empress of Russia and Emperor of Germany offered their mediation for the purpose, which was accepted. The original cause of the war, the dispute between Great Britain and her colonies, was first brought to an accommodation; and on November 30th, provisional articles were signed at Paris between the commissioner of the King of Great Britain and those of the United States. By this treaty the sovereignty and independency of the Thirteen United States was recognized in the most ample manner; and in fixing the boundaries between them and the remaining British possessions in North America, imaginary lines were drawn, which assigned to the American States vast tracts of land and water not before within their limits. A great number of Indian nations were comprized in these boundaries, which, however, could not properly be said to be granted by those, and to those, who had no right over them. Among the concessions was that of an unlimited right of fishery on the banks of Newfoundland, and all the other fishing grounds which had before been frequented by the Americans.

The other negotiations were brought to such a degree of forwardness, that on November 23d letters were sent from the secretary of state to the lord mayor and the governor of the bank, acquainting them for the information of the public, and to prevent speculations in the funds, that a decisive conclusion, either for peace or war, might be expected before the meeting of parliament, which on that account was prorogued to December 5th. On that day the session was opened by a speech from the throne of uncommon length, and comprehending a great variety of political topics. The independence of the colonies was mentioned in the following terms. "In thus admitting their separation from the crown of these kingdoms, I have sacrificed every consideration of my own to the wishes and opinion of my people. I make it my humble and earnest prayer to Almighty God, that Great Britain may not feel the evils which might result from so great a dismemberment of the empire; and that America may be free from those calamities which have formerly proved, in the mother country, how essential monarchy is to the enjoyment of constitutional liberty." The consequent addresses passed without opposition in both houses; but some severe remarks were made by the different parties in opposition on particular parts of the speech. It was not, however, till the meeting after the recess that important debates took place relative to the conditions of peace.

1783

23^d & 24th Year of the Reign

BEFORE we enter, according to our usual order, upon the domestic events of the year, it may be convenient to finish the narrative of warlike transactions, of which the East Indies were now the only remaining theatre.

General Matthews receiving intelligence of Tippoo's repulse by Colonel Macleod, and subsequent retreat, changed his intention of proceeding farther to the south, and marched to lay siege to the city of Onore, in the Lower Canara, one of Hyder's annexations. On January 5th, this place was carried by storm, its only defenders being the native polygars or militia, who were little conversant with war, and a cruel slaughter is said to have been made not only of the garrison, but of the inhabitants of both sexes and every age. A great booty was obtained on this occasion, in the division of which the army was much dissatisfied with the general. In consequence of the positive orders of the president and council of Bombay, that if the reports of Hyder's death should be confirmed, Matthews should endeavour to penetrate through the Ghauts to the Bednore country and attack its capital, that commander proceeded along the coast, where he took Cundapore. In its progress, the army is accused of a shameful massacre at the storming of the fortress of Annampore. The Ghauts being at length passed, the city of Bednore was surrendered by capitulation early in February; and the conduct of Matthews is represented as being now so dishonourable, that Colonels Macleod and Humberstone, with other officers of the royal forces, quitted the army and returned to Bombay. He however still proceeded in a career of success, and in March he took the town and fortress of Mangalore, an important seaport. Tippoo, who now bore the title of Sultan, on the intelligence of these events, collected a very powerful army and marched to oppose the invaders. He appeared in sight in the beginning of April, and a disparity of force is stated, of more than 100,000 men on his part, and about 600 Europeans and 1600 sepoys on that of the English. Matthews, who certainly did not want courage, marched out of Bednore to meet this mighty host, but was soon driven back with the loss of 500 of his men; and abandoning the town, he took refuge in the citadel. He was presently surrounded in a manner to preclude all possibility of escape; and Tippoo sent a detachment to attack the posts in the Ghauts, which were easily carried. The garrison of Cundapore in a panic took to flight; and all the magazines and stores deposited there were set on fire, and a train of artillery was abandoned. On April 28th, the garrison at Bednore capitulated upon liberal terms, which the conqueror did not think himself bound to observe. The troops, after piling their arms, were led out of the place, and were surrounded by some battalions of sepoys. Matthews was brought before Tippoo, who ordered him and those who accompanied him into close confinement, whence they never returned. That they and several of the principal officers, were barbarously put to death is not doubted, though different reports prevailed as to the mode. The troops were plundered of all they possessed, and under the most rigorous treatment were sent to be imprisoned at a fort in the interior. Thus terminated this unfortunate and ill-conducted expedition.

Tippoo, after the reduction of Bednore, laid siege to Mangalore, which, by the aid of his French auxiliaries, would probably have fallen into his hands, had not the intelligence of peace between France and Great Britain induced the French commander positively to refuse acting any more against the English. Tippoo blockaded the place some time longer; but General Macleod arriving on the coast from Bombay, threw in supplies, and no military events of importance afterwards occurred in that quarter.

General Coote who, after transferring the command of the army on the Coromandel coast to General Stuart, had proceeded to Bengal, embarked at Calcutta on his return, with a large sum of money for the further prosecution of the war in the Carnatic, when his constitution being entirely broken by the voyage, he died in two days after his arrival at Madras, April 26th, to the great regret of all who had benefited by his eminent services.

Early in June, General Stuart marched against Cuddalore, which had been strongly fortified by the French, and was held by a considerable body of troops under the command of the Marquis de Bussy. Immediately after his arrival, General Stuart directed an attack on the outworks of the place, which, after a bloody action, were carried. Soon after, Suffrein arrived on the coast from Trincomalee, at which time Sir Edward Hughes was cruizing before Cuddalore with a fleet greatly weakened by sickness. On June 20th, the French fleet, consisting of 15 ships of the line, made an attack, favoured by the wind, upon the English with 17, and a heavy but not close cannonade took place during three hours, at the end of which time the French drew off and repaired to Pondicherry roads. Hughes followed them thither, but was afterwards obliged to go to Madras for water, and Suffrein returned to Cuddalore, where he landed a reinforcement for the garrison. The French on the 25th made a vigorous sally for the purpose of destroying the works of the besiegers, but were repulsed with loss.

Soon after, all hostilities were terminated by the intelligence of a general peace.

The preliminaries of the treaty between England and France, and England and Spain, were signed at Versailles on January 20th. By the first of these, France obtained an extension of her rights of fishery at Newfoundland, and unrestricted possession of the isles of St. Pierre and Miquelon on that coast. In the West Indies, St. Lucie was restored, and Tobago ceded to her, whilst she restored to Great Britain the islands of Grenada, the Grenadines, St. Vincent, Dominica, St. Christopher's, Nevis, and Montserrat. In Africa, France obtained the cession of the river of Senegal and its dependencies and forts, and a restoration of Goree; and England, the possession of Fort James and the river Gambia. In the East Indies, all that France had lost was restored to her with considerable additions; in particular, England was bound to procure certain districts round Pondicherry and Karical, to be annexed to those places. England further consented to the abrogation of all the articles relative to Dunkirk which had been inserted in the treaty of Utrecht and in every posterior treaty. By the preliminaries with Spain, England relinquished all claim to Minorca and West Florida, and ceded East Florida, but obtained the restitution of the Bahama islands. The right of logwood-cutting was left in its former uncertainty.

On the meeting of parliament after the recess, a bill was brought in for removing and preventing all doubts respecting the exclusive right of the parliament and courts of Ireland in matters of legislation and judicature, and for preventing writs of error or appeal from being received from that kingdom in the English courts. The occasion of this bill was the decision in the court of King's Bench on a writ of error, which had been brought from Ireland previously to the passing of the declaratory act in favour of Irish independence, which circumstance had excited jealousy in that country. The bill was carried without opposition.

The provisional treaties with America, and with France and Spain, having been laid before parliament, the 17th of February was the day appointed for taking them into consideration by the House of Commons. After the papers were read, a motion was made by Mr. Thomas Pitt for an address of thanks to his Majesty for the communications, in which was expressed, first, their satisfaction with the treaty of peace with the States of North America, and their expectation that these States would carry into effectual execution the measures which the congress was bound to recommend in favour of such persons as had suffered for the part they had taken in the war; and secondly, to acknowledge their sense of that paternal regard for the happiness of his subjects which had induced his Majesty to relieve them from a burdensome and expensive war. To this address amendments were moved by Lord John Cavendish, and by Lord North, as representatives of the two parties now in opposition; and a debate ensued in which the subject of the peace was canvassed by all the principal speakers in and out of the ministry. The necessity of peace was argued by its defenders from the deplorable state of the finances, the magnitude of the national debt, amounting to upwards of 250 millions, and the enormous load of taxes under which the nation was groaning. The prospects on the supposition of a continuance of the war were also affirmed to have been highly discouraging; and the comparative force in the different quarters of the world, of Great Britain and its enemies, was stated greatly to our disadvantage. The particular articles of the treaty were then gone over, and excused as being the best that could be obtained. On the other side, many of these assertions were controverted or denied, and an ability in this country to have treated on the principle of mutual restitution was insisted upon. Many of the concessions were severely censured, and the lavish augmentations of the American boundary, with the desertion of the loyalists, were especially exclaimed against. So copious were the topics, and numerous the debaters, on this occasion, that the house did not divide till eight o'clock in the morning, when the ministers were left in a minority, the votes for the amendments to the address being 224, against them, 208. In the House of Lords, where proceedings of a similar kind took place, and the same train of argumentation was gone through, the result was different, an amendment moved by the Earl of Carlisle being rejected by 72 against 59.

On February 21st, the subject being resumed in the House of Commons, Lord John Cavendish moved four resolutions, the three first of which went to pledge the House to maintain the peace agreed upon, and to improve the blessings of peace; and also to affirm the propriety of his Majesty's acknowledgment of the independence of America. The fourth was in these terms: "That the concessions granted to the adversaries of Great Britain were greater than they were entitled to either from the actual state of their respective possessions, or from their comparative strength." On this last resolution the force of the parties was again tried in a long and earnest debate, which concluded in a division, for the resolution 207, against it 190. In consequence of this decisive proof of the disapprobation of the House of Commons, Lord Shelburne resigned his post of first commissioner of the treasury; and the chancellor of the exchequer declared that he held his place only till a successor should be nominated.

Now began a ministerial interregnum, filled with the intrigues and vacillations necessarily attending an emergency which had not been foreseen long enough to be provided against, and in which the arduous task was undertaken of forming a new division of power among parties lately in a state of open and apparently irreconcilable hostility. After much time had passed without any appearance of a determination, Mr. Coke, member for Norfolk, on March 19th, gave notice in the House, that if an administration should not be formed on or before the following Friday, he would move for an address to his Majesty on the subject; and a negotiation which commenced on the next day having broken off abruptly, he made the proposed motion on the 24th, which was received with general approbation. The address, which besought his Majesty to form an administration entitled to the confidence of his people, and such as might tend to bring to a close the unfortunate divisions and distractions of the country, was presented, and a gracious answer was returned; and on the following day Mr. Pitt resigned his office.

On April 2d, the *coalition ministry*, so noted in the political history of this reign, was announced. It was formed by the Duke of Portland, first lord of the treasury; Lord North, secretary of state for the home department, and Mr. Fox for the foreign; Lord J. Cavendish, chancellor of the exchequer; Viscount Keppel, first lord of the admiralty; Viscount Stormont, president of the council; the Earl of Carlisle, lord privy seal; the Earl of Hertford, chamberlain, and the Earl of Dartmouth, steward of the household; Viscount Townshend, master-general of the ordnance; Mr. Burke, paymaster-general; Mr. C. Townshend, treasurer of the navy; Mr. Fitzpatrick, secretary at war. The Earl of Northington was nominated to the viceroyalty of Ireland. The seals were put in commission. In this mixture of persons and principles, the Rockingham party were considered to possess the predominancy, four out of the seven cabinet ministers bearing that denomination; but names are of little consequence, when there are acts to judge from.

A loan for 12 millions, brought forward on April 16th, by the chancellor of the exchequer, underwent censure, on account of the high premium it speedily bore: the apology for a disadvantageous bargain for the public was that the late ministry had left an empty treasury, and that the wants were urgent. On May 7th, Mr. Pitt made a promised motion for a reform in the parliamentary representation. For this purpose certain specific propositions were offered, one of which was for an addition of knights of the shire and representatives of the metropolis to the present number of members, which addition he left undetermined, but said he should propose it to consist of one hundred. From the paucity of petitions in favour of reform in this point, it appeared that the ardour for it was much abated in the nation; and on a division, the motion was quashed by the order of the day, the numbers being 293 to 149.

On June 23d, a message was delivered from his Majesty to the House of Commons, recommending to its consideration the forming of a separate establishment for the Prince of Wales. The House was at the same time informed that the King had taken upon himself the annual charge of this establishment, by assigning to the Prince £50,000 out of the civil list, and that nothing more was demanded than £60,000 by way of equipping him for his outset. This sum was accordingly voted.

In a committee on a bill for regulating certain offices in the exchequer, the chancellor proposed, that after the interest of the present auditors and tellers of the exchequer, and the clerk of the pells, in their places, should expire, the salaries of them in future should be fixed and certain; and a rate was offered and adopted, according to which it was calculated that on an average of peace and war, the salaries would be reduced about one half.

The session of parliament closed on July 16th.

In this year, Ireland was decorated with an order of knighthood appropriated to herself, by the style of Knights of the illustrious order of St. Patrick, of which the reigning King was nominated sovereign, and the Lord Lieutenant for the time being, grand master. The date of the institution is February 5th.

Preliminary articles of peace with the States General of the United Provinces, were signed at Paris on September 2d. Of these the most important were, the cession of Negapatam to Great Britain, but with a proviso of treating for its restitution in case of an equivalent offered by the States; and the restoration to the States, of Trincomalee, and of all the other places conquered from them. The definitive treaties of peace between

Great Britain, and France, Spain and the United States of America, were signed on the following day.

The two committees on East India affairs in the House of Commons had paid unremitting attention to the matters before them during the late session of parliament, but the unsettled state of the government had prevented them from bringing forward the result of their enquiries. On the renewed sitting of parliament, however, November 11th, a leading topic of the speech from the throne was the situation of the East India Company, and the expectation of some fruit of those investigations which had so long been carrying on; and Mr. Fox soon after moved for leave to bring in a bill "for vesting the affairs of the East India Company in the hands of certain commissioners, for the benefit of the proprietors and the public;" and also a bill "for the better government of the territorial possessions and dependencies in India." By the first of these it was proposed to commit the whole management of the territorial possessions, revenues, and commerce of the company, with all the powers before vested in the directors or general court of proprietors, to *seven directors* named in the act during the space of four years. Under the orders of this board, and for the sole purpose of managing the commercial concerns of the Company, *nine assistant directors*, proprietors of £2000 India Stock, were to be appointed: vacancies in the directory to be filled up by his Majesty; and in the assistant-directory, by a majority of proprietors at an open election; the assistant directors to be removable by five directors on reasons specified; and both classes to be removable by the King on address of either House of Parliament. The second bill chiefly related to the powers granted to the governor-general and council in India, and to the conduct to be observed towards the natives.

The bold and comprehensive ideas displayed in these bills made a powerful impression upon the public in and out of parliament; at the same time their innovations and

extraordinary delegations of power excited a strong
opposition against them. In the House of Commons the
two principal grounds of objection were the arbitrary
invasion of the chartered rights of the East India proprietors and
directors, without a justifiable plea of necessity, and the
dangerous authority lodged in the hands of the new direction.
On both these heads issue was joined in debates maintained
by the principal speakers, among whom were distinguished, in
support of the bills, the two secretaries of state, Messrs. Burke,
Sheridan, Adam, and Sir Grey Cooper; against them, Messrs.
William and Thomas Pitt, Dundas, Powis, and Jenkinson;
and the contests frequently lasted till near five in the morning. Numerous pamphlets and satirical prints also appeared,
in order to render the bills odious in the eyes of the nation,
and petitions against them were presented by the East India
Company and the City of London. Their progress through
the House of Commons, however, marked the strength of the
coalition from which they originated, and the first bill passed
by a majority of 208 to 102. On December 11th, it was first read
in the House of Lords, when it was reprobated in the strongest
terms by the Duke of Richmond, the Earl of Temple, and Lord
Thurlow, the latter of whom pronounced a high panegyric on
Mr. Hastings, and dwelt on the flourishing state into which
the Company's affairs had been brought by his administration.
No division, however, occurred at this stage. In the meantime
some extraordinary movements were taking place at court. It
is affirmed, that Earl Temple, having requested an audience of
the King, represented so forcibly to his Majesty the thraldom
to which the crown would be reduced by the power now proposed to be constituted, that a note was put into his hands
in which his Majesty declared, "that he should deem those
who should vote for the bill, not only not his friends, but his
enemies; and that if Lord Temple could put this into stronger
words, he had full authority so to do." That the royal influence
was really employed, is undoubted; for several lords who had

entrusted the minister with their proxies, withdrew them a few hours before the House assembled for the second reading of the bill; and others whose support of it had been relied on, gave their votes on the opposite side. The result was, that on a division upon the question of adjournment, the ministers were left in the minority of 79 to 87.

The House of Commons on the same day, December 15th, on the motion of Mr. Baker, took into consideration the rumours above-mentioned, and moved that it was *now* necessary to declare, that to report any opinion of his Majesty upon any proceeding depending in either house of parliament was a high crime, and a breach of the fundamental privileges of parliament; which was carried by 153 to 80. And a resolution then passed, that on the next Monday the House would resolve itself into a committee of the whole House, to take into consideration the state of the nation. A dissolution of parliament being now apprehended, Mr. Erskine made a motion, importing that the House would consider as a public enemy any one who should advise his Majesty to prevent it from discharging the important duty of providing a remedy for the abuses prevalent in the government of the British dominions in the East Indies, which was also carried.

On December 17th, the India bill was rejected by the House of Lords on a division in which the numbers were 95 to 76; and on the same day a messenger brought to the two secretaries of state an order from the King that they should deliver up the seals of their offices and send them by the under secretaries, as a personal interview would be disagreeable to his Majesty. On the following day the rest of the cabinet were dismissed, and a new ministry was appointed. In this arrangement Mr. Pitt, then at the age of 24, was made first lord of the treasury and chancellor of the exchequer; Earl Gower, president of the council; Lord Sydney, secretary of state for the home department, and the Marquis of Carmarthen for the foreign; Lord Thurlow, high chancellor; the Duke of Rutland, lord privy seal; Viscount Howe, first lord of the admiralty; the Duke of Richmond, master-general of the ordnance; Mr. W. Grenville and Lord Mulgrave, joint paymasters; Mr. Henry Dundas, treasurer of the navy. As this change in the ministry left the majority of the House of Commons in a state of opposition, it was not doubted that a dissolution of parliament was in meditation; and on the day fixed for a committee on the state of the nation, Mr. Erskine moved an address to the King deprecating such a measure. The address passed without a division; and a reply was obtained, in which his Majesty assured the House that "he would not interrupt their meeting by any exercise of his prerogative, either of prorogation or dissolution." In this extraordinary situation of political affairs, parliament broke up for the holidays.

The early part of this year was rendered fatally memorable to Calabria and Sicily from the disasters occasioned by a series of violent earthquakes. The first and most destructive shock occurred on February 5th, and villages, towns, and whole cities were totally ruined by it, with the death of numbers of people. The city of Casal Nuova was entirely swallowed up, and the Princess Gerace Grimaldi with more than 4000 people perished in an instant. The inhabitants of Scylla, who, with their prince, had descended from their rock, and taken refuge on the sea-shore, were all swept away by an enormous wave on its return from the land which it had inundated. Messina and the north-east part of Sicily were also great sufferers. The shocks continued through the months of February and March, and their effects extended to both Calabrias.

Spain in this summer employed its marine force in another expedition against Algiers. In July, Don Barcelo set sail with a powerful force, the object of which was a cannonade and bombardment of Algiers by sea, for the former experiment had taken away any desire of renewing an attempt against the place by land. He arrived in the bay on July 29th, where he found preparation made to give him a warm reception. On

August 1st, Barcelo drew up his fleet in line of battle, and began his fire with shot and shells, which was continued for several days with great fury, and was fiercely returned by the Algerine batteries. The effects were not, however, correspondent with this great consumption of ammunition, for though Algiers was frequently set on fire, the flames were prevented from spreading. At length, a Spanish council of war determined that it was advisable to sail back to their own coast; and thus the expedition ended, having only served to give proof that the siege of Gibraltar had improved the practice of Spanish gunnery.

From the period of the conclusion of peace between Russia and Turkey, the peninsula of the Krimea had been a scene of tumult and civil war. The Khan set up by Russia was expelled, and a new one was elected by the Tartars, probably under the influence of the Porte. This event afforded a pretext for the court of Russia to march an army into the country, the result of which was the reduction of the Krimea and the adjacent parts of Tartary, and the cession of these territories in full sovereignty to the Empress Catharine by the restored Russian Khan, who was indemnified by a grant of estates in Russia. In the summer of this year the empress published a manifesto, in which the Krimea, the Kuban, and the island of Taman, were declared to be perpetually annexed to her dominions, and reasons were assigned for this assumption in the usual style of that ambitious sovereign. The Porte issued a counter manifesto, in which the over-bearing and encroaching spirit of the court of Petersburgh was severely animadverted upon, and a declaration was made of the resolution to oppose by force of arms its new claim if persisted in. War being now apparently inevitable, vast preparations were made on both sides for the approaching conflict. Russian troops in great bodies advanced through Poland and the countries from the Don to the Dnieper, towards the borders, and the Emperor of Germany, who had contracted a close alliance with the Empress Catharine, filled Hungary and the provinces adjacent to the Danube with his forces;

whilst the Porte drew the greatest part of its Asiatic troops into Europe. Negotiations for peace under the mediation of France were still carried on to the close of the year.

One of the remarkable occurrences of this year was the first experiment of air balloons in France, invented by M. Montgolfier.

1784

24th & 25th Year of the Reign

T HE meeting of parliament on January 12th exhibited the extraordinary spectacle of a ministry and House of Commons at open variance, the former yet maintaining its ground. In order to prevent, or at least delay, the apprehended dissolution of parliament, two resolutions were carried: one declaring the payment of public money for services voted in the present session, after parliament shall be prorogued or dissolved, if such event shall take place before an act shall have passed appropriating the supplies to such services, a high crime and misdemeanour; the other, deferring the second reading of the mutiny bill to February 23d. Other motions were made and carried hostile to the ministry; when, on January 14th, Mr. Pitt moved for leave to bring in a bill "for the better government and management of the affairs of the East India Company." Of the principles of this bill it is unnecessary here to give an account, since at its second reading, the motion for its being committed was negatived by 222 votes against 214. Mr. Pitt was now strongly urged to give the house some satisfaction respecting the measure of dissolution in which the members were so nearly concerned, but he absolutely refused answering to the interrogatories put to him; and whatever be thought of the propriety of this refusal, it was certainly a remarkable instance of firmness of mind in one so young in public life, to remain unshaken in a situation so awful, especially as he was left almost singly to brave the storm, his brother ministers scarcely affording him any aid. Several independent members of the House of Commons, desirous of putting an end to this disordered state of things by promoting a coalition between the parties, held meetings for that purpose at the St. Albans tavern, where they drew up an address to the Duke of Portland and Mr. Pitt, expressing their wishes for a free communication between them. Both of these persons declared themselves desirous of complying with the wishes of the meeting, but the duke thought it a necessary preliminary to his having an interview with Mr. Pitt, that the latter should previously resign his office, which Mr. P. declined doing. Further attempts for obtaining this concession from him proved fruitless, and all ideas of a coalition between members of the present and past ministry were given up. A motion having passed for laying before his Majesty a resolution of the House, that the continuance of the present ministers in office was an obstacle to the forming a firm, efficient, extended, and united administration Mr. Pitt, on February 18th, when a question of supply was to be brought under consideration, informed the House that his Majesty, after considering all the circumstances of the country, had not thought proper to dismiss his ministers, and that they had not resigned. A long debate ensued, the result of which was a postponement of the supplies, carried by 208 to 196.

The House of Lords, which had for some time appeared no more than a spectator of this interesting contest, had now begun to interfere, and on the motion of the Earl of Effingham two resolutions were passed by a considerable majority in opposition to those of the Commons of December 24th and January 16th. The latter then passed six resolutions in defence of their conduct, and in assertion of their privileges. An address from the House of Commons to the King, pointing to the removal of the ministers, having been carried on February 20th, his Majesty's answer was reported on the 27th, the tenor of which was that no charge having been brought against his ministers, but, on the contrary, numbers of his subjects having expressed to him the utmost satisfaction on the change of his councils, he could not see that any salutary effect would be produced by their dismission. A second address, and a second answer, followed; after which a long representation to the King was voted, but by a majority only of one, the numbers being 191 to 190. On March 10th the mutiny bill was passed without a division, and on the 24th parliament was prorogued, and on the next day dissolved.

This measure was in reality attended with little hazard; for the coalition ministry, powerful as the union on which it was formed had rendered it in the House of Commons, was extremely unpopular in the nation at large. By a coalition as singular as its own, opposite parties concurred in regarding it with hostility. They whose attachment to principles of reform, and whose jealousy of the power of the crown, had rendered them zealous friends to the Rockingham administration, were shocked to see those whom they had looked up to as their champions, in close league with the very men whose measures they had been in the habit of condemning with the utmost acrimony. They, on the other hand, whose reverence for royalty led them to disapprove of every thing which tended to infringe the prerogatives of the crown, and fetter the exercise of its constitutional authority, could not forgive the attempt, as they considered it, to set up a power beyond its controul by the provisions of Mr. Fox's India bill. Addresses had therefore been pouring in from every quarter expressive of gratitude to his Majesty for dismissing a set of ministers who had rendered themselves unworthy of the public confidence. From this concurrence, added to the whole weight of the East India Company, the succeeding elections presented the most unprecedented results. The oldest and best established interests in many counties and towns were overthrown, and candidates who reckoned their return a matter of course, found themselves deprived of a seat. Upwards of 160 members, almost all of them friends of the coalition ministers, were rejected in consequence of the junction of local parties which never joined before. This event would have afforded a satisfactory proof of the efficacy of popular opinion, notwithstanding the inequality of the representation, had the crown stood neuter on the occasion.

The new parliament met on May 18th, when a speech was delivered from the throne, in which were some pointed allusions to the circumstance of having recurred to the sense of the people, and to the demerits ascribed to the first India bill. The addresses, containing strong expressions of gratitude to the King for having dissolved the late parliament, occasioned a debate in which an amendment was proposed, but it was rejected by a large majority.

On June 21st, Mr. Pitt moved several resolutions as the base of his bill known by the title of the Commutation Act. He stated that the illicit trade of the country had risen to such a height as to endanger almost the existence of several branches of the revenue, especially that arising from the duty on tea, of which article only five and a half millions of pounds were sold annually by the East India Company, whereas the annual consumption of the kingdom was supposed to exceed 12 millions. The only remedy of this evil that he could devise, was a reduction of the duty upon tea, the deficiency to be made good by some other tax; and his proposal was to lower the duty on tea from fifty per cent, as it now stood, to twelve and an half, and to raise the window-tax in proportion; and he gave a scale by which he calculated that this *commutation* would be a gain to families in common life. The farther effect would be the absolute ruin of the smuggling trade, and a considerable and timely relief to the East India Company. The principle of this bill was strongly combated, both as to its justice, and its policy. The resolutions were however passed.

The affairs of the East India Company were next brought forward. The minister first moved a bill to enable it to divide an interest of eight per cent on its capital, which passed the House of Commons without a division, and the House of Lords by 28 votes to 9. The second bill proposed, was to allow the Company a farther respite of duties due to the exchequer, to enable it to accept bills beyond the amount prescribed by former acts, and to establish its future dividends: this, likewise, after several divisions, passed both Houses. The important act followed, "for the better government of the affairs of the East India Company," which was framed upon the model of that brought in by Mr. Pitt in the former parliament, but with several material alterations. By its first part, a board was established of commissioners to be nominated by the King from the members of the privy council, and authorized to superintend, check, and controul all operations in any wise relating to the civil or military government or revenues of the Company in the East Indies: hence it has been usually denominated the *Board of Controul*. To this board was given free access to all papers belonging to the Company, and the right of demanding copies of them, and of all proceedings of the courts of proprietors and directors, and of all dispatches received from its servants in the East Indies, and of orders and directions proposed to be sent thither. The copies of the latter were to be returned to the court of directors, with the approbation, disapprobation, or amendment of the board, and then to be dispatched to India; and no orders or instructions were to be sent by the directors without such previous communication to the board on any pretence whatsoever. Although this mutual communication between the directors and the board was made the general rule, yet the latter was empowered, in *cases of urgency* and *cases of secrecy*, to transmit their own orders to India, without being subject to the review of the court of directors. The nomination of the commanders in chief was vested in his Majesty, in whom also was vested the power of removing any governor-general, president, or member of council in the settlements of India: vacancies in these offices to be supplied by the court of directors, but subject to the approbation or rejection of the King. The governor-general and council were vested with an absolute power over the other presidencies in all points relative to transactions with the native powers, and in applications of the revenues and forces.

The second part of the bill contained a variety of internal regulations respecting the affairs of India.

The third part related to the punishment of crimes in India; and by its provisions all British subjects were rendered amenable to the courts of justice in England, for acts done in India. Power was also given to the governors of settlements to seize all persons suspected of carrying on illicit correspondence, and send them to England if necessary. Every servant of the Company was required, within two months after his return to England, to deliver in upon oath to the court of exchequer an inventory of his real and personal estates; and in case of any complaint thereon from the board of controul, or the court of directors, he was to be examined by the court of exchequer, and imprisoned till he should answer interrogatories to its satisfaction. Further, a new court of justice was instituted for the prosecution of crimes committed in the East Indies, consisting of three judges, four peers, and six members of the House of Commons, whose judgment was to be final, and to extend to fine and imprisonment.

This bill was warmly combated in every part and stage; the judicial part, in particular, was vehemently opposed, as an infraction of the right of trial by jury, and as inconsistent with the established principles of English jurisprudence. These objections were answered on the ground of the total inadequacy of the ordinary courts of law to do substantial justice upon Indian delinquency; and the bill passed both houses by great majorities.

On June 30th the minister produced his budget, which comprized a loan of six millions, and some new taxes, and encountered little opposition. The terms of the loan were favourable to the public, and regarded as creditable to the financial talents of the minister. A motion was afterwards made by Mr. Dundas for the restoration of the estates in Scotland forfeited on account of the rebellion in 1745 which passed without the least opposition in the House of Commons. In the upper House it was objected to by the Lord Chancellor, but was carried, and received the royal assent. The session closed on August 20th.

The affairs of Ireland were in this year interesting and important.

Projects for the reform of the parliamentary representation had for some time been warmly entertained by the volunteer corps of that country, and delegates had been appointed for the purpose of furthering that object.

In September 1783 a general meeting of delegates from the province of Ulster was held at Dungannon, at which a plan of reformation was proposed and agreed upon, and it was resolved that a convention of representatives from the whole volunteer army should assemble on the 10th of November following at Dublin. This was accordingly held, and the plan was produced and considered. On the next day Mr. Flood brought the topic before the House of Commons, by moving for leave to bring in a bill "for the more equal representation of the people in parliament." The motion was received with much displeasure by a great majority of the members, as being a proposal tendered to them at the point of the bayonet, and it was rejected by 157 votes to 77. An address to the King was then voted, in which the Lords also concurred, to express the happiness enjoyed under his government, and their determination to support the present constitution with their lives and fortunes. The convention, informed of these measures, agreed upon a counter-address to the King, beseeching that their wish for the remedying of certain perversions in the parliamentary representation might not be imputed to a spirit of innovation, but a sober desire for upholding the constitution, and perpetuating the union of the two nations. The change in the administration which raised to the first seat the person who had been one of the most zealous advocates for the reform of the British representation, gave new hopes to the friends of the cause in Ireland; and in March 1784, Mr. Flood again moved his bill, supported by a great number of petitions: it was, however, rejected at the second reading by nearly the same majority as before. Exasperated at this defeat, and also at some unpopular acts of the new government, the citizens of Dublin, on June 7th, held an aggregate meeting, at which another petition to the King was resolved upon, and also a circular address to the people for the purpose of stimulating their exertions in the cause of reform. In this last, a proposal was made that five persons should be elected from every county, city, and considerable town, to meet in Dublin in *national congress.* The very name of this projected assembly was sufficient to excite an alarm in the government, and vigorous measures were determined upon to prevent the design from taking effect. The attorney-general for Ireland wrote a letter to the sheriffs of Dublin, expressing his surprise at seeing a summons under their signature for a meeting to choose delegates to the assembly in question, and threatening them with a prosecution if they should proceed; and the high-sheriff for the county of Dublin, who had convened and presided at an assembly of freeholders for the purpose of electing and instructing their delegates, was proceeded against by attachment from the court of King's Bench, and condemned in a small fine and a short imprisonment. Attachments were also granted against the magistrates of other counties who had called the meetings, and signed their resolutions; and prosecutions were instituted against the printers and publishers of newspapers in which such resolutions had been inserted. The congress however met on October 25th, though in an incomplete form, and passed a number of resolutions of the same import with those agreed on at the former assembly, together with earnest exhortations for rendering a future meeting complete; after which they adjourned.

This was not the only cause of discontent and popular commotion in Ireland. The distress of the manufacturers of Dublin had proceeded to such a length about the close of 1783, that a state of anarchy would have been the consequence, had not some public measures been taken for their relief. A committee of the Irish House of Commons was appointed to take into consideration the condition of the manufacturers in that kingdom, and a gentleman, Mr. Gardener, went to England for the purpose of conferring with the ministers on the subject. After his return, he brought forward in the house, on March 31st, a plan of protecting duties in favour of Irish manufactures, and began by moving that a duty of 2s. 6d. per yard be laid on all drapery imported into that kingdom; intimating at the same time his intention of moving proportionate duties on other articles. The rejection of this motion, by a majority of 110 to 36, occasioned a violent ferment among the populace; and at the next sitting of the house a mob broke in, and reproached the members with having sold themselves to England; they were, however, dispersed by the guards without bloodshed. Their rage having been excited by inflammatory addresses inserted in the newspapers, prosecutions were commenced against several of the printers, and a rigorous bill was brought in by Mr. Foster, "for securing the liberty of the press, by preventing the publication of libels." This being strongly opposed, its most obnoxious clauses were withdrawn, and it passed into a law.

Notwithstanding the great preparations for war between Russia and the Porte, and the strong indignation displayed by the latter on occasion of the empress's annexation of the Krimea and Kuban to her dominions, such were the difficulties under which the Ottoman empire laboured, that the mediation of France was successful in effecting an accommodation between these powers. On January 9th, a treaty was signed, by which Russia was left in full possession of its new acquisitions, the river Kuban being fixed as its limits on the side of Asia. A preceding treaty of commerce regulated every thing respecting the intercourse of trade and navigation between the two empires. At the same time the differences between Austria and the Porte were temporarily adjusted by some concessions on the part of the latter.

The court of Spain, being resolved to renew its attempt against Algiers, called in the assistance of Portugal and Naples; and in July, a combined armament of those powers and of the Maltese, consisting of more than 130 vessels of all sizes, with 16,000 seamen on board, sailed for that place, and on the 12th commenced the attack. The Algerines had improved their means of defence since the last year, and both the attack and the resistance were conducted with the greatest gallantry. So formidable, however, was the fire of the Algerines that in seven attacks after the first, the combined forces were never again able to approach near enough for their shells to take effect. A council of war being then held, it was agreed that no farther attempts could be made with any probability of success; and a tempest supervening, they hastily put to sea and returned to Spain.

The Emperor Joseph, who had already taken possession of and dismantled the fortresses in the Netherlands constituting the Dutch barrier, began at this time to manifest a disposition to take advantage of the weak and disordered state into which the United Provinces were plunged in consequence of the disasters of the late war, and of their internal dissentions. The latter were owing to the machinations of the aristocratical party to subvert the stadtholderian system of government; one effect of which was the resignation, by Prince Lewis of Brunswick

Wolfenbuttle, of the post of field-marshal of the Dutch army, which he had long held as the guardian and representative of the Prince of Orange during his minority. This hostility to the stadtholderate involved the ruling party in differences with the King of Prussia, uncle to the Prince Stadtholder, and his natural and political protector, whilst on the other hand they looked to France for their own support. Military associations under the term of volunteers, were forming in the principal towns, and affairs seemed to be tending to a civil war. This state of things induced Joseph to advance obsolete claims upon the United Provinces, among which the most serious were those respecting the city and country of Maestricht, and a free navigation of the Scheldt. In April the States General sent two plenipotentiaries to Brussels for the purpose of settling their disputes with the imperial court, but on the very day of their arrival a small detachment of Austrian troops entered the Dutch territory, and took possession of Old Lillo, a fort which was neglected since the construction of New Lillo near it. The Austrians afterwards violated the Dutch territory in another part, and demolished the barriers. These transactions excited a great alarm in Holland, and troops were sent to Maestricht and other places. Recourse was also had to the French court, to procure its mediation with the emperor, which was readily granted. The opening of the Scheldt being the principal object of the latter, who, among his other projects, had entertained that of reviving the ancient commerce of Antwerp, an experiment was made of the acquiescence of the Dutch in this respect. A small Flemish vessel was sent down the river, which having passed the Fort of Lillo and the guard-ship stationed near it without notice, was remarked on its return, and hailed by the captain of the guard-ship to bring to for the usual examination. The Fleming replied, that he had positive orders not to pay any respect to the fort, or submit to a search; and a magistrate on board said to the Dutch officer, that they did not acknowledge any Dutch or Zealand authority in that port. The trial being afterwards repeated, a gun was fired at the vessel, and officers were sent on board when the master entered a formal protest against the proceeding. The emperor soon after presented a statement of his claims to the Dutch ministers at Brussels as an ultimatum, among which were the free navigation of the Scheldt from Antwerp to the sea, the demolition of all the Dutch forts erected to command the river, and an uninterrupted commerce in the East and West Indies. Discussions of considerable length were now entered into, and the States displayed a disposition to make some concessions; when, to render the experiment on the Scheldt complete, an imperial brig was sent down in October with orders to proceed to the sea without submitting to any detention or examination whatever. The result was, that a broadside was fired into her by a Dutch armed cutter, with a threat of sending her to the bottom if she did not immediately bring to, with which she was obliged to comply. On the intelligence of this transaction, the imperial ambassador was recalled from the Hague, the negotiations at Brussels were broken off, and a large Austrian army was placed under orders to march for the Netherlands. The French court now seriously interfered to prevent hostilities, and intimated that it would be under the necessity of assembling troops on the frontier, if the emperor persisted in the design of using force. The Dutch on their part made active preparations, and in November a dyke near Lillo was broken down, and the adjacent tract was laid under water. In this state affairs were left, when the severity of winter had suspended farther operations. The Austrian dominions in Transylvania and Wallachia were at this time in a state of disorder, from a revolt of the peasants, who assembled in great numbers, attacked the nobility in their castles, many of whom they massacred with their whole families, and committed ravages and cruelties of every kind.

In the early part of this year, the Prince Royal of Denmark, having attained his 17th year, was declared major, and took his seat at the council board. This occurrence was immediately followed by a total change in the Danish ministry which had before consisted almost entirely of the adherents of the queen-dowager and her son. The counts Rosencrantz and Bernstorff were recalled from exile, and placed at the head of a new administration, and a new plan of government was framed, to which the signature of the incapable King was obtained. This court revolution was elected without the least disturbance, and great moderation was shewn by the new possessors of power towards their predecessors. The queen-dowager retired to a castle which had been conferred on her in Holstein.

In the month of June a volcanic eruption broke out in Iceland, more extensive and dreadful in its ravages than that island had ever before experienced, and perhaps unparalleled in Europe with respect to the quantity of lava and other matter which was ejected from the bowels of the earth. It continued its devastations to the month of May in the following year.

1785

25th & 26th Year of the Reign

THE session of Parliament after the recess was re-opened on January 25th, by a speech from the throne, in which the object particularly recommended to consideration was the commercial intercourse between Great Britain and Ireland. One of the first subjects brought under discussion in the House of Commons was the scrutiny which had been demanded by Sir Cecil Wray, against the majority of votes obtained by Mr Fox at the last election for Westminster. The legality of this scrutiny had been strongly contested by the opposition immediately after the meeting of the new parliament, but had been supported by the ministry, and the high bailiff of Westminster had been ordered to proceed in it with all practicable dispatch. After its continuance during eight months at a vast expence, not quite two out of the seven parishes in that city had been gone through; and it was calculated that at this rate it would take more than two years longer to finish the scrutiny. A petition from several of the electors brought the matter again before the House in February, and various motions were made by each party respecting it. In the debates some severe personal altercation took place between Mr. Fox and Mr. Pitt, the former representing himself as ungenerously made the victim of the minister's persecuting resentment; the latter reproaching Mr. F. as wishing to recover that esteem with the public which he had forfeited by his detestable politics. In conclusion, after the ministry had carried some questions, they were defeated by a majority of 162 to 124, and the scrutiny was terminated on the next day by the return of Lord Hood and Mr. Fox. An action was afterwards brought by Mr. Fox against the high bailiff for not returning him after the election, and £2000 damages were awarded to him.

The debts of the nabob of Arcot had long been a subject of investigation by the East India Company, and had obtained notice in the regulating bills both of Mr. Fox and Mr. Pitt. In pursuance of the directions in the latter, the court of directors had prepared orders to be sent to the council at Madras, in which they were enjoined to proceed to a more complete investigation of the nature and origin of these debts. The board of controul, to which these orders were communicated, rejected them, and caused a new letter to be drawn up, by which the claims of the creditors were established, with a few limitations, and a fund for their payment was assigned out of the revenues of the Carnatic. In consequence of this proceeding, a motion was made in the House of Lords by the Earl of Carlisle, on February 18th, for copies or extracts of all letters or orders issued by the court of directors, in pursuance of the injunctions contained in two clauses of the regulating act, to be laid before the House. A debate ensued, in which the propriety of the interference by the board of controul in this instance was warmly canvassed. The motion was, however, rejected without a division. A similar motion was made in the House of Commons, where a still more strict scrutiny was entered into, of the nature of the nabob's debts, and the right of the board of controul to act as it had done. On this occasion Mr. Burke particularly distinguished himself by his eloquence, and the extent of his information. The motion was lost on a division, by 164 to 69.

Mr. Pitt, who stood deeply pledged to the advocates of
parliamentary reform to use his endeavours both "as a man
and a minister" for promoting their cause, on April 18th, after
an introductory speech of considerable length, made a motion
for leave to bring in a bill "to amend the representation of
the people of England in parliament." The plan which he
proposed was to transfer the right of electing representatives
from 36 decayed or decaying boroughs, to the counties, and the
principal unrepresented towns, giving a pecuniary compensation to the owners and holders of the disfranchised boroughs;
and to extend the right of voting for knights of the shire to
copy-holders. The scheme of compensation was not approved
even by some of the friends to the system in general; and, after
a long debate on the motion, attended with much personality,
it was negatived by 248 against 174.

Much time, during this session of parliament, was
occupied with the discussion of propositions for
adjusting the commercial intercourse between Great Britain
and Ireland. A plan for this purpose, which had been framed
in a conference between the British cabinet and commissioners deputed from the sister kingdom, was laid before the Irish
House of Commons in February, and a set of resolutions was
formed upon them; which, having passed both Houses, was
transmitted to England as the base of the agreement. Mr.
Pitt then introduced the business in the English House of
Commons with a review of the past concessions to Ireland;
and proceeding to those which were now proposed, observed
that this might be reduced to two heads: 1. The importation
of the produce of our colonies in the West Indies and America
through Ireland into Great Britain: 2. A mutual exchange
between the two countries of their respective productions and
manufactures upon equal terms. With regard to the first he
acknowledged that it seemed to militate against the navigation
laws; but as Ireland had already been allowed to trade directly
with the colonies, he thought that the importation of their

produce into Great Britain circuitotisly through Ireland could not injure the direct colonial trade of this country. In return for these concessions he proposed that Ireland should consent to the payment of a certain annual sum out of the surplus of her hereditary revenue towards the general expences of the empire.

Before the subject was again brought into the House, a report was drawn up by a committee of the board of trade and plantations, stated as being founded upon the opinions of some of the principal merchants and manufacturers in the kingdom who had been examined by them; and in the meantime, these persons, joined by a great number of others from all parts of the nation, had held conferences among themselves relative to the Irish propositions. The statement of their opinions was so contradictory to that in the report, that it was thought necessary to examine the representatives of the different commercial interests at the bar of the House, and more than two months passed in receiving petitions and examining evidence on these topics. On May 12th Mr. Pitt again introduced his propositions, with a variety of amendments, and the addition of ten new ones. Of the latter, the principal objects were to provide, that whatever navigation laws the British parliament should hereafter enact, the same should be passed by that of Ireland — that there should not be imported into Ireland, and thence into Great Britain, any West Indian commodities, except such as were the produce of our own colonies — and that Ireland should not trade to any country beyond the Cape of Good Hope and the Streights of Magellan, as long as the charter of the East India Company should be continued. After long discussions in both Houses, a bill was framed upon these propositions, which was read for the first time in the House of Commons on July 28th. An address was then voted to the King, informing him of what had been done, and saying it remained for the parliament of Ireland to judge and decide upon it. When the bill was transmitted to that country, it met with a very unfavourable reception; several public bodies petitioned against it, and in the House of Commons much disapprobation was manifested of the additions that had been made to the original plan. On August 12th the secretary to the Lord Lieutenant moved for a bill corresponding to that of the English minister, when very animated debates ensued, especially on the part of the opposition. On a division, the votes were for bringing in the bill 127, against it 108. So small a majority in the House, with so much discontent without, was insufficient to encourage the administration to push the bill; and the mover, having procured it to be read the first time and printed, declared that he should proceed no further in the business during the present session.

The national congress of Ireland for the purpose of parliamentary reform, held their second meeting on January 2d, which was attended by about 200 persons, of whom were the delegates of 27 counties. They had afterwards several adjourned meetings, the last of which was on April 20th. In May the bill, formerly moved by Mr. Flood, was again introduced to the House of Commons, and again rejected.

The city of Dublin continued through the whole of this summer in a state of perturbation; and, after the rising of parliament, non-importation agreements became frequent in the capital, and spread into every quarter of the kingdom. They were even sanctioned by the grand juries, and the merchants in the ports found it necessary to comply with them. In order to restrain the violences of mobs, the military were posted in the most disorderly parts of the capital, where their presence naturally inflamed the passions of those whom their arms kept in awe; and the Lord Lieutenant, the Duke of Rutland, though a nobleman of popular manners, underwent some mortifying proofs of the odium which his government had incurred.

The Emperor of Germany, ever busied with projects often inconsistent with each other, and rarely brought to execution, had, in the last year, formed a secret scheme for the exchange of the Low Countries (for the interests of which he was at the eve of a war with the Dutch) against the electorate of Bavaria, which would doubtless have been a very desirable accession to the Austrian dominions. He carried on a negotiation with the Elector Palatine, also Elector of Bavaria, on the subject, which was not made public till the Empress of Russia, Joseph's political ally, wrote to the Duke of Deux-Ponts, presumptive heir to the Elector Palatine, to obtain his concurrence in the plan. The Duke disclosed the affair to the King of Prussia, and claimed his interposition as guarantee of the treaty of Teschen; and Frederic, the perpetual opposer of the aggrandizement of Austria, formed a confederation among the German princes, (the Elector of Hanover being one) signed on July 23d, for the purpose of maintaining the indivisibility of the empire, and the rights of the Germanic body. Joseph, greatly incensed, made vigorous preparations for war, which were carried on with equal activity by the other party. On mature consideration, however, the Emperor found it most prudent to proceed no further in the meditated exchange, and the threatened storm insensibly died away.

Whilst the Emperor's attention was thus drawn towards Germany, the Dutch were intent upon warding off the blow with which they were menaced; but their principal reliance was upon the protection of the court of France, which, chiefly at the instigation of the Count of Vergennes, had sent the Marshal de Maillebois to take the chief command of their forces. Negotiations for an accommodation were carried on during the summer at Paris under the mediation of France; and on the Emperor's return to Vienna after a long tour, towards the close of July, he gave audience to the Dutch deputies, who, with much humility, apologized for the insult offered to his flag. On September 20th, preliminary articles of peace were signed at Paris between the Emperor and the States General, which were the base of a definitive treaty concluded on November 8th. By its articles, the Emperor's sovereignty over every part of the Scheldt, from Antwerp to the limits of Saftingen in Dutch Flanders, was recognized, but from that point to the sea, the river, with all its mouths, was to remain under the sovereignty of the States; and thus the free navigation of Antwerp was frustrated. The Emperor renounced all his claims upon Maestricht, on consideration of the payment of a large sum of money by the States; and as he had already obtained a considerable loan from the States of Brabant on the ground of his exertions for the Netherlands, his pecuniary projects, at least, were not without success.

A treaty of alliance between the Dutch republic and the King of France immediately followed the peace which the latter had mediated. Its stipulations were calculated to draw as closely as possible the bonds of amity and mutual defence, which proceeded so far, that each promised not to contract any future alliance or engagement whatever which should be directly or indirectly contrary to the present treaty. In matters of commerce, each was to be treated by the other as the most favoured nation; and in every other point they were, on all occasions, to give each other mutual assistance. The French having now a preponderant influence over the Dutch councils, that party in the state which had always been opposers of the high authority vested in the stadtholderate, was urged to pursue with vigour their schemes for abolishing that office, or at least greatly abridging its prerogatives; and the bodies of volunteers, to which the late dissensions and dangers had given rise, excited a democratic spirit, which, though it militated against the authority of the ancient aristocracy, was still more hostile to that of the Stadtholder. A riot which occurred at the Hague, in consequence of the appearance of some volunteers with their badges in that town, the inhabitants of which are zealously devoted to the House of Orange, gave a pretext to the acting committee of the States of Holland for depriving the Prince of his government of the Hague and his body guard, in consequence of which affront he withdrew to his own city of Breda, and sent his Princess and family to West Friseland. The King of Prussia on this occasion remonstrated with the States of Holland on the treatment of his nephew, but was so little attended to, that they issued an order to transfer all the military honours usually paid to the Stadtholder, to their own president and pensionary; which was followed by another to discharge the troops from the obligation of their oath to the Stadtholder, and enjoin a new oath to the States alone. Such was the prospect of affairs in Holland at the close of the year.

From the time of the seizure of the Krimea by Russia, a petty war was carried on between the Russians and the Tartar tribes of Caucasus and the regions about the Caspian sea. It was subsisting in the present year, and the capture of a Tartar Khan and his family, who were brought prisoners to Petersburgh, attested a victory of the Russians. The latter were also successful against the Tartars of the Kuban; and a pretended prophet, Sheik Mansour, with his fanatical disciples, were defeated with great slaughter.

Destructive inundations occurred in several parts of Europe, particularly in Germany, where vast losses were sustained. This calamity, joined to the inclemency of the seasons, occasioned a scarcity approaching to a famine in the north of Europe.

1786

26th & 27th Year of the Reign

I<small>N</small> the speech from the throne with which the session of Parliament was opened, January 24th, after notice was taken of the amicable conclusion to which the disputes had been brought that threatened the tranquillity of Europe, and of the suspended state of the attempt to adjust the commercial intercourse between Great Britain and Ireland, the attention of the House of Commons was particularly called to the establishment of a plan for the reduction of the national debt. In the debate on the usual address, Mr. Fox took occasion to censure the ministry for their neglect in cultivating continental alliances, to which he attributed the ascendancy which France had gained in the concerns of the United Provinces. He then entered into a wide field of European politics, and alluded to several instances in which ministers had been blameable in not taking advantage of the occurrences of the time. He was replied to by Mr. Pitt in a tone of sarcasm; and the debate would not here have been touched upon, had it not served to display the different sentiments of these eminent persons relative to the important subject of the degree in which this island ought to involve itself in the affairs of the continent.

The first question of importance that came under parliamentary discussion related to a measure proposed by the Duke of Richmond, master-general of the ordnance, which was that of fortifying the dock-yards of Portsmouth and Plymouth. A board of naval and military officers, of which the Duke was president, had been appointed by the King, which had taken into consideration the plan proposed for that purpose, and made their report upon it; and an estimate of the expence had been given by a board of engineers, amounting to £760,000. After the estimate, and as much of the report as was thought advisable, had been laid before the House of Commons, Mr. Pitt, on February 27th moved a resolution importing a general approbation of the design of fortifying the dock-yards of Portsmouth and Plymouth. A debate followed in which the measure was fully discussed by speakers for and against the question. Among the opposers Mr. Sheridan was particularly distinguished, and his speech had probably a considerable effect on the decision. When the division took place, the Ayes and Noes were exactly equal, the numbers of each being 169; and the Speaker, as usual in such cases, being called upon for his casting vote, he gave it on the negative side, which put an end to the project.

The suggestion concerning the reduction of the national debt, introduced into the King's speech, was followed up, early in the session, by the minister's motion for a select committee to examine and report what might be expected to be the future annual amount of the income and expenditure. This report having been laid before the House, Mr. Pitt, on March 29th, brought in his proposition for the gradual diminution of the debt, which has since produced such remarkable effects. After a statement at large of the actual and probable financial resources of the country, he drew the following conclusions. 1st, That the yearly income of the state exceeded the permanent level of its expenditure by £900,000: 2d, that this sum might be augmented to a million by means nowise burdensome to the people: 3d, that although the present establishment exceeded in some points those stated in the report of the select-committee, yet there were ample resources to over-balance such excesses without having recourse to new taxes: 4th, that the ways and means of the present year would be sufficient to furnish the supplies, together with £250,000 quarterly, towards a fund for paying the national debt. With respect to the mode for securing the due application of this fund to its object, he proposed to vest in a certain number of commissioners the full power of disposing of it in the purchase of stock in their names for the public, to whom should be issued from the exchequer the annual million in quarterly payments, previously to any other money, except the interest of the national debt itself. He calculated that the interest of the stock so purchased, accumulating at compound interest, together with the annuities which would fall into that fund, would in 28 years amount to a sum that would leave a surplus of four millions annually to be applied, if necessary, to the exigences of the state. In appointing the commissioners he said he should endeavour to choose persons of weight and character corresponding to the importance of the trust; and he mentioned the Speaker of the House of Commons, the chancellor of the exchequer, the master of the rolls, the governor and deputy governor of the bank of England, and the accountant general in chancery, as proper to be of the number. He concluded with moving an annual grant of one million to commissioners for the purpose above-mentioned, to arise out of the sinking fund.

The policy of the principle of making the income of the state so far exceed its expenditure as to leave a surplus for the discharge of the national debt, being universally acknowledged, the motion was carried without a division. Various objections, however, were made to the mode proposed by Mr. Pitt for effecting this purpose, which were a subject of debate; and Mr. Sheridan formed upon them a series of resolutions, which were negatived without a division. Additional clauses were also proposed, and admitted; and the bill, having passed both houses, received the royal assent.

On May 22d, Mr. Pitt brought in a bill for transferring certain duties on wines from the customs to the excise. He stated that the amount of the duty on wines was considerably less at this time than it had been in the middle of the last century, which defalcation he attributed, partly to the importation of large quantities of foreign wine without paying the duty, and principally to the sale of a spurious home-made liquor under its name, both which causes would be removed by the present bill. Objections were made, which especially regarded the mode of trial adopted by the excise laws, as being abhorrent to the law of the land; and Mr. Beaufoy moved an amendment, to give the subject, in cases of information consequent upon this bill, an optional right of being tried by jury; which was negatived by a majority of 95 to 30. The bill afterwards passed into a law.

On June 23d, in pursuance of a message from the King, Mr. Pitt moved for a bill to appoint commissioners for enquiring into the condition of the woods, forests, and land-revenues belonging to the crown. A strong objection against this bill was taken from the unlimited power it gave to the commissioners to call for and keep all titles, plans, and documents relating to land holden of the crown. Mr. Jolliffe, who made this objection, moved amendments for the protection of title deeds, and for obliging the commissioners to report their proceedings to the House, which were admitted without a division, and the bill passed the Commons. In the House of Lords it was severely animadverted upon by Lord Loughborough, on account of the ministerial and other new powers conferred by it, but on a division it was carried by 28 votes against 18.

A motion of Mr. Marsham for a bill to extend the disqualifications for voting at elections for members of parliament to persons holding places in the navy and ordnance offices, was opposed by the minister, and negatived by a large majority.

This session of parliament was remarkable for the commencement of that public prosecution of Mr. Hastings for his conduct as governor-general of British India which so long engaged the public attention. The subject was first introduced to the House of Commons by Mr. Burke in February. After causing the clerk to read the resolutions of censure and recall of Mr. Hastings moved by Mr. Dundas in May 1782, and observing that he agreed with the friends of Mr. Hastings in the opinion that these resolutions should not be suffered to remain a mere calumny on their journals, he took a view of the different modes of proceeding against the delinquents, and gave reasons for preferring that of impeachment. He concluded by moving for copies of the correspondence which, from January 1782, had passed between Warren Hastings, Esq. and the court of directors, relative to presents and other money received by him; which was carried. After various other motions for papers, some of which passed, and others were rejected, Mr. Burke, in his place, on April 4th, made a charge against Warren Hastings, late governor-general of Bengal, of sundry high crimes and misdemeanours; and delivered in the nine first articles of this charge, the rest, amounting in the whole to 22, being presented in the following week. Mr. Hastings on the 26th, requested by petition to the House that he might be permitted to be heard in his defence to the several articles, and might be allowed a copy of the same; which was granted.

As the vast compass of this celebrated prosecution renders it impossible to give a clear view of the nature of the several charges, and the arguments produced in their support and refutation, within the limits of a succinct narrative, no more will be attempted than to record the principal facts of its long annals.

On June 1st, Mr. Burke brought forward his accusation on the Rohilla war, and moved that it afforded ground for charging Mr. Hastings with high crimes and misdemeanours. He caused a resolution of 1782 to be read in order to show that the House had already, in strong terms, reprobated his conduct in that war. The motion was, however, rejected by the majority of 119 to 67.

On June 13th, the charge respecting the Rajah of Benares was opened by Mr. Fox; and the result was that it was voted by 119 to 79, "that there was matter of impeachment against W. Hastings in the said charge."

Mr. Pitt was on the affirmative side in this article, for which he was severely reproached by some of the friends of the accused, who declared that it was in the full confidence of the minister's protection that they had urged Mr. Burke to bring forward his charges.

During the course of these proceedings, Mr. Dundas brought in a bill for amending Mr. Pitt's act for regulating the government of the East India Company, by enlarging the powers of the governor-general.

The proposed augmentation consisted in vesting in him the nomination to vacant seats in the council; in uniting the office of governor-general and commander in chief; and in authorizing him to decide upon every measure, whether his council agreed with him or not. The bill was warmly opposed in both Houses, but was supported by great majorities, and passed into a law.

The session of parliament closed on July 11th.

In July a convention was signed at London by the Marquis of Carmarthen on the part of the King of Great Britain, and Don Bernardo del Campo on that of the King of Spain, for the purpose of settling the differences between the two crowns relative to the logwood cutters in South America. By its terms, the English and those colonists who have enjoyed the protection of England were to evacuate the country of the Mosquitos, continental and insular, as far as a described line; in return for which, more extensive limits than those specified in the last treaty of peace were assigned to them beyond another line, within which they were allowed to cut, not only dying woods, but mahogany, and to gather all other products of the earth, but without the permission of establishing plantations of sugar, coffee, cocoa, or the like. The Spanish sovereignty was likewise preserved over the country, which was granted to the English only for the purposes above specified.

A treaty of commerce and navigation between the Kings of Great Britain and France, founded upon the principle of mutual advantages and privileges, and embracing a great variety of objects, was signed at Versailles on September 26th by William Eden, Esq. and the Sieur Joseph Matt. Gerrard De Rayneval. Its leading commercial object was the admission, upon easier terms, of the staple products and manufactures of each country into the other, so as to form a balance of trade between the two, and promote the demand for their respective commodities; an object which the jealousy and frequent disputes between the two nations had for a long time past rendered unattainable. A liberal and enlightened spirit was also displayed with respect to the reciprocal treatment of subjects of each kingdom while residing in the other; and the inhospitable *droit d'aubaine*, or right claimed by the crown of France to the property of foreigners dying in that country, was abrogated with respect to British subjects.

The French government at this time manifested uncommon attention to every point connected with naval and commercial improvement. For the former purpose stupendous works were undertaken in order to render the harbour of Cherbourg capable of receiving men of war; and in June the King paid a visit to that port, and was present at the launching of one of the vast cones which were to form the base of a mole. A colony of American whale fishers, chiefly quakers from Nantucket, arrived at Dunkirk, to be settled there with every security for their civil and religious rights, under the auspices of M. De Calonne. Some indulgences were granted to the protestants in

France; and the peasantry were relieved in regard to some of their most burdensome services.

The United Provinces were in this year thrown into a state of the greatest ferment and disorder through the violence of their political contests. In the assembly of the states of Holland and West Friseland, held at the Hague in March, after extremely warm debates on the question of restoring the Prince of Orange to his command of the Hague, it was carried in the negative by a majority of one only in nineteen votes. This resolution produced a letter from the new King of Prussia to the States General, in which he strongly urged that body to interpose with the states of Holland and West Friseland for the restoration of the Stadtholder to his rights, and offered his mediation, with that of other friends of the republic, for terminating the differences among them. Five of the provinces referred the consideration of this letter to the committee for foreign affairs; but that of Holland refusing to admit any foreign interference in its domestic concerns, paid no regard to the application.

The Prince of Orange, who for some time had taken up his residence at Middleburg with his family, at length thought proper to remove to Guelderland, the states of which province, as well as those of the neighbouring province of Utrecht, were much attached to him, and which immediately borders upon the Prussian territories. He still retained the military command of five provinces, the forces of which were about equal to those of Holland. In Guelderland, the burghers of the towns of Hattem and Elburg, encouraged by the states of Holland, proving refractory to the authority of the states of the province, the latter passed a resolution charging the Stadtholder, as captain-general, to send a body of troops for the purpose of reducing them to obedience. The burghers of Hattem, joined by volunteers from different quarters, mounted cannon, and made a show of resistance, but a few discharges from the regular troops so much intimidated them, that they abandoned their town at one gate as the regulars entered at the other; and Elburg was deserted in the same manner with less resistance. In resentment of this proceeding of the Prince of Orange, the states of Holland suspended him from all the functions appertaining to his office of captain-general within their province; and recalling their troops from Maestricht and other garrisons, they formed a line of defence on the inland frontier. They also directed their general to attend to the succour of the city of Utrecht if any attempt should be made against it by the states of that province, who, after violent contests, had been obliged to withdraw to Amersfort. Such was the deplorable condition of the United Provinces at the close of this year.

Frederic King of Prussia, who has perhaps, of all modern sovereigns, best merited the title of the Great, sunk under the rapid decline of an exhausted constitution on August 17th, in the 75th year of his age. Chargeable as all the early part of his career may have been with unprincipled ambition, rapacity, and despotism, his latter years exhibited him in the character of a mild and beneficent sovereign, whose cares were devoted to the happiness and prosperity of his subjects; and of a patriotic assertor of the rights of that Germanic body of which he was the most illustrious member. His death produced no change in the political system of the court of Berlin, and it has been already seen that his nephew and successor, Frederic William III interfered in favour of his brother-in-law the Prince of Orange, with as much vigour as the old King could have done.

The first Swedish diet since the revolution assembled in the month of May. Although there appeared the greatest cordiality between the King and the States, yet the latter preserved so much of the spirit of their ancient freedom as to reject some of his Majesty's proposals. The diet broke up after a very short session. The practice of torture was totally abolished by the King of Sweden.

The Emperor of Germany proceeded in his multifarious plans of reform, civil and ecclesiastical; among which was the abrogation of the old laws, and the establishment of an entire new code. In this system capital punishment was nearly abolished, but the substitutions were, in many cases, so severe, that humanity rather lost than gained: the suppression of religious orders was persisted in, and a list was this year published of 413 monasteries and 211 nunneries suppressed since 1782.

The court of Bavaria, the most bigoted in Germany, having at this time invited a papal nuncio to reside at Munich, the German prelates, in alarm at the measure, applied to the Emperor for his protection, who published a memorial in which he positively declared against any jurisdiction of the court of Rome in the ecclesiastical affairs of Germany. This declaration was confirmed at a conference of the ecclesiastical princes.

The Empress of Russia, who had planned a most magnificent progress to her new kingdom of Taurida, or the Krimea, and its vicinity, was obliged to defer it on account of the increased confederacies of the Tartars, who maintained the war against the Russians with great vigour, and gave them a considerable defeat in the region of Caucasus.

Egypt having been long a prey to the contentions of the rebel beys, of whom, Murad and his party had taken possession of the lower part of that country, the Porte sent out a powerful armament under the command of Hassan Bey, the captain pashaw, who sailed for the Nile, and landed his forces at Rosetta. Proceeding to Cairo, he gave Murad and the beys a total and bloody defeat in the suburbs of that city, which he entered, and obliged the rebels to take refuge in Upper Egypt.

The aged Emperor of China, Kien Long, after a reign of more than fifty years, died at Pekin, leaving the character of one of the best and most enlightened sovereigns of his dynasty.

Some differences among the Chinese and Russians at the place where trade is carried on between the two empires had previously occasioned an interruption in that commerce on the part of China.

Among the remarkable domestic incidents of this year was an attempt on his Majesty's life by a woman, who presenting a paper to him as he was alighting from his post chariot at the garden-gate of St. James's, made a stroke at his breast with a concealed knife. The blow was happily avoided by a backward movement, and as she was about to make another thrust, her hand was caught by a yeoman of the guard, and the knife taken from her, the King, with his characteristic humanity, exclaiming, "I am not hurt — take care of the poor woman — do not hurt her." On examination she was found to be one Margaret Nicholson, a person in obscure life from the North of England, whose reason was bewildered by some insane ideas of rights to the crown. Her insanity being fully apparent to the privy council, she was committed to custody as a lunatic.

1787

27th & 28th Year of the Reign

AFTER an unusually long recess, parliament was opened on January 23d by a speech from the throne, the leading topics of which were the treaty of commerce lately concluded with France, and the state of the revenue. On the 5th of February, Mr. Pitt moved that the House should form itself into a committee for taking into consideration that part of his Majesty's speech which referred to the commercial treaty with France. Some motions for delay by the opposition having been negatived, the minister, on the 12th, took up the subject in a long explanation and defence of the treaty in question. As the foundation of a commercial connection between the two countries, he stated it as an allowed fact, that France had the superiority in her natural products, and Great Britain in her manufactures and artificial productions. Upon this relative condition, a valuable intercourse of trade between the two nations might be established, each having its own distinct staple; and instead of clashing in their respective pursuits of wealth, they might resemble two opulent traders in different branches, carrying on a mutually beneficial traffic with each other. After going through a variety of particulars to show that the demand for our manufactures was likely fully to balance that for the French commodities, and that whatever reduction our revenue might undergo from the diminution of duties on some articles, would be compensated by increase in others; he proceeded to answer some objections made to the political tendency of the treaty. It had been said that its effects would be to compose that jealousy and rivalry between the two countries which was so essential to the welfare of Great Britain, France being naturally and necessarily its enemy. This principle he held to be a national prejudice, unworthy of an enlightened people; and he regarded it as a libel upon the constitution of political societies to suppose that any two states were necessarily enemies. He concluded with moving a resolution, that all the articles of the produce and manufactures of the European dominions of the French King, not specified in the tariff of the treaty, shall be imported into this kingdom on the payment of duties as low as any payable on the like articles from any other European nation. Mr. Fox followed in a long speech, the principal object of which was to prove, that the only situation in which Great Britain could stand in the general system of Europe with honour, dignity, and safety, was as a counterpoise to the power of France. Having with all his energy maintained this political point, he proceeded to consider the treaty in a commercial view, and supported a petition which had been presented from an association of manufacturers called the Chamber of Commerce, for further deliberation on so important a subject. He then moved an amendment, which, after several other speakers had joined the debate, was negatived, and the resolution was agreed to by a majority of 248 to 118.

The committee of the house being again formed, Mr. Pitt moved his second resolution, that the wines of France be imported upon as low duties as the present duties upon Portugal wines. This motion brought on a warm discussion of the general commercial merits of the treaty, as well as of the resolution in question, which was strongly opposed as militating against the Methuen treaty with Portugal, and Mr. Fox moved as an amendment, that the duty upon Portugal wines should at the same time be reduced one-third. This was negatived; and the report of the committee was afterwards brought up and agreed to by a great majority. It is unnecessary to notice the further debates which took place in this House, or those which occurred in the House of Lords, relative to the commercial treaty. It was finally approved in both Houses by large majorities; and an address, in which both concurred, was presented to the King, thanking him for having entered into the treaty. It appears that upon the whole, the manufacturing interest of this country was better satisfied with it, than that of France.

About this time a constitutional point relative to the peerage of Scotland was decided by the House of Lords. Two peers of the sixteen representing that body in parliament, the Earl of Abercorn, and the Duke of Queensberry, having during the late prorogation been created peers of Great Britain, the question occurred, whether, after such creation, they could continue to sit in their former representative capacity. The act of union was silent on this subject, and the only precedent was that of the Duke of Athol, who, upon succeeding to an English peerage, had continued to sit in both qualities. The discussion was introduced on February 13th by Lord Stormont in a motion that the Earl of Abercorn, one of the sixteen representing the peerage of Scotland, having been created Viscount Hamilton, doth thereby cease to sit as a representative of the Scotch peerage. In his speech supporting this motion, his lordship principally dwelt upon the incompatibility of the two characters, a peer possessing a temporary seat by election, and one holding a hereditary seat. The motion was opposed by the Lord Chancellor and the Earl of Moreton, and was supported by Lord Loughborough. Upon a division it was carried by 52 votes to 38; and was followed by a motion of the same tenour relative to the Duke of Queensberry, created Baron Douglas.

A plan for the consolidation of the several duties upon articles in the customs, and the excise, so as to convert them into single duties upon each article, was introduced by Mr. Pitt on February 26th, and met with the general concurrence of the House. Objections were, however, made to an intention of including in the plan the duties to be imposed upon merchandize to be imported in consequence of the new commercial treaty with France; but they were over-ruled, and the bill framed upon this proposal passed into a law.

On March 28th Mr. Beaufoy made a motion for taking into consideration the repeal of the corporation and test acts. With respect to the latter of these acts, he shewed, from its title, that its design was to prevent dangers from popish recusants; and he related from the history of the time, that the dissenters had determined not to oppose it, considering it as then essential to the safety of the kingdom, and confiding in the justice of parliament that a bill for their relief should afterwards be passed — that such a bill was actually passed, but was first defeated by a prorogation of parliament, and afterwards by the clerk's stealing the bill. With respect to the corporation act, it was passed in the year after the restoration, when men's minds were under the agitation occasioned by the late troubles. He then entered into the general right of every man to follow his own religious principles without being liable to penalties for so doing, unless they were injurious to the community, and endeavoured to prove that the present dissenters were no just objects of jealousy to the state. The motion was opposed first by Lord North, and then by Mr. Pitt, and was supported by Mr. Fox. Other members joined in the debate, and the question being put, the motion was negatived by 178 to 100.

The debts contracted by the Prince of Wales, since the allowance settled upon him on his coming of age in 1783, had for some time been a subject of conversation, and had been made known to the public by a great reduction of his establishment at Carlton-house. No overture having been made for his relief by his Majesty or the ministers, his Royal Highness, whose political connections lay among the opposition, consented to an appeal being made in parliament to the generosity of the nation, in his behalf; and on April 20th, Mr. Alderman Newnham demanded of the chancellor of the exchequer, whether it was the intention of the ministers to bring forward any proposition for rescuing the Prince of Wales from his present embarrassed situation. Mr. Pitt having replied that he had received no command on the subject from his Majesty, the alderman signified his intention of making a motion on the subject upon a day which he named. On some subsequent conversation in the House relative to the nature of the intended motion, Mr. Rolle rose and declared that the question involved matter by which the constitution both in church and state might be materially affected, and which it would be necessary to enquire into; in which he was understood to allude to a connection between the Prince and a lady of the Roman Catholic persuasion, which was rumoured to have been attended with a ceremonial forbidden by the laws of the country. Some very warm conversation took place on this topic, which at length produced an assertion from Mr. Fox, that the supposed fact not only could never have happened legally, but never did happen in any way whatsoever, and had from the beginning been a base and malicious falsehood; and this he affirmed was spoken by him from direct authority. Before the day arrived for which Mr. Newnham had announced his motion, Mr. Pitt informed the Prince by his Majesty's command, that if the intended motion were withdrawn, every thing should be settled to his Royal Highness's satisfaction. This being assented to, a message from the King was delivered to both Houses on May 21st, in which it was mentioned that his Majesty had directed £10,000 a year from the civil list to be added to the allowance of the Prince, who had given full assurance of confining his future expences within his income; and that he had ordered an estimate of the Prince's debts to be laid before parliament, for which he hoped his faithful Commons would make a provision. The result was, that the Commons voted an address to the King, requesting that the sum of £781,000 might be made payable on the Prince's account out of the civil list, which they promised to make good.

On April 26th Mr. Pitt brought in a bill for authorising the treasury to let out to farm the duty on post horses. It was proposed that the island should be divided into districts, on each of which the tax was to be put up to public auction for three years, and in order that the public might lose nothing, the bidders were to begin from the highest sum which the district had yet produced. The reason which he gave for this proposal was the fraudulent evasion of the tax through the collusion between the innkeepers and collectors, which prevailed to such a degree, that a large proportion of it never found its way into the exchequer. No greater powers were to be conferred upon the farmers than were possessed by the present collectors, and it was from their superior vigilance alone that they could derive any profit. The bill was opposed chiefly as being a novelty, not analogous to the principles of the constitution, and likely to lead the way to other plans of the same kind: it was, however, carried on a division by 162 votes to 95.

During these parliamentary transactions, the great cause of Mr. Hastings was proceeding. On February 7th, Mr. Sheridan opened the third charge against that gentleman relative to the resumption of the jaghires, and the confiscation of the treasures of the begums or princesses of Oude, the mother and grandmother of the reigning nabob. The subject was particularly favourable to a display of that kind of impassioned eloquence in which the orators of antiquity, when acting as public accusers, so much excelled; and it was universally agreed that never in the British senate, nor probably elsewhere, was a speech of this class delivered comparable to that with which Mr. Sheridan during five hours and a half rivetted the attention of a full house, and an audience of distinguished visitors. Its effect was such, that the friends of the accused had no other means of appeasing the storm of indignation raised against him, than that of procuring an adjournment. On a renewal of the debate, after the charge had been discussed in a cooler moment, the house divided, when there appeared for admitting it 175 votes, against it 68. Several other articles of accusation were afterwards successively discussed, many of which were decided to furnish matter for impeachment. At length, the resolutions of the House being read and agreed to, Mr. Burke moved that they should be referred to a committee to prepare articles of impeachment upon them; and the members of the committee were accordingly nominated. The articles being read and agreed to, Mr. Frederick Montague moved "That Mr. Burke in the name of the House of Commons, and of all the Commons of Great Britain, do go to the bar of the House of Lords, and impeach Warren Hastings, Esq. late Governor-General of Bengal, of high crimes and misdemeanours, and do acquaint the Lords, that the Commons will, with all convenient speed, exhibit articles against him, and make good the same." The motion having passed, the majority of the House immediately attended Mr. Burke, who pronounced the impeachment at the House of Lords in the form above recited. Mr. Hastings, having been taken into custody by the usher of the black rod, was admitted to bail, himself in £20,000 and two sureties in £10,000 each, and was told to prepare his answer against the next session of parliament.

Nothing further of importance occurred in parliament to its prorogation on May 30th.

Before the important affairs of Europe in this year are touched upon, it may be proper to pursue the narrative of home transactions, although they have a reference to the former; since they will be rendered sufficiently intelligible by a slight allusion to the leading facts.

The court of France having, by a private memorial to those of London and Berlin, declared that it had determined not to interfere in the disputes of Holland except as a mediator, provided other powers observed the same moderation, but if any other power should take up arms against the republic, France would act as the exigency of affairs might require; measures were taken by the British ministry to equip a fleet with all expedition; the land-forces were recruited, and a subsidiary treaty was entered into with the landgrave of Hesse for the hire of troops. France on its part also made hostile preparations both by land and sea, The contests in the United Provinces, however, being speedily settled by a Prussian army, whilst the French government was fully occupied with its internal concerns, a convention took place between England and France on October 27th, for mutually disarming and reducing their naval forces to the establishment formerly agreed upon.

These events caused the parliament to be assembled for the winter session as early as November 27th, when it was opened by a speech from the throne, in which notice was taken of the occurrences on the continent which had induced his Majesty to adopt the measures that were to be laid before them. His interference to maintain the lawful government of the United Provinces was avowed; and to the declared intention of the French court to assist the party which had usurped that government, was attributed the warlike preparation which had been directed. The address in return to the speech, moved in the House of Commons, was generally approved; and Mr. Fox took credit to himself for having always maintained the opinion, that this country ought to assume an active and vigorous part in preserving the balance of power in Europe, as well as for having warned the house against the perfidious designs of France, in contradiction to those assertions of her amicable disposition which had been made when the commercial treaty was in agitation.

Nothing of interest occurred in parliament during the remainder of the year, except some debates relative to the Hessian treaty, and to a proposed augmentation of the troops, and the erecting of fortifications, in the West Indies. A motion for a grant for the latter purpose occasioned a division in the House of Commons, when it was carried by the majority of 242 to 80.

In the beginning of the year negotiations were still carrying on under the mediation of France and Prussia for conciliation between the Stadtholder and the States of the United Provinces. The demands of the States of Holland, however, were so high, that nothing could be agreed upon, and in January the ambassadors of the two courts returned home. It was to the advantage of the stadtholderian cause, that its opponents were split into the two parties of the favourers of the old aristocracy, and the votaries of the new democratical principles, which, since the American revolution, had made great progress in Europe. This dissention among themselves rendered their measures wavering and inconsistent, and enmity to each other occasioned them sometimes to lean towards the party to which both were originally adverse. The senate of Amsterdam, as far back as the middle of 1786, had so far changed its principles as to use all its efforts for procuring the restoration of the Prince of Orange to the command of the garrison of the Hague, and the State of Holland began to display an inclination to the same cause. The democratical party, however, was still strong in numbers; and in April the armed burghers of Amsterdam and Rotterdam surrounded the senate house in each city, and forcibly deposed some of the senators, filling their places with others of their own nomination. The city of Utrecht had for some time past given the example of a constitution entirely popular, and, as already mentioned, had obliged the states of the province to retire to Amersfort. This body, thinking that the change of sentiments which had taken place in favour of the ancient government afforded an opportunity for recovering its authority, resolved upon making an attempt for reducing Utrecht, and began by sending troops to take possession of some posts round that city. A skirmish brought on by this movement ended in favour of Utrecht; and the States of Holland, according to a former determination, caused troops to march into the province for the protection of the city.

Parties in Amsterdam, in the meantime, were so nearly balanced, that an address to the States of Holland for restoring the stadtholder to his prerogatives was signed by a great number of inhabitants, which circumstance was the occasion of some alarming riots, and put a stop to all mercantile business. The States General, which for a considerable time had taken no decided part in the contests of the provinces, now acted openly against the States of Holland, and issued an order to the general of the troops of Holland, to break up the line of troops formed by them on the frontiers of Utrecht; which order not being obeyed, they suspended the general from his command. It was a more alarming circumstance to the States of Holland, that, in June, the greatest part of their troops were induced to go over to the stadtholder.

A circumstance now occurred which suddenly produced a great change in the affairs of the United Provinces. The Princess of Orange, a lady possessing the vigour of character belonging to the royal house of Prussia, left Nimeguen, where the prince then held his court on a journey to the Hague, for the purpose of a conference with the chiefs of the stadtholderian party. Being near Schoonhoven, on June 28th, she was stopt by a guard of armed burghers, and placed under arrest, but was afterwards allowed to return to Nimeguen. This occurrence being made known to the King of Prussia, he sent a strong memorial to the States of Holland demanding satisfaction for the insult offered to his sister, to which the States, who had already passed a resolution justifying the conduct of their officers, gave an unsatisfactory answer. The king also applied to the States General, and to the court of France, both of which concurred in the necessity of an apology from the States of Holland. In the meantime great preparations for war were carrying on by the Prussians on the Dutch frontier; and the stadtholder, making the first movement, took possession of the towns of Wyk Duerstede and Harderwyk, and advanced near Utrecht, while the whole province of Zealand declared in his favour. These approaches of danger only stimulated the anti-stadtholderian party in Holland to measures of greater violence, and the whole country exhibited lamentable proofs of the rage of civil discord. The states of the province, however, sensible of the inequality of a contest with such a power as Prussia, returned an answer of great respect and humility to the king's last memorial respecting his sister, though they still justified the proceeding of interrupting her journey. But condescension was now too late. The King of Prussia had determined to make use of the opportunity for restoring the stadtholder to his hereditary authority; and on September 13th a Prussian army of about 18,000 men under the command of the Duke of Brunswick (formerly celebrated under the title of the hereditary prince) entered the province of Guelderland. Scarcely any resistance was made, whilst the Provinces of Utrecht and Holland were over-run by the invaders, and the city of Utrecht was abandoned by the party of which it was the strong-hold, without a shot fired. All the other towns opened their gates as the Prussian army approached; the Hague declared for the stadtholder; and in Amsterdam alone the resolution was adopted of attempting a defence. The natural strength of its situation, and some degree of military skill in the defenders, assisted by French officers, obliged the Duke of Brunswick to make regular approaches, and retarded the submission of the city till October the 10th, when it received a foreign garrison. The triumph of the stadtholderian party was now complete, and the Prince of Orange was restored to all the rights and prerogatives which he formerly possessed.

The part of the Netherlands under the dominion of Austria was also in this year the seat of violent tumult and disorder. The Emperor Joseph, who in several instances had offended the people by his reforms and innovations, which in general displayed a despotic and rapacious spirit, promulgated on January 1st some new edicts, by which the existing tribunals of Brabant were abrogated, and new courts of judicature, and a new form of government, upon arbitrary principles, were established in contravention of the constitution of those provinces, as recognized by the ancient treaty denominated the *Joyous Entry*. The States of Brabant made a vigorous opposition to these alterations, which threw the whole country into confusion and alarm; and they were joined by the States of Flanders and Hainault. In Brussels, the syndics of the trading companies had so well learned the language of public liberty, as openly to assert in a memorial, that "if the sovereign shall infringe the articles of the *Joyous Entry*, his subjects shall be discharged from all duty and service to him, until due reparation shall be made for such infringement." The general spirit of resistance that manifested itself at the time when the new edicts were to take place, intimidated the Austrian governors-general so much, that they issued a declaration suspending all arrangements contrary to the *Joyous Entry*, till the emperor's determination could be known. This, however, was far from being favourable to such a concession, and the imperial forces were put in motion, with orders to advance to the Low Countries. But when nothing was expected less than a renewal of the scenes under the Duke of Alva, the emperor, who had at first received the deputies from the Netherlands with sternness, and given them no hopes of conciliation, on a sudden relaxed; and in conclusion, the new tribunals were suppressed, and the *Joyous Entry* with all the ancient privileges of the nation were restored. This change was attributed not so much to the usual mutability of the emperor's councils, as to his engagements with Russia, and an impending war with Turkey.

To the political agitations of this year are to be added certain domestic events in France, which may be regarded as the immediate preludes of that awful change in its condition, external and internal, which for so long a period has excited the interest and influenced the fortune of all Europe.

The disordered state of the French finances, occasioned by the debts contracted in the late war, and the extravagancies of the court, had suggested as the only effectual remedy, an application to the body of the people, in the form of a convention of *notables,* or principal persons in the different classes throughout the kingdom. This assembly met at Versailles on the 22d of February, and was opened in high solemnity by the king, accompanied by the princes of the blood and the great officers of state. The minister of finance, M. de Calonne, in an elaborate harangue, after laying before them the vast deficiencies of the public revenue, proposed different sources of supply, particularly a territorial impost, in the nature of a general and equal land-tax. The assembly did not possess public virtue enough to consent to such a proposal; and so great was the clamour raised against the minister, that he found it necessary to resign his post, and even to take refuge in England. He was succeeded by M. de Brienne, archbishop of Toulouse; but all that could be carried in the assembly was some regulations and reforms with respect to levying the taxes; and these being agreed upon, the meeting was dissolved on May 25th.

The inefficacy of this measure led to a resolution of the parliament of Paris, carried at length after two failures, for a petition to the king for convoking the States General of the nation. In the meantime the necessities of the government caused a recurrence to the usual mode of levying money by royal edicts, which the parliament refused to register. A bed of justice having been held by the king to compel the registry, the parliament made a decree declaring the edict of no force, and denouncing penalties against all who should attempt to put it in execution, which proceeding was sanctioned by the other parliaments. The royal authority was now absolutely at stake, and for its support it was judged advisable to punish the parliament of Paris for contumacy, by banishing all the members to Troyes. The derangement of public business and general tokens of dissatisfaction which followed this step alarmed the court, already vacillating and divided, and a compromise took place, by which the parliament was recalled, and the edicts of taxation were withdrawn. As a proof of the rapid progress which the spirit of liberty was now making in France, it may be mentioned, that the parliament of Grenoble issued a decree, by which it was rendered a capital crime for any person to attempt executing a *lettre de cachet* within their jurisdiction.

The apparent return of a good understanding between the court and the parliament of Paris was not of long duration. The wants of the government becoming more and more urgent, at a very full meeting of parliament on November 19th, attended by the princes of the blood, the peers, and all the great officers, the king appeared, bringing with him two edicts, one for a new loan to the amount of 450 millions of livres, the other, for the re-establishment of the protestants in their ancient civil rights; the latter being a measure which had been warmly recommended by the parliament. The king opened the way for his edicts by a long speech, in which he reminded the parliament of the principles from which they ought never to have deviated, and which, as part of the essence of the monarchy, he would not suffer to be evaded or changed. He then explained the nature of the loan he demanded, and pointed out his necessity; and having exhorted them to confine themselves within their proper functions, he gave them permission to deliver their sentiments individually without restraint. A very warm debate on the subject of the loan then followed, with the length and freedom of which the king being out of patience, he suddenly rose and commanded the registry of the edict without delay. This proceeding was opposed by the Duke of Orleans, who entered a protest against the whole business of the day, as thereby rendered null and void; and after the king's departure, a resolution to the same import was entered into by the parliament. The result was a royal order for the duke to retire to one of his seats, and the imprisonment of two members of the parliament. Very bold remonstrances were made against this act of power, and the parliament demanded, in the name of the laws, the trial or the liberation of the persons thus punished; and with this open assertion of the leading principle of a free government, the year closed.

The Ottoman Porte, still indignant at the occupation of the Krimea by Russia, and further irritated by the intention of the Empress Catharine to make a triumphant progress to that country, as well as by the various manifestations of her ambitious designs against the Turkish empire, commenced hostilities in its usual manner by committing M. Bulgakow, the Russian ambassador at Constantinople, to the Seven Towers, after which, on August 18th, war was formally declared against that power. Mauro Cordato, the Hospodar of Moldavia, being suspected of a traitorous correspondence with Petersburgh and Vienna, was deposed, and narrowly escaped being seized by the Turkish emissaries. The Captain Pashaw was recalled from pursuing his success in Egypt, and was placed at the head of the army on the Russian frontiers, where he was opposed by Prince Potemkin; and various enterprizes were undertaken by the Turks and Tartars; in all of which, to the close of the year, they were defeated. The Emperor of Germany declared his intention of acting as an ally to Russia with a large army, and assembled a great number of troops for the purpose. The Porte, however, was so determined upon war, that it rejected the proposal of the French ambassador for a suspension of arms in order to give time for a negotiation. A remarkable spectacle was afforded at Constantinople by a splendid embassy from Tippoo Sultan to the Grand Seignior, for the purpose of establishing a solemn league between these two Mussulman powers, though the remoteness of their several dominions rendered mutual aid impracticable. The Indian ambassador, however, was received with honours superior to those ever paid to the envoy of a Christian prince, and his appearance served to augment the religious and warlike enthusiasm of the Turks.

1788

28th & 29th Year of the Reign

O N the meeting of Parliament after the recess, the first subject brought under consideration was a naval promotion declared by the board of admiralty, in which, while 16 captains were advanced to a flag, more than 40 had been passed over. This selection was authorized by an order, dated 1747, which permitted the lords of the Admiralty to place on the superannuated list such captains of long service as were disabled by age or infirmity to act as admirals. In the present case, the exercise of this right was in general regarded in the navy as partial, and capricious; and on February 20th the matter was taken up by Lord Rawdon in the House of Lords, who moved that an address should be presented to his Majesty, praying him to take into consideration the services of such captains in his navy as had been passed over in the last promotion of admirals. Lord Howe, the first commissioner of the admiralty, then rose to defend his conduct on the occasion, which he justified on the ground of the necessity of a discretionary power in the appointment of flag officers, without following the exact order of seniority; and he affirmed that in the present instance he had acted to the best of his judgment, and with strict impartiality. A debate ensued, in which Lord Sandwich ably defended the propriety of lodging such a power in the admiralty, and shewed the mischiefs that would arise from rendering navy promotions a subject of parliamentary discussion. The motion was at length negatived without a division. On the following day the same topic was brought into the House of Commons by Mr. Bastard, who moved for an address to the King requesting him to confer some mark of his favour upon two navy captains by name, who had received the thanks of the House for their behaviour on the 12th of April 1782. Finding, however, that this mode of bringing on the investigation was not generally agreeable to the House, he moved on the 18th, that the House should go into a committee for enquiring into the conduct of the admiralty touching the late promotion. In the debate which followed, several names of officers who had been passed by were mentioned, and their professional merits were stated in proof of the injustice of their omission; on the other hand, arguments were repeated in favour of the conduct of the admiralty, and of the propriety of leaving the matter to their decision. The division, however, shewed that a considerable impression had been made to the contrary; for notwithstanding the efforts of the minister, the motion was rejected by no greater majority than 150 to 134. This division encouraged Mr. Bastard to bring on the subject again by a somewhat different motion, which was negatived by a larger majority; and thus the matter terminated.

A resolution had been formed by government during the apprehensions of a rupture with France in the last year, of sending four additional regiments to India on board of the Company's ships, and this had been unanimously approved by the court of directors; but the alarm having passed over, and government still adhering to the measure of sending the regiments, with the view of forming a permanent establishment of king's troops in India, it became a question on whom the expence of their conveyance and subsequent maintenance should fall. By an act in 1781 it was stipulated that the Company should be bound to pay for such troops only as were sent out on their requisition; but the board of controul in 1784 had determined that they were invested with a power, in case of the Company's refusal to pay for troops sent out, to defray the expence of them from its territorial possessions. Several eminent lawyers had given their opinion against such power in the board of controul, and on their authority the directors had refused to take the troops in their ships. Mr. Pitt, in consequence, moved, on February 25th, to bring in a bill for removing the doubts in question, and for declaring that the intention of the legislature in the act of 1784 was agreeable to the construction put upon it by the board of controul. He argued that there was no step which could have been taken by the court of directors previously to the act of 1784 relative to the military and political concerns of India, and the management and application of the territorial revenues, which the board of controul had not now a right to take by virtue of that act; and in this opinion Mr. Dundas fully concurred. The motion was strongly opposed, but was carried without a division on the second reading of the bill, however, counsel being heard against it on the part of the East India Company, its grounds and merits were fully canvassed, as also in the several debates which followed. In one of these, Mr. Pulteney and others who usually supported the minister, declared that the construction now attempted to be put upon the act of 1784 rendered it as obnoxious as the rejected India bill of 1783, and that the only difference was, that the object openly professed by one, was attempted to be obtained clandestinely and fraudulently by the other. Upon this ground, Mr. Fox and his friends triumphed in the complete justification which, they asserted, the measure they had proposed received from the tacit confession of their adversaries, who now assumed for the board of controul all the powers which they had vested in a board of commissioners. In the progress of this declaratory bill every step was warmly contested, and it passed the Commons by a majority of only 54. In the House of Lords it also encountered a powerful opposition, but was carried by 71 against 28, and finally passed into a law.

A matter of some constitutional importance which engaged the attention of parliament, was the proposed addition to the mutiny act, of a clause for incorporating in the army a corps of military artificers newly raised, conformably to a plan of the Duke of Richmond. This was objected to as unnecessarily putting a body of men under martial law, and depriving them of the privileges of Englishmen; the clause however passed both Houses.

On May 6th, Mr. Grenville moved for leave to bring in a bill for certain emendations and additions to his father's bill for the regulation of controverted elections. The first object he had in view was to limit the great number of groundless petitions for undue elections, which had been presented in the first session of every parliament since the passing of that act; and this he proposed to do by empowering the election committee to adjudge that the party presenting a petition which should turn out frivolous, and also that the party offering a frivolous defence to a petition, should pay reasonable costs. The second object was to lay down a rule for establishing the rights of election, and rendering them immutable for the future; it being now no uncommon thing for two gentlemen to be sitting in that House at once as representatives of the same borough, on different rights of election. The bill for these purposes was immediately brought in, and, having passed both Houses, received the royal assent.

The abolition of the African slave-trade, so long an object of the warmest interest to the friends of humanity in this country, was first introduced to parliament in this year. A petition for the purpose had been presented to parliament in the preceding year by the society of Quakers, who, with that spirit of general philanthropy for which they are so much distinguished, took the lead here, as well as in America, in this work of reformation; and the cause being rendered popular by their efforts and those of others animated by a kindred spirit, petitions to the same effect had been presented from the two English Universities, and from several of the most considerable towns and corporations. It was now thought proper by the ministers that an enquiry should be instituted before a committee of the privy council into the facts and allegations of the parties for and against the abolition; and the business was brought into the House of Commons on May 9th, by Mr. Pitt, in the absence of Mr. Wilberforce, to whom the conduct of the parliamentary measures for obtaining the abolition had been delegated by common consent. His motion was for a resolution to the effect that the House would in the next session take into consideration the circumstances of the slave-trade complained of in the petitions which had been presented. In the conversation which followed, Mr. Fox and Mr. Burke objected to the reason given by Mr Pitt, for delaying the proceedings of the House to that period, namely, that the privy council would by that time have brought their enquiry to a state fitted to direct the investigation in parliament; and maintained that parliament ought rather to lead than follow. At length, Sir William Dolben, after observing that some of the greatest evils of the trade arose from the sufferings of the negroes in their passage, for which an immediate remedy might be applied, moved for a bill to regulate the transportation of the natives of Africa, to the British colonies in the West Indies, the provisions of which should go to the limiting of their number in proportion to the tonnage of the vessel conveying them, and also to other points, for their health and comfort. This proposal was generally approved; the bill was brought in and carried, notwithstanding a petition from Liverpool praying that no alteration in the slave-trade might take place, and the examination of witnesses to prove that the evil which the bill was to remedy did not exist. It afterwards went through the House of Lords with some amendments, and passed into a law.

On June 8th, Mr. Pitt introduced to the House of Commons the subject of the compensation to the American loyalists for their sufferings during the war. He stated a proposition for adjusting their claims by arranging the claimants into different classes according to their different demands upon the sympathy and generosity of the country, which obtained the general approbation of the House; and concluded by moving that a sum amounting to about £1,340,000 be voted to the several American claimants, which was agreed to. He had before mentioned in the committee of ways and means his idea that the sum should be paid by instalments, by means of an annual lottery, till the whole should be cleared, which was approved.

On February 13th, the trial of Mr. Hastings commenced at the House of Lords, with the usual formalities; and two days being occupied in reading the articles of impeachment and the answers to them. Mr. Burke, on the 15th, opened the cause in a very eloquent and impressive speech, which was continued through several days. The managers of the impeachment having then stated their intention to proceed to a conclusion of each article of the charge singly, on both sides, before another was entered upon, this mode was objected to by Mr. Hastings's counsel; and after a vigorous debate by the Lords, a large majority determined that the whole of the charges collectively should be gone through by the impeachers, before the accused should be called upon to make his defence — a decision which probably had a great influence on the final result. During the subsequent months various articles of accusation were gone through by the managers, till the court on June 15th, adjourned to a day after the next meeting of parliament.

Early in the present session, proceedings commenced in the House of Commons relative to the impeachment of

Sir Elijah Impey, against whom charges of high crimes and misdemeanours were presented by Sir Gilbert Elliot. The discussion of these continued till the month of May, when their further consideration was adjourned for three months.

A treaty of defensive alliance between the King of Great Britain, and the States General of the United Provinces, was signed at the Hague on April 25th. By its tenor, each country was bound to succour the other by sea and land, if attacked by any European power in any part of the world, and to guarantee each other in the possession of all their dominions. Further, his Britannic Majesty "guaranteed in the most effectual manner the hereditary Stadtholderate, as well as the office of hereditary governor of each province, in the house of Orange, with all the rights and prerogatives thereto belonging, as forming an essential part of the constitution of the United Provinces."

A provisional treaty of defensive alliance between the Kings of Great Britain and Prussia having been signed at Loo in June, the same was made the foundation of a definitive treaty of defensive alliance signed at Berlin on August 13th, the terms of which were similar in effect to that above-mentioned.

Important events took place in different parts of Europe during this year.

The Emperor of Germany, at the close of 1787, had decidedly shown his intention of joining Russia in the war against the Ottoman Porte; and an attempt to surprize Belgrade previously to any declaration of hostilities, was a commencement, which, not being attended with success, could only throw discredit on the sovereign or his generals. It was followed by another act of hostility, that of an attack on the fortress of Turkish Gradisca, which was repulsed with considerable loss to the assailants. After some other enterprizes of the like kind, a formal declaration of war against the Turks was issued at Vienna on February 10th, in which the sole assigned cause of enmity was the conduct of the Porte towards Russia. In April, the Emperor in person joined his grand army on the

Danube, and an active campaign ensued, which, without any great events, was attended with much waste of lives and desolation of country. The Turks, singularly exasperated against the Austrians for what they regarded as unprovoked aggression, behaved with uncommon intrepidity, and at the same time appeared improved in the art of war, and upon the whole the advantage was on their side. Besides their losses in the field, the Austrians suffered extremely from the diseases which are endemic in these unhealthy regions, and the Emperor here began to feel that decline in his constitution which brought him to an early end. The Grand Vizier opened the campaign with an army of 200,000 men, of whom the main body was encamped at Silistria, whilst detachments occupied almost the whole frontier of the Turkish territories. The Russians co-operated little with their allies, except at the siege of Choczim, which, after an obstinate defence, was taken by their united forces. The Grand Vizier made an irruption into the Bannat of Temeswar, and over-ran the greatest part of the country, which he evacuated at the approach of winter, and in November an armistice was concluded between the Turkish and Austrian commanders. The Emperor Joseph returned to Vienna broken in health and spirits, having obtained no other fruits from his military exploits than a few fortresses on the borders, and Choczim, with some of the adjacent part of Moldavia, purchased at a prodigious cost of men and treasure. He was farther disquieted by the discontents of his Hungarian subjects, whom he had alienated by his harsh and arbitrary measures, and particularly by carrying away their crown and regalia, which they regarded with singular veneration. The Grand Seignior having endeavoured to avail himself of this disaffection by a manifesto calling upon the Hungarians to assert their rights and place themselves under his protection, Joseph hastily issued a proclamation, in which he promised to them the restoration of their ancient constitution and peculiar privileges.

The Russian operations in this campaign were chiefly directed to the coasts of the Black sea, the quarter to which their interests pointed. A powerful fleet was fitted out early in the year at Cronstadt for the purpose of entering the Mediterranean and attacking the Turks on that side; but the power and ambition of the Empress Catharine had at this time impressed most of the states of Europe in such a manner, that the re-appearance of a Russian fleet in that sea was discountenanced by almost all the powers which bordered upon it; and even the English court issued a prohibition for its shipping or sailors to engage in the service of Russia. A flotilla was at the same time prepared for the Black sea which, though unequal in force to the Turkish fleet in that part, was well supplied with seamen and soldiers, and rendered extremely strong in artillery. An army computed at 150,000 men, under Potemkin, Romanzow, and other distinguished Generals, assembled in June on the banks of the Bog, the first object of which was the siege of Otchakof. The Captain Pashaw having the command of the Turkish squadron on the Black sea, appeared off the mouth of the Dnieper, and some warm actions occurred between it and the Russian flotilla under the Prince of Nassau, on the lake called the Liman, in which the shallowness of the water gave an advantage to the latter; and the Turkish admiral, after sustaining considerable loss, returned to the port of Varna. Prince Potemkin in July invested Otchakof which had a garrison of 20,000 select troops; and the bravery of the defenders protracted the siege to the month of December, when a winter of unusual severity had set in, and little advance had been made. As a last effort, Potemkin ordered a general bombardment and cannonade with red-hot balls, which occasioned the explosion of the principal powder magazine, attended with a great breach in the wall. An assault was instantly made by the Russian troops, and after a dreadful slaughter on both sides, the fortress was carried, and the greatest part of the garrison was put to the sword.

In the meantime a new enemy had made his appearance against Russia. The King of Sweden, irritated against the court of Petersburgh, which had constantly fostered the discontented party in his own country, and who was also supposed to have received a subsidy from Turkey, had from the beginning of the year been making warlike preparations, and at length assembled an army of 35,000 men in order to embark them for Finland. This measure occasioned the Russian minister at Stockholm to present a memorial to the Swedish ministry, addressed exclusively to them without noticing the King, in which, while the greatest goodwill was expressed towards the government of Sweden, complaint was made of the hostile indications that were displaying. The King, indignant at this attempt to separate him from the nation, ordered the ambassador to quit the kingdom, and presented a circular note on the subject to all the foreign ministers. He then departed for Finland, where, soon after his arrival, hostilities with the Russians commenced, June 21st. They were presently followed by a declaration of war from the court of Petersburgh, in which care was taken to remind the Swedes that by a solemn compact the King was bound not to engage in any war without the consent of his subjects. The Swedish troops were for the most part successful in the petty actions which took place about the borders of Finland; and their approach towards Petersburgh spread an uncommon alarm in the capital. Measures were taken for its defence against any sudden attack, and Admiral Greig sailed with a strong fleet from Cronstadt to oppose, in the gulph of Finland, that of Sweden commanded by the King's brother, the Duke of Sudermania. The fleets meeting in a fog, an action was brought on, attended with much bloodshed, and in which many ships were disabled on each side, but rendered indecisive by the obscurity under which it was fought. Both fleets returned to their ports; but the Russian being first refitted and reinforced by fresh ships, came unexpectedly upon the Swedish in the road of Sweaborg, and after burning a ship of the line, forced the rest to take shelter under their forts. During the remainder of the campaign, the Swedes lay blocked up in the harbour of Sweaborg, whilst the Russians rode masters of all the seas within the Sound. The influence of the Empress afterwards diffused a general disaffection among the officers, especially those of rank and family, in the Swedish army in Finland; and the King laying siege to a fortress, was severely mortified by a refusal of the officers to lead on the troops to an attack, and the laying down of their arms by the soldiers.

The embarrassment of the King was greatly increased by the declaration which the court of Denmark issued on August 19th, of its intention to act as an auxiliary to Russia, pursuant to the treaties subsisting between the two nations. The plan of operations formed by that court was that Prince Charles of Hesse, the viceroy of Norway, should invade Sweden on the side of that country with the stipulated number of troops. The King upon this intelligence hastened to Stockholm, whence he proceeded to Dalecarlia for the purpose of animating its martial and loyal inhabitants to the defence of himself and the country. On September 24th the Prince of Hesse, accompanied by his nephew the Prince Royal of Denmark, entered Sweden by the sea coast, with 12,000 men, and found no more than 5 or 6000 to oppose him. He gained possession without resistance of Stromness and Uddewalla, and having crossed the river Gotha, came within sight of the principal commercial town of Sweden, Gottenburg. That important place was on the eve of capitulating, when the King, having with great celerity performed a long journey alone, suddenly, on October 3d, arrived at Gottenburg, and put an end to every idea of surrender. His means of defence were, however, so inadequate, that nothing but the immediate and powerful interference of England, Prussia, and Holland, as mediators for maintaining the peace of the north, could probably have saved the town from capture or destruction. Mr. Elliot, the British minister at the Danish court, was the most active agent on this occasion; and by his explicit declaration to the Danish commander and the Prince Royal, that a Prussian army was ready to enter Holstein, and an English fleet to sail for the Baltic, unless all farther progress of the Danish arms against Sweden were suspended, an armistice was concluded, and the Prince of Hesse withdrew his troops into Norway about the middle of November.

In France, the spirit of political reform, and of resistance to arbitrary power, was proceeding in accelerated course. The parliament of Paris, which in answer to their last remonstrance respecting the imprisonment of two of their members, had been told by the King "not to demand from his justice, what solely depended on his will," at a meeting on January 4th passed strong resolutions against *lettres de cachet*, as subversive of all the foundations of the constitution; and repeated their declaration, that they would not cease their demands of what was essential to the personal security of every Frenchman. The contest upon this point still continued, and new acts of authority were followed by fresh remonstrances, till at length the court adopted the project of instituting a *cour pleniere*, which was to be possessed of such powers as to render the parliaments unnecessary for all the purposes of government, and to reduce them to mere courts of justice. This design, notwithstanding the secrecy with which it was conducted, came to the knowledge of M. D'Epremenil, a member of the parliament of Paris, who communicated it to his colleagues, the consequence of which was a sudden meeting of that assembly, who made a formal protest against any change in the frame of the national government. An attempt to arrest D'Epremenil and another member having produced a strong remonstrance from the parliament, the King refused to receive the deputies who were to present it; and causing the hall to be surrounded by a regiment of guards, the two obnoxious members delivered themselves up, and were committed to different prisons. The parliament, instead of being intimidated by this exertion of authority, were rendered only the more resolute in their measures, and entered a formal protest against the seizure of their members. On May 8th the King held a bed of justice at Versailles, which he opened with a long speech, severely reflecting upon the parliament, whom he charged with a constant deviation from their duty for a year past, but declared it not to be his intention to dissolve them, but to bring them back to their original institution. Certain ordinances were then brought forward, ready signed by the King, the first of which was the establishment of the *cour pleniere*, and the rest related to alterations and improvements in the judicial system, attributed to M. de Lamoignon, keeper of the seals. These were registered, the parliament meantime keeping profound silence, and the meeting broke up. A protest was on the next day drawn up against the new court by the parliament, in which they were seconded by several of the peers. In the meantime great disturbances prevailed in several of the provinces, and the authority of government was resisted in a manner that in some instances rendered necessary the interference of the military. At length, the opposition to the new system became so great and general, that the King, whose mind appears to have been in a perpetual agitation during this struggle, was obliged to retract, or at least suspend, all his ordinances. The financial difficulties now became more and more urgent, public credit sunk to the lowest ebb, while inclement seasons augmented the general distress. The Archbishop of Toulouse, now promoted to the see of Sens, resigned his uneasy post at the head of the finances, and M. Necker, the celebrated banker of Geneva, who had held it previously to M. de Calonne, and who more than any other man possessed the confidence of the French nation, was called a second time to occupy the arduous station. A new convention of the Notables was summoned for the purpose of giving their advice concerning the organization of the States General, which it was now determined to convoke.

Although the Emperor of Germany, occupied with his preparations of war against the Turks, had entered into an accommodation with his subjects of the Low Countries, it was by no means conformable to his temper and principles to renounce the projects he had formed for reducing them to compliance with his arbitrary will. In order to prepare the way for the resumption of his authority, he removed from the command of the army the Count de Murray, who had distinguished himself by his lenient conduct, and conferred it upon General Dalton, a soldier of fortune, of a despotic character; and at the same time he nominated Count Trautsmandorff to the civil government. The first exertion of power under the new authorities was a positive mandate to the university of Louvain to admit that system of reform which the Emperor had some time before attempted to force upon it, and which went to a total subversion of constitution, especially with regard to the theological department. For this purpose, Trautsmandorff urged the council of Brabant to publish a declaration in support of the Emperor's decree against that university; but instead of complying, they issued a strong remonstrance against the violence offered to their rights. It being determined by the government to quell this spirit of resistance, a letter was sent by the minister to the council at Brussels on January 22d, commanding them, in the language of an absolute sovereign, to publish the required declaration, and allowing but two hours for their determination. While they were sitting, Dalton had drawn up at no great distance a body of infantry and cavalry with cannon, and a crowd of people having assembled round them, a young ensign, on the pretext of some stones thrown by boys, ordered a platoon to be fired upon the unarmed multitude, which killed some and wounded more. This act meeting with approbation from the Emperor himself, the soldiery were let loose upon the people; and in many other considerable towns, such as Mechlin, Louvain, and Antwerp, the smallest tumult occasioned by instances of oppression was punished by military execution. A strong garrison was sent to Louvain to coerce that refractory place, and the university was thoroughly purged of all who had shewn any opposition to the Emperor's decrees. A college for education at Antwerp having rendered itself distinguished by a similar spirit among the students, the government resolved upon its entire suppression, and August 4th being appointed for the day of shutting it up, a body of soldiers with cannon attended to enforce the execution. The riot naturally occasioned by this arbitrary act was revenged by the slaughter of above forty men and women on the spot, and double the number sent to the hospital. The Emperor's applause was given to all these sanguinary measures; and the state of the Low Countries was rendered so wretched by martial law, and the violation of all chartered rights, that many of the most respectable inhabitants quitted the country, and commerce and manufactures were almost annihilated. The states of Brabant, however, continued with firmness to oppose the inroads of despotism, and refused to grant the ordinary supplies.

In December died Charles III, King of Spain, and was succeeded by his son, Charles IV.

The latter part of this year was made unfortunately memorable at home by the occurrence of that mental malady, which has thrown so deep a gloom upon the close of his Majesty's reign. Some time in October it became known to the public that the King was labouring under an indisposition, which was announced in such a manner, that an alarm prevailed of great danger to his life. His appearance at a levee dissipated this fear; but it could not much longer be concealed that the real case was a derangement of the understanding, of which, indeed, symptoms had more than once before appeared, though they had been kept as a state secret. This lamentable event, unprecedented in English history, produced a general consternation, and occasioned extraordinary movements among the heads of parties. Parliament having met on November 20th, the day to which it had been prorogued, it was unanimously adjourned for fifteen days longer; and a privy council being held on the day before the expiration of that term, the physicians in attendance on his Majesty were summoned, to whom three questions were put. Their answers will indicate the questions; namely, that his Majesty was incapable of business; that there was a great probability of his recovery, but it was impossible to limit the time; and that they formed this opinion from experience, having observed that the majority of those afflicted with the same disease had recovered.

Parliament having assembled on December 4th, a committee was appointed in each House for fully ascertaining his Majesty's state, which being done, with the same result as above-mentioned, Mr. Pitt, on the 10th, moved "that a committee be appointed to examine the journals of the house, and report precedents of such proceedings as may have been had in cases of the personal exercise of the royal authority being prevented or interrupted by infancy, sickness, or infirmity, or otherwise, with a view to provide for the same." To this motion Mr. Fox objected, as nugatory, and productive of unnecessary delay, it being his decided opinion, that when the sovereign from any causes became incapable of exercising his functions, the heir apparent had an indisputable claim to the exercise of the executive power; though, indeed, the two houses of parliament were alone competent to pronounce when he ought to take possession of his right. Mr. Pitt, in reply, declared this doctrine to be little less than treason to the constitution; and he maintained, on the contrary, that the heir apparent had no more right in such a case than any other subject in the kingdom, and that it belonged to the two remaining branches of the legislature, in behalf of the people to make provision for the temporary deficiency. This great constitutional question was debated with ardour in both houses, and in both, the majority appeared adverse to the Prince of Wales's claim to the regency as a matter of right.

On the 16th, the House of Commons being in a committee, Mr. Pitt moved three resolutions, of which the first, asserting his Majesty's present incapacity for public business, passed unanimously. The others were: That it is the right and duty of the Lords and Commons of Great Britain assembled, to provide the means for supplying the defect of the personal exercise of the royal authority in such manner as the exigency of the case may seem to require; and that for this purpose, and for maintaining entire the constitutional authority of the King, it is necessary that the Lords and Commons should determine on the means whereby the royal assent may be given to such bill as may be passed in the two houses of parliament respecting the exercise of the powers of the crown during the continuance of his Majesty's indisposition. After these points had been debated; and a motion by Lord North for immediately proceeding to declare a regent had been negatived by 268 against 204, the two resolutions were carried with out farther discussion.

Mr. Pitt, on December 19th, being called upon to inform the House of the mode of proceeding he intended to adopt, stated that he should propose that their proceedings should be under the royal authority, delegated by a commission under the Great Seal: that the commissioners should open the parliament in his Majesty's name according to the usual form, and afterwards give the royal assent to such bill as might be passed by the two houses for appointing a regent to exercise so much of the royal authority as was necessary during his Majesty's indisposition. The resolutions which had passed in the committee being now brought up, long arguments, in which much historical and constitutional knowledge was displayed, were adduced on both sides; and the conclusion was, that they were agreed to, and ordered to be delivered to the Lords at a conference. Similar debates took place in that house, which ended in passing the resolutions by a majority of about one third on December 29th. A protest against this concurrence was however signed by the Dukes of York and Cumberland, and 46 other peers.

In the nation at large these proceedings were viewed with much interest; and addresses were sent from a considerable majority of the counties and corporations in the kingdom approving of the measures adopted by the ministers.

This year having completed a century from the Resolution, the memory of that event was celebrated by rejoicings in various parts of the kingdom. The birthday of King William was in particular kept with more than usual solemnity at Dublin.

1789

29th & 30th Year of the Reign

THE speaker of the House of Commons, Mr. Cornwall, dying on January 2d, the House adjourned to the 5th, when two members were proposed for the vacant office, the Hon. Mr. W. Grenville, and Sir Gilbert Elliot. On a division, the former was chosen by 215 votes to 144.

The great business of the regency was then resumed, and a re-examination of his Majesty's physicians having been agreed upon, the report of the committee appointed for this purpose was brought up on January 13th, from which it appeared that all those gentlemen agreed on the probability of the King's recovery, though they were not equally sanguine in their expectations, and that none would venture to fix the time when such a change was likely to take place. On January 16th Mr. Pitt took up the subject of the regency by observing, that what they were to provide for was a deficiency in the executive government for an interval, and as he hoped, a short one; and also, against any embarrassment in the resumption of the royal authority upon his Majesty's recovery. He should therefore propose to invest the Prince of Wales with the whole royal authority, subject only to certain limitations and restrictions. The first of these was, that the regent should not have the power of creating peers. The second that he should not grant any place or pension for life or in reversion, other than such place as from its nature is to be held for life or during good behaviour. The third, that he should be restrained from any power over the King's personal property. Besides these resolutions he proposed one, to intrust the queen with the entire care of the royal person during his illness, and to place under her authority the whole of the King's household, with full power to dismiss and appoint at her pleasure; and another, for the nomination of a council to assist her Majesty with their advice. These five resolutions were then moved in succession, when a warm opposition was made both to the whole plan of restriction, and to the particular articles. The bestowing of the whole power and patronage of the household upon the queen was especially objected to, as setting up a party in the court opposed to the administration of the regent; it being well known that an entire change of ministers was intended by the regent, whilst her Majesty would naturally be inclined to favour those who had conferred upon her such high authority. The resolutions, however, after several divisions, were agreed to, and ordered to be delivered at a conference to the Lords. In the upper house they underwent a discussion similar to that in the Commons, and being at length voted, a protest against them was signed by 57 lords.

On January 27th, Mr. Pitt proposed the appointment of a committee to wait on the Prince of Wales with the resolutions which had been agreed to by parliament, and endeavour to know whether his Royal Highness was willing to accept of the regency on the terms therein proposed. This motion being carried, not without some severe animadversions on the part of opposition upon the want of respect with which, as they alleged, the Prince had been treated, and a similar motion having passed the Lords, the two committees presented the resolutions to the Prince and the Queen. The answer received from his Royal Highness contained an assurance that, his duty to the King, his regard for the interests of the people, and his respect for the desires of the two Houses, outweighing every other consideration, he would undertake the weighty trust proposed to him conformably to the resolutions, though sensible of the difficulties that must attend its execution, in the peculiar circumstances in which it was committed to his charge, and of which he was acquainted with no other example.

The next process was that of enabling the two Houses, which as yet sat merely in convention, to act as a legislative body; and for this purpose, the lord president (Lord Camden) moved that letters patent under the great seal be impowered to be issued by the authority of the two houses in the usual form appointing commissioners to open the parliament. This being carried in the House of Lords, and concurred in, after a warm debate, by the Commons, Mr. Pitt, on February 3d moved for leave to bring in the regency bill, which being granted, it was read for the first time. This bill consisted of thirty-two clauses, many of which were subjects of debate; but as it never passed into a law, there appears no necessity for attending upon its farther progress. Whilst it was under discussion in the House of Lords, the Lord Chancellor, on February 19th, after observing that it had appeared from the reports of the physicians that his Majesty for some time past was in a state of convalescence, and that the accounts just received affirmed the improvement to be progressive, said, that in this situation of things he conceived they could not possibly proceed with the bill before them, and therefore moved an adjournment. On the 24th the Lord Chancellor acquainted the House that he had on that day attended his Majesty by his express command, and had found him to be perfectly recovered. Further adjournments took place till March 10th, when the Commons with their Speaker, attending at the bar of the House of Lords, the chancellor informed them that the King had caused a commission to be issued authorizing the commissioners appointed by former letters patent to hold that parliament, to open the same. This being done, the chancellor acquainted them, that his Majesty being recovered, and capable of attending to public affairs, had commanded the commissioners to convey his warmest acknowledgments for the additional proofs they had given of attachment to his person, and of concern for the honour of his crown and the good government of his dominions. Other topics were then alluded to, as in an usual speech from the crown, and congratulatory addresses were unanimously voted in both houses. This was the termination of the public proceedings in an emergence which will ever stand as an event of high moment in the constitutional history of this country.

It is proper, however, before the subject is dismissed, to advert to the very different measures taken on the occasion by the parliament of Ireland. The session was opened on February 5th by the Marquis of Buckingham, lord lieutenant, who informed the Houses of his Majesty's indisposition, and acquainted them that he had directed all the necessary documents to be laid before them. The secretary then moved in the House of Commons, that the House should, on the Monday se'nnight, resolve itself into a committee to take into consideration the state of his Majesty's health. This motion being regarded as made for procuring a delay to prevent the Irish parliament from coming to any resolutions on the subject previously to the determinations of the British parliament, it was vehemently opposed as derogatory to the independence of that kingdom, and a motion by Mr. Grattan for the House to meet on the next Wednesday was carried by a majority of 128 to 74. On that day, Mr. Connolly moved that an address should be presented to the Prince of Wales requesting him to take on himself the government of that kingdom during his Majesty's incapacity, which, after a violent debate, was carried without a division. The Earl of Charlemont moved for a similar address in the House of Lords, which was voted by a majority of 19; and both Houses waited on the Lord Lieutenant with their address, requesting him to transmit it, which he refused to do. The result was the appointment, by both Houses, of a deputation for the purpose of presenting the address. Mr. Grattan further moved a vote of censure on the Lord Lieutenant for his refusal, which was carried by 115 to 83; and also votes of supply for two months only, which were carried. The deputies arrived at London time enough to present their address to the Prince of Wales, who, returning them his warmest thanks, informed them at the same time of the King's convalescent state, and of his hopes that within a few days his Majesty would be able to resume the government.

The national rejoicings on the happy event of his Majesty's recovery exceeded every thing before known. More splendid illuminations than had ever been exhibited were universal throughout the kingdom. A day of general thanksgiving was appointed, which was observed with unusual solemnity; and the King in person, attended by the royal family, the great officers of state, and both houses of parliament, went in grand procession to St. Paul's.

Among the proceedings in parliament, one of the first was a renewal by Mr. Fox of an annual motion for the repeal of the shop tax. That impost had become more and more unpopular ever since it was laid, and various meetings had been held in the metropolis for petitioning against it. The minister therefore thought proper at length to give way to the public feeling, and the repeal was agreed to. At the same time, on the motion of Mr. Dempster, a kind of countervailing additional tax on hawkers and pedlars was taken off.

A renewed application for the repeal of the corporation and test acts as far as related to protestant dissenters, was made in a motion by Mr. Beaufoy, supported by Mr. Fox and Mr. W. Smith, and opposed by Lord North and Mr. Pitt, and was rejected by 122 votes against 102.

The resumed consideration of the slave trade in the House of Commons, promised in the last session, was, from the circumstances of the time, deferred to May 12th. A large report on the subject from the privy council being laid before the House, twelve resolutions founded upon it were presented by Mr. Wilberforce, after which, and some evidence heard before the House, the farther consideration of the subject was adjourned to the next session. Sir W. Dolben's bill for regulating the transportation of slaves was, by a new act, continued in an amended form.

Mr. Grenville having in the month of June been appointed one of the secretaries of state on the resignation of Lord Sidney, he resigned the office of speaker of the House of Commons, for which Mr. Addington and Sir Gilbert Elliot were proposed by the different parties, and the former was chosen.

In June Mr. Pitt brought in a bill for repealing the subsisting duties on tobacco, and substituting others of excise. The information of this intended change occasioned a general alarm among the manufacturers of that article, and many petitions were presented against it. In parliament it was also strongly opposed, and various alterations were made in its progress, to remove objections. In fine, it passed into a law just before the close of the session.

The trial of Mr. Hastings was proceeding during this time, though with much delay and interruption. Mr. Burke having, in a speech upon one of the charges, adverted to his treatment of Nundcomar, one of his accusers in India, and asserted that he had at last murdered him by the hands of Sir Elijah Impey, Mr. Hastings petitioned the House to be heard against such a charge, and after many debates, a censure was moved upon Mr. Burke's expression, and carried.

Parliament was prorogued on August 11th.

In this year was effected the great *Revolution* in France, which for so long a period has rendered the affairs of that country not only the most interesting political spectacle afforded by modern history, but the hinge upon which the principal public events of all Europe have turned. In an especial manner it has influenced the state of these kingdoms; so that from this time it becomes absolutely necessary to entwine a thread of French history with the whole fabric of the annals of the present reign. As, however, the remainder of this work would be rendered wholly disproportionate by relating the transactions belonging to the French revolution upon the same scale with that assigned to domestic occurrences, nothing more will be attempted than such an outline as may mark out the continuous chain of cause and effect, and the series of the most important events.

The embarrassments of the French government could not have been more forcibly displayed than by its consent to the convocation of those States General, the disuse of which ever since the year 1614 sufficiently proved the aversion with which they were regarded by the arbitrary princes and ministers who had succeeded. It was indeed obvious, that if constituted so as to be a representative of the whole community, they must hold in their hands the mass of public power; hence their organization was a subject of warm contest in the body of notables appointed for that purpose, and was a topic of general interest in the nation. The two material points for determination were, whether the three orders of which the States were composed should sit in one chamber, and vote by heads, or in three chambers and vote by orders; and whether each order should consist of about the same number of individuals, or the *tiers etat* or commons should equal in number the orders of nobles and of clergy together. The importance of these questions with respect to the influence of the crown will be at once apparent, especially of the latter, on which, in fact, the circumstance of a revolution almost entirely depended. The popular party, now become predominant in France, was so ardently bent upon the measure of doubling the representation of the *tiers etat*, that M. Necker, to whom the King committed the whole decision of the matter, either not foreseeing the consequences, or convinced that the desire of the nation could not be resisted without the danger of a general tumult, gave his advice in its favour. It was therefore determined in council on December 27th, that the number of deputies to the States should not fall short of a thousand, to be apportioned conformably to the population and financial contributions of the different bailliages; and that the representation of the *tiers etat* should be equal to the sum of the representation of the two other orders.

On May 5th the meeting of the States General was opened at Versailles with great solemnity by a speech from the King. It was followed by a long speech from M. Necker in which exact details were given of the state of the national finances, and plans were proposed for remedying their disorders. The first business of the assembly was the verification of the powers of the members, on which subject differences immediately arose, the third estate insisting that it should be done in a common assembly of the three orders, whereas the nobles and clergy adhered to the ancient practice of each verifying in its own house. This dispute was rendered important from the plan annexed to it by the democratic party, of voting by *pole* and not by *orders,* which would clearly give the third estate the preponderance; since their number was equal to that of the other two conjoined, and they might expect adherents from both. The nobles were resolute, and formed their separate house; the clergy wavered; and after an inaction of six weeks, the third estate, being joined by a few of the clergy, and feeling themselves strong in the public opinion, declared themselves the legislative body, and assumed the title of the *National Assembly.* The majority of the clergy were brought to acquiesce in this assumption; but the King, supported by the nobles, declared these proceedings null, and commanded the deputies to separate. Violent tumults followed, in some of which, that very dangerous symptom of fallen authority appeared, an attachment of the soldiery to the popular cause; and in fine, the King prevailed on the nobles to give way, and an union of the three orders took place.

In the meantime an army was collecting round Paris; and as soon as the court felt its strength, the step was taken on July 11th, of suddenly dismissing Necker, with an order to quit the kingdom in twenty-four hours. The intelligence of this event excited a furious commotion in the capital, and an attempt to disperse the populace by means of a foreign regiment having been defeated, the citizens armed, and were joined by the French guards. On the 14th that extraordinary action, the storming of the Bastille by the people of Paris, aided by some of the military, made a bloody commencement of the revolution. The lives lost by the assailants were revenged by the massacre of the governor and several others, whose heads were carried about the streets upon poles; and that sanguinary spirit was fully imbibed, which characterized the whole revolutionary period. The King, in great alarm, issued orders for the removal of the troops stationed in the vicinity of Paris, and immediately recalled Necker. He also, with that disregard of personal danger which he displayed through the most trying scenes, resolved upon visiting Paris, while several of the princes of the blood and principal courtiers sought their safety in flight. His Majesty was received at first with no other cry than that of *Vive la nation*! but having accepted the national cockade from the hand of M. Bailly, elected mayor of Paris, the usual tokens of that affection which the French have habitually borne to their sovereign were bestowed on him. After various succeeding scenes displaying the agitation, the enthusiasm, and the ferocity which had taken possession of the minds of the public, as well in the provinces as in the capital, and some of them truly shocking and atrocious; several decrees passed the national assembly abolishing ancient abuses, particularly all the relics of the feudal system. On August 20th, a declaration of rights was agreed upon to serve as the base of the new French constitution. This frame of government was a limited hereditary monarchy, in which the legislative authority was rendered superior to the executive, the latter being only allowed a suspensive veto. The person of the King was declared inviolable, and the throne indivisible. The decrees having been sent to the King, with a requisition for their promulgation, a letter was received from him containing objections to certain articles, among which were the abolition of rents originally founded in personal service, and of tithes. The national assembly, however, still urging the promulgation, the King at length acceded to its desire, and on September 20th sanctioned the decrees.

It seemed now that nothing was wanting to restore the public tranquillity, but the regulation of the finances, on which M. Necker was incessantly employed; but the royal or aristocratical, and the democratical parties were too adverse in their principles cordially to coalesce; and suspicions, either real or feigned, were diffused among the latter relative to the sincerity of the Court and higher orders in the sacrifices which they had concurred in. Under the influence of those suspicions, and the distress arising from a scarcity of bread, a fresh insurrection broke out at Paris among the lowest of the populace, and an infuriated mob of both sexes, escorted by some armed men, proceeded to Versailles, where, on October 6th, they made an attack by night on the palace. Amidst massacre and plunder the royal family were brought into great danger of their lives, but were at length rescued by the national guard; and the King and Queen, conducted by the Marquis De la Fayette, who had been made commander of that corps, were brought to Paris, and placed in the Tuilleries under guard. This triumph of the popular party occasioned a new change in the constitution by the national assembly, which had followed the King to the capital, and from which several of the aristocratical members seceded, taking refuge in foreign countries. Among those who left the country for a time was the Duke of Orleans, a man universally represented as tainted with every vice, and fit for any villainy; who, beginning his political career as an opposer of arbitrary power, is supposed always to have entertained a party of his own, and to have been the secret instigator of every mischief, in order to make way for his ambitious projects. Having fallen under the suspicion of criminal views towards the crown, he found it expedient for the present to withdraw to England.

The national assembly was now closely occupied in wholly regenerating the frame of polity, laws, and government, the King unconditionally acceding to every thing which they chose to establish. The first object was to reform the representation of the people, and abolish all local differences, by entirely breaking the ancient division of France into provinces, and substituting a new one founded upon a combined ratio of territory, population, and taxation. In this scheme the whole kingdom was distributed into 83 nearly equal sections, named departments, and which took their denominations from circumstances of geographical situation. These were subdivided into districts and cantons, and a plan of representation and administration was formed corresponding to this partition. The further changes were the abolition of all distinction of orders, the resumption of tithes and all ecclesiastical property, with the suppression of monastic institutions, and the extinction of all the provincial parliaments, instead of which new courts of justice were instituted, with trial by jury. To this last change great opposition was made; and in the midst of the agitations consequent upon such radical alterations, and the still urgent financial difficulties, this year, so memorable in the French annals, concluded.

While these events were passing in France, the neighbouring Austrian provinces of the Low Countries were the scene of violent commotions tending alike to a revolution in the government, but of a nature entirely different from that in the former country, since its object was to restore a popular constitution abrogated by arbitrary power. It has been mentioned that the preceding year closed with a refusal from the States of Brabant to vote the usual supplies to a government now become a mere tyranny. This resistance inflamed the resentment of the Emperor Joseph to such a degree, that he addressed an edict to the province, in which he not only annulled all his late concessions, but recalled his oath to observe the terms of the *Joyous Entry*. At the same time all the rigours of a military administration were continued, and many persons, on suspicion of disaffection, were thrown into prison. The Flemings now finding that they had no alternative between absolute submission and resistance, boldly took the latter part, and whilst the Austrian armies were chiefly occupied in the Turkish war, they rose in arms in the different provinces, and attacked the imperial garrisons. After some successful actions, the insurgents obtained possession of many of the principal towns without a contest, and even the city and citadel of Ghent were deserted by the garrison. On November 30th, the States of Flanders assumed the supreme authority in that province, and issued resolutions declaring the forfeiture by the Emperor of his title as their sovereign, and ordaining the levy and maintenance of an army, and an union with the States of Brabant. Brussels was soon after delivered from the Austrian power; and no regard being paid to the Emperor's conciliatory proposals, the States of Brabant, on the last day of the year, bound themselves, in presence of the citizens of Brussels, by a solemn oath, to preserve the rights, privileges, and constitution of their country; and soon after joined in an offensive and defensive league with Flanders.

Great discontents took place at Constantinople on account of the loss of Choczim and Otchakof; and an additional misfortune befell the Ottomans in the death of the Grand Seignior Abdul Hamet, one of the best and most enlightened sovereigns who for a long time past had occupied the Turkish throne. He was succeeded by his nephew Selim, who soon displayed his rapacious and sanguinary temper by the confiscation and execution of the Grand Vizier, who had been honourably acquitted of the charge brought against him in the former reign, as having by misconduct occasioned the loss of Otchakof. On the expiration of the armistice, the war recommenced between the Turks and Austrians along the frontiers of Transylvania and the banks of the Danube, whilst the Russians acted partly as allies to the Austrians, and partly pushed their successes in other quarters. Fortune or conduct now entirely deserted the Ottomans. Marshal Laudohn took Turkish Gradiska in June, and afterwards laying siege to Belgrade, obliged that important place to surrender in October. The Prince of Saxe-Coburg, and the Russian General Suwarrof, entirely defeated the main Turkish army under the new Grand Vizier near Martinesti in Wallachia, on September 22d, the relics of the vanquished re-crossing the Danube. Bucharest afterwards fell. Hassan Pashaw was defeated by Potemkin and Repnin, and Bender, Bielgorod, and other places, were the prize of victory.

The King of Sweden, involved at the same time in a foreign war, and in party differences at home, found no other means of extricating himself from his embarrassments, than appealing to the nation at large, the inferior orders of which were generally attached to him. He summoned a diet to meet at Stockholm, which he opened on January 26th, in a long and eloquent speech. He found the nobles for the most part in opposition to him, but the other three orders were in his favour; and confiding in their support, he ventured upon the bold measure of seizing by military force, and committing to prison, twenty-five among the principal nobility. These were officers lying under the charges of treason, treachery, disobedience, and mutiny. A great number of resignations followed, of persons in every department of the state, civil and military, but the King steadily pursued his purpose. He totally abolished the senate, and instituted in its place a new court, the model of which he is said to have taken from the French *cour pleniere*: and he framed an act of confederation by which all Swedes were bound to mutual defence, and to the preservation of the existing constitution and laws. This last he procured to be passed in the diet, notwithstanding the opposition of the order of nobles, whose consent, in their absence, he caused to be declared by the signature of Count Lowenhaupt, the Marshal of the diet: and against this direct infraction of the constitution only one noble had the courage to enter a protest. The trials of the persons arrested commenced in March, and after occupying many months, terminated in very severe sentences, some of them extending to capital punishment; but the King's disposition not being sanguinary, few lives were sacrificed. With respect to foreign foes, the King's first care was to procure the neutrality of Denmark, which was effected by the interposition of the British minister. He then returned to Finland, and pursued the war with Russia. Some actions of no great moment ensued, and at length the King was obliged to make a hasty retreat from the Russian territory, which he had incautiously entered. At sea a bloody engagement took place, August 25th, in the Gulph of Finland, between the Swedish and Russian fleets of galleys, in which the Swedes, who were considerably inferior in force, were finally obliged to take shelter under the cannon of Sweaborg. This result gave a superiority to the Russians for the remainder of the campaign.

1790

30th & 31st Year of the Reign

THE efforts of the French people to liberate themselves from arbitrary power, and establish a constitution upon the principles of rational freedom, had in their commencements been regarded with general favour by the English nation, which could not but recognize the same rights in another people, that they had themselves so happily asserted. But the violence with which their revolution had finally been effected, and the subversion of so many ancient and venerable institutions by which it was attended, now began to render their proceedings alarming and obnoxious, not only to all the habitual supporters of authority, but to those who were attached to the establishments of their own country, and dreaded the progress of a spirit of innovation. On the other hand, the friends of reform, civil and ecclesiastical, whose expectations had so often been frustrated, generally rejoiced in an event which afforded so striking a proof of the power of a nation when exerting its energies, and hailed the propagation of the principles by which the revolution was effected, as the introduction to a new and happier era in human affairs. Under this persuasion, some of the societies instituted for purposes of reform sent letters of congratulation to the French leaders, and opened a correspondence with them. The example of France was even so far imitated, that clubs were formed in many of the most considerable towns in the kingdom, with the intention of promoting some of those reforms which there appeared no prospect of obtaining by means of the representatives of the people.

Parliament was opened on January 21st with a speech from the throne, in which the internal commotions which disturbed the tranquillity of different parts of Europe were lamented, but without any particular reference; and a persuasion was expressed that all would be sensible of the invaluable blessings which this nation derived from its excellent constitution. Occasion being soon after given in the House of Commons to speak of the French revolution, which Mr. Fox mentioned in terms of approbation, Mr. Burke rose, and in a speech of considerable length employed the powers of his eloquence in a very severe and opprobrious censure of the principles and conduct of that event, which was received with great applause by the House in general. He was replied to by Mr. Fox and Mr. Sheridan, who defended the principle of the revolution, while they joined in detestation of the outrages with which it had been accompanied; but Mr. Pitt and several other members expressed their entire concurrence with Mr. Burke, and their sense of the obligations he had conferred on his country by the part he had taken. These differences of opinion spread through the kingdom, and parties began to take their respective ground with a spirit of hostility even more acrimonious than that which prevailed during the American war.

These feelings were aggravated by a renewed attempt of the dissenters to obtain a repeal of the corporation and test acts. Zeal to carry their point had induced them in some places to hold public meetings, at which they entered into resolutions for supporting at future elections such members only as should have voted in their favour. This policy, injudicious for a minority, was turned against them by the established clergy and their adherents; and the warmth with which some distinguished characters among the dissenters had publickly maintained the principles of reform, and the justice of the French revolution, rendered them still more the objects of apprehension. When, therefore, Mr. Fox, on March 2d, brought their cause before the House of Commons, his motion for taking the subject into consideration was negatived by the decisive majority of 294 to 105.

At the same inauspicious period Mr. Flood moved for a bill to amend the representation in parliament. The plan proposed for this purpose was the addition of a hundred members, to be elected by the resident householders in every county. In the debate which ensued, the sense of the House appeared so adverse to any measure of kind, that Mr. Flood agreed to withdraw his motion.

A motion by the Honourable Frederic Montagu for augmenting the salary of the Speaker of the House of Commons, was carried with only one dissentient voice; and to the sum of £5000 which he proposed, another thousand was voted on the motion of Sir James Johnstone.

The opening of the annual financial budget in April gave the minister the opportunity of laying before the House a very favourable statement of the national revenue under his management. The produce of the consolidated fund he stated as being half a million more in the last year, than the average of the three last years; and he gave a total of ways and means amounting to near six millions, which he said was more than sufficient to meet the supply.

On May 5th the public was surprized by a message from his Majesty to parliament containing information of the vio-lence committed on two vessels belonging to his subjects, on the north-western coast of America, by a Spanish naval officer; also, of his applications to the Court of Spain for satisfaction; of the exclusive claims of that Court to the navigation of those seas, and its hostile preparations. This dispute was a consequence of the establishment, by an English trader, of a small settlement for the purposes of commerce at Nootka Sound, on the coast of California, the liberty for which he had purchased from the Indian chief of the district. In May and June 1789 two English vessels were seized in that bay by the commander of a Spanish frigate, who made the crews prisoners, took possession of the lands on which the building for a settlement was erected, pulling down the British flag, and hoisting the Spanish in its stead, with a declaration that all the lands comprized between Cape Horn and the 60th degree of north latitude belonged to his Catholic Majesty. Negotiations respecting this act had been carried on between the two courts, which had not produced an accommodation, and the King's message on the occasion expressed a determination to support the honour of his crown and the rights of his people. The House of Commons unanimously voted an address to the King corresponding to this resolution, and passed a vote of credit for a million. Vigorous preparations for war were made on both sides; but the Spaniards not choosing to proceed to extremities, the dispute was adjusted by a convention, in which Spain agreed to the restoration of the settlement at Nootka, with reparation for the injury sustained; and also to a free navigation and fishery in the Pacific ocean and South seas by British subjects, with a proviso, in order to prevent smuggling, that they should not come within ten leagues of any part of the coasts already occupied by Spain.

During this session the subject of the slave trade was still under consideration in the House of Commons and evidence was examined both for and against the abolition.

The trial of Mr. Hastings recommenced on February 16th, but proceeded with still less dispatch than before. Mr Burke, after some observations on this protraction, moved two resolutions, the first of which was to authorize the managers of the impeachment to insist only upon such articles as should seem to them the most conducive to the obtaining speedy and effectual justice against the culprit; the second, that the House of Commons was bound to persevere in the impeachment till judgment should be obtained on the principal charges. Complaint having been made to the House of a publication in a newspaper by Major Scott grossly reflecting on the conduct of the managers and the justice of the House, after considerable debate, the major was ordered to be reprimanded by the speaker.

On June 10th the session was terminated by a speech from the throne, and on the following day the parliament was dissolved.

The session of the Irish parliament was opened on January 21st by the new Lord Lieutenant, the Earl of Westmorland. During a very short session various motions were made in both houses for the purpose of controuling the corrupt influence of ministers, by abolishing unnecessary places and pensions, all of which were defeated by large majorities. Parliament was then prorogued and on April 8th was dissolved.

This summer was rendered remarkable from the heat of political controversy occasioned by the principles of the French revolution. The anniversary of that event having been celebrated with great triumph in several parts of the kingdom by the zealous friends of those popular rights which it asserted, Mr. Burke soon after published his celebrated work, entitled "Reflections on the French Revolution," in which he had employed all the undiminished powers of his wit, eloquence and reasoning to stigmatize and ridicule that great change, and the principles which led to it, not without many severe strictures on the English societies and writings by which the cause was patronized. The work was most extensively circulated and highly applauded, and had a powerful effect in inspiring confidence in that party of which he was now regarded as the champion. On the other hand it produced many replies and criticisms, to which the author's violence and exaggeration rendered it in some parts liable; and it was lamented by the rational friends of political freedom, that in his zeal to overthrow the abuses of that principle, he had employed arguments which would apply against resistance to the most oppressive tyranny. Of his literary antagonists the most distinguished was Thomas Paine, a writer who had made himself noted in the American war by a pamphlet styled "Common Sense," which was very efficacious in persuading the Americans to make their declaration of independence. His present work, entitled "The Rights of Man," though not comparable to that of Mr. Burke as a literary composition, was so well adapted to common feeling and comprehension that it greatly contributed to the diffusion of democratical principles and a spirit of reform throughout the kingdom.

In France, from the time of the King's compelled residence in Paris, no opposition appeared to the will of the National Assembly. The King even thought proper voluntarily to repair to that Assembly, on February 4th, and make a solemn declaration of his purpose to defend the new constitution to the last moment of his existence, and to educate his children in the love of liberty. The country was however still far from being in a state of tranquillity. The seizure of all the church property to the use of the public, leaving only a slender pittance for the maintenance of the officiating clergy, though a measure which passed with little opposition at Paris, excited serious commotions in several of the provinces, where a zealous attachment to the ancient religion still continued. In the French West Indies, particularly in St. Domingo, dreadful tumults arose from the communication of the principles of equality to the negroes and people of colour, which the decrees of the National Assembly were unable to quell. A storm also began to threaten on the German border on account of the dissatisfaction of those princes who were deprived of their feudal rights in Alsace, and who declined the offered compensation. The dispute between Great Britain and Spain was another source of embarrassment to the National Assembly, since the alliance between France and Spain rendered it probable that the aid of the former would be demanded in case of a rupture. The consideration of this subject led to the question, to whose hands ought the nation to delegate the right of making war and peace? After a long discussion, it was finally determined that to the King should be entrusted the prerogative of announcing to the Assembly the necessity of war or peace, which, after due deliberation, should be declared "on the part of the King in the name of the nation." In the debate, M. Petion proposed a resolution "that the French nation renounced for ever all idea of conquest, and confined itself entirely to defensive war;" which passed with universal acclamation!

In June a decree passed the Assembly which, perhaps, more than any thing that had yet been done, excited the hostility of the superior classes throughout Europe: it was for the abolition of all hereditary titles, orders, armorial bearings, and other marks of the distinction of ranks in society. When it is considered how fondly, even in the most enlightened countries, men are attached to honours, how futile soever, which elevate them above the mass of their fellow-citizens, the indignation excited by such an example of levelling will readily be conceived.

Preparations for a splendid and imposing solemnity, under the name of a General Confederation, for the purpose of a national administration of oaths of fidelity to the new constitution, for some time occupied the attention of the Parisians; and on July 14th, the anniversary of the taking of the Bastille, it was celebrated in the Champ de Mars. The King, for whom a throne was erected in the midst of a wide space, and the whole National Assembly, surrounded by an immense concourse of people, solemnly swore to maintain the constitution; and the armed citizens repeated the oath, which was taken on the same day throughout the extent of the kingdom.

The legislature then proceeded to the organization of the judicial system for the nation, in which several useful regulations were established. The protestants were restored to the possessions of which their ancestors had been deprived by the repeal of the edict of Nantes; the extraordinary taxes levied upon the Jews were suppressed; and the *droit d'aubaine* was abolished. The Duke of Orleans, who had returned to France, and the celebrated Mirabeau, were tried upon the charge of a conspiracy to murder the Queen and raise Orleans to the throne, but were acquitted. But amidst some favourable appearances, the relaxation of the usual bands of authority, and the unqualified principles of equality which had been diffused through all ranks, were productive of serious disturbances in various parts, and M. Necker felt the difficulties of his situation so sensibly, that he determined to resign his post. His popularity had for some time been on the decline, in consequence of his maintaining sentiments of government too moderate for the period, and of Mirabeau's intrigues against him. On September 4th he sent a letter of resignation, on the plea of ill health, to the National Assembly, of which no notice was taken; and he was at length obliged to quit like a fugitive, the country which he had twice entered in triumph, and which he had certainly served with zeal and integrity, if not with judgment.

Contests with the clergy chiefly occupied the National Assembly for the remainder of the year. An oath had been imposed upon them in July, by which each beneficed clergyman was, among other articles, to swear to maintain to the utmost of his power, the new constitution of France, and particularly the decrees relative to the civil constitution of the clergy. This injunction had been little regarded till November 27th, when a decree passed, declaring that all who should neglect to take the oath, would be considered as ejected from their benefices, and be condemned to severe pains and penalties if refractory. As the pope had strongly declared his disapprobation of this oath, it was declined by a great number of the clergy, including almost the whole of the episcopal order. Numerous emigrations were the consequence, and a schism in the church took place, all the most devout persons in the nation adhering to the non-juring deprived clergy, and refusing to acknowledge their successors.

On February 20th died the Emperor Joseph, leaving to his brother Leopold, Grand Duke of Tuscany, a throne miserably shaken by his ill-concerted projects, and unjust enterprises. Almost on his death-bed he had the mortification of receiving from the Hungarian nobility a memorial in lofty terms, demanding the restoration of their ancient rights and privileges, the return of the royal crown of Hungary to Presburg, liberty to the people of laying aside the German dress which had been forced upon them, and resuming that of the nation, and that the Hungarian or Latin language should be used in public acts, instead of the German. On these conditions they promised to defend the kingdom to the last drop of their blood, and to supply the imperial armies with every necessary. The Emperor, now additionally humiliated by disease, readily consented to the restoration of all the privileges of the Hungarians, insisting only on retaining three articles of his innovations which did him honour: these were, a general toleration in matters of religion, provision for the parochial clergy out of the revenues of some suppressed monasteries, and the security of a degree of liberty to the peasants.

Leopold repaired to Vienna on the intelligence of his brother's death and assumed a sovereignty involved in difficulties on all sides. His first care was to free himself from the Turkish war. The campaign on the Danube had opened early on the part of the Austrians, and the fortress of Orsova surrendered to Prince Coburg in April. Attempts were then made against Widdin and Giurgewo, but without success. In the meantime, negotiations for peace had been opened at Reichenbach under the mediation of England, Prussia, and the United Provinces, which had for their farther object an accommodation of the differences between the Austrian court and its subjects in the Low Countries. An armistice was immediately concluded with the Turks, and conditions of peace were settled on the basis that each party should return to the state they were in before the war, and that Austria should stand neuter, if Russia should refuse to accede to this treaty. The repossession of the Low Countries by Austria was guaranteed by the mediating powers, on the condition of the re-establishment of their ancient privileges and constitution. The malcontents of Hungary were at this time very numerous, and many among them even entertained the design of liberating that country from the Austrian dominion: but differences among themselves, and the politic management of Leopold, produced an accommodation, in which he took care not to bind himself to any concessions derogatory from the rights of the crown. On his first accession to the Austrian sovereignty, Leopold had cause to apprehend some opposition to his succession to the imperial crown, especially on the part of Prussia; but the convention of Reichenbach having conciliated him with that power, he was elected King of the Romans without competition on September 30th, and was crowned Emperor on October 9th.

The affairs of the Belgic provinces were in this year an object of the greatest interest to the Austrian court, and attracted the notice of all Europe. In the month of January the United Belgic States in congress issued the plan of a constitution which, being aristocratical in its frame, as well as highly intolerant in matters of religion, was much objected to by the democratical party, a portion of the community which the example of France had now rendered very numerous in the Netherlands. Great disturbances ensued from the contests of the different parties, in which, besides the principles of political liberty and national independence, that of religious fanaticism, congenial to the Flemish character, acted a part; and through these differences, the defence of their newly declared sovereignty was greatly impeded. In August, the King of Prussia sent a letter to the congress, in which he acquainted them that he had acknowledged Leopold as Duke of Brabant; an intimation which implied that, in conformity with the articles of the treaty of Reichenbach, the mediating powers intended to interfere in the affairs of the Belgic provinces. The Emperor, immediately after his coronation, issued a manifesto dated October 14th, in which he solemnly engaged, under the guaranty of the courts of London, Berlin, and the Hague, to govern his provinces in the Netherlands according to their ancient constitutions and charters, and to pass a general amnesty in favour of all who should lay down their arms before the 21st of November following. A notification of these terms of agreement was also sent by the mediating powers to the congress. This body, however, was still resolved to maintain the independency which had been assumed, and the different parties seemed animated by the same spirit. Meantime an Austrian army under General Bender was advancing to decide the point, and on December 2d, Brussels was surrendered to it without resistance. The example was followed by all the other towns of Brabant and Flanders; the members of congress, and those who had been most active in the revolution, took refuge in the neighbouring countries; and the whole of Belgium again submitted to the Austrian government. A convention took place at the Hague, between the ministers of the Emperor and those of the confederated powers, by which the provinces were not only restored to the rights and privileges which they possessed before the usurpations of Joseph, but were secured in additional liberties; and thus another example was given of the final advantages obtained by a determined resistance to tyrannical power, notwithstanding temporary reverses.

The King of Sweden, pursuing his plan of humiliating the nobles, and ingratiating himself with the other classes, issued a declaration that all orders of the state had an equal right to serve their country in situations for which they were qualified; and in consequence, appointed persons belonging to the inferior orders to offices in the different public departments. This policy answered his purpose so as to obtain for him supplies in the diet to an amount beyond what had ever been before known; and several of the towns equipped armed vessels and raised volunteers for his service at their own expence. He was thus enabled to open the campaign against Russia earlier than usual; and, commanding in person, he gained some advantages in Finland. Some bloody actions were likewise fought at sea, with various success. The last of these was a complete defeat by the King, of the Russian fleet under the Prince of Nassau, in July. The mutual losses, and the exhausted state of Sweden, produced overtures for a peace, which was concluded in August, on the condition of a restitution of conquest on both sides. This desertion by the King of Sweden of the alliance with the Ottoman Porte, by which he had been subsidized, excited great indignation at Constantinople, but was apparently necessary to prevent another revolution.

The Empress Catharine was still as much as ever bent upon her further aggrandisement at the expence of the Turks; and to the pacific proposals offered to her by the mediating powers, she returned a haughty, and disdainful answer. During the early part of the year war was suspended on the banks of the Danube, and the Black sea was the chief scene of contest between the Turks and Russians, in which the success chiefly remained with the latter. An attempt made by the Turks to penetrate into the Russian conquests between the Black sea and the Caspian was frustrated by a defeat given to the Turkish army as it was passing the river Kuban. Prince Potemkin, who at the close of the preceding year had taken Kilia Nova, a town at one of the mouths of the Danube, now projecting farther conquests in Moldavia and Walachia, moved in the end of October to invest the strong fortress of Ismail, the key of the lower Danube. Its importance caused a numerous garrison, the flower of the Turkish troops, to be posted in it. The task of reducing this place was committed to Suwarof; and on December 22d, the approaches having allowed batteries to be erected on all sides, a terrible cannonade was ordered, which prepared the way for a general assault. The attack and resistance long continued with mutual fury; at length the Russians burst in, and a slaughter ensued scarcely paralleled in modern war. About 24,000 of the Turkish soldiers are said to have perished, either by the sword or in the stream of the Danube, and the Russian accounts stated the whole loss of the Ottomans at more than 32,000. That of the assailants was also very considerable, but was little regarded in the triumph of victory with which the year concluded.

In the East Indies the English Company were involved in a fresh war by the ambition of Tippoo Saib, Sultan of Mysore. Having seized upon a pretext for making war upon the Rajah of Travancore, an ally of the Company, he had in 1789 entirely over-run and occupied the greatest part of the dominions of that sovereign. The government of Bengal had in vain interposed to restrain his hostilities; and having formed a close alliance with the Mahrattas and the Nizam of the Decan, it declared war against Tippoo. Two armies were formed for the purpose of carrying it on; one, of 15,000 men, in the Carnatic, under General Meadows; the other, commanded by General Abercrombie, of about half that strength, in the presidency of Bombay. Tippoo, after having without effect attempted to avert the storm by negotiation, left Travancore, and returned to his capital, Seringapatam. The Carnatic army marching from Trichinopoly in June 1790, advanced towards the enemy, reducing several fortresses in its progress. Tippoo, however, making an irruption into the Carnatic, recalled General Meadows in pursuit of him; and in the meantime General Abercrombie, having landed at Tellicherry from Bombay, reduced several places on that side, and re-established the Rajah of Travancore in his kingdom. The campaign, however, though upon the whole successful, effected nothing decisive against the power of Tippoo; and Lord Cornwallis, who was now the Governor-general in India, resolving to take the supreme command upon himself, arrived at Fort St. George in December.

The new parliament assembled on November 25th, when Mr. Addington was unanimously re-chosen Speaker of the House of Commons. The King's speech, among other topics of foreign politics, took some notice of his endeavours to terminate the dissentions in the Netherlands, but made no allusion to the affairs in France. An address in favour of the Spanish convention was carried in each House by a large majority. The expence incurred by the armament against Spain was defrayed by some temporary taxes, and a loan of half a million without interest from the Bank. Before the recess, an important question was brought on in the House of Commons: whether an impeachment by the Commons did not remain *in statu quo*, notwithstanding the intervention of a dissolution of parliament? and Mr. Burke moving, that the impeachment of Warren Hastings is now depending, it was carried in the affirmative without a division. He afterwards made a motion for limiting the impeachment to the articles on which the managers had already closed their evidence, with the exception of what remained, relative to contracts, pensions, and allowances, which was also carried.

1791

31st & 32d Year of the Reign

Mr. Hippisley having, previously to the recess of parliament, made a motion for laying before the House the correspondence relative to the attack of Tippoo on the lines of Travancore, which was carried, the subject was introduced on February 28th by the same gentleman, in a motion for reading the clause in the East India act of the 24th of the King, disavowing all schemes for the extension of the British territories in India, and also various resolutions of the House of Commons. These being read, he entered into an argument to prove that we were under no obligation to take part with the Rajah of Travancore in the present contest, and that the Rajah, and not Tippoo, was the aggressor. A debate followed, in which Mr. Francis made various motions to censure the principles of the war into which we had entered with Tippoo, and prevent its farther prosecution, all of which were negatived; and Mr. Dundas moved opposite resolutions, which were carried without a division. The same was the result of the attack and defence of the war in the House of Lords.

The solicitor-general moved in February for a committee of the whole House to enable him to bring in a bill to relieve from the penalties to which they were legally liable, those English catholics who were termed protesting catholic dissenters, on account of their protestation against certain dangerous opinions attributed to the papists. The motion being agreed to, he brought in a bill to that effect, which passed the House without opposition, the only objection made being, that it did not carry the principle of toleration far enough. In its passage through the House of Lords, it was observed by Bishop Horsley that the terms of the oath of allegiance enjoined by the bill might offend the feelings of some of those whom the bill was intended to relieve; and it was in consequence expunged, and another substituted. The bill was cordially supported by the episcopal bench, and passed unanimously.

Very different was the fate of a petition from the general assembly of the Church of Scotland for a repeal of the test acts as far as concerns Scotland, brought before the House of Commons by Sir Gilbert Elliot. It was supported by several members, particularly by Mr. Fox, who argued upon the disparity in which the members of the established church of Scotland were placed by an obligation imposed upon them of complying with a rite of the English church before they could be admitted to an office. Mr. Pitt represented this as an imaginary hardship, as he understood that the members of the Church of Scotland had no objection to give such a pledge of amity to the sister church. The motion for taking the petition into consideration was negatived by 149 to 62.

A message from his Majesty having been delivered to parliament recommending to its attention some new regulations for Canada, Mr. Pitt on March 4th, brought before the House of Commons a bill for that purpose. By its tenor, Canada was divided into two distinct governments, those of the Lower, and of the Upper Province, and for each of these a legislative council and assembly were established, after the model of the British constitution. Particularly, the council was formed on an imitation of the House of Lords, by lodging a power in the governor to summon members to it; and in his Majesty, that of annexing to hereditary titles of honour a right to a seat in the council. In the ecclesiastical establishment, to the former provision for the Protestant clergy, was added an allotment for their support out of the crown lands, and the appropriation of one-seventh in all future grants of land to that purpose. Future grants of land in Upper Canada were to be held in common soccage as in England, and also in Lower Canada, when desired. The discussions on this bill were rendered remarkable by the introduction of a warm debate between Mr. Fox and Mr. Burke relative to the principles of the French revolution, which produced a renunciation by the latter of the private friendship which had so long subsisted between them; a determination which moved Mr. Fox to tears, but in which the other persisted to his death, unshaken by all kind advances. The Canada bill, after a full discussion in both houses, passed into a law.

The matter of the slave trade was again brought under consideration by a motion from Mr. Wilberforce in a committee of the whole House, that the chairman be instructed to move for leave to bring in a bill to prevent the further importation of slaves into the British colonies in the West Indies. Being supported chiefly by arguments of humanity, and opposed by those of interest, the motion was negatived by 163 votes to 88.

On March 28th, Mr. Pitt delivered to the House a message from the King, importing that his endeavours in conjunction with his allies to effect a pacification between Russia and the Porte having been ineffectual, he had thought it requisite, in order to add weight to his representations, to augment his naval forces. The minister, in moving a correspondent address, argued that we had a direct interest in this war, both in supporting our ally, and in checking the progress of the Russian arms, which was becoming dangerous to the political system of Europe. Mr. Fox and Mr. Burke joined in opposition to the measure, contending that the sole question was whether Russia should retain, of her conquests, the town of Otchakof and an adjacent tract, an object by no means of consequence enough to justify our armed interference. The address was however carried by a majority of 93. Mr. Grey next moved a set of resolutions, concluding with one declarative that the expence of an armament was, under the present circumstances, inexpedient and unnecessary; and these were negatived by a majority only of 80. Other motions to a similar effect were made by different members; and in the House of Lords an address in answer to the message was also opposed, and motions were made by Earl Fitzwilliam against a war with Russia. In all these cases administration was supported by majorities, but in the meantime the war was manifestly becoming unpopular in the nation, so that in the end it was thought advisable to give up the point.

A bill was brought into parliament in May for the establishment of a colony at Sierra Leone on the coast of Africa, by way of experiment whether the culture of sugar and other tropical products might not be carried on by free negroes; and notwithstanding a strong opposition by the West India planters, it passed both Houses by a great majority.

On May 30th, the managers of the impeachment of Mr. Hastings having closed their case, that gentleman requested that a day might be allowed him for stating what he thought of importance respecting the farther progress of his trial. This being granted him, on June 2d, the Lords being seated in Westminster-hall, he rose, and delivered from writing a speech of considerable length, in which, after expressing a willingness and desire to wave his formal defence to the charges exhibited against him, and to refer himself to their lordships immediate judgement, he went into a statement of the substance of these charges, to which he gave brief and clear answers. He concluded with re-tracing the principal events of his public life, in which, with the confidence of a man conscious at least of having well and faithfully served his employers, he pronounced an eulogy of his administration. The following apostrophe in his speech will serve to show what he himself regarded as the distinguishing points of his Indian government. "To the Commons of England, in whose name I am arraigned, for desolating the provinces of their dominion in India, I dare to reply that they are, and their representatives annually persist in telling them so, the most flourishing of all the states of India — It was I who made them so. The valour of others acquired, I enlarged, and gave shape and consistency to the dominion which you hold there: I preserved it: I sent forth its armies with an effectual but economical hand through unknown and hostile regions, to the support of your other possessions, to the retrieval of one from degradation and dishonour, and of the other from utter loss and subjection. I maintained the wars which were of your formation, or that of others, not of mine: I won one member of the great Indian confederacy from it by an act of seasonable restitution: with another I maintained a secret intercourse, and converted him into a friend: a third I drew off by diversion and negotiation, and employed him as the instrument of peace. When you cried out for peace, and your cries were heard by those who were the object of it, I resisted this and every other species of counteraction, by rising in my demands; and accomplished a peace, a lasting, and I hope an everlasting one, with one great state; and I at least afforded the efficient means by which a peace, if not so durable, more seasonable at least, was accomplished with another. I gave you all; and you have rewarded me with confiscation, disgrace, and a life of impeachment."

The Lords afterwards passed a resolution to proceed farther in the trial of Mr. Hastings on the first Tuesday in the next session of parliament.

This session concluded on June 10th.

Party spirit in this year raged with redoubled violence throughout the kingdom, food being constantly administered to it by the events of the French revolution, which was continually more and more tending to those changes in government, which, one party detested as subversive of all legitimate authority and wholesome subordination, and the other rejoiced in, as the demolition of old prejudices and usurpations, and an assertion of the true principles of civil society. The anniversary of July 14th was by the latter celebrated in various places with no other consequences than the aggravation of political hatred; but at Birmingham it was the cause of a dreadful riot. The populace of that town, collecting in a great mob, and uncontrouled by the magistrates, burned to the ground some meeting houses, and the dwellings of several of the principal dissenters. In particulars the house, books, papers, and apparatus of that eminent divine and philosopher, Dr. Priestley, were consumed, and himself compelled to become a fugitive in order to preserve his life. This tumult, after raging four days, and spreading over the adjacent populous district, was quelled by military force.

His Royal Highness the Duke of York was married in September to the Princess Frederica, daughter of the King of Prussia.

France continued to be the great object of interest and solicitude to all the courts in Europe, which could not but be sensible how deeply they were concerned in the issue of the political changes begun and still proceeding in that country. Emigrants of the royal family and the first nobility were every where endeavouring to render their's a common cause among the superior orders, and several sovereigns shewed themselves well disposed to become the champions of degraded royalty.

The King of France, on January 22d, communicated to the National Assembly a letter from the Emperor of Germany, in which, with strong protestations of his amicable intentions with respect to the French, he intimated the necessity of revoking the decree for the suppression of feudal rights, as being injurious to several German princes possessing fiefs in Lorraine and Alsace. The Assembly, not confiding in the Emperor's professions, and regarding his application as only a pretext for advancing troops to the frontier, voted a large augmentation of the army, and defensive preparations on the borders. At this time their apprehensions were further excited by insurrections of the royal party in different parts of the kingdom; and also by the departure of the King's aunts, daughters of Louis XV, for Italy. An emigrant army was likewise assembled on the German border, commanded by the Prince of Condé. Under these circumstances, it is no wonder that suspicion was easily roused; and on April 18th the King and his family preparing to set out for St. Cloud to pass the Easter holidays, his carriage was surrounded by the populace who imagined he was taking flight to commence a counter revolution, and he was compelled to return. On the following day the King repaired to the assembly, and in a dignified manner complained of the insult offered him. The president answered him very respectfully, and he proceeded on his journey. Further to allay suspicion, he sent at this time a circular dispatch to all his ministers at foreign courts, notifying his full acceptance of the new constitution; and he dismissed from his person those courtiers who were the objects of jealousy. The King and the National Assembly now seemed to be on terms of mutual confidence and good will.

This, however, was a fallacious appearance. The King, probably persuaded by the anti-revolutionists to consider himself as in a state of durance which rendered him incapable of contracting obligations, consented to join in a plot for his liberation, the chief agent in which was the Marquis de Bouillé, now military governor of Metz. As a prelude which might justly renew former suspicions, the emigrations had greatly encreased, the specie of the kingdom all disappeared, and the royalists and non-juring priests were unusually active in disseminating their principles. On the night of June 20th, the King, Queen, the King's sister, Monsieur and his wife, escaped from the Tuilleries through a subterraneous passage, and set off for the frontiers; the King leaving behind him a paper in which he protested against all the decrees which he had sanctioned while under a state of restraint, and recited all the deprivations and indignities he had undergone from the National Assembly. That body displayed great firmness at the receipt of this alarming intelligence and took every necessary measure for securing the public tranquillity and intercepting the fugitives. The King and his party were stopped at Varennes, and brought back under escort of the national guard. Monsieur and Madame, taking a different route, reached Brussels in safety. The Marquis de Bouillé fled to Germany. This event greatly strengthened the power of the National Assembly, which passed some strong decrees against emigrants, and for preventing any attempts against their own authority. The majority still determined for the continuance of a monarchical form of government; and the republican party having on July 17th, instigated a mob to assemble tumultuously in the Champ de Mars for the purpose of enforcing measures against the King, they were dispersed, not without bloodshed, by the national guard. The National Assembly then, after much debate, decreed the inviolability of the royal persons and proceeded without interruption to the termination of their labours on the constitution. Upon the 3d of September the *Constitutional Act* was presented to the King for his consideration, and on the 13th he signified his acceptance of it in writing. Appearing at the Assembly on the following day, he confirmed this assent, and took an oath to be faithful to the law and the nation. The constituent National Assembly on Sept. 30th dissolved itself after a session of two years and four months, having, by a kind of self ordinance, determined that none of its members should be eligible to the next assembly. This dismission from authority of the men who by their talents and experience were best qualified to conduct public affairs, was a national misfortune, especially at a time when the popular societies were acquiring a dangerous influence. Of these the principal was the famous Jacobin club, which, originating in an association of about 40 men of letters and free enquiry, became noted for the boldness of its political discussions, and increased in numbers and consequence so much as to become a kind of national assembly in miniature, and an instrument of the most violent faction.

In the month of August an interview took place at Pilnitz in Saxony between the Emperor of Germany, the King of Prussia, and the Elector of Saxony, and which was attended by the Count d'Artois, Calonne, and Bouillé, in which an engagement was entered into by the two first powers, in certain eventual cases, to interfere for the support of the royal authority in France. This circumstance becoming known to the French, suspicions of the court again pervaded the minds of the public, and the republican party acquired additional influence. The new assembly, termed the Legislative, met on October 1st, consisting chiefly of representatives from the provinces unacquainted with business, and of men of letters, mostly of the inferior order, generally republicans, and votaries of the new French philosophy. Their oath on admission bound them to the maintenance of the constitution, and to fidelity to the nation, the law, and the King. Louis appeared in the assembly, and made a patriotic speech which was much applauded: assurances were given by the Emperor and the King of Prussia of their amicable dispositions, and for a time affairs proceeded in tranquillity. The hostile appearance of the emigrants on the borders however occasioned alarm; and on November 9th a decree was passed, declaring such emigrants conspirators and liable to capital punishment if found in that situation after January 1st; and the French princes and public functionaries who should not return before that time, also obnoxious to the same punishment. In the same month some very severe decrees passed against such of the clergy as should still refuse the civic oath. Both these and the former, the King, by virtue of the *veto* or negative lodged in him by the constitution, refused to sanction; which circumstance was employed by the violent party to augment the suspicions prevailing against him. Towards the close of the year, the hostile intentions of the emigrants and German princes on the borders became still more manifest; and on December 21st the court of Vienna gave official notice to the French ambassador, that Marshal Bender had been ordered to march to Treves with succours to the elector of that place, in case of an attack upon him, which had been threatened on account of the encouragement he had given to the emigrants.

Whatever difference of feeling there might be with respect to the French revolution, the fate of an attempted reform in the constitution of Poland could not fail of exciting the regret, and rousing the indignation, of every one interested in the improvement of human societies. That unfortunate country, after its sufferings from the rapacity of its neighbours and its own dissentions, was anxiously desirous of obtaining a compensation by a change in its disorderly government, and the establishment of its independence; and for that purpose the army was augmented and an alliance was cultivated with Prussia, as the power best able to counterbalance the overbearing influence of Russia upon the Polish affairs. At the same time it was endeavoured to animate and render general the patriotic spirit, by admitting the inferior orders into a participation of the sovereign power. The diet, which had opened in October 1788, resolved to continue its sittings till the plans for the public defence should be completely organized; and in the meantime a system of government was framed upon the basis of general rights, which was to abolish the former aristocratic tyranny, and remedy the disorders which had so long been inseparable from the administration of the executive and legislative departments of the state. Although the King of Prussia had signed, in March 1790, a treaty of alliance and reciprocal defence with Poland, yet he soon displayed his selfish views by a demand for the cession of the towns of Dantzic and Thorn; and when the farther proceedings of the diet evidently pointed at a free constitution with an hereditary monarchy, he concurred with the other two partitioning courts in resolving to oppose a plan calculated to render Poland really independent. The new constitution was introduced to the diet on May 3d in this year by a speech from King Stanislaus, who represented it to be of his own framing; and after a long debate, in which the article rendering the crown hereditary was the principal subject of opposition, the King was called upon by a great majority formally to accept and swear to it. He immediately complied, the majority joining with him by holding up their hands; and repairing to the cathedral, the oath was there solemnly renewed, and announced to the public. The essence of the constitution was an hereditary crown (the house of Saxony being nominated in the first succession), a legislative diet in two Houses, one of senators, the other of deputies, equality of civil rights, and a complete toleration of different religions.

This revolution in government was too favourable to the principles of liberty, and too well calculated to raise Poland from her state of depression, to be acquiesced in by her despotic and ambitious neighbours; and although the King of Prussia, when the event was communicated to him in form, as it was to all the other European powers, expressed the most unqualified approbation of all that had been done, it was not doubted that he was at the same time concerting measures with the courts of Vienna and Petersburgh for its defeat. The latter, regarding any political operations in Poland to which it was not a party as a kind of rebellion, was fully determined, as soon as the Turkish war was brought to a close, to interfere with open force; but its purposes could not be carried into effect during the present year. In the meantime, the Poles, sensible of the severe trial their new constitution was to encounter, were actively preparing for resistance to foreign arms. It was, however, unfortunate that a plan of defence formed by the King upon the principle of training the whole nation, was defeated by the pride and prejudices of the nobility.

War between the Russians and Turks was renewed in the Spring, and the former, frequently crossing the Danube, kept the Turks in constant alarm, and defeated them whenever they came to action: they were however repulsed with great loss in an attack of the strong fortress of Brahilow. Another Russian army invaded the province of Kuban, and took the town of Anapa with the camp of Turks and Circassians posted for its defence. Both parties being now wearied of the war, a peace was suddenly concluded in August at Galatz by which Otchakof, and all the country between the Bog and the Dnieper which had previously belonged to the Turks, was ceded to the Russians. In other respects, affairs were left in the same state between the two empires as before.

In the East Indies, Lord Cornwallis having formed the plan of penetrating directly from Madras to the heart of Tippoo's dominions, whilst General Abercrombie should lead his army to Trincomalee, began his march at the end of January, and proceeding to Bangalore, invested that place. The pettah or town being carried by assault, batteries were raised against the fort, and on February 21st it was taken by storm. In the beginning of May Lord Cornwallis set forward on his advance to Seringapatam, the capital of Mysore, where Tippoo had strongly posted himself. He arrived after a laborious march, and on May 15th gained a victory over Tippoo which laid the city fully open to his view. Scarcity now began to prevail in the British camp, the Mahrattas, whose assistance had been relied on, not making their appearance. General Abercrombie, however, had reached Periapatam with a large store of provisions and battering cannon. As he was not strong enough to make his way to Seringapatam, Lord Cornwallis marched up the Cavery with the intention of joining him. This was rendered impracticable by a sudden swell of the river, and the army becoming greatly distressed by want and disease, it was necessary to give up the attempt against Seringapatam for that season. Directions were sent to General Abercrombie to return to the Malabar coast, and Lord Cornwallis marched back to Bangalore.

1792

32^d & 33^d Year of the Reign

PARLIAMENT opened on January 31st. The speech from the throne was chiefly remarkable from the prediction of a continuance of the tranquillity at present enjoyed by this country, inferred from the friendly assurance received from foreign powers, and the general state of Europe. This prospect was said to justify some immediate reduction in the naval and military establishments, and to afford the hope of a gradual relief from a part of the existing taxes. The debates on the address, and several succeeding discussions in both Houses, principally turned upon the line of policy pursued by the ministry in their interference in the quarrel between Turkey and Russia, and in the hostility they had displayed towards the latter power. All interest on that subject being at an end, it would be useless to recite the particulars of those debates; one circumstance, however, was so remarkable an exemplification of the political sentiments at that time entertained by the government, that it may deserve to be recorded. Mr. Jenkinson (now Earl of Liverpool) in a maiden speech much admired for its extensive views of the existing state of Europe as bearing upon this country, said, "the strength and influence of France being at an end, we had no further danger to apprehend from that once formidable rival; but a power had succeeded to France, no less deserving of attention from its restless politics and ambitious views — this was Russia."

In a committee of the House of Commons to consider the state of the finances, Mr. Pitt gave a most encouraging statement of the national prosperity. The revenue of the last year had so much exceeded the average of the last four years, that the permanent income would surpass the permanent expenditure, including the annual million for extinguishing the national debt, by £400,000; whence, he said, government would be enabled to take off taxes which bore chiefly upon the poorer classes, to the amount of £200,000 and to apply the other £200,000 to the increase of the sinking fund. As future prosperity would greatly depend upon the continuance of peace, he did not hesitate to confirm the language of the King's speech by asserting that "unquestionably there never was a time when a durable peace might more reasonably be expected, than at the present moment."

When, in the committee of supply, the minister proposed the raising of more than £800,000 by lottery, he was severely reflected on by Mr. M.A. Taylor for having recourse, at such a time, to a method of levying money so extremely pernicious to the morals and happiness of the people. Several other members joined in the reprobation of lotteries, and a petition against them was presented from the grand jury of Middlesex. The impression made on the House from these representations was such, that a committee was appointed for enquiring into the evils arising from this source.

In this session the question of the abolition of the slave trade was again agitated in parliament, and all the force of argument was adduced on both sides in the different discussions which it underwent. The House of Commons having gone into a committee of examination on the subject, Mr. Wilberforce, ever the most active and zealous friend of the oppressed Africans, after a minute exposure of the evils and cruelties attending the slave trade, moved for its immediate and total abolition. After a keen debate, in which some members, among whom were Mr. Fox and Mr. Pitt, spoke in favour of the motion as it stood; others supported the trade throughout; and others, among whom Mr. Dundas was the leader, argued for a gradual abolition; the latter measure was carried by a majority of 68. On a following day the subject of debate was the period at which its total cessation should take place. Much of the same ground was again gone over, and the friends of the trade endeavoured to defer the abolition as long as possible. At length, a compromise being agreed on, the term was fixed for January 1st, 1796.

The resolutions of the Commons being carried to the House of Lords, it appeared that there was much less zeal for the abolition in that assembly. After a debate, in which the ministerial lords in general spoke against that measure, and a prince of the blood, the Duke of Clarence, openly avowed himself a friend to the slave trade, a motion was carried for the appointment of a committee for the hearing of evidence on the subject at the bar of the House; and thus the means were given of an indefinite protraction of a decision.

The police of the metropolis, especially of that largest portion of it which lies beyond the verge and jurisdiction of the city of London, being notoriously insufficient for preserving order among such a vast population, a bill was brought into the House of Commons for the establishing of five different offices in Westminster and the adjacent parts, at each of which three justices, paid by an annual salary, were to sit; and also for vesting a power in constables to apprehend such persons as did not give a satisfactory account of themselves. Although the necessity of some regulation of the police could not be controverted, yet objections were made to this bill as adding to the power of the crown, and as authorising a dangerous infringement of personal liberty. It was however approved by the majority, especially as its proposed duration was only for a limited time; and it passed into a law.

An enquiry was moved by Mr. Sheridan, April 18th, into the grievances complained of in petitions from the Royal Burghs of Scotland. These were, in substance, infringements of the rights and properties of the burghs, through the authority of self-elected magistrates, against whose usurpations the law had provided no remedy. The case was strongly made out, and the deficiency of a tribunal to judge of the proceedings of the magistrates was admitted by the Lord Advocate of Scotland; but a peculiar aversion to any reforming project of the popular kind subsisting at this period, the motion for referring the petitions to a committee was negatived. A similar fortune attended a motion from Mr. Fox for the repeal of certain penal statutes particularly levelled against persons of Unitarian principles. On the other hand, an extension of toleration to the Scotch episcopalians was carried in both houses without opposition.

A bill declaratory of the rights of juries in matter of libel, namely, that they are empowered to give a general verdict of *guilty* or *not guilty* upon the whole matter put to issue, which had been introduced by Mr. Fox in the last session, but postponed, was again brought in by him; and notwithstanding the opposition of the law lords it passed into a law.

Whilst the dread of that innovating spirit which the French revolution had fostered, operated as a motive with many to oppose every thing that bore the name of reform, there were others who thought that the safest and most rational method would be to conciliate the nation by concession in that object which seemed to have taken the firmest hold on the public mind — the reform of the parliamentary representation. A society was accordingly formed for obtaining this end, which, under the name of *Friends of the People*, comprehended a number of persons of character and consequence, among whom were about thirty members of parliament. They published their resolutions on this topic with great freedom;

and Mr. Grey, on April 30th, gave notice in the House of Commons of his intention to bring forward the design of the society in the ensuing session. This declaration was inveighed against with great warmth by Mr. Pitt, who took occasion to announce the change of his opinions on this topic, since experience had taught him the danger of altering the established forms of government. In order still more effectually, to discountenance every attempt by writing or association to excite discontent with any thing sanctioned by the forms of the constitution, a royal proclamation was issued on May 21st for preventing seditious meetings and publications, in which magistrates were enjoined to oppose them by all legal means, and the people were strongly exhorted to submission. This proclamation was supposed particularly to have had in view Paine's celebrated "Rights of Man," which had been printed in the cheapest forms, so as to give it the most extensive circulation, and its success in making proselytes would have been a truly formidable circumstance, had their rank in society borne a proportion to their numbers. When an address was moved in the House of Commons in consequence of the proclamation, several extracts were read from this work to show its dangerous tendency; but on the other hand it was remarked, that twelve months had elapsed since its publication, and that if it were really of so noxious a quality, ministers had been highly culpable in not taking notice of it before. This address, which passed, and the tenor of which was highly loyal, was the model of a great number of others sent up from every part of the kingdom. Prosecutions were now commenced against many persons on account of their share in circulating obnoxious publications; among the rest, of Paine himself, who avoided the effects of his conviction by taking refuge in France.

The session of parliament concluded on June 15th.

At the commencement of this year, the designs of the courts of Vienna and Berlin against France were becoming continually more apparent, although the Emperor Leopold employed every art, with that duplicity which belonged to his character, to lull suspicion. In the meantime, jealousies of the court were industriously propagated by the republican party at Paris; to which, the frequent departure of the nobles to join the emigrant army at Coblentz, and the language held by persons about the King and Queen, gave too much occasion. The King, reduced to perpetual difficulties, wavered in his conduct, and frequently changed his ministers as they fell under the displeasure of the prevailing parties. The sudden death of Leopold on March 1st, which was strongly suspected to have been occasioned by poison, appeared likely to have effected some change in the state of affairs. His son and successor, Francis II, however, immediately holding a conference with the Prussian minister, desired him to inform his master that he was determined to adhere to the resolutions entered into at the convention of Pilnitz.

A correspondence now went on for some time between the French and Austrian courts relative to the hostile preparations on both sides upon the borders; and Louis, having, categorically required from Francis a renunciation of any armed coalition against France, which was refused on his part, on April 20th came to the legislative assembly, and proposed formally to declare war against the King of Bohemia and Hungary, which was accordingly done. Louis, however, in order to throw from himself the responsibility of a measure which he did not approve, but probably could not have avoided, took care to make each of his ministers sign his opinions and reasons for going to war, which he transmitted to Francis for his own justification.

An attack on the Austrian Netherlands was the measure by which the war began, and which was undertaken with three divisions of troops, under the chief command of General Rochambeau. The French were at this time for the most part raw and undisciplined levies, ill fitted for such an enterprize, and more formidable to their officers than to the enemy. A division commanded by M. Dillon, advancing from Lisle against Tournay, being seized with a sudden panic, took to flight, and revenged themselves by murdering their general on pretence of treason. This plan having failed, the command in that quarter was conferred on Marshal Luckner, whilst a separate force acted under the orders of La Fayette. The subsequent events varied in their fortune, but in the end Luckner found it necessary entirely to evacuate Flanders.

In the meantime the assembly was a scene of much tumult and faction. The republican party having conceived a suspicion of the national guard of Paris, were desirous of possessing an army under their own influence, and for that purpose proposed the formation of a camp of 20,000 men, consisting of volunteers from every part of France, under the walls of the capital. A decree to this effect passed the assembly; and also another, authorizing the banishment of any non-juring priest on a petition presented to the directory of the district by twenty citizens. The King firmly refused to give his sanction to these decrees; and assuming a resolution to maintain the authority conferred upon him by the constitution, he dismissed his ministers, Roland, Claviere and Servan, and nominated Dumouriez, and some others, to their posts. The public discontents on these accounts, inflamed by the Jacobin club, broke out into a violent tumult on June 20th, when a vast crowd of the lowest class, armed with pikes, broke into the Tuilleries, and offered insults to the King, who acted with great coolness and intrepidity on the occasion, and persisted in his resolution respecting the decrees. La Fayette, for the purpose of preventing a repetition of these shameful and dangerous outrages, unadvisedly quitted his army, and presented himself before the assembly, demanding the dissolution of the factious clubs, but was sent back with a reprimand.

On July 1st, the assembly declared that the country was in danger, and on the 6th, the King announced to it that the King of Prussia had marched 52,000 men to co-operate with the Austrians. Marshal Luckner, who had obtained some success in the Netherlands, sent dispatches about this time signifying that the combined forces were bearing down upon him, and that it was necessary for him to retreat, to avoid being cut off from La Fayette's army. As danger approached, the first movement was an union of all parties for the defence of their country, and the anniversary of the confederation was celebrated in Paris with great unanimity. But this calm did not long continue, and the arrival of the federates, or volunteers, from different parts of the kingdom, filled the capital with ferocious and turbulent spirits, among whom the Marseillois were particularly conspicuous. In this inflammable state of the public mind appeared the two declarations of the Duke of Brunswick, commander in chief of the combined Prussian and Austrian armies, dated at Coblentz on July 25th and 27th, as he was about to commence his march towards Paris. They were drawn up in a style of haughty and sanguinary menace, of which another example is scarcely to be found in the case of a general entering a foreign country at the head of an army; and they espoused the cause of Louis and the royal authority in a manner that could not fail of confirming every suspicion of his participating in the councils of the allied powers. It was in vain that the King, in communicating these documents to the legislative assembly, implied a doubt of their authenticity, and in his message expressed the most faithful attachment to the constitution. A member audaciously affirmed, "that the King has asserted what was not true;" and on August 3d, Petion, the late mayor of Paris, at the head of the sections of the city, appeared at the bar of the assembly and demanded the deposition of Louis. The members in general seeming to revolt from such a proposition, means were employed by the Jacobin party to augment the fury of the populace, already raised to a high pitch by the fatal declarations, and the desperate measure was planned of an attack upon the Tuilleries. That palace, the residence of the King and Royal Family, was defended by the Swiss guards, a party of the national guard, and a number of gentlemen attached to royalty. On the 10th, numerous bands of men, armed with all the weapons they could procure, and provided with artillery, marched to the palace, and having forced open the gates, rushed in. The King, at the beginning of the alarm, had been induced to take shelter with his family in the hall of the legislative assembly, which was sitting. A bloody action ensued in the court of the palace, and the national guards having joined the assailants, the Swiss were overpowered, and most of those who did not fall in the fight were massacred in cold blood. The slaughter extended to the gentlemen ushers, pages, and all of the royal suite who came in the way of the insurgents; while the mob without vied with them in ferocity by assassinating the objects of their suspicion or hatred: it was a day of terror and savage frenzy. A calm being in some measure restored, the assembly issued decrees declaring the executive power suspended, and the authority given to Louis XVI by the constitution revoked, and inviting the people to form a national convention, the meeting of which was fixed for the ensuing September 20th. The ministers were discharged from their functions, and a new executive council was nominated, consisting of Roland, Servan, and Claviere. The King and Queen were placed under confinement in the Temple. The assembly, apprehensive of the resistance of La Fayette and his troops, sent three commissioners to the army in order to counteract his motions. His influence caused them at first to be imprisoned; but finding that he could not rely on the fidelity of the soldiers, he quitted the camp, and on his way fell in with an Austrian party, by whom he was arrested, and sent prisoner to Namur. Dumouriez was appointed his successor in command, and he and all the other generals submitted to the assembly and provisional government.

The allied army in the meantime was slowly advancing in the French territory. On August 21st Clairfait appeared before Longwy, which surrendered within a few hours; and on the

31st the Duke of Brunswick summoned Verdun, which was delivered to the Prussians by capitulation without resistance. This approach of an enemy whose declarations had taken away all hope of mercy from a great part of the public, and devoted the capital to destruction, hardened men's hearts to all the cruelty of despair. Danton, whose boldness had raised him from a low origin to the office of minister of justice, made a proposal in the assembly, of taking all the arms in the possession of private persons at Paris, and equipping with them a volunteer army, which should march out to meet the danger. This was immediately adopted, and decrees passed ordering all citizens capable of bearing arms to hold themselves in readiness at a moment's warning, and for disarming all suspected persons. On September 2d, the tocsin was sounded, the country declared in danger, and the populace was summoned to meet in the Champ de Mars. A multitude obeyed the call, among whom a number of voices was heard, exclaiming that they were ready to march against the foreign enemies, but that they must first purge the nation of its domestic foes. This cry was the signal of one of the most horrid massacres recorded in modern history. The first victims were some non-juring priests under detention till an opportunity should occur of sending them into banishment. The assassins then went to other prisons; and with the form of a pretended jury pronounced sentence on, and immediately executed, upon that and the following day, prisoners to the shocking number of 1085. Among these, sympathy was particularly excited for the beautiful Princess de Lamballe, the confidante of the Queen, whose head was stuck upon a pole and carried about the streets. This detestable massacre was imitated in other places, and several private assassinations were perpetrated during the general confusion.

With the ferocity, the energies of the French nation were also increased. Dumouriez, though much inferior in force, kept the allied troops in check, so that the farthest of their advance was the extremity of Champagne. He received reinforcements which at length enabled him fairly to meet the foe; and on September 20th, his advanced guard under Kellerman completely repulsed an attack of the Duke of Brunswick. The allied armies were now in want of provision; and disease spread among them. On the 24th their commander desired a conference with the French general and proposed an armistice. His tone was now so much lowered, that he acknowledged the full authority of the French nation to make laws for itself; and only desired the admission of the King into their government, however limited in power. On the last day of that month he began his retreat, and the French recovering Verdun and Longwy, the territories of France were entirely evacuated by the Prussians before the close of October.

The National Convention met on September 20th, — a body for the most part composed of the most violent and least respectable of the two last assemblies, but with a mixture of some men of talents and character. The first president was Petion. They immediately voted by acclamation the eternal abolition of royalty in France. Various decrees passed for the establishment of republicanism and the use of its forms and language; and the equalising principle was carried to a degree of puerility. The common titles of respect, Monsieur and Madame, were laid aside, and those of citizen, male and female, were substituted in their place. All distinctions in society were abolished; dress was made slovenly, and every thing that had graced and decorated polished life was abandoned with contempt. Decrees of the greatest severity were passed against emigrants; and several generals were denounced and deprived of their commands upon vague charges. In the midst of all this folly and misgovernment, there existed a kind of civic spirit that preserved order in the community beyond what might have been expected; and the conflict of factions and changes of administration did not prevent the nation from being triumphant abroad.

The King of Sardinia had been one of the powers confederated for the overthrow of the new French constitution, on which account war was declared against him on September 16th. General Montesquiou soon after entered Savoy, and in a short time the whole country submitted to him without resistance. It was afterwards, in contradiction to the resolution against making conquests, annexed to France as an additional department. Custine, collecting his army at Landau, September 29th, marched into the circle of the Upper Rhine, where he took Spire, Worms, and Metz. Frankfort submitted to him on October 23d, but was afterwards recovered by the Prussians.

The successes of Dumouriez were still more brilliant. The Austrians, who had laid siege to Lisle in September, and almost ruined the city by a bombardment, were foiled in their attempt by the courage of the garrison and inhabitants, and broke up their camp before it in the first week of October. The attack was retaliated by a renewed invasion of the Austrian Netherlands under the command of Dumouriez, who, on November 6th, gained the bloody battle of Jemappe, the first of the great victories which have signalised the French arms. This engagement decided the fate of the Netherlands. Brussels was entered by the victor on the 14th, and before the year closed, every place fell into the possession of the French, Luxemburg excepted.

The party then in power was not of a complexion to bear so much good fortitude without running into excesses. On November 19th the National Convention passed a decree calculated to involve them with every regular government in Europe: they declared, in the name of the French nation, that they would grant *fraternity* and assistance to all people wishing to obtain liberty: and they charged the executive power to order the generals to give aid to such people as had suffered or were then suffering in the cause of freedom. A measure by which they were certain to incur still deeper odium was that of the trial of the King, whose person had been declared inviolable by the constitution. The violent or mountain party, of whom the leaders were such men as Robespierre, Marat, and Danton, never ceased to urge on the fate of the unhappy monarch; and an extraordinary commission of 24 members was appointed to examine and draw up evidence against him. On December 11th he was ordered to the bar of the convention, where the act of accusation was read, and the King was summoned by the president Barrere to answer to each article. Counsel was afterwards allowed to him, and the year closed whilst this great cause was still pending.

Among the sovereigns whom conformity of interests engaged in the support of the ancient monarchy of France, the earliest in their declarations were the Empress of Russia and the King of Sweden. The former, however, contented herself with supplying the French Princes at Coblentz with money, and urging the Emperor of Germany to active measures; but Gustavus undertook the cause with all the ardour of his character, and appeared ambitious to stand forth as its principal champion. In the summer of 1791 the two northern powers, in conjunction with Spain, concerted a plan, by which Gustavus, at the head of a combined army of Swedes and Russians, was to be landed as near to Paris as possible, and Spain was to contribute money and troops in aid of the design. Full of his project, the King of Sweden went in July to Spa, where he held a conference with the Marquis of Bouillé; and at the subsequent meeting at Pilnitz, his plan was laid before the assembled sovereigns, but was not approved. Spain afterwards receded from her engagements; but Gustavus persevered regardless of obstacles. On January 23d he assembled a national diet at Geffle for the purpose of raising supplies for the intended expedition; but though he met with no direct opposition, the place of assembly being a small solitary town, surrounded with soldiers, yet the Swedes in general were little disposed to plunge into a new war, the object of which was exclusively royal. The nobles, in particular, irritated by the loss of their privileges, and disaffected to a change of government which had rendered the crown nearly arbitrary, avowed their disapprobation of the King's design, and held secret councils for its defeat. In one of these a resolution was taken to put an end to his life and projects together by assassination; and one Ankerstrœm, a disbanded officer, who had been condemned under a charge of high treason but pardoned, agreed to be the perpetrator. At a masked ball in the opera house to which Gustavus went in spite of warnings given him of a conspiracy, he received a shot in the side from a pistol, on March 16th, of which he died some days after, having nominated to the regency during the minority of his son, the Duke of Sudermania, his brother. The Regent immediately declared for a system of neutrality with respect to France, which was also the policy of Denmark, and of the Italian and Swiss republics. The court of Spain wavered.

The Empress of Russia, now freed from the Turkish war, had leisure to turn her attention to Poland; and in May, her ambassador delivered to the diet at Warsaw a declaration, warmly complaining of the late change in the constitution of that country, and announcing her intention of taking active measures for restoring the former order of things. The King thereupon made an exhortation to the diet to resist any aggression by force; and a resolution was unanimously adopted for exerting every effort in the public defence. An army was levied, of which Prince Joseph Poniatowski, nephew to the King, was appointed general, but it was extremely deficient in point of military requisites. A Russian army of 60,000 men entered Poland, and some actions ensued, at first favourable to the Poles. Their situation, however, becoming more and more difficult, application was made by the King to the court of Berlin to furnish those succours which he was by treaty bound to contribute in defence of the Polish independence: but the answer returned was that the change in the government made without his concurrence had cancelled this obligation. The court of Vienna returned a similar reply to an application of the like kind; and after some more actions in the field, it was found absolutely necessary to submit to superior force. The Polish army was required to surrender to the Russians, Russian garrisons were placed in every considerable town, and the constitution and independence of Poland sunk together.

The later transactions in France excited strong emotions in England. On the deposition of the King, the British ambassador, Lord Gower, was recalled, and M. Chauvelin, the French ambassador, who remained in London, was not acknowledged in a public character. The successes of the French in Flanders, and their declaration of the free navigation of the Scheldt, gave occasion to an offer from the English ministry of assistance to the Dutch, should it become necessary; and an exclusive embargo was laid upon the exportation of corn to France, which was in want of that article. *French principles* were now particularly obnoxious, and those societies which held correspondence with the convention in France, and propagated their doctrines in this country, were looked upon with increased suspicion. By way of counteracting their effects, and affixing a strong stigma upon such societies, an association was formed in London under the influence of government, professedly "For preserving liberty and property against republicans and levellers," which, at a meeting on November 20th, at the Crown and Anchor tavern, agreed upon a set of resolutions for promoting that purpose. These were signed by a number of the principal inhabitants of the metropolis, and were copied by similar associations in different parts of the kingdom. On December 1st a royal proclamation was issued, announcing danger to the constitution from evil-disposed persons within the kingdom, acting in concert with persons in foreign parts, whereby a spirit of tumult and disorder had been excited, which had shewn itself in acts of riot and insurrection; and declaring his Majesty's intention to embody such part of the militia as might enable him more immediately to provide for the public safety. In consequence of calling out the militia, a proclamation, according to statute, was also issued for assembling the parliament on December 13th, which had been prorogued to January. The public alarm occasioned by these measures was augmented by drawing troops round the metropolis, doubling the guard of the bank, and repairing the fortifications of the tower.

Parliament was opened by a speech from the throne, in which the internal disposition to riot and insurrection was adverted to in terms similar to those of the proclamation relative to the militia. With respect to continental affairs, it was said, that his Majesty had carefully observed a strict neutrality in the present war, and had uniformly abstained from interfering in the internal concerns of France; but that it was impossible for him to see without serious uneasiness the indications which had appeared there of an intention to excite disturbances in other countries, to disregard the rights of neutral nations, and to pursue views of aggrandisement. Under these circumstances, he had thought it his duty to have recourse to the means of prevention and defence with which he was entrusted by the law, and also to take measures for the augmentation of his naval and military force.

The address was moved by the Lord Mayor of London, Sir James Sanderson, who spoke of the numerous societies established in the capital, and corresponding with others in different parts of the kingdom, the aim of which was to subvert the constitution. On the other hand, Mr. Fox declared it to be his belief that all the insinuations in the speech were unfounded, that no insurrection existed, and that the alarm was occasioned only by the artful designs and practices of ministers. After dwelling with much animation upon this topic, and deprecating the idea of a war, to which the speech seemed to point, he moved an amendment to the address, proposing that the House should enter into an immediate examination of the facts stated in his Majesty's speech as the causes for assembling the parliament. He was answered by

Mr. Windham, who asserted facts to prove the real existence of those dangerous machinations which had occasioned the alarm. Several other speakers on each side entered into the debate, which as concluded by a division: for the address, 290; for the amendment, 50. In the House of Lords the motion for the address produced a debate of a similar tenor, in which an amendment moved by the Marquis of Lansdowne was negatived without a division. When the report of the address was brought up in the House of Commons, Mr. Fox moved an amendment, beseeching his Majesty to employ every species of honourable negotiation to prevent a war with France. This having been negatived, he rose on the following day to introduce a motion in these terms: "That an humble address be presented to his Majesty that he will graciously be pleased to give directions, that a minister may be sent to Paris, to treat with those persons who exercise provisionally the functions of executive government in France, touching such points as may be in discussion between his Majesty's allies and the French nation." The motion being seconded by Mr. Grey, a warm debate ensued, in which a negotiation with France in its present state was reprobated by the majority in the severest language. The motion was negatived without a division. It was now evident that the opposition party had been much weakened by the defection of many of the old whigs, who were strongly impressed with the idea of dangers threatening the constitution from French principles and designs.

On December 9th Lord Grenvile brought in a bill respecting the aliens, of whom there were a great number now in the kingdom; and though the major part were French loyal emigrants, yet some of these had conducted themselves in such a manner as to excite the suspicions of government. The object of the bill was to place all aliens under strict supervision, to distribute those who received eleemosynary support into certain districts, and to require passports from them on removal; the prerogative asserted to be vested in the crown, of sending them out of the kingdom, was left as before. The bill occasioned a good deal of discussion in both Houses, and was chiefly remarkable for the reasons given by some of the members who had deserted their former party, for their change of opinion. It was also in this debate that Mr. Burke exhibited the noted stroke of oratorical acting, that of throwing down on the floor of the House one of the daggers of Sheffield manufacture. The bill passed both Houses; and during its progress another bill connected with French affairs was moved and carried, the purpose of which was to prevent the circulation of assignats and other paper issued under the authority of France.

The war with Tippoo Sultan was in this year brought to a close. Lord Cornwallis, on February 5th, arrived with his allies a second time before Seringapatam, at which time Tippoo occupied a fortified camp opposite the city, on the north bank of the Cavery. An attack was made by the British on the night of the 6th upon this post, which succeeded; and all the attempts of Tippoo to recover it being frustrated, the capital was completely invested. The siege was pushed with great vigour till the 24th, when the Sultan, finding his affairs in desperate situation, signed the preliminary articles of the peace imposed on him. The conditions of this treaty were, that he should cede half his dominions to the allied powers, should pay a vast sum by way of indemnities, should release all the prisoners taken by the Mysoreans from the time of Hyder Ally, and should deliver two of his elder sons as hostages for the due performance of these articles. The young princes were delivered up on the 26th at a grand and interesting ceremonial; and a definitive treaty being signed on March 19th, this dangerous war was terminated to the great glory of the British arms and the distinguished commander. The ceded territories were divided into three equal portions, and shared between the Company, the Nizam, and the Mahrattas.

In the autumn of this year a splendid embassy, of which Lord Macartney was the head, for the purpose of establishing an amicable intercourse with the empire of China, sailed from England.

1793

33^d & 34th Year of the Reign

THE progress towards open hostilities between Great Britain and France was too apparent at the close of the preceding year to admit any doubt of the result; and it is not easy to say which nation advanced with more eagerness towards such a conclusion. In England, the majority of the people, including almost all who were connected with public establishments, and a great proportion of the possessors of rank and opulence, had imbibed such a detestation of the principles and practices of the French revolutionists, and such a dread of their adoption in this country, that they were impatient to break off all intercourse between the two nations, and thought the evils of direct war much less to be feared than the machinations of insidious policy. They also doubtless expected that a general confederacy of the principal powers of Europe must in the end prove successful against a new government full of frenzy and faction. In France, besides the presumptuous confidence inspired by the late victories, an opinion prevailed, that a mass of disaffection existed in Great Britain which could not fail to overturn the established government in case of a rupture, with such aid as they might be able to afford it. A letter from the minister of the marine, addressed to all friends of liberty in the seaports, contained the following passage quoted, among others, by Mr. Pitt in the House of Commons. "The King and his parliament mean to make war against us. Will the English republicans suffer it? Already these free men shew their discontent, and the repugnance which they have to bear arms against their brothers the French. Well! We will fly to their succour — we will make a descent in the island — we will lodge there fifty thousand caps of liberty — we will plant there the sacred tree, and will stretch out our arms to our republican brethren — their tyrannical government shall soon be destroyed."

Every sentiment of abhorrence towards the French republic was kindled to a flame, on the intelligence of the condemnation and public execution of the unfortunate Louis, which took place on January 21st. The first political result was an order from his Majesty, transmitted by Lord Grenville, to M. Chauvelin, for his departure from the kingdom within eight days. On the 28th a message from the King was sent to parliament, acquainting both Houses that he had directed copies of several papers received from M. Chauvelin, and the answers to be laid before them, together with a copy of the order abovementioned and also, that he thought it indispensably necessary to make a further augmentation of his forces by sea and land. Of the papers communicated, the first, from M. Chauvelin, dated December 27th was an interrogation in the name of the French republic, whether France ought to consider England as a neutral power, or an enemy; accompanied with an exculpatory explanation of the offensive decree of fraternization, and of that declaring the opening of the Scheldt, and an assurance that France has no intention to attack Holland provided she confines herself to a strict neutrality. Lord Grenville, in his answer, begins with informing M. Chauvelin that he is acknowledged in no other public character than that of minister of his most Christian Majesty. He then proceeds to consider the explanations given of the points above referred to, and shews that they are unsatisfactory. An official note of the executive power of France in answer to that of the British minister succeeds, dated January 7th and signed Le Brun. It repeats, more at large, the explanation of the points of complaint; and ends with saying, that if all their efforts to avoid extremities prove fruitless, they will fight the English, whom they esteem, with regret, but without fear. A note of the same date from "Citizen Chauvelin" minister-plenipotentiary from the French Republic, contains a strong remonstrance against the alien act, as a particular measure of hostility towards the French. Lord Grenville, in reply, returns the note as wholly inadmissible, M. Chauvelin assuming in it a character which is not acknowledged. Lord Grenville then, in the form of extra-official communication, again points out the insufficiency of the explanations given, and positively assures him that our warlike preparations will be continued, to place us in a state for protecting the safety and rights of this country and those of our allies, and to set up a barrier against those views of ambition and aggrandizement, which are peculiarly dangerous as being supported by the propagation of principles destructive of all social order. M. Chauvelin then requests an interview with Lord G. which is declined; and the correspondence ends with the order for his departure.

The King's message being taken into consideration by both Houses, corresponding addresses were moved and carried by great majorities. Among the accessions to the ministerial party at this time was Lord Loughborough, who, on January 26th, succeeded Lord Thurlow in the post of high chancellor.

War was declared by the National Convention against England and Holland on the 1st of February; and on the 11th a message from the King was brought to both Houses of Parliament, informing them of this fact, and expressing his reliance on their support in resisting a wanton and unprovoked aggression, and maintaining the honour of his crown and the rights of his people. On the following day, the subject of the message being brought before the House of Commons by Mr. Pitt, he entered into a statement of the circumstances which had preceded the declaration of war from the time of the dismission of M. Chauvelin, and then commented on the various reasons alledged by the convention for this declaration. He concluded by moving an address in answer to the royal message. A debate followed in which Mr. Fox objected to voting that ministers had given no cause or provocation for the war; and moved an amendment, promising an effectual support to his Majesty in repelling every hostile attempt against this country, and in such other exertions as might induce France to consent to a pacification on safe and honourable terms. This was negatived without a division, and the address was agreed to. In the House of Lords similar debates took place, and amendments were moved by Lord Stanhope and Lord Lauderdale, both of which were negatived.

The opposition, notwithstanding the predominant voice for war in and out of parliament, did not renounce their endeavours to prevent an extremity which they probably regarded as a greater evil than any with which the nation was threatened; and on February 18th Mr. Fox introduced a series of resolutions, the object of which was to declare that war with France on the grounds alleged was neither for the honour nor the interest of this country; that ministers, in their late negotiations with the French government, had not taken the proper means for procuring an amicable redress of the grievances complained of; and that it was their duty to advise his Majesty against entering into engagements which might prevent a separate peace. These resolutions were rejected by the previous question, the division being 270 against 44. A motion by Mr. Grey for an address to his Majesty, expressing at great length the opinion that the differences between this country and France might have been adjusted by negotiation, and requesting him to embrace the first opportunity of restoring peace, was negatived without a division.

Various motions were made in this session for proceeding in the business of abolishing, or at least farther regulating, the slave trade, which were all defeated. It appeared to be the general feeling that the present time was improper for entering into measures of this kind; and though Mr. Pitt spoke largely in favour of a motion by Mr. Wilberforce, it was evident that he gave it no support *as a minister*.

On March 4th Mr. Sheridan brought forward a motion for appointing a committee to enquire into the truth of the reports of sedition in this country. He said, he should not attempt to prove that there never existed any sufficient reason for apprehending the danger of sedition, or that there had not been any acts of insurrection to warrant the propagation of such reports, but he would contend that nothing had happened to justify the alarm that had followed. He then made a variety of remarks to prove that government and its agents had officiously propagated this alarm, the purpose of which he supposed to be diverting the public attention from the question of parliamentary reform. He adverted to an expression of the attorney-general, "that he had 200 cases to bring forward for prosecution," and said that very few had been brought forward, and these were chiefly for selling Paine's works. He reprobated the practice of employing attornies as agents in discovering the distributors of seditious books, and severely animadverted upon the conduct of the Crown and Anchor association, which received and took into consideration anonymous informations. Mr. Sheridan's speech was answered by Mr. Windham, who asserted his belief, from his own knowledge and observation, of the existence of alarming discontents actively propagated by seditious publications. The debate was continued by Mr. Fox and Mr. Burke, not without considerable acrimony; and in the end, Mr. Sheridan's motion was negatived without a division.

A message from his Majesty was presented on March 6th to the House of Commons, acquainting them with his having engaged a body of his electoral troops in the service of Great Britain for the purpose of assisting his allies, the States General, and that he had directed an estimate of the charge of the troops to be laid before the House, in reliance on their zeal to make the necessary provision. The House being formed into a committee of supply on the 11th, Mr. Pitt made his statement of ways and means, the deficiencies of which he proposed to supply by a loan of four millions and an half, and an issue of four millions of exchequer bills; and resolutions were passed for that purpose.

On March 15th, the attorney-general made a motion in the House of Commons for a bill, the object of which was to prevent all traitorous correspondence with the King's enemies during the war. Its provisions went to prohibit under the penalty of high treason all persons from supplying the French government or armies with arms, military stores, provisions bullion, or woollen cloths; also, under other penalties, from purchasing lands in France or property in the funds of that country; from going from this country to France without a licence under his Majesty's Great Seal; and from insuring vessels either coming from or going to France. An amendment was afterwards proposed by the solicitor-general, to confine the operation of the bill to persons residing in Great Britain. In every stage of its progress it was warmly opposed, Mr. Fox particularly stigmatizing it as a violation of justice and human-ity, and a tyrannical extension of the law of treason. Mr. Burke took a leading part in its defence, and at its third reading it passed that House by a majority of 154 to 53. It was likewise vigorously opposed in the House of Lords, where it received several alterations, which were agreed to by the Commons; and it finally passed into a law.

A petition having been presented to parliament by the East India Company for the renewal of their charter, Mr. Dundas introduced the subject to the House of Commons on April 23d, in an elaborate view of the nature of the present government of British India, and the advantages derived to this nation from its connection with that country. The scope of his observations was to shew the expediency of continuing the present administration of India affairs, foreign and domestic, upon the same principles; and in conclusion he proposed thirty-three resolutions for the future government of our East-Indian possessions. After some discussion, the first resolution was moved and carried; and on May 8th the whole of them being agreed to, a bill was brought in upon them and passed, by which the possession of the British territories in India was continued to the Company for a further period.

The spirit of unlimited commercial speculation, and the vast extension of paper currency, having produced great embarrassments in trade, and an alarming state of public credit, Mr. Pitt, April 25th, moved for a select committee to take the subject into consideration. From its report the minister moved for an issue of exchequer bills, to the amount of five millions, to commissioners, to be advanced by them under certain regulations to those who should apply for such assistance, and should give proper security for the repayment at a limited time. After much discussion of the provisions of the bill, it passed both Houses, and received the royal assent.

The Lord Advocate of Scotland moved, in April, for a bill to relieve the Roman Catholics of that country from certain penalties and disabilities imposed upon them by acts of parliament in Scotland, by which they were incapacitated from holding or transmitting landed property. The bill was unanimously received, and passed to a law without opposition.

A number of petitions on the subject of parliamentary reform being presented to the House of Commons, a motion was made by Mr. Grey for referring them to a committee. On this occasion a debate ensued, in which the arguments for and against such a reform were gone over by several speakers; those against the measure being enforced by particular objections respecting the time, and the small proportionate number of persons concurring in the desire. The motion was rejected by 282 to 41.

In this session a motion was made by Sir John Sinclair for an address to his Majesty recommending the institution of a board of Agriculture, which was carried, and the institution took place accordingly.

A short time before the close of the session Mr. Fox made a motion for an address to the King, beseeching him to employ the earliest measures for procuring peace on such terms as were consistent with the professed objects of the war, and with the good faith, strict justice, and liberal policy which have distinguished the British nation. This motion brought on a renewed discussion of the original objects and causes of the war, and of the actual state of the French government, which terminated in a division, for the motion 47, against it 187.

Parliament was prorogued on June 21st, by a speech from the throne, in which the general concurrence of the nation in support of the established constitution was mentioned as what could not fail to check every attempt to disturb the internal repose of the kingdom; and it was announced that measures were taken, in concert with our allies, for an effectual prosecution of the war, so as to bring it to a happy issue.

In France, that atrocious act which had manifestly been preparing at the close of the preceding year, was early brought to a conclusion in the present. It has been mentioned, that notwithstanding all the efforts of the violent party in the convention, a resolution had passed for indulging the unhappy King with counsel at his trial. Among those who pressed forwards to take this honourable office, Louis selected Lamoignon Malesherbes, one of the most virtuous and noble characters in France, who, having been a zealous advocate for freedom in the reign of Louis XV had been appointed minister of state by his successor. He was joined with two others in the defence, which was begun in a very able speech by M. De Seze, who dwelt with much force upon the provision made in the constitutional code for punishing the greatest national crimes of which a King could be supposed guilty, namely that of his forfeiture of the crown. After the defence had been concluded, judgment was hurried on by the violent party, especially by the jacobins in the gallery, who, to the disgrace of all the discussions in the convention, had always a great influence over the decision. The members, however, though generally agreeing in the imputed guilt of Louis, differed in opinion respecting the penalty incurred; the Rolandists, Brissotins, and Girondists, thinking that both justice and policy opposed capital punishment, whilst Danton and Robespierre with their parties, furiously urged the death of the victim. It having been determined on January 15th, that "Louis Capet, late King of France, had been guilty of a conspiracy against liberty, and of attempts against the general safety of the state," and also that the judgment to be pronounced upon him should *not* be submitted to the ratification of the people in their primary assemblies, (a decision which, in fact, sealed his fate), on the following day the convention passed to the vote respecting his punishment. Out of 721 votes, 366 declared for death, 321 for imprisonment, the rest for death, but conditionally. The sentence of death being declared, Louis by his counsel made a solemn appeal against it to the nation at large. On a second division, relative to a respite from the execution of the sentence, it was carried against the delay by 380 votes to 310. On this occasion, Thomas Paine, who had been elected to a seat in the convention, and had voted against the King's death, made a speech, (read for him by the secretary) in favour of the respite, which was deemed very forcible and well reasoned.

Louis, during the short interval of life that was left to him, displayed a dignified serenity befitting his character and station, and passed through the severe trial of parting from his family with all the fortitude which the sensibility of a feeling heart would permit. He was prepared for death by a truly venerable ecclesiastic of Irish descent, the Abbé Edgeworth de Fermont, and received the consolations of religion with all the marks of genuine piety. On January 21st, he was taken to the scaffold, and decapitated by the guillotine. His body was thrown into a common grave, which was filled with quicklime, and a guard was placed upon it till the corpse was consumed. After his death, some of the members of the convention who had been most zealous in their endeavours to preserve his life resigned their seats, and Roland quitted his place in the ministry.

The consequences of this catastrophe as far as they related to England have been already related. After the declaration of war by the French convention against Great Britain and Holland, Dumouriez assembled an army at Antwerp for the purpose of an attempt against the latter country. On February 17th, he attacked Breda, which surrendered by capitulation; and Klundert and Gertruydenburg soon after made their submission. His next object was the fortress of Williamstadt which commands the passage across an arm of the sea into the province of Holland. Its garrison being strengthened by a detachment of English guards, and the place being farther defended by some Dutch and English gun-boats, the attack of the French was successfully resisted, and they drew back to Antwerp. General Miranda, in the meantime, invested Maestricht with a force of 20,000 men, and having completed his works on February 23d, summoned the town to surrender in a menacing proclamation. The Prince of Hesse, however, who was the commandant, determined on a resolute defence. General Clairfait having passed the Roer on the 28th, repulsed the French army with loss in that quarter; and on the following day the Archduke Albert carried some French batteries. On the 8th of March the Prince of Saxe-Coburg obtained a complete victory over the French at Aix la Chapelle, and drove them as far as Liege; and on the same day Prince Frederic of Brunswick defeated a body of them at Bruges. These successes obliged Miranda to raise the siege of Maestricht and retreat with precipitation.

Dumouriez now returned from Holland to place himself at the head of the French army of the Low Countries, and on March 17th, he attacked the imperial army at Neerwinden, but was repulsed, and at length was routed with great loss, which misfortune he imputed to Miranda. After some other actions he fell back as far as Tournay, having given orders for the evacuation of the citadel of Namur and other places, and thus the Austrian Netherlands were recovered from the French as rapidly as they had been lost. Dumouriez, who had formed a design of marching to Paris to effect a counter-revolution, now entered into a negotiation with the Austrian generals, by which he was to remain in his quarters undisturbed, and to be after assisted by them if necessary. Having, however, fallen under the suspicion of the convention, they sent commissioners to suspend him from his command and call him to account. These he arrested in his camp, and delivered up to the Austrians, to be kept as hostages for the good treatment of the royal prisoners in the Temple. He was himself, however, near being seized by a corps of French volunteers, and was obliged to take refuge in the imperial territories. Afterwards, intending to repair to his camp at St. Amand, he was informed that the army was in such a disposition, that it would not be safe to venture among them; for which reason, accompanied by some superior officers and his staff, he went over to General Clairfait, and was followed by a small body of his troops. When the defection of Dumouriez and the arrest of the commissioners was made known to the convention, the event was regarded as so important, that they decreed a permanent sitting, and employed themselves in measures for preserving the tranquillity of the capital, and defending the frontiers. They sent other commissioners to the army, who appointed General

Dampierre the provisional commander in chief. He occupied a fortified camp at Famars, from which, on May 8th, he made an attack on the Austrian and Prussian posts. A severe action was the result, which terminated in favour of the allies, Dampierre having received a wound of which he died on the following day. In this engagement the British troops under the command of the Duke of York greatly distinguished themselves. The camp of Famars was afterwards attacked by the allies and carried; and Valenciennes being thereby laid open, the siege of that town was committed to the Duke of York. Condé, which had been invested by the imperialists from the beginning of April, capitulated in July; and Valenciennes, after a great part of it had been reduced to ashes by a bombardment, surrendered on July 26th.

The campaign on the Rhine had been attended with various fortune in a number of small actions. Its most important event was the surrender of Mentz to the King of Prussia after a long siege, on July 22d.

Whilst France was undergoing these reverses abroad, it was disquieted at home by all the violence of contending parties. A declaration of war against Spain on March 4th, one cause of which was stated to be the zeal of that court in behalf of Louis, proved the inconsiderate warmth which prevailed in the conventional government. In the same month a revolutionary tribunal for trying offences against the state was established, armed with powers which rendered it a dreadful engine of party. It was made a court without appeal, and its sentences against persons absent were to have the same effect as if they were present. On the 29th, a decree passed denouncing the punishment of death upon all persons convicted of composing or publishing writings for the restoration of monarchy, or the dissolution of the national representation; and on April 1st, another decree abolished the inviolability of the deputies of the convention when accused of crimes against the state. On the 7th, a committee of public safety was appointed, with powers greater than had hitherto been conferred for the prevention of insurrection and conspiracy: its duration was limited to one month. This measure was doubtless suggested by the dangerous commotions which were now subsisting in those parts of Britany and Poitou which bore the names of La Vendée and Le Loire. The inhabitants of these parts were firm royalists and much attached to their religion. They assumed the title of the Christian army acting under the authority of Monsieur, as Regent of France; and being stimulated by the harangues of their priests, they engaged in action with the national guards, and were successful on various occasions. They laid siege to Nantes, and obtained possession of a large tract of country. In April General Berruyere was sent to command against the insurgents; but the latter defeated the republican forces in two general engagements.

The convention about this time decreed that all the branches of the Bourbon family, as well as such officers of the Austrian army as had been taken prisoners, were to be considered as hostages for the safety of the commissioners whom Dumouriez had delivered up to the imperialists. The paper currency of France being greatly depreciated, a decree was passed for the payment of all contracts and bargains in assignats, not in specie.

The contest between the two parties which divided the convention, the Brissotine or Gironde, and the Mountain, was now coming to a crisis, and Paris was long kept in a state of violent tumult from their contentions. The former as the most moderate, fell into suspicion among the people, whose passions were continually excited by the inflammatory publications of Marat, president of the Jacobin club. This detestable incendiary having put his signature to a paper of the most sanguinary tendency, he was committed to the abbey prison by a great majority of votes; but such was his influence over the public, that he was unanimously acquitted by the jury which tried him. After his liberation he became more furious than before, and the convention was frequently a scene of the wildest uproar. On June 1st, its place of assembly was surrounded by a clamorous multitude, which compelled the members to pass a decree of arrestation against the Gironde deputies, and the ministers Claviere and Le Brun. The Jacobin party being now triumphant, proceeded to complete the constitution, and issued a large declaration of the rights of man. The constitutional act soon followed, consisting of 134 articles, of a character essentially democratical. About this time Marat was assassinated by a young woman, an enthusiast in favour of liberty, named Charlotte Cordé, who displayed in the act, and at her condemnation and execution, the most heroical firmness of mind. A variety of decrees were afterwards issued for regulating the civil and military affairs of the republic, and bringing to punishment the enemies of the state. On August 15th, Barrere proposed a declaration from the French people, by the mouth of their representatives, that they would rise in one body in defence of liberty, equality, independence, and the constitution, which was adopted by general acclamation. He then presented a plan for putting this purpose in execution, which consisted of a number of articles, the effect of which was to place all the force and property of the nation at the disposal of the existing government. It was afterwards matured and introduced by the committee of public welfare.

The remainder of the year was extraordinarily marked by the energy, as well as by the merciless cruelty, of those who now conducted the affairs of France.

On August 18th, the Duke of York marched to a camp near Menin where the Dutch, stationed at that place, were so closely pressed by the French, that the hereditary Prince of Orange requested assistance from the English. Three battalions were accordingly sent under the command of General Lake, who with great gallantry drove the enemy from a strong redoubt at the village of Lincelles. The Duke of York in the latter part of the month took his ground before Dunkirk for the siege of that town; but the delay in the arrival of his heavy artillery, and the want of the early co-operation of a naval force, caused the loss of so much time, that the French were enabled to collect a powerful force for its defence before any progress had been made. The result was that the Duke found himself obliged to raise the siege, leaving behind him his battering cannon, and a large quantity of ammunition. The French now made attacks upon several places on the frontier of the Austrian Netherlands, but were in general repulsed: the Prince of Coburg, however, who had been blockading the French in the neighbourhood of Maubeuge, was driven by General Jourdan across the Sambre in October.

Besides the necessity of providing for the war with the allies on the borders, the conventional government had to contend against foes within the heart of France. The disturbances in La Vendee continued; and in the south a formidable confederation had taken place between the cities of Marseilles, Lyons, and Toulon. General Cartaud, who was sent against the latter, having in August taken Aix, the populace of Marseilles opened their gates to him. The people of Toulon having, in conjunction with Admiral Turgot, entered into a negotiation with Admiral Hood, then commanding a fleet in the Mediterranean, possession was given to him of the town and shipping under the express condition that they should return to the French monarchy whenever it should be re-established. The Lyonnese resolved to stand upon their defence, and though ill prepared for resistance, they sustained a siege of two months. On October 8th, a great part of the city being reduced to ash by a bombardment, they found it necessary to surrender, and there are few examples of such vindictive treatment inflicted upon a conquered city in a civil war. The victims, too numerous for the guillotine, were driven in crowds into the Rhone, or massacred in the public squares by discharges of musquetry and artillery; and the convention decreed that the walls and public buildings of Lyons should be demolished, and that she should lose her name in that of *La Ville Affranchie*.

After General Cartaud had gained possession of Marseilles, he made preparations for the recovery of Toulon, and on August 30th appeared before it with a small force. Various petty actions ensued, in which the French were repeatedly checked in advancing their works towards the town. At length, they received so many reinforcements, that their troops amounted to between 30 and 40,000 men; and it being impossible with the defensive force in the place to maintain the works by which it was protected, a resolution was taken for its evacuation. This was effected in December, the whole of the troops being brought off without loss, and some thousands of the inhabitants being sheltered on board the British ships. A conflagration then took place, under the direction of Sir Sydney Smith, of the magazines, store-houses, and arsenals, with the ships in harbour, on which occasion fifteen ships of the line, with several frigates and smaller vessels, were consumed, and an immense quantity of naval stores. Three ships of the line and some frigates sailed away with the British fleet. This was very severe stroke on the French navy; and however advantageous to the rival nation, may be marked as an example of the criminality incurred by a party in a state which calls to its assistance a foreign and hostile power.

The French were at this time worked up to a pitch of ferocity which rendered them capable of every thing cruel and atrocious. The trial of Marie Antoinette, late Queen of France, was one of the resolutions contained in Barrere's decree of August 1st; and she was on that day suddenly removed to the prison of the Conciergerie. She there remained ten weeks, treated as the meanest criminal, and was at length brought before the bloody revolutionary tribunal, charged with a number of state crimes. Not one of these was proved, but her doom was already determined. She suffered at the guillotine on October 26th, and her body was interred in the same manner with that of her husband, in a grave filled with quick-lime. Marie Antoinette possessed talents and virtues, and her errors have perhaps been magnified; but it is certain that, as consort to the unfortunate Louis, she exerted an influence which contributed to the fall of the monarchy.

The execution of the Queen was soon followed by that of twenty Brissotine deputies, the person from whom they took their name being at the head. The charge against them was that of having conspired against the unity and indivisibility of the republic by exciting a rebellion in the departments of the south; and their defence was abbreviated by the judicial maxim then prevalent, that a jury might pronounce sentence, when convinced, without waiting to hear the whole of the evidence. Several other distinguished persons who deserved a better fate were the next victims. The death of the Duke of Orleans, then known by the name of Egalité, who had given his vote against the life of the King, and was contaminated by every vice, was pitied by none. Very different was the feeling on the execution of Madame Roland, the wife of the minister, whose noble character was the object of general admiration. She died with exemplary fortitude, having on her way to the scaffold apostrophized the statue of liberty, by exclaiming "O Liberty, how many crimes are committed in thy name!"

Among other circumstances marking the times and the nation was the publication of a new calendar, which, with much that was futile and fanciful, was well calculated to promote an end which the men in power at this period manifestly had in view, that of abolishing from France the christian religion. It divided the year into twelve months of 30 days each, all denominated from some occurrence of the season, and five supplementary days, ridiculously termed *sansculotides*. The subdivisions of the months were decades, the first days of which were festivals, intended gradually to obliterate the memory of Sundays; and nothing in the calendar bore any stamp of former religious observances.

Some foreign transactions of the year remain to be mentioned. The allies under the Duke of Brunswick and

General Wurmser were victorious for some time on the Rhine in the autumnal campaign; but in the latter part of November the French were rendered so much superior in number, that they were always able to outflank their opponents. Wurmser, having failed in an attempt to gain possession of Strasburg, retired to Haguenau, where the French, after repeated attacks, forced the strong lines, and obliged the Austrians to retire across the Rhine. The Prussians afterwards relinquished the siege of Landau; and the Duke of Brunswick went into winter quarters at Mentz.

On the Spanish border, various actions took place between the troops of Spain and of France, in which the former were successful. The war in this quarter, however, was of very subordinate importance.

In Italy, the county of Nice was the scene of some actions between the troops of the King of Sardinia and of the French republic, and the latter were repulsed with considerable loss in two attempts upon the Sardinian posts. Genoa, which had manifested a disposition to take part with the French, was overawed by the English fleet; and the Duke of Tuscany was induced by the representations of the British minister to declare against France.

Early in the year the English arms were actively employed in the West Indies. On April 12th an expedition under Admiral Laforey and General Cuyler sailed from Barbadoes for the reduction of Tobago, which was effected with an inconsiderable loss. An attempt on Martinico, in consequence of an invitation from the royalist inhabitants, was rendered abortive by the conduct of the latter.

The French planters of St. Domingo, which island had been in a deplorable state of civil war from the commencement of the revolution, and was now groaning under the tyranny of the commissioners sent by the French convention, having requested the English government to take them under its protection upon certain conditions, General Williamson sailed from Jamaica in September, with a force to take possession of the town and forts of Jeremie, which was effected without resistance. Commodore Ford then proceeding to Cape Nicholas Mole, a deputation came to him, and desired him to occupy that place on the same conditions which had been granted to Jeremie, which was complied with.

In the East Indies, intelligence of the declaration of war by France was received at Fort William in June, and immediately all the small factories belonging to that country on the coast, and the ships in the ports, were seized, and preparations were made for an attack on Pondicherry. This place presently surrendered to Colonel Braithwaite; and the settlements near Bengal and on the Malabar coast soon after being yielded, the French flag no longer waved on the continent of India.

General Washington was in this year unanimously re-elected President of the United States of America.

The vigour and success of the French government, and the hope that the revolution would finally be the means of promoting the cause of liberty throughout Europe, still rendered many persons in Great Britain well-wishers to France, and admirers of its political principles, notwithstanding the enormities by which it had disgraced itself, but which they attributed to the aggression of the coalesced powers. In Scotland, a party zealous for reform had projected what they termed a national convention, and in framing it, had foolishly assumed the titles and proceedings of the French republicans. They had thereby attracted the notice of government, and prosecutions were instituted against some of the leading members upon the old Scottish statute concerning *leasing-making*, or sowing discord between the King and his people — a law of very wide and dangerous application. In consequence, the Court of Justiciary at Edinburgh, and the Circuit-court of Perth, adjudged Mr. Muir and Mr. Palmer to transportation; which sentences being the first instances of the imposition of that punishment for such a crime, and pronounced against persons in decent life and of good character, were generally regarded as unreasonably severe.

The Courts of Petersburgh and Berlin having determined upon a farther partition of Poland, the King of Prussia in the beginning of this year seized upon Thorn and Dantzic, issuing a manifesto on the occasion, in which he justified the proceeding by pretended apprehensions of a jacobinical party in Poland. The diet assembled at Grodno made a protest against this injustice, and applied to the Empress of Russia for her protection; but in March that sovereign also published a manifesto, in which she gave her imperial reasons for resolving to annex a large share of Poland to her own dominions. It was in vain that the diet declared against this second dismemberment of their country, and looked for the interposition of the other powers of Europe against this shameful violation of all national rights. It was obliged to negotiate with its spoilers respecting their demands; and at length Poland was compelled to surrender to Prussia territory occupied by more than 1,136,000 inhabitants, and to Russia as much as contained more than 3,500,000.

1794

34th & 35th Year of the Reign

PARLIAMENT met on January 21st and was opened with a speech recommending a vigorous prosecution of the war, on the success of which depended the preservation of the Constitution, laws, and religious establishment of this kingdom, and the security of all civil society. The efforts of France were said to be founded solely on an usurpation of power which rendered the present rulers absolute masters of people's lives; and the system they had adopted was represented as tending rapidly to exhaust the natural strength of the country. The speech was warmly applauded by the supporters of the administration in both Houses; and the amendments to the corresponding addresses, in which his Majesty was requested to avail himself of the earliest opportunity for concluding an honourable peace, were rejected by great majorities.

The landing of a body of Hessians on the Isle of Wight in order to recruit them from the fatigues of a voyage from Germany till a projected expedition should take place, was a subject of warm debate in both Houses; the opposition contending that such an introduction of foreign troops into the kingdom without the previous consent of parliament was absolutely illegal; whilst the ministers and their supporters maintained that there was no precise law on the subject, and that nothing irregular had been done in the case. The motions for declaring the illegality of such a transaction were negatived by the usual majorities, and the ministers refused to accept of a proposed bill of indemnity. An augmentation of the navy to 85,000 men was unanimously agreed to. The proposal of augmenting the regular army to 60,000 men was opposed, and produced some severe strictures on the conduct of the last campaign. Mr. Pitt's expression on speaking in favour of the augmentation, that "France had been converted into an armed nation," was afterwards much commented upon. On February 2d, the minister laid before the House an account of the supplies necessary for the prosecution of the war, and the ways and means for raising them. On this occasion he stated the interior strength of the kingdom at 140,000 men, and the foreign troops in our pay at 40,000. The total of the requisite supply he calculated at nearly 20 millions; and the ways and means included some new taxes, and a loan of eleven millions. The double taxation to which the Roman Catholics had been long subjected was liberally cancelled.

The subject of the slave trade was again brought before the consideration of parliament by a motion from Mr. Wilberforce for the abolition of that branch of it which went to the supply of the islands and territories belonging to foreigners. This motion was supported by Mr. Pitt, and passed by 63 votes against 40. Petitions having been presented against the bill by the West India merchants of London and Liverpool, a motion was made for deferring it for six months, which was negatived. On the introduction of the bill into the House of Lords it was, however, thrown out by the majority of 45 to 4. In the same House a motion by Bishop Horsley for referring to a committee the hearing of evidence concerning the slave trade, was negatived.

On February 17th, the Marquis of Lansdowne introduced, by a long argumentative speech replete with censure on the conduct of the ministry, a motion for an address to his Majesty, the tenor of which was to show the great improbability of the reduction of such a country as France, the small reliance to be placed on the coalition, the losses and burdens to be expected by this nation from persisting in the contest, and the folly of maintaining a war against principles; and for these reasons to request that he would immediately declare his readiness to enter into a negotiation. He was seconded by the Duke of Grafton, who, after a long absence from parliament, had thought it incumbent on him to declare his sentiments on this important occasion. An active debate ensued, in which the principal speakers on each side took a part; and the motion was finally negatived by 103 against 13.

The ministers, though triumphant in parliament, were now rendered fully sensible of the arduousness of the foreign contest in which they were engaged; and on March 6th, a motion was made by Mr. Pitt for an augmentation of the militia in order to provide for the better security of the kingdom against a menaced invasion by the French; and another for the levy of a volunteer force of horse and foot in every county, which were carried. The ministry having by their own authority issued a requisition under the name of a recommendation, for the raising of volunteer companies of horse and foot, the measure was warmly censured by the opposition as unconstitutional, particularly as notice was publicly given in the papers that those who refused compliance would be considered as enemies to government. A question being put on the subjects it was carried in favour of the ministers. The attempt to procure subscriptions without authority of parliament however, created much dissatisfaction and was vigorously opposed in several counties. On March 28th, Mr. Sheridan moved in the House of Commons a declaration "that it was dangerous and unconstitutional for the people of this country to make any loan of money to the crown." A debate followed, which was terminated by voting the previous question. The same topic was discussed in the House of Lords, where a motion to the same effect was defeated by a large majority. Mr. Pitt on April 1st, moved for a bill for the encouragement of those who should voluntarily enroll themselves for the general defence of the kingdom during the war. This was succeeded by a proposal to enable the subjects of France to enlist in the King's service on the continent of Europe, and to employ French officers as engineers under certain restrictions. By all these measures government acquired a great accession of influence, and the warlike spirit became universally diffused.

The subsidiary treaties concluded with the Princes of the coalition were a subject of discussion in parliament; and on March 6th, Mr. Grey moved in the House of Commons for an address to the King, for the purpose of expressing their concern that his Majesty should have formed an union with powers whose apparent aim was to regulate a country wherein they had no right to interfere. In the subsequent debate, and in a debate in both Houses consequent upon a message from the King informing them of a treaty concluded with the King of Prussia, by which a larger subsidy was stipulated with that monarch for carrying on the war, many observations were made by the opposition relative to the objects and prospects of the war, and the small confidence to be placed in subsidized powers, who were chiefly attentive to their own interests. The ministers, however, were supported by the usual majorities.

At this time the British government became involved in those differences with the United States of America consequent upon the war with France, which were finally attended with such serious effects. Soon after the commencement of the war, orders were given for stopping all American vessels carrying corn to France, and detaining their cargoes, paying for them and the freight; which proceeding was much resented by the Americans, as an infraction of their independence. It was followed by an order for seizing all American ships carrying provisions and stores to the French colonies, and also for obliging American ships sailing from the British islands to give security to land their cargoes in British or in neutral ports. More than 600 American vessels were seized in consequence of this order within five months. Further cause of displeasure and alarm was given to the States, by the occupation of some forts on the Canadian border by the British troops, which had been ceded to the Americans in the peace of 1783; and by a conference held with several Indian tribes by Lord Dorchester, Governor of Canada. The American government shewed its resentment of these proceedings by an embargo of 30 days on the British shipping; and appointed Mr. Jay, chief justice of the United States, its minister for settling the subsisting differences.

Mr. Jay arrived in England in the summer of this year, and delivered a memorial on the subject, in which, among other topics, was also contained the frequently recurring complaint of the severity used to American seamen, and their being compelled to serve on board of English men of war. Lord Grenville made a moderate and conciliatory answer; and both parties being pacifically disposed, the dispute was for the present compromised.

On the 30th of May, the Duke of Bedford in the House of Lords, and Mr. Fox in the House of Commons, moved a set of resolutions for terminating the war with France. In the debates attending these motions, the topics of the origin, objects, and prospects of the war were again brought into discussion by both parties, with no other effect than to display their irreconcilable differences of opinion, and the great superiority of numbers by which the measures of government were supported.

Amidst this attention to foreign politics, the parliament and public found at least equal matter of interest in the internal affairs of the nation. The progress of French principles, as they were termed, excited a very serious alarm in the higher orders of society, and in the friends of all existing establishments, which was probably in some degree participated by the ministers, since they now resolved upon taking the most effectual measures for arresting that progress. The most obvious cause of apprehension was the formation of societies for the declared purpose of legitimate reform, but the organization of which, and their mutual connections, together with the attachment which they generally displayed to the French republic, rendered them objects of suspicion. It has already been mentioned that the arm of the law had been extended against a society of this kind in Scotland, which had assumed the title of a national convention; and *that* arm had been exerted with a vigour which gave occasion to an alarm of an opposite nature.

Early in the session, Mr. Adam gave notice of an intention to propose some alterations in the criminal law of Scotland, particularly on appeals from the Court of Justiciary; and the sentences against Messrs. Muir and Palmer induced him afterwards to enlarge his plan by inserting a clause for a retrospect to the judgments pronounced by that court in 1793, which should render it competent for these persons to appeal on the ground of error in law. His motion being rejected, he gave notice of a motion for the relief of Messrs. Muir and Palmer in another form; and in the meantime Mr. Sheridan presented a petition from Mr. Palmer, stating that he conceived the sentence passed upon him, and from which there was no appeal, to have been unjust. It being intimated by Mr. Dundas that the sentence was already executed, the warrant for Mr. Palmer's transportation (to Botany Bay) being signed and issued, this proceeding was loudly complained of; and a motion was made to stop the sailing of the transport, which was negatived. On March 10th, Mr. Adam moved for a review of the trials of the two culprits; and in the subsequent debate, the sentence by which they were condemned was severely censured by that gentleman, Mr. Fox, and Mr. Sheridan, and was strenuously defended by the lord advocate of Scotland, Mr. Pitt, and Mr. Windham. The motion was negatived by 77 against 24. Similar motions in the House of Lords by the Earls of Lauderdale and

Stanhope were negatived, and the Lord Chancellor carried a resolution, that there were no grounds for interfering in the courts of criminal justice as now established.

The two principal political societies in England were the Society for Constitutional Information, and the Corresponding Society; both avowing for their object the reform of the representation in parliament. Government had kept a vigilant eye upon them since the last year, when the alarm from such associations was first roused; and thinking it had now procured sufficient matter of legal charge against them, some of the principal members of both societies were apprehended in the month of May and committed to the tower.

On the 12th a message was delivered to both Houses of parliament from the King, informing them that seditious practices had been carried on by societies in London in correspondence with other societies for the purpose of assembling a convention to represent the people of England, and that their papers had been seized and would be laid before parliament, to which the examination of them was recommended, with the adoption of such measures as might appear necessary. In the House of Commons Mr. Pitt moved an address of thanks to his Majesty, and proposed that the papers should be referred to a committee of secrecy consisting of 21 members chosen by ballot, which was agreed to. The report of the committee was brought in on the 16th. It contained the proceedings of the two societies, most of which had been already published by themselves in the newspapers. Mr. Pitt then, after commenting on the facts discovered, moved for a suspension of the Habeas Corpus act. This measure was strongly opposed by the minority, as not warranted by any actual necessity. It was supported with equal warmth; and Mr. Windham went so far as to say, that the evils threatened must be obviated at all events; and if the laws in being were inadequate to that purpose, others more effectual ought indispensably to be framed. This menace called forth some very animated remarks from Mr. Fox, as portending a gradual deprivation of their liberties to Englishmen. Mr. Pitt, in answer, said that no undue severities would be resorted to, and that the measure did not affect the right of the people to meet for lawful purposes, or to petition for a reform, or for the redress of abuses.

The progress of the suspension bill in the other House was attended with similar debates; and Lord Thurlow, in acceding to the bill, said that it was only on the presumption that its necessity had been proved; and that the report, in his opinion, contained many facts amounting to sedition, but not to any higher crime. It passed into a law on May 23d. An address to his Majesty was afterwards moved and carried in both Houses, to assure him of their determination to punish the participators in the conspiracy laid before them, and to invest him with additional power for the suppression of attempts against government.

The session of parliament was terminated on July 11th with a speech from the throne, in which the designs against the constitution were adverted to in language similar to that of the royal message.

Before proceeding to the other events of the year, it may be interesting to conclude the topic which has occupied the last pages. A bill of indictment having been found against thirteen members of the reforming societies, the trials began with that of Thomas Hardy, who, with his fellow-prisoners, was accused of nine overt acts of treason. Few state trials have excited more solicitude in the public, as it was generally understood that upon its event would depend the fate not only of his partners in accusation, but probably of many more who were within the reach of government. The charge was opened by the attorney-general in a speech of nine hours, in which all the particulars mentioned in the reports of the secret committee were dwelt upon, and the papers of the society to which Hardy was secretary were produced in evidence. It was much in the prisoner's favour that none of the witnesses who deserved credit criminated him personally, that the proceedings of the society were of public notoriety, and that their sole apparent object had been parliamentary reform. He was assisted by the admirable powers of his counsel Mr. Erskine and Mr. Gibbs; and after a trial which lasted eight days, he was pronounced *not guilty*, to the unspeakable joy of all those who entertained similar political sentiments, and the satisfaction of the greater part of the public, who were convinced that the charge went beyond the crime, and that nothing could be more dangerous to liberty than the attempted extension of the doctrine of constructive treason.

The trial of Mr. Horne Tooke which followed was chiefly remarkable for the perfect ease of the accused, while the persons he summoned as witnesses, among whom was Mr. Pitt, were sometimes not a little disconcerted by his questions. He was acquitted by the jury after a very short consultation; and the subsequent trial of Mr. Thelwall terminated in the same manner. The crown then declined all farther prosecution, and the remaining prisoners were dismissed. Thus concluded a transaction which furnished an additional and very striking proof of the excellence of the judicial branch of the English constitution, and the high importance of the trial by jury in criminal cases.

The beginning of this year, whilst it displayed the vast preparations of the French to push their success in the Low Countries, gave tokens of a disunion among the coalesced powers on the continent, which boded ill to the operations of the campaign on their parts. One of its consequences was the resignation, on January 6th, of the supreme command of the Prussian army by the Duke of Brunswick. Soon after, a friendly communication took place between the French and Prussian governments, on the pretext of an exchange of prisoners, but attended with circumstances which inspired a suspicion of further views. In fact, the King of Prussia's hopes of the subjugation of France being at an end, and the farther expence of a war being beyond his means to supply, he resolved to withdraw from the confederacy, unless he could find a power willing to take upon it the burden of indemnifying him from all charges. This power was Great Britain; and the notice taken in parliament of the subsidy granted to him has been already mentioned. By the stipulations of the treaty between the Kings of England and Prussia and the States General of the United Provinces signed on April 19th, an army of 62,400 men was to be furnished by the Court of Berlin, to be employed in concert with the two other powers, for which the sum of £2,200,000 was to be paid, in the proportion of £400,000 by Holland, and the rest by England.

When the Austrian army in the Netherlands was about to commence its operations, disputes arose respecting the command, the Duke of York refusing to serve under General Clairfait. It was at length adjusted that if the Emperor Francis should personally assume the supreme command, the Duke would serve under him; and accordingly the Emperor repaired to Brussels in April, whence he proceeded to the army. The siege of Landrecy was soon after commenced. Several attempts for its relief by the French were defeated with great loss on their part, and the place was obliged to surrender; but in the meantime Pichegru had forced the encampment of Clairfait, and had taken Courtrai and Menin. General Jourdan in the beginning of March entered the province of Luxemburg, where he was opposed by the Austrian General Beaulieu. On April 17th, Jourdan made an attack upon the Austrian lines which, after a conflict of two days, he carried. In May, the French attacked the army under the Duke of York near Tournay, and were repulsed with loss. They afterwards marched in great force from Courtrai against Clairfait, whom, after a very obstinate engagement, they put to the rout, and followed across the Sambre. A variety of other hard fought actions ensued, attended with much slaughter on both sides; but upon the whole, the forces and the confidence of the French seemed to increase. Jourdan was engaged in the siege of Charleroy, when, on June 26th, a general attack was made on his posts by the allies on the plain of Fleurus. Its result was the total defeat of the assailants, who retreated in confusion as far back as Halle; and the success of this day decided that of the French for the remainder of the campaign. Charleroy fell; and some time before, General Moreau, after defeating Clairfait, made himself master of Ypres. Bruges submitted to the victors on June 24th. The Duke of York found it necessary to retreat to Oudenarde, thus leaving Tournay exposed, which came into the possession of the French without resistance. The Duke then drew back to the vicinity of Antwerp, where he was joined by Lord Moira with ten thousand British troops.

The garrison of Ostend being withdrawn, the French entered it and were received with joy. It was, indeed, manifest through the whole of their invasion of the Belgic provinces, that the remembrance of the Austrian tyranny had disposed the people in general readily to admit a change of masters. This was especially observable at Brussels, which Prince Coburg in vain attempted to cover by strong entrenchments in the forest of Soignies. He was driven from them with great loss, and the Austrians taking their flight through Brussels in the night, left the capital open to their pursuers, who entered it in triumph on July 9th. Ghent had opened its gates to the French on the 5th of that month. The Duke of York and Lord Moira, after taking shelter in Mechlin, evacuated that place, and proceeded to Antwerp. The French now advancing from Brussels marched against Clairfait, who was protecting Louvain, and having defeated him, obtained possession of that city on July 15th. Antwerp surrendered undefended on the 23d, and thus the whole of Austrian Flanders and Brabant fell under the French dominion. The strong city and citadel of Namur were evacuated by General Beaulieu on the 17th; and the Austrians were soon after driven from Liege and its territory. In Dutch Flanders, Cadsandt and Sluys were reduced by Moreau.

The campaign on the German borders was not less successful to the French republic. It began early with the reduction of Kaiserslautern and Spire, and other fortresses in that quarter. An obstinate engagement took place on July 12th and 13th between the French and Prussians, which ended in the discomfiture of the latter. Two subsequent days of fighting obliged the Imperialists to cross the Rhine, and the Prussians to retreat towards Mentz. The French army on the Moselle on August 8th took possession of Treves. The next object of the republican arms was to recover those towns within the limits of France which had been taken by the allies; and Landrecy, Quesnoy, Valenciennes, and Condé, were brought to a capitulation with little resistance, the garrisons being threatened with military execution if they should hold out. In all these places vast stores of ammunition and provision were found.

The Emperor had now returned to Vienna; and so much was he dissatisfied with the conduct of Prussia as an ally, and disheartened by the state of the war, that apprehensions were entertained of a design in the Austrian councils, to propose a pacification. In order to prevent a dissolution of the confederacy, the English ministry deputed Earl Spencer and the Honourable Thomas Grenville as ambassadors extraordinary to Vienna, for the purpose of keeping that court steadfast to its engagements, which was effected by the stipulation of a large subsidy. In the meantime the French were advancing on the German border. Jourdan in September carried a strong post not far from Liege, defended by a force under General Latour. Clairfait was afterwards defeated and obliged to retreat to Juliers, and in the meantime the French took Aix la Chapelle. Another engagement, continued from September 29th to October 3d, so much exhausted the Austrian army, that the French could not be prevented from entering Cologne. They afterwards reduced several places in that electorate; and on October 23d Moreau carried with scarcely any opposition Coblentz, which had been fortified at great expence. The possession of this place, which had been the head-quarters of the emigrant army, was particularly gratifying to them. Worms and several other places in that vicinity yielded to the French troops on the Rhine.

The Duke of York, having assisted the Prince of Orange in putting Breda and Boisleduc in a state of defence, posted his army along the Dommel, where, on September 14th, he was attacked by a powerful force under Pichegru. Finding his posts untenable, he retreated, after an action, to a position near Grave. An invasion of Holland was now the great object of the French, and their first operation was the siege of Boisleduc, which capitulated on October 10th. The Duke of York had quitted Grave and was encamped under the walls of Nimeguen. The French, crossing the Maes, made an attack on the British posts in front of that town, and having obliged them to change their position, invested the place. Nimeguen, being strong by situation, and well garrisoned, was expected to have made a long resistance; it was however suddenly carried after a siege of a few days. The important town of Maestricht, which was besieged by General Kleber, held out for 40 days, and surrendered on November 4th. The loss of these two places excited a general alarm in Holland, and at the close of the year all eyes were turned to that country as the expected scene of great events.

The arms of France were in this year equally successful, in other parts of Europe. The advantages which had been obtained by the Spaniards at the close of the preceding year were so much beyond its military character, that their continuance was not to be expected when the French were able to turn their attention towards that quarter. Early in February the French army took the field, and routed with great loss a Spanish force posted at St. Jean de Luz. After some other considerable success General Dugommier on May 23d obtained a complete victory over a Spanish army near Collisare, in which, beside those who fell in battle, 7000 men laid down their arms, and all the artillery and baggage came into the possession of the French. The strong fortress of Bellegarde, which had been taken by the Spaniards in the preceding campaign, was in the meantime invested by a large body of French, who defeated a spirited attempt by a Spanish general for its relief; and after a long resistance, it surrendered to Dugommier in September with its garrison of 6000 men. To avenge this loss, the Spaniards collected the flower of their troops and advanced against the French, who met them at Spanilles on October 17th, when a bloody action ensued, which terminated in a victory on the part of the French; purchased however by the death of their very able commander, Dugommier. It was followed three days after by a furious attack upon the Spanish entrenchments defended by 40,000 men, which were carried by the French in three hours; and such was the panic inspired by this action, that the neighbouring strong town of Figueras, garrisoned by near 10,000 men, surrendered almost without resistance. On the northern frontier, Fontarabia, Passages, and St. Sebastian, were reduced by the French in the course of the four first days of August, the Spaniards being entirely deprived either of courage or of will to resist the invaders. The remaining Spanish army kept on the defensive within a line of fortified posts, the extent of which was near 40 leagues. They were not, however, suffered to be unmolested, and their line was forced by their impetuous enemy in twelve different places at once, on which occasion the whole army narrowly escaped destruction.

Italy was another theatre of the French successes. It being resolved that the King of Sardinia should be made to feel the power of the republic against which he had declared hostility, his harbour of Oneglia on the gulf of Genoa was attacked and taken in the beginning of April. The French then having defeated a body of combined Sardinians and Austrians, penetrated into Piedmont, some districts of which they reduced, with the capture of large quantities of provisions and military stores. They next attacked a Sardinian fortified camp, which they carried, taking a number of prisoners, and a large train of artillery. A strong entrenchment in the Col de Tenda, one of the difficult passes into Piedmont on the west, was then assailed and forced. Meantime, the French General Dumas entered on the north side, and undertook the arduous task of clearing the passage of Mount Cenis. On the 10th of May, he began his operations by storming a fort which commanded the first pass. In the sequel he attacked and carried, after a vigorous resistance, all the redoubts and batteries by which the mountain was defended, and compelled the Sardinian army to retreat, leaving behind them all their cannon and warlike stores. In several ensuing actions the French were successful, but they were resisted with so much pertinacity that they were unable to make further progress on this side. On the southern quarter the French gained a decisive victory over the Sardinians and Austrians, whom they pursued to the gates of Alessandria. During the remainder of the campaign, the allied troops stood on the defensive, and by occupying advantageous posts, prevented the invaders from advancing farther into Piedmont.

At sea alone the French arms experienced a reverse, having on that element to contend with a foe certainly not inferior in ardour, and undoubtedly superior in skill and discipline. By vast exertions, notwithstanding the disaster at Toulon, they were enabled to fit out a powerful fleet, which, after having for some time been blocked up in Brest by the Channel fleet commanded by Lord Howe, put to sea during his absence about the middle of May. It was followed by the British fleet, which came within sight of the enemy on the 28th off the coast of Britany. After some partial actions and manœuvring, by which Lord Howe gained the weather-gage, the two fleets came to close action on the morning of June 1st, their respective force being 26 ships of the line on the part of the French, and 25 on that of the British. The French steadily waited the attack; but in less than an hour after the centre was engaged, their admiral, whose opponent was Lord Howe in the Queen Charlotte, went off with crowded sails, and was followed by most of his van, who were in condition to carry canvas. Of those who were left crippled, some escaped on account of the disabled or separated state of the English fleet. Seven were captured, one of which sunk almost immediately on being taken possession of. One French ship sunk in the action, and not a man of her crew was saved. The slaughter on board the French fleet was very great, that in the captured ships alone amounting in killed and wounded to 1270. The British total loss was 904. This action conferred great glory on the admiral and all his fleet; and was received at home with uncommon rejoicing, as a triumph over an enemy become formidable by his victories.

A short-lived accession to the British empire was made in this year by the annexation of the island of Corsica to its crown. The town and citadel of Bastia having for some time been under siege by a British force from the squadron in the Mediterranean commanded by Lord Hood, assisted by a party of Corsicans, a proposal for capitulation was made by the French commandant on May 19th, which being accepted, the surrender took place on the 22d. A circular letter had previously been addressed by General Paoli to his countrymen, for the convocation of the General Consult or representatives of the nation, at Corte on June 8th, which, on the 14th of that month, was opened by an eloquent speech from that veteran chief. This assembly then unanimously voted the separation of Corsica from France, and its union to the crown of Great Britain. A committee was appointed to prepare the articles of union, which being presented to Sir Gilbert Elliot with a tender of the crown to his Majesty, he accepted them in his name, and took the oath prescribed. A constitution was then agreed upon, framed according to the model of that of Great Britain; and his Majesty was enabled to add King of Corsica to his other titles.

The maritime superiority of England ensured success to her arms in the West Indies. The attempt for the reduction of Martinico was renewed in the spring, when 5000 men under the command of Sir Charles Grey, convoyed by a fleet commanded by Sir John Jervis, landed on the island. After a gallant resistance by the French at the different forts, it was entirely reduced on the 25th of March, by the surrender of Fort Bourbon. The victors proceeding to Guadaloupe, that island was brought to a capitulation on April 21st, which included its dependencies, Mariegalante, Deseada, and the Saintes. St. Lucie also surrendered to a British force. It was unfortunate that at this time the yellow fever raged among the West India Islands with unusual virulence; and the English troops in Guadaloupe were so much weakened by it, that a small armament from Brest landing 2000 men on the island under the commissioner Victor Hugues, they made themselves masters of the Fort of Grand Terre. Reinforcements being collected from the other islands, an attempt was made to recover the fort, which failed. Another effort about the end of June was also unsuccessful; and the few surviving English left at the other posts being obliged to surrender, Guadaloupe was entirely restored to its former possessors.

The domestic events of France during this period were marked with the same features of violent action as those which characterised its foreign exertions, but coloured with the ferocity peculiarly belonging to civil contention. The insurgents of La Vendee who, after many sanguinary actions, had at length appeared nearly extirpated by the sword in the field, and by the most savage and merciless executions when reduced to submission, began to collect again in arms and became formidable. At the same time another body of malcontents, named Chouans, arose in Britany, and joining forces with the Vendeans, gave much employment to the republican troops. The unremitting efforts of the convention however, which spared neither its own commanders nor the enemy, gave a prospect at the beginning of this year of a favourable termination of these disturbances. As it was a great object with the republic, at the same time that the generals were held under a strict responsibility, to encourage the citizen-spirit in the soldiers, it was ordained that every commander condemned for treason should be executed at the head of the army which he had attempted to betray, whilst the punishment of flogging was abolished in the army and navy, as unworthy of freemen. Universal liberty and equality being the fundamental principle of the constitution, a display was made of its application, by admitting to seats in the convention three deputies from St. Domingo, two of them mulattoes, and the other a negro; and soon after, a decree passed for the abolition of slavery in every part of the French dominions. In order to ease the lower classes of the people, who were labouring under a dearth of provisions, a maximum was established — a measure by which temporary popularity was sought, at the expence of true policy. If humanity might seem to have been consulted in some of these ordinances, the decrees for the extension of the powers granted to the Committee of safety, and against those who were construed enemies of the revolution, sufficiently proved that nothing was more foreign from the present rulers of France than a spirit of lenity and moderation; and this year has been particularly distinguished in its domestic history as the *reign of terror.*

After the overthrow of the Gironde party, the powers of government fell into the hands of a triumvirate consisting of Robespierre, Danton, and Barrere. The first of these, a man of a most ferocious character, and formed by nature for the part of a tyrant, gained the ascendancy, and for some time might be regarded as the master of France. There existed at this period a society called the Cordelier club, which being an offset from that of the Jacobins, carried its principles to the extreme, and under the conduct of one Herbert, became its rival. The destruction of this society was the first object of the triumvirate, and by their engine, the revolutionary tribunal, Herbert, and eighteen other persons, were found guilty of treason, condemned and executed. Robespierre, now looking upon his colleague Danton with jealousy, and trusting in his own superior influence with the people, brought an accusation against him, Camille Desmoullins, Fabre D'Eglantine and others, of a conspiracy to effect a counter-revolution in favour of monarchy; and by the assistance of their venal or intimidated judges, procured their capital condemnation. Such an act could not fail of raising many enemies to the tyrant, and his next victims were General Dillon and some others who had shewn an attachment to the late sufferers. He obtained some credit by a decree to prevent peculation by the members of the convention, his own character being pure in that respect; and by several useful regulations for the speedy administration of justice in the civil courts: and the increased severity with which he acted towards the royal party was probably in conformity with the public feeling. If it had been possible to shock the people by atrocities of this kind, the execution of the Princess Elizabeth, sister to the late King, a person of the most exemplary character, against whom none but frivolous charges could be produced, would have brought down execrations on his head. She suffered with calm dignity on a scaffold which had already streamed with the blood of 26 victims.

Immediately after this deed, Robespierre, on May 7th, pronounced a speech in which he appeared as a votary of religion. It was preparatory to a decree, by which the French nation recognized the existence of a Supreme Being, and the immortality of the soul, declared the freedom of public worship, and appointed decades and other religious festivals. His sanguinary disposition, meantime, seemed to acquire continual aggravation; and he established such a system of domestic treachery, that no one was safe in his own house from accusations, of which death was an immediate consequence. All means were employed to inflame the animosity of the nation against the English; and a decree passed, prohibiting quarter to be given to the British or Hanoverian soldiers in battle. The military character, however, would not permit the French army to act upon it; and the spirit of the decree was finely contrasted in orders issued by the Duke of York to his troops on the occasion.

The intolerable tyranny of Robespierre at length raised a party against him in the convention, consisting of some of its most resolute members, who, like those of the Roman senate under the worst Emperors, saw their own safety in perpetual hazard under his domination. A decree procured by him for empowering the committees of public safety to consign whomsoever they should think proper to the revolutionary tribunal, was the immediate signal for resistance. Contrary decrees passed in the convention denoted his decline of power. He attempted to raise the Jacobin and other popular clubs in his favour, and for a considerable time the balance of parties was in a state of suspence. At length a decree passed the convention unanimously, that their sittings should be permanent till the law was executed upon the guilty, and that Robespierre with his accomplices should be arrested. An insurrection excited by Henriot, commander of the national guards, for his deliverance was suppressed; and on July 28th he was apprehended in the Hotel de Ville, wounded, condemned, and executed, with a number of his adherents, amidst the execrations of the Parisian populace. All France appeared to breathe after the removal of the tyrant, and congratulations were sent up to the convention from every part, and every class of society. From that time a more moderate and humane spirit began to prevail. The revolutionary tribunal was new modelled; numbers of prisoners were enlarged; and conciliation instead of terror became the leading principle of public measures. A plan of republican government was resolved upon, which should effectually prevent the power of the state from being engrossed by one person; and Barrere, who had detached himself in time from his connection with Robespierre, was entrusted with drawing up the articles of a temporary government upon that system which was adopted. The meetings of the Jacobin clubs were suspended; and punishments were inflicted upon some of the chief actors in the barbarities perpetrated on the Vendeans.

In this year was effected with respect to Poland, what had been augured in the beginning of the French revolution by Mr. Burke with regard to France — it was blotted out of the map of Europe. The tyranny exercised by the partitioning powers over the poor remnant of that country proved so intolerable, that the Poles rose in insurrection, headed by that patriot chief Kosciusco. In February he attacked the Prussians and expelled them from part of their new acquisitions. Marching next to Cracow, it was deserted by the Russians, and he was declared commander in chief of a confederacy of nobles. He then advanced towards Warsaw, and defeated a Russian corps under Woronzof; and soon after, the Russians posted in that capital were driven out by the citizens and the Polish garrison. The King of Prussia now entered Poland with a powerful army, and made himself master of Cracow. He then proceeded to Warsaw, joined by the Russian troops in the neighbouring district. He had invested the city, when the resistance of the inhabitants, the approach of Kosciusco, and an insurrection in the Polish provinces seized by Prussia, obliged him to abandon the attempt. Meantime a Russian army, led by the formidable Suwarof, was advancing. It was met by Kosciusco on October 10th, and a bloody engagement ensued, which ended with the entire defeat of the Poles, of whom half were killed or made prisoners. Their brave general was severely wounded and taken captive. Suwarof after the victory marched to Warsaw, and assailed it as he had done Ismail. The Russians, forcing their way after an obstinate resistance into the suburb of Praga, put to the sword all whom they met with, and it is computed that

20,000 perished in this horrid massacre. The fate of Poland was now decided. The three partitioning powers divided among them all that still bore the national name; and King Stanislaus, who bore to survive his crown and country, was sent to reside at Grodno, and live in obscurity as a pensioner of the Empress Catharine.